PENGUIN BOOKS

THE RISE AND FALL OF N

'Ruchir Sharma is a shrewd and thoughtful observer ~~~~~~~ ~~~~~~. His insights deserve the attention of all who care about the future of the global economy' Lawrence H. Summers

'Globalization has gone into reverse gear. Into the wreckage steps Ruchir Sharma, author of the bestselling *Breakout Nations*. The result is ambitious . . . also entertaining, acute and disarmingly honest. Instead of pious statements about poverty, or portentous mutterings on the importance of American leadership, Mr Sharma sees the world from the ruthless and restless perspective of an investor . . . He has a knack for sharp comparisons between countries . . . a fine guide to the great emerging market boom and bust' *Economist*

'Embarking on an economics discussion with Ruchir Sharma is a bit like golfing with Tiger Woods. Like Woods . . . it is the way he goes about his business that makes him interesting. In a profession marked by dour punditry, he brings an élan that enlivens his commentary . . . As his career progressed, so did recognition come his way as something of an oracle for the world economy' *Straits Times*

'For insights into the forces operating in our world today, *The Rise and Fall of Nations* is a stimulating and useful guide . . . compelling' Henny Sender, *Financial Times*

'Compelling . . . The local insight adds colour, while the data reassures us that his analysis is underpinned by more than a series of conversations with taxi drivers . . . Much more than an investment primer. The issues he deals with, from growth to inequality, are of much broader interest . . . Sharma's book provides a good guide for working out what will come next' Duncan Weldon, *Prospect*

'Sharma's new book is filled with amazing data . . . fascinating insights and revealing anecdotes, this is quite simply the best guide to the global economy today. Whether you are an observer or an investor, you cannot afford to ignore it' Fareed Zakaria

'What determines whether countries succeed or fail? That's the big question Ruchir Sharma sets out to answer in *The Rise and Fall of Nations* . . . Ambitious, compelling and credible . . . The author backs up each of the rules with a combination of hard facts and colourful anecdotes gathered on his travels . . . Sharma's tried and tested tenets and eloquent delivery will reward anyone hoping to understand what determines the fickle fortunes of nations' Katrina Hamlin, *Reuters*

'If you have been wondering what's happening to the world – why for example has England voted to commit economic suicide by leaving the European Union? . . . The Americans have voted for Donald Trump . . . Donald Trump? What's going on? Is there a rightwing, anti-immigrant backlash, or is it more complex? In fact much of what is happening is following a pattern, a pattern of global trends that this book has in great detail and mastery documented . . . an amazing read, I learned a lot from it, and its out-of-the-box thinking'

Prannoy Roy, NDTV group

'The book is so lively and wandering that it is possible to miss the 10 rules and enjoy it just as a record of Sharma's learning them'
Indian Express

'The most interesting question of all time is why countries are poor . . . *The Rise and Fall of Nations* is a wonderful attempt to answer that question by asking 10 questions . . . This book is a wonderful way to travel the world, understand the issues countries should care about'
Manish Sabharwal, *India Today*

'A vital guide to the new economic order . . . Sharma's book is ambitious in positing new rules that investors should take into consideration as they think about the growth prospect of all nations, developed and developing, in the coming economic era . . . he looks to help readers navigate this turbulent world with rules that can help them identify which countries might, over 5 to 10 year time horizons, rise, fall, or muddle through'
Rana Foroohar, *Time*

ABOUT THE AUTHOR

Ruchir Sharma is Head of Emerging Markets and Chief Global Strategist at Morgan Stanley Investment Management. His acclaimed book, *Breakout Nations: In Pursuit of the Next Economic Miracles* (2012), was an international bestseller. Sharma began his career as a writer and still contributes regularly to the *Wall Street Journal*, *Financial Times*, *Foreign Affairs* and other publications. Now a countributing opinion writer at *The New York Times*, he was named one of *Foreign Policy*, Magazine's Top Global Thinkers in 2012 and one of *Bloomberg Market's* 50 most influential thinkers in 2015.

THE RISE AND FALL OF NATIONS

*Ten Rules of Change in the
Post-Crisis World*

RUCHIR SHARMA

PENGUIN BOOKS

PENGUIN BOOKS

UK | USA | Canada | Ireland | Australia
India | New Zealand | South Africa

Penguin Books is part of the Penguin Random House group of companies
whose addresses can be found at global.penguinrandomhouse.com.

Penguin
Random House
UK

First published in the United States of America by
W. W. Norton & Company, Inc. 2016
First published in Great Britain by Allen Lane 2016
Published in Penguin Books 2017
007

Printed and bound in Great Britain by Clays Ltd, Elcograf S.p.A.

A CIP catalogue record for this book is available from the British Library

ISBN: 978–0–141–98070–6

www.greenpenguin.co.uk

MIX
Paper from
responsible sources
FSC
www.fsc.org   FSC® C018179

Penguin Random House is committed to a
sustainable future for our business, our readers
and our planet. This book is made from Forest
Stewardship Council® certified paper.

CONTENTS

Prologue

INTO THE WILD

For each of the past twenty-five years, I have gone on a safari, either to India or Africa. On one trip to Africa, I heard the story of a king who sends his son out to learn the rhythms of the jungle. On his first outing, against the din of buzzing insects and singing birds, the young prince can make out only the roar of the lions and the trumpet of the elephants. The boy returns again and again and begins to pick up less obvious sounds, until he can hear the rustle of a snake and the beat of a butterfly's wings. The king tells him to keep going back until he can sense the danger in the stillness and the hope in the sunrise. To be fit to rule, the prince must be able to hear that which does not make a sound.

The rhythms of the jungle are far removed from those of New York, where I live, but this old African tale is quite relevant to a world reshaped by the global crisis of 2008. The crisis turned the world on its head, disrupting trade and money flows, unleashing political revolts, slowing the global economy, and making it more difficult to discern which nations would thrive and which would fail in such a transformed landscape. This book is about how to filter out the hype and noise and pick out the clearest signals that foretell the coming rise or fall of nations. It's an attempt to recreate the education of the prince, for anyone interested in the global economy.

People in the world of global finance often think of themselves as big cats, predators alert to the rustlings of the economic jungle. But in Africa the difference between the cats and the rest quickly dissolves. Each year on the Mara-Serengeti plains of Kenya and Tanzania, more than a million wildebeest walk a nearly two-thousand-mile loop that they have traced and retraced for generations. Moving behind the rains and accompanied by zebra and gazelle, the ungainly wildebeest are shadowed by the lion, the leopard, and the cheetah.

The contest looks stacked, but lions are relatively slow and short-winded and catch their prey on less than one attempt in five. Cheetahs are faster, but because they are smaller and often hunt alone, they are forced to concede many kills to scavengers working in packs. Less than one cheetah in ten lives longer than a year. Lions do a bit better, but many males die young in territorial battles with other males. The circle of life and death turns as brutally for the predator as for the prey, a fact that might give pause to the would-be lions of the global economy.

I've lived in fear for my own survival since I entered this jungle. I started out in investing as a twenty-something kid in the mid-1990s, when the United States was booming and emerging nations were still seen as wild and exotic. Financial crises swept from Mexico to Thailand and Russia, triggering painful recessions and reshuffling the ranks of rising economies and world leaders. The collateral damage in global markets wiped out many big investors, including a good number of my mentors, colleagues, and friends.

Looking back, the demise of national leaders (and global investors) followed a pattern. They initially followed a path that led to economic or financial success, but then the path shifted and led to quicksand. It happened in the emerging-world crises of the 1990s, in the dot-com bust of 2000–2001, and again in 2008. Each time people got too comfortable doing what they were doing in good times, then got swallowed when the earth shifted under their feet.

The cycles of market euphoria and despair often produce clichés about "herd behavior," but even in the jungle life is more complicated than that stereotype. A certain "swarm intelligence" guides the wilde-beest, ensuring the survival of the group even when it means an early death for many individuals. The wildebeest's circular migration has been mocked with the old proverb "the grass is always greener on the other side," but the herd is right about where the grass will be greener. It follows the rains, north into Kenya in the spring, back south into Tan-zania during the fall.

The critical dangers appear twice a year at "the crossing" of the Mara River, which the herd must ford while traveling both north and south. Normally, to avoid predators, the herd heeds an ancient warning system—the shrieks of baboons, the harsh calls of jungle babblers. But this system fails on the banks of the Mara, where the wildebeest mass by the tens of thousands, with danger in plain sight: floating crocodiles, rain-swollen waters, lions in ambush on the far side.

Heads down, the wildebeest appear to be talking all at once, their distinctive bellows like so many Wall Street analysts on a conference call, plotting their next move. The herd waits for one member to go. If this animal takes a step and retreats, fear paralyzes the multitude, but memories are short. Within minutes another will try, and if it plunges in, the mass follows—many into waiting jaws and deadly currents. An estimated 10 percent of the wildebeest population perishes each year, a large number of them during the crossing.

People working in global markets from New York to Hong Kong can get sucked into a culture that is programmed, like the wildebeest, to remain in constant motion. Every day research reports bombard these financial capitals, urging the crowd to chase the next Big Thing or to run from the next Big Correction. The compulsion to move gives rise to a new consensus every season or every quarter, an impulse that has only grown since the global financial crisis. Just take the year 2015. During the first quarter the chatter was all about how you had to either get in or get out of the way of the surging Chinese stock market, which then seemed like a one-way bet. The second quarter was all about how Greece was going to take down the global economy, and during the third quarter the financial panic in China dominated the conversation. Sometimes the reports are right, and sometimes they're wrong, but always they move forward, forgetting what they were saying the day before, and why. At times the shifting conversation appears to have no rhyme or reason.

Wall Street is fond of old sayings about how only the paranoid and the fittest survive. I would phrase the issue a bit differently. The challenge is how to channel a wise paranoia in the service of survival. Every crisis is greeted as a renewed call to action, and the bigger the crisis, the more frantic the action. Years after 2008 the fear of more big losses still runs so high that Wall Street's biggest players are likely to watch returns monthly rather than yearly, which pressures money managers to trade constantly in the hope of avoiding even a single bad month. This is happening despite evidence that gains are now more likely to accrue to investors who trade less, proving, as one wag put it, that "sloth is a virtue."

In the summer of 2014, after many safaris, I saw a big cat actually catch its prey for the first time, in Tanzania. Late one afternoon my friends and I came upon a cheetah, panting hard after, our guide told us, two failed chases earlier in the day. Over the next two hours, the cheetah waited in a little dugout as it recovered its breath; the light faded with evenfall, and the wind shifted to carry its scent away from a solitary male gazelle. When conditions were right, the cheetah made its move, creeping slowly, slowly, low and unseen through the short savannah grass to within fifty yards of its target. Then it accelerated to sixty miles per hour and—in a zigzag final dash that took fractions of a second—brought down the gazelle.

More telling than the burst of speed was the stillness that preceded it. Big cats are programmed to survive by conserving energy, not to waste it in constant motion. The most common sighting of a lion involves watching them take a nap; they are known to sleep eighteen to twenty hours a day. When cats do succeed on the hunt, they try not to expend much effort on battles over the meal. And they don't panic over cyclical turns in the weather. During the violent afternoon rains that sweep the Masai Mara plains in Kenya, I've watched the wild animals stop where they are and stand stock still—predators within striking distance of their prey—until the deluge ends. They seem to understand instinctively that cloudbursts are one beat in the normal rhythm of their days and that panic will only lead to greater chaos.

Many accomplished survivalists inhabit the jungle, and not all are big cats. The best defenses belong to the hulking vegetarians, the elephants and the rhinos. Even a lion pride will rarely take on a seven-ton elephant with six-foot tusks. The best spies may be the wildebeest, with their network of baboons and birds. The best hunters may be the hyenas, who despite their popular depiction as thieving scavengers are among the most successful large predators. Unlike the cats, a hyena has endurance, can run down virtually any animal, and does not target mainly the old and infirm. Moving in packs of up to sixty, hyenas fear no prey. On the plains of the Serengeti, I once saw a pride of lions cede its kill to a pack of twenty persistent hyenas.

Early on in my career, painful experience taught me that anyone who wants to survive longer than the five-year political and economic cycles that buffet the global economy needs to absorb a few laws of the jungle. Do not expend energy on daily or quarterly blips in the numbers. Adapt to a changing landscape rather than let ego obstruct a strategic retreat. Focus on big trends, and watch for the crossings. Build a system to spot important signs of change, even when everyone around you is comfortably going with the current flow. Over the past twenty-five years I have spent long hours on the road, trying to build a system of rules for spotting telltale shifts in economic conditions.

What goes for survival in the wild and on Wall Street also goes for the survival of nations in the world economy. There is no one role model. Every nation is equally vulnerable to the cycles of boom and bust that kill off most runs of strong economic growth and that ultimately transform sprinting cheetahs into exhausted cats. The waves of crisis following the 2008 global meltdown crippled many economies, weak and strong, developed and developing. Following the well-established patterns of economic development, the new stars of a new era are likely to emerge from nations that are overlooked as scavengers and slow-footed vegetarians and whose rise is starting without a lot of hype. Anyone trying to understand the rise and fall of nations needs to internalize the fact that the global economy is a noisy jungle; booms, busts, and protests are part of its normal rhythms. What follows is my guide to identifying the ten telltale signs of major turns for the better or worse, even those that don't make a sound.

Introduction

IMPERMANENCE

IN THE YEARS BC—BEFORE THE CRISIS OF 2008—THE WORLD enjoyed an unprecedented economic boom that extended from Chicago to Chongqing. Though the boom ran for only four years and its foundations were thin, many observers saw it as the beginning of a golden age of globalization. Flows of money and goods and people would continue to expand at a record pace, increasing wealth and spreading it as well. More poor nations would enter the ranks of the rich nations. More of their citizens would escape poverty and earn a comfortable living, narrowing the gap between the 1 percent and the rest. With their newfound clout, the rising global middle class would put pressure on dictatorships to loosen censorship, hold genuine elections, and open up new opportunities. Rising wealth would beget political freedom and democracy, which would beget greater prosperity.

Then came 2008. The years BC gave way to the years AC. After the Crisis, the expectation of a golden age gave way to a new reality. Hype for globalization yielded to mutterings about "deglobalization." The big picture is complicated and contradictory, because not all the flows that globalization traditionally describes have slowed or reversed. The flow of information, as measured by Internet traffic, for example, is still surging. The flow of people, as measured by the number of tourists and airline passengers, is rising sharply. But overall the number of economic migrants moving from poor countries to rich ones has fallen, despite the heated controversy that broke out in 2015 over Muslim refugees from Syria and Iraq. And the flows of money that most directly influence economic growth—capital flows between nations and trade in goods and services—have slowed sharply.

Nations have been turning inward, rebuilding barriers to trade and fencing themselves off from their neighbors. In the 2010s, for the first time since the 1980s, global trade has been growing more slowly than the global economy. Big international banks have pulled back to within their home borders, afraid to loan overseas. After surging for more than three decades, flows of capital reached a historic peak of $9 trillion and a 16 percent share of the global economy in 2007, then declined to $1.2 trillion or 2 percent of the global economy—the same share they represented in 1980.

When money dries up and trade recedes, so does economic growth. National economies often suffer recessions, but because there are always fast-growing nations somewhere in the world, the global economy rarely shrinks as a whole. The International Monetary Fund therefore defines a global recession not in terms of negative GDP growth but in terms of falling income growth, job losses, and other factors that make the world feel like it is in the grips of a recession. According to the IMF, there have been four such instances: in the mid-1970s, the early 1980s, the early 1990s, and 2008–9. In all four cases, global GDP growth fell below 2 percent, compared to its long-term growth rate of 3.5 percent.[*] Global growth also dropped under 2 percent in 2001, when the U.S. tech bubble burst. For practical purposes, then, it can be said that there have been five worldwide recessions since 1970, and they had one thing in common. They all originated in the United States.

But the next global recession is likely to be "made in China," which in recent years has risen to become the world's second largest econ-

---

[*] Global GDP growth is measured here in market-determined exchange-rate terms.

omy and single largest contributor to annual increases in global GDP. In 2015, owing to the slowdown in China, the global economy grew at a pace of just 2.5 percent, and by year end was teetering on the brink of another recession. China's slowdown is hitting fellow emerging nations particularly hard. Excluding the Middle Kingdom, the other emerging nations are growing at an average pace of barely above 2 percent, which is slower than the much richer economy of the United States. The average income of these poor and middle-class nations is no longer catching up to that of the world's leading economy. From Brazil to South Africa, emerging economies are falling down the development ladder. The sense of possibility created by rising global prosperity has transformed into a scramble to find a survivable niche.

This is a world disrupted. The hope that prosperity would beget freedom and democracy has faded as well. Every year since 2006, according to Freedom House, the number of countries registering a decline in political rights has outstripped the number registering an increase. In all, 110 countries, more than half the world's total, have suffered some loss of freedom during the past ten years.[1] The number of democracies has not changed dramatically, but repression is on the rise even in countries, like Russia, that keep up the appearance of elections. Few observers argue anymore that prosperity in China will lead to democracy. They point instead to the rise of a new and increasingly assertive form of authoritarianism, led by Russia and China and marked by regimes that reject democracy as a universal value while defending softer forms of political repression as expressions of unique national cultures.

The big blow to global prosperity and political calm came around 2010, as the economic slowdown spread from the United States and Europe to the emerging world. In the previous decade, the world had seen an average of about fourteen episodes of major social upheaval each year, but after 2010 that number shot up to twenty-two, fueled in many cases by growing middle-class anger at rising inequality and at aging regimes that had grown corrupt and complacent in the comfortable BC era.

The first big wave of revolt came in the Arab Spring, when protests fueled by rising food prices stirred hopes that new democracies would take root in the Middle East. Those expectations were dashed by the return of dictatorship in Egypt and the outbreak of civil war from Libya to Syria. By 2011, the revolts were spreading to the bigger emerging nations. These protests were driven by economic grievances compounded by the global slowdown: by inflation in India, political cronyism in Russia, and wages and working conditions in South Africa. This unrest culminated in the summer of 2013, when millions of people joined demonstrations in cities across the fading-star economies of Brazil and Turkey.

The American playwright Arthur Miller once observed that an era has reached its end "when its basic illusions are exhausted."[2] Today the illusions of widening prosperity that defined the pre-crisis era are finally spent. The last to die was the faith that China's boom would last indefinitely, lifting up countries from Russia to Brazil, from Venezuela to Nigeria, which had been thriving mainly by exporting commodities to the Chinese. Ever-growing demand from China would drive a "super cycle" of rising commodity prices and growing wealth from Moscow to Lagos. This storyline began to strain credulity by 2011, when prices for copper and steel started to fall. It collapsed completely in late 2014, when the price of oil dropped by more than half in a span of months.

Nothing illustrates the impermanence of global trends better than the fate of the most-hyped emerging nations of the 2000s, Brazil, Russia, India, and China. Marketers rolled them into the acronym BRICs, to capture the idea that these four giants were poised to dominate the global economy. Today the acronym is often qualified with an adjective like *broken* or *crumbling*, dismissed as a "bloody ridiculous investment concept," or reshuffled into a new acronym like CRaBs, to capture how ungainly China, Russia, and Brazil look now. In the AC era, the annual GDP growth rate of China has fallen from 14 percent to private estimates of less than 5,[3] of Russia from 7 percent to negative 2, and of Brazil from 4 percent to negative 3. Of the original BRICs, only India has any hope of growing anywhere near as fast in the 2010s as it did in the 2000s.

The unease of the AC era has been magnified by the rosiness of the preceding boom and by the fact that so few observers saw the crisis coming. The world looked forward to endless good times and instead got hard times. It anticipated rising demand from the emerging middle class and instead, in many countries, got falling demand from an angry middle class. In this tense global scene, the standard fear of inflation has given way to fear of deflation, or falling prices, which in some cases can be even more damaging for economic growth.

The hot names of the BC era have fallen deeply out of fashion. As money flows dried up and reversed, the currencies of emerging nations have weakened sharply. After attracting positive flows of capital every year since recordkeeping began in 1978, the emerging world saw an outflow of capital for the first time in 2014 and in 2015 the dam burst, with a massive outflow of more than $700 billion. This sudden loss of funding makes it more difficult for these nations to pay foreign debts. Many emerging nations that fought hard to dig their way out of debt are relapsing, becoming troubled borrowers again. At the height of the BC-era boom in 2005 the IMF had conducted zero rescue operations and looked about ready to fold its bailout business, but it came roaring back in 2009 and since then has been launching ten to fifteen new assistance programs each year, from Greece to Jamaica.

In the AC era, the perils of growth are more widely acknowledged. The global expansion that began in 2009 is on track to be the weakest in post–World War II history. In 2007, just before the financial crisis hit, the pace of growth was slowing in only one emerging economy out of every twenty. By 2013, that ratio was four out of five, and this "synchronized slowdown" was in its third year, the longest in recent memory. It had carried on longer than the synchronized slowdowns that hit the emerging world after Mexico's peso crisis in 1994, or the Asian financial crisis in 1998, or the dot-com bust in 2001 or even the crisis of 2008.[4] As the sluggishness spread, the old hunt for the next emerging-world stars gave way to a realization: Economic growth is not a God-given right. Major regions of the world, including the Byzantine Empire and Europe before the Industrial Revolution, have gone through phases stretching hundreds of years with virtually no growth.

At Goldman Sachs, researchers looked back 150 years at countries that had posted long runs of subpar growth and had seen their average income slip relative to their peers. They found ninety such cases of stagnation that lasted at least six years, including twenty-six that spanned more than ten years. These slumps hit countries ranging from Germany in the 1860s and '70s to Japan in the 1990s and France in the 2000s. The longest stagnation lasted twenty-three years and struck India starting in 1930, while the second longest lasted twenty-two years in South Africa, starting in 1982. These stagnations are not as famous or well studied as the postwar Asian growth "miracles" that ran for decades and lifted Japan (before 1990) and some of its neighbors to rich-nation status. But stagnations are at least as common as miracles and are perhaps more relevant to the AC era.

It's vital to understand that even the business cycle cannot be relied on to revive nations in a predictable, linear way. Once an economy contracts beyond a certain point, it can lose its capacity to self-correct. For example, a normal recession will raise unemployment and lower wages, which will eventually lead to a new cycle of hiring and a recovery. If the recession is too long and deep, however, it can destroy the skills of the labor force, trigger widespread bankruptcies, and gut industrial capacity, leading to an even longer downturn. The buzzword for this threat is "hysteresis," which describes a period in which slow or negative growth begets slower growth rather than recovery. In the sluggish AC era, the new fear is that some nations may now be stuck in this condition.

The fleeting and difficult nature of strong growth is now plain to see, and it raises a simple question. How, in an impermanent world, can we predict which nations are most likely to rise and which to fall? What are the most important signs that a nation's fortunes are about to change, and how should we read those signs? To help navigate the normal condition of the world—an environment prone to booms, busts, and protests—this book outlines ten rules for spotting whether a country is on the rise, on the decline, or just muddling through. Together the rules work as a system for spotting change. They are most applicable to emerging nations, in part because those nations' economic and political institutions are less well established, making them more vulnerable to political and financial upheaval. However, as I will show along the way, many of the rules find useful applications in the developed world.

Pattern Recognition: The Principles Behind the Rules

A few basic principles underlie all the rules. The first is impermanence. At the height of the 2000s boom, a variety of global forces—easy money pouring out of Western banks, spiking prices of commodities, and soaring global trade—doubled the growth rate of emerging economies. The scale of the boom was unprecedented—by 2007, the number of nations expanding faster than 5 percent reached one hundred, or five times the postwar norm—but forecasters assumed this freak event was a turning point. Extrapolating from existing trends, they figured that if all the hot economies stayed hot, the average incomes of many emerging nations would soon catch up or "converge" with those of rich nations.

This form of straight-line forecasting was hardly new. In the 1960s Manila won the right to host the headquarters of the Asian Development Bank (ADB) based in part on the argument that fast growth in the Philippines made it the future of Asia. By the next decade, under the dictatorship of Ferdinand Marcos, growth was stalling, but the ADB headquarters was in Manila for good. In the 1970s similar exercises in extrapolation led some American scholars and intelligence analysts to predict that the Soviet economy was destined to become the largest in the world. Instead, it collapsed at the end of the 1980s. By then forecasters had handed the next century to Japan, but it became the next economic star to falter.

None of that prevented a new round of excitement in the early

2000s, focused on the rise of the BRICs, or BRICS (some included South Africa in the group), and the commodity super cycle. As the hype was peaking around 2010, the historical pattern for commodity prices—which tend to boom for a decade, then fall for two decades—was about to reassert itself. Today talk of these nations fulfilling their destinies as regional economic powerhouses seems like a dim memory.

Recognizing that this world is impermanent leads to the second principle, which is to never forecast economic trends too far into the future. Trends in globalization have ebbed and flowed ever since Genghis Khan secured commerce along the Silk Road in the twelfth century, and the cycles of business, technology, and politics that shape economic growth are short, typically about five years. The election cycle, too, runs for around five years on average, and it can usher in reform-minded leaders with the potential to shake up stagnant economies. As a result, any forecast that looks beyond the next cycle or two—five to ten years at most—is likely to be upended. It also makes nonsense of recent talk of the coming Asian or even African century.

One aim of this book is to nudge our discussion of the world economy away from the indeterminate future to a more practical time horizon of five to ten years and to the job of spotting the next booms, busts, and protests. Predictions for the next twenty to one hundred years cannot possibly be fulfilled when new economic competitors can arise within five years, as China did in the early 1980s, as eastern Europe did in the 1990s, and as much of Africa did in the 2000s. In any five-year period, a new technology can spring seemingly from nowhere, as the Internet did in the 1990s and as new digital manufacturing techniques like 3-D printing are doing now. In the postwar period, even the twenty-eight longest periods of "super-rapid" growth—in which per capita GDP was rising faster than 6 percent a year—have lasted less than a decade on average.[5] So the longer a streak lasts, the less likely it is to continue. When a country like Japan, China, or India puts together a decade of strong growth, analysts should be looking not for reasons the streak will continue but for the moment when the cycle will turn.

The tendency to believe good times will last forever is magnified by a phenomenon known as "anchoring bias." Conversations tend to build on the point that starts (or anchors) them. In the 2000s, people who handicapped global economic competition came to believe that double-digit annual GDP growth was normal for China and that a rate of more than 7 percent was standard in emerging economies. Those superhigh rates were unprecedented but came to anchor the conversation. In 2010 the notion that the emerging world was about to see its average growth rate drop to 4 percent was so far below the anchor that it would have seemed implausible, even though 4 percent is the average growth rate of emerging economies in the post–World War II era. In general, the correct anchor for any forecast is as far back as solid data exists, the better to identify the most firmly established historic pattern. The patterns of boom and bust described in this book are based on my own research, including a database of the fifty-six postwar emerging economies that managed to sustain a growth rate of 6 percent for at least a decade.

The habit of hanging on to a poorly chosen and improbable anchor is compounded by the phenomenon of "confirmation bias," the tendency to collect only the data that confirm one's existing beliefs. During the runaway optimism of the 2000s, there was a lot of confirmation bias in hype for the BRICS, but in most periods the prevailing intellectual fashion is pessimism. That is certainly the greater risk today, when it is hard to convince people that any nation has a chance to rise, given the rough global conditions. The question to ask, in any period, is not the typical one: *What will the world look like if current trends hold?* It is, rather, *What will happen if the normal pattern holds and cycles continue to turn every five years or so?* In a sense, the rules are all about playing the right probabilities, based on the cyclical patterns of an impermanent world.

To critics who are thinking that the five-to-ten-year horizon reflects a narrow and short-term Wall Street worldview, I would say wait. The chapters in this book will show that long runs of strong growth last because leaders avoid the kinds of excesses that produce credit and investment bubbles, currency and bank crises and hyperinflation—the various kinds of busts that end economic miracles. The rules double as a rough guide to long-term economic success.

In countries like Brazil and India, one often hears the argument that if the government focuses too narrowly on economic growth, then health, education, and other measures of human development will suffer. But this is a false choice. The countries with the lowest per capita income also tend to have the worst human development records. Every year the UN puts out a Human Development Index (HDI) ranking countries by educational measures like years of schooling, health measures like life expectancy, and basic infrastructure measures like access to running water and electricity. A nation's overall rank on the HDI often aligns very closely with its ranking for per capita income, which is the result of its long-term growth record. India, for example, ranks 135 out of 187 countries on the latest list. Only ten countries with lower per capita income rank higher for human development. Only five countries with higher per capita income rank lower for development.

India has risen in the rankings, but only as its economy grew. Back in 1980, when there were only 124 countries on the HDI, India ranked one hundredth. Over the subsequent decades, India's economy expanded by 650 percent, while the global economy expanded by less than 200 percent, and as a result India climbed in the HDI rankings. It now stands at eighty-ninth among the original 124 countries, up eleven spots. However, countries with stronger economic records made bigger gains. China's economy expanded by 2,300 percent, and its HDI ranking climbed 30 places, from ninety-second to sixty-second. These gains are not confined to the poorest countries, either. South Korea's economy expanded by 700 percent, and its HDI ranking rose 30 places, from forty-fifth to fifteenth. There are of course exceptions—the people of South Africa live unusually short lives for a country with an average income of $6,500, due in part to a high murder rate and the AIDS epidemic. In countries that have fallen way behind their peers on specific development measures, a focus on these issues can make sense. In general, however, if a country focuses on growth, development will follow.

The Impractical Science

Public disillusion with the economics profession has been growing, since it failed to foresee not only the events of 2008 but also the many crises that have shaken the world before and since. Economists are under attack even within their own ranks for being too academic and for being too focused on elegant mathematical models and theories that pretend humans always act rationally and on historical data that change too slowly to capture what may come next. Whether they are players in politics, diplomacy, or business, or are just engaged citizens, practical people cannot begin to make plans without making an educated guess as to what is coming next. This book is for those practical people. They are duly skeptical of crystal balls, but they need to look forward, and to recognize misleading economic futurology when they see it.

Increasingly, economics is seen as an impractical science. For some academics, forecasting is an intellectual exercise, and rewards flow from publishing big ideas. The result is often a one-dimensional or ideological worldview. Some American and European intellectuals hint that Islamic culture is too backward to promote rapid growth. Some people on the extreme right believe every government action is by definition bad. Liberals often trace strong growth to democratic institutions, an explanation that can't account for many things, including the long boom in Asia from 1980 to 2010, when most regimes in the region were illiberal.

Often economists and writers oversell the importance of a single growth factor—the challenge of a remote geographic location, the advantage of liberal institutions or the favorable demographics of a young and growing population—as the key to understanding the rise and fall of nations. These factors, the subject of compelling recent best sellers, are often important in shaping long-term growth, but in my experience no single factor works well as a sign of how an economy is likely to change over the next five years. For example, "the curse of oil" is real: In poor nations that are not prepared to hit the oil lottery, large oil discoveries tend to breed corruption and retard development. But a gut distaste for corrupt petrostates can blind forecasters to the high likelihood that when global oil prices enter a boom decade, many oil economies will follow.

It's important to understand economic theories, but it is equally important to learn how to apply them and in what combinations and situations. An economy's growth rate is the product of multiple factors, and the balance of these factors will shift over time, as a country grows richer and as global conditions change. Most mainstream forecasters understand this well but wind up with numbingly complex systems. Institutions including the World Bank and the IMF count dozens to hundreds of factors that have a statistically relevant impact on growth, including everything from the share of university students who are studying law to "ethno-linguistic fractionalization," and whether the country in question is a former Spanish colony.

Practical forecasters need to weed out data that is not forward looking, reliable, and up to date. People in developed nations who worry about information overload may be surprised by how difficult it is in emerging countries to obtain solid current information on basic issues like the size of the economy and by how erratically these numbers are revised. In early 2014 Nigeria announced an official GDP number of $500 billion, thus almost doubling the size of the economy overnight. This transformation attracted relatively little attention, because people who watch emerging markets have grown more or less numb to such statistical drama. Only one year before, Ghana had issued an equally large revision, effectively promoting itself from a poor to a middle-class country. Commenting on the Indian statistical bureau's frequent revisions of official economic data, former central bank governor Y. V. Reddy once cracked to me that while the future is always uncertain, in India even the past is uncertain.

Numbers coming out of the emerging world have a strange fluidity and a way of morphing to meet the self-interest of major players. In China, analysts skeptical of official GDP growth figures have started checking them against other indicators, such as cargo traffic and electricity consumption. That check can be pretty reliable, except that in 2015 reports emerged that government authorities were instructing developers to keep the lights on even in empty apartment complexes. The aim was to drive up electricity consumption data so that it would confirm official economic growth claims. This is a classic case of Goodhart's Law, which says that once a measure becomes a target, it ceases to be useful, partly because so many people have an incentive to doctor numbers to meet it.[6]

One useful and timely data source is the prices in global financial markets, which in normal times will accurately capture the world's best collective guess about the likely prospects of an economy. What author James Surowiecki has called "the wisdom of crowds" has substance, and the market embodies it, second by second, subject to emotional contagions but not wild revisions.[7] A sharp decline in the price of copper has almost always been an ominous sign for the global economy, earning the base metal the moniker "Dr. Copper" in financial circles. In the United States, one of few countries where most lending is done through bonds and other credit market products rather than through banks, the credit markets started sending distress signals well before the onset of the last three recessions, in 1990, 2001, and 2007. The credit markets also send false signals on occasion, but for the most part they have been a fairly reliable bellwether.

Despite their periodic bouts of euphoria and panic, stock markets also have a track record of anticipating economic trends. Back in 1966 the Nobel Prize–winning economist Paul Samuelson quipped that the stock market had "predicted nine out of the last five recessions," and writers aiming to disparage the predictive power of markets have often cited him. But Samuelson was no more impressed by professional economists, who in fact have a worse record than markets. In a 2014 note Ned Davis Research showed that despite a few big misses, in which the market tanked in anticipation of a recession that never came, the market has been a consistently good predictor of both good and bad times for the economy. Going back to 1948, the benchmark S&P 500 Index has on average started to turn down seven months before the peak of an expansion, and it has started to turn up four months before the bottom of a recession. On the other hand, Ned Davis reviewed the track record for professional forecasters who are regularly surveyed by the Philadelphia branch of the Federal Reserve and found that as a group, these mainstream economists "called exactly none" of the last seven recessions, dating back to 1970.[8] In the United States, the National Bureau of Economic Research is the official documenter of recessions, and on average it has declared recession starts eight months after recessions actually began.

Market indicators aside, numbers alone cannot provide a handle on any nation's real prospects. Most economists tend to ignore any factor that is too soft to quantify or incorporate into a forecasting model, even something as basic as politics. Instead, they study "policy" through hard numbers, like government spending and interest rates. But numbers can't capture the energy unleashed by a new leader's intolerance for monopolists, bribe takers, or stonewalling bureaucrats. No nation has an entitlement to economic greatness, so leaders need to push for it and keep pushing. My rules, therefore, offer a mix of ways to read hard data on things like credit, prices, and money flows, as well as softer signs of shifts in politics and policy.

These are the basic principles: Avoid straight-line forecasting and foggy discussions of the coming century. Be skeptical of sweeping single-factor theories. Stifle biases of all kinds, be they political, cultural or "anchoring." Avoid falling for the assumption that the recent past is prologue for the distant future, and remember that churn and crisis are the norm. Recognize that any economy, no matter how successful or how broken, is more likely to return to the long-term average growth rate for its income class than to remain abnormally hot (or cold) indefinitely. Watch for balanced growth, and focus on a manageable set of dynamic indicators that make it possible to anticipate turns in the cycle.

The Practical Art

These rules emerged from my twenty-five years on the road, trying to understand the forces of change both in theory and in the real world. The reason I developed rules at all was to focus my eyes and those of my team on what matters. When we visit a country, we gather impressions, storylines, facts, and data. While insight is embedded in all observations, we have to know which ones have a reliable history of telling us something about a nation's future. The rules systematize our thoughts and have been back-tested to determine what has worked and what has not. Eliminating the inessential helps steer the conversation to what is relevant in evaluating whether a country is on the rise or in decline.

I have narrowed the voluminous lists of growth factors to a number that is large enough to keep the most significant forces of change on our radar but small enough to be manageable. In theory, growth in an economy can be broken down in a number of ways, but some methods are more useful than others. Growth can be defined as the sum of spending by government, spending by consumers, and investment to build factories or homes, buy computers and other equipment, and otherwise build up the nation. Investment typically represents a much smaller share of the economy than consumption, often around 20 percent, but it is the most important indicator of change, because booms and busts in investment typically drive recessions and recoveries. In the United States, for example, investment is six times more volatile than consumption, and during the typical recession it contracts by more than 10 percent; while consumption doesn't actually contract, its growth rate merely slows to about 1 percent.

Growth can also be broken down as the sum of production in various industries, such as farming, services, and manufacturing. Of these, manufacturing has been declining worldwide—it's now less than 18 percent of global GDP, down from more than 24 percent in 1980—but it is still the most significant force of change, because it has traditionally been the main source of jobs, innovation, and increases in productivity.

So the rules have a lot to say about investment and factories and much less about consumers and farmers. Some say manufacturing is going the way of farming, as machines largely replace jobs, and my rules are evolving to account for this shift. But for now manufacturing remains central to understanding economic change.

This is not an argument for tossing out the textbooks, just for zeroing in on the forces of change that have the strongest predictive qualities. As a case in point, textbooks talk about the importance of savings in driving investment and growth, because banks funnel the money saved by households and companies into investments in roads, factories and new technology. But savings is a chicken-or-egg issue: It is not at all clear which comes first, strong growth or high savings. Similarly, this book elaborates on subjects that will be familiar to many, like the impact of overinvestment and debt binges, the scourges of inflation and inequality, and the vagaries of political cycles. But there are hundreds of ways to track and measure these factors, and the issue I try to address is, for example, exactly how to parse the debt burden of a nation and how to understand when debt signals a turn for the better or worse.

I eschew factors that matter to growth in the long run but that don't work well as signs of change. For example, education is everyone's favorite way to boost the talent of the labor force and raise productivity, but my rules pay little attention to it. The payoff from investment in education is so slow and variable that it is almost useless as a predictor of economic change over a five-to-ten-year period. Many studies have linked the post–World War II booms in the United States and Britain to the advent of mass public education, but that change began before World War I. A recent study by the Centre for Cities think tank found that the British cities that grew fastest in the 2000s were the same ones that had invested most in education—in the early 1900s. The economist Eric Hanushek found in a 2010 report that a twenty-year education reform program could result in an economy one-third larger—but that increase would register seventy-five years after the reform program began.

In many postwar cases the economy took off in educationally backward nations like Taiwan and South Korea. As the Asia expert Joe Studwell has pointed out, in Taiwan 55 percent of the population was illiterate in 1945, and that share was still high at 45 percent in 1960. South Korea in 1950 had literacy levels comparable to Ethiopia's. In China, as the economy took off in the 1980s, local officials spent heavily on roads, factories, and other investments that had a fast impact on growth, because their careers depended on producing high growth numbers immediately. Schools came later.

Investing in education is often seen as a sacred obligation, like defending motherhood, and too few questions are asked about whether it is getting the job done. In some countries huge expenditures on the university system have had almost no economic impact, even over the long term. The emerging nation in which the population has the highest average years of schooling (11.5) and the largest share of university grads (6.4 percent) is Russia, where the Soviet era legacy of excellence in science and technology education has yet to affect the economy. Russia is still dependent on raw materials, and although it has a few dynamic Internet companies, it lacks a tech sector to speak of and has been one the world's slowest-growing economies in the 2010s.

I also see limited use for various surveys that try, in essence, to make a science of measuring some of the factors that can contribute to productivity. The World Economic Forum's Global Competitiveness Report focuses on twelve basic categories, but many are slow-moving forces like institutions and education. Finland, for example, has been near the top of the forum's ranking system for a long time, and in 2015 it ranked fourth in the world and first in a dozen subcategories ranging from primary schools to antimonopoly policies. Finland was also the survey's top-ranked European Union country. Yet it suffered one of the slowest recoveries from the crisis of 2008, far behind the United States, Germany, and Sweden, and was about on par with the hardest-hit countries of southern Europe. Finland was paying the price for having let its debts and wages rise quickly and for its heavy dependence on exports of timber and other raw materials at a time when global prices for these commodities was collapsing. Having good primary schools was no defense for Finland when more important forces of change were at work.

The World Bank also puts out rankings of countries for everything from quality of roads to how many days it takes to open a business, and these rankings have become very popular. That creates a problem, as more than a few countries have started hiring consultants to help them raise their rankings (another example of Goodhart's Law in action). In 2012 President Vladimir Putin set a goal of raising Russia's rank for "ease of doing business" from 120 to top 20 within six years, and he soon saw results. By 2015, Russia was ranked at 51—more than thirty places ahead of China, and sixty places ahead of Brazil and India. That raised a question: If it was so easy to do business in Russia, why wasn't anyone doing business there? Moscow in 2015 is increasingly hostile to and isolated from international business, far more so than China or Brazil or India. To the extent possible, I try to avoid relying on numbers that are vulnerable to political manipulation and marketing.

The most significant forces of change vary from year to year and country to country. In the AC era, the dominant economic storyline has been about debt: which countries did the most to pay down debts amassed before 2008, and the surprising number that have dug themselves deeper into debt trying to fight the subsequent slowdown. As a whole, the world has a bigger debt burden now than it did in 2008, which is a real issue. But my first chapter is not about the rule on debt—it's about people and population, which could have a bigger impact going forward.

Another simple way to define economic growth is as the sum of the hours that people work plus their output per hour or productivity. But productivity is hard to measure, and the results are subject to constant revision and debate. On the other hand, the number of hours people work reflects growth in the workforce, which is driven by population growth, which is relatively easy to count. Unlike economic forecasts, population forecasts depend on a few simple factors—mainly fertility and longevity—and have a strong record for accuracy. Before the start of the new millennium, the United Nations predicted global population for the year 2000 a total of twelve times going back to the 1950s, and all but one of those forecasts was off by less than 4 percent. The first rule addresses the economic impact of population growth, and most of the others deal one way or another with productivity. But I don't use productivity growth data directly because they are not reliable.

In a way, population trends are half the story. Since 1960 the global economy, including both developed and developing countries, has had an average annual growth rate of about 3.5 percent.* Half of it came from population growth, more specifically labor force growth, or more people working more hours. The other half came from gains in productivity. This 50-50 split still holds, with one distressing change, which is that both sides of the equation are slumping.

The impact of population is very straightforward: a 1 percentage point decline in growth in the labor force will shave about 1 percentage point off economic growth. That is roughly what has been happening in the last decade. Global GDP growth has been trending lower and is now running more than a full percentage point below its long-term pre-crisis average. It is no coincidence that since 2005 the growth in the global labor force, ages 15 to 64, has slowed to 1.1 percent, from 1.8 percent over the previous five decades. The implications of this new population threat to the world economy are dark but not uniform across countries. The working-age population is already shrinking in Germany and China; it is growing, but very slowly, in the United States; and it is still booming in Nigeria, the Philippines, and a few other countries. Slower growth in the world population may curb but won't stop the constant rise and fall of nations.

The rest of the rules deal one way or another with the other half of the global growth story, which is captured in a loose way by the productivity growth numbers. Here too the global picture appears at

---

* This figure refers to potential growth, which we calculate by taking the sum of productivity growth and employment growth from the Conference Board Total Economy Database.

best mixed. Between 1960 and 2005, the average annual productivity growth rate was around 2 percent, but that rate downshifted by almost a full percentage point in the last ten years. Like population growth rates, officially recorded productivity growth rates have fallen by varying degrees, from less than a percentage point in the United States to more than 2 points in South Korea and nearly 4 points in Greece. But while the demographic downshift is indisputable, debate rages as to whether the productivity decline is real.

Productivity growth is the sum of hard-to-quantify improvements in the skill of workers, in the number and power of the tools they use, and in an elusive x factor that tries to capture how well workers are employing those tools.[*] That x factor, which can be influenced by everything from experience using a computer to better management or better roads to get workers to their workplaces faster, is the fuzziest part of this difficult calculation. Technoskeptics say that the last decade's decline in productivity growth reflects the fact that most recent innovations involve relatively trivial advances in communications and entertainment: Twitter, Snapchat and the like. Even with worker training and experience, these advances will do much less to raise productivity than previous innovations like electricity, the steam engine, the car, the computer, or air conditioning, which was a huge boost to human output per hour in a stuffy office setting.

Optimists respond that productivity growth measurements aren't capturing the cost and time savings produced by new technologies, ranging from artificial intelligence to increasingly powerful broadband connections and the nascent "Internet of things." In the United States, for example, the cost of broadband Internet access has remained flat for many years, but broadband connections have grown much faster and gone mobile—a huge time savings that is not captured in the productivity growth data.[9] If the optimists are right, productivity growth is considerably faster than current measurements show, and therefore so is economic growth. Whichever side is right, both would agree that it is

---

[*] Technically, productivity growth is the sum of increases in labor quality, capital deepening, and total factor productivity.

easier to measure population growth, which has a more clear-cut impact on the economy. Fewer working people mean less economic growth, and this impact has become more visible worldwide in the last five years.

All the rules try to capture the delicate balances of debt, investment, and other key factors required to keep an economy humming. Over the course of this book, it will—I hope—become clear how the ten rules work together as a system. To foreshadow the story in brief, an economy is most likely to begin rising steadily when the nation is emerging from crisis, has fallen off the radar of the global markets and media, and has chosen a democratic leader with a mandate to reform. That leader will create the business conditions to attract productive investment, particularly in factories, roads, and technologies that will strengthen supply networks and thus help contain inflation. The probability that a boom is about to end will rise as a nation gets too comfortable and as private companies and individuals run up debts to buy frivolous luxuries, particularly imported luxuries. This period of extravagance will make it impossible for the nation to pay its foreign bills, while widening the gap between billionaires and the rest, and between the countryside and the nation's capital, provoking a political backlash that brings down the now aging regime, after which the cycle can begin again.

The book's final chapter sketches how the top emerging and developed nations rank on the ten rules at a given point in time. The rankings change constantly, so the last chapter merely offers a snapshot of how the rules work as a system. The approach makes no promise of certainty in an impermanent world, and the most it can hope to achieve is to improve the probability of spotting the next shifts in the constant rise and fall of nations. It is a system for handicapping global economic competition as a practical art rather than as an impractical science. There are no sweeping forecasts for the year 2050, only an objective effort to identify the most plausible outlook for the next five to ten years. The aim: a practical person's guide for spotting the rise and fall of nations, in real time.

1

PEOPLE MATTER

Is the talent pool growing?

A T FIRST I DIDN'T THINK THERE WAS MUCH MYSTERY TO the lackluster global recovery. After 2008, when the United States fell into a deep recession and the world soon followed, economists argued that the recovery would be painfully slow because this was a "systemic crisis," not an ordinary recession, and I was persuaded. Their research showed that following a crisis that devastates the financial system, an economy typically experiences weak growth for four to five years even after the end of the recession. But as each year passed—five, six, seven—the global economy continued to perform more weakly than expected. By 2015, there was still not a single major region of the world where economic growth had returned to its pre-crisis average. I became convinced that the sluggish recovery was not normal. It was a mystery: Where was the missing growth?

Economists have put forth many reasons to explain why the world has been slogging through its weakest recovery in the postwar era. Most of the explanations focus on the way severe credit crises can depress the demand side of the economy, as consumers and companies struggle to work off their debts and slowly regain the confidence to spend money. Others blame weak demand on rising income inequality, the regulatory crackdown on bank lending, or some other symptom of post-crisis stress disorder. While all these arguments may have some merit, the evidence is mixed as to what impact these factors had on economic growth. In the United States, there are clear signs that consumer demand fully recovered by 2015: Car sales have hit new highs and job growth is running at a brisk pace, yet the headline GDP growth number is still well below its pre-crisis pace. As often happens in a good mystery, perhaps the detectives have been looking in the wrong place.

My team and I turned our attention from the arguments that primarily focus on demand to those concerning supply, the side of the economy that supplies labor, capital, and land, the basic inputs to growth. We found an unexpected culprit. One critical cause of the missing growth was, of all things, a shrinking supply of people in the active workforce. This finding was so thoroughly at odds with popular fears about how human jobs are being replaced by the rise of robots and artificial intelligence, it seemed hard to accept at first. How could too few workers be a problem if technology has made them obsolete? But in this case at least, numbers don't lie.

A collapse in population growth was already under way before the 2008 crisis, and in fact it can explain a good chunk of the persistently disappointing recovery since. As we've seen, one simple way to measure an economy's potential to grow is by adding productivity growth and labor force growth, and while both have slumped worldwide, the productivity slowdown is widely disputed, since many experts think the official statistics are undercounting the impact of new digital technologies. In the United States, by the official numbers, productivity grew at an average pace of 2.2 percent between 1960 and 2005 before slowing to just 1.3 percent in the past ten years. The population slowdown was even more dramatic, and it is not in dispute. In the five decades before 2005, the U.S. labor force grew at an average annual pace of 1.7 percent, but slowed to just 0.5 percent over the past decade. In short, the clearest explanation of the missing economic growth in the United States is the roughly 1 percent decline in labor force growth, which is largely a function of growth in the population of working-age people, between 15 and 64.

The world still echoes with recurring fear about the "population bomb" scenarios, which suggest that the number of people will outstrip supplies of food and other resources, with explosive results. Those scenarios rely on the United Nations' oft-cited forecast for the year 2050, which shows that population will rise by 2.4 billion people, from 7.3 billion to 9.7 billion. A number close to ten billion may sound frighteningly high, but the UN forecast in fact takes into account a dramatic slowdown in the population growth rate. Many fewer babies are being born, and fewer young people are entering the working-age cohort, while the overall population is growing mainly because people are living longer. This mix is toxic for economic growth.

For much of the post–World War II era, global population grew at an average of nearly 2 percent annually, which meant that the world economy could also expect to grow at a baseline rate of close to 2 percent— and a couple of percentage points more than that when output per worker was also growing. Then around 1990 global population growth just fell off a cliff. The growth rate has since halved to just 1 percent. The difference between 1 and 2 percent may not sound like much, but if the population growth rate had stayed at 2 percent since 1990, the global population today would be 8.7 billion, not 7.3 billion. The world would not be aging so rapidly, and we would not be talking about population's impact on economic growth.

The economic impact of the decline in the population growth rate has taken time to show up, because it takes a while for babies to reach the working age of 15. Of course, in many places people don't actually start working until they reach 20 or 25, depending on how long they stay in school. So it takes fifteen years or more for a baby bust to have a clear impact on the population contribution to economic growth, which has become increasingly clear in the last five years.

The fall in the global population growth rate was the delayed result of aggressive birth control policies implemented in the emerging world in the 1970s, particularly the one-child policy China instituted in 1978. In emerging and developed countries, the population slowdown was also fueled by rising prosperity and education levels among women, many of whom decided to pursue a career and have fewer children or none at all.

The roots of this demographic shift lie in basic changes in mortality and fertility rates over the last half-century. Since 1960 advances in science and health care have allowed people to live longer. Worldwide, the length of the average human life has been extended from 50 years in 1960 to 69, and it is still rising. Already, most of global population growth is occurring among people over 50, and by far the fastest-growing segment of the population is people above 80. The overall population will continue to grow, albeit at a much-reduced rate, even as the segment that drives economic growth—working-age people—continues to shrink.

The period since 1960 has also seen a global baby bust, as the average number of births per woman has fallen from 4.9 to 2.5 worldwide. In emerging nations, the collapse has been more dramatic, encouraged by those aggressive birth control policies. Fertility rates in India and Mexico, two countries that were once a focus of fear about accelerating overpopulation, have plummeted from more than 6 to 2.5 or less since 1960. Both countries are now very close to the replacement fertility rate of 2.1—the rate below which the population eventually starts shrinking. As the world's fertility rate slips toward the critical level of 2.1, more and more countries are falling below the replacement level. Nearly one of every two people on earth already lives in one of the eighty-three countries where on average women have fewer than two children, from China, Russia, Iran and Brazil to Germany, Japan, and the United States.[1]

Working-age populations are already shrinking in some advanced countries, including Japan, Italy, and Germany, and while that shrinkage has been obvious for years, the same process is now unfolding or is poised to unfold even faster in many large emerging nations, including

China and India. Moreover, the global population growth rate is projected to keep falling over the next decade and beyond. This changes the planet's economic prospects in fundamental ways.

The slowdown in population growth is already sending economic shockwaves through society, affecting relations between generations, sexes, nationalities, and even the contest of man versus machine. When the United Nations recently rereleased its population forecast for nearly ten billion people by the year 2050, alarmists naturally repeated their warnings about overpopulation. Some are neo-Malthusians, who fear that population growth will outstrip growth in food supply, leaving a hungry planet. Some are neo-Luddites, who fear that the "rise of the robots" will make human workers obsolete, a threat all the more alarming if the human population is exploding. And some are anti-immigrant forces in Europe and the United States, who favor building border walls to keep out a "rising tide" of what one British cabinet minister calls "desperate migrants marauding around."

What all these alarms miss is that while ten billion sounds like a lot of people, the slowing rate of growth is what matters for the economy, including the food supply. Slower population growth means there will be less pressure on the entire chain of production, which doesn't have to supply as much clothing or housing or food. Farms won't have to increase production as fast as they have in the past to feed everyone, and they will have to expand mainly to meet the needs of elderly people, who consume up to a third fewer calories than young people. I don't want to minimize the real problems of hunger in many countries, but the economic driver of these problems is not population. For most countries, the primary economic threat is not too many people but rather too few young people, and the arrival of robots may simply help relieve the impending labor shortage. Farmbots may be the answer to retiring farmers.

In a world where more and more countries are going to face labor shortages, the current controversies over "marauding" migrants will give way to—or perhaps rage alongside of—aggressive campaigns to attract or steal labor and talent from other countries. For countries confronting a rapidly aging and declining workforce, it doesn't matter whether immigrants arrive as "economic migrants" seeking opportunity or as "political refugees" fleeing war or persecution: Either group will boost the size of the labor pool. The pressure to attract or retain workers will be particularly acute in the emerging world, where fertility rates have fallen faster and life expectancy has increased much faster than they did in the past, when wealthy countries like Britain or the United States were in their early economic development stages.

For a nation's economic prospects, the key demographic question is: Is the talent pool growing? The first part of the rule for finding the answer is to look at the projected growth of the working-age population over the next five years, because workers (more than retirees or schoolchildren) are the drivers of growth. The second part of the rule is to look at what nations are doing to counteract slower population growth. One way is to try to inspire women to have more babies, an approach with a spotty record at best. The other is to attract adults—including retirees, women, and economic migrants—to enter or reenter the active labor force. The big winners will come from among those countries that are blessed with strong growth in the working-age population or are doing the best job of bringing fresh talent into the labor force.

The 2 Percent Population Pace Test

To get a better handle on how demographics will limit national economies in coming years, I studied population trends in the countries on my list of postwar growth miracles—the fifty-six cases in which a country sustained an average economic growth of at least 6 percent for at least a decade. I found that during these booms the average growth rate of the working-age population was 2.7 percent. In other words, a significant part of the growth in these miracle economies could be explained by the fact that more and more young people were reaching working age. This clear connection between a population explosion and an economic miracle has played out in dozens of cases, from Brazil in the 1960s and '70s to Malaysia from the 1960s through the 1990s.

As for how fast the working-age population needs to grow to raise the likelihood of an economic boom, it turns out 2 percent is a good benchmark. In three out of four of the miracle economies, the working-age population grew at an average pace of at least 2 percent a year during the full duration of a decade-long boom. A country is thus unlikely to experience a decade-long growth boom if its working-age population is growing at a rate less than 2 percent. And one striking change in the post-crisis world is that there are now very few countries with a population growing that fast. As recently as the 1980s, seventeen of the twenty largest emerging economies had a working-age population growth rate above 2 percent, but that number has fallen steadily from seventeen to only two in the 2010s, Nigeria and Saudi Arabia. And the number is still falling. By the next decade, between 2020 and 2030, there will be just one, Nigeria. A world with fewer large, fast-growing national populations will witness fewer economic miracles.

To be sure, economic booms don't always require population booms: in a quarter of the cases, above, the country did manage to generate a decade of rapid economic growth without the boost of 2 percent population growth. But most did so in unusual circumstances. Some were already relatively well off, such as Chile and Ireland in the 1990s, when some combination of reform and new investment increased productivity and compensated for weak population growth. Others were witnessing a return to economic calm during a period of reconstruction, as Japan, Portugal, and Spain were in the 1960s, and as Russia was a decade after the fall of the Soviet Union, with an added boost from high oil prices. Today no country can expect a similar boost, not when commodity prices are falling and political unrest is spreading.

This does not bode well for the emerging world, where more and more countries face the prospect of weak or even negative population growth. Over the course of the 2010s, all the major emerging economies are projected to have working-age population growth rates below the 2 percent mark, including India, Brazil, Mexico, Indonesia, and Thailand. Already the working-age population is actively contracting in three large emerging countries: Poland, Russia, and most important, China. There the working-age population growth rate hovered under 2 percent as recently as 2003, then dropped steadily until it turned negative for the first time in 2015.

Population decline is now high on the list of reasons, alongside its heavy debts and excessive investments, to doubt that China can sustain rapid GDP growth. Since 2010 a credit binge has run up China's debts to around 300 percent of GDP, which has been widely discussed. The investment boom that was driving China's rapid growth has started to unravel and is now leaving development ghost towns all over the country. But the fallout from the depopulation bomb is at least as damaging to growth.

To produce strong economic growth in a country with a shrinking population is close to impossible, or as the European Commission warned in 2005, "Never in history has there been economic growth without population growth."[2] Based on the record for nearly 200 countries going back to 1960, there are 698 cases in which data for both population growth and GDP growth are available for a full decade. Among these cases, there were 38 in which a country's working-age population was shrinking over the course of the decade, and the average GDP growth rate for these countries was just 1.5 percent. And in only three of the 698 cases did a country with a shrinking population manage to sustain a GDP growth rate of 6 percent or more. All three were small countries bouncing back from a period of political turmoil, postwar chaos, or post–Soviet collapse: Portugal in the 1960s, and Georgia and Belarus between 2000 and 2010. This record suggests that an average growth rate of 6 percent or more is extremely unlikely in China, even though the official target is still above that threshold.

In a few other populous countries, the number of working-age people is growing at a rate near or above 2 percent, including the Philippines and some emerging countries with economies too small to make the top twenty, such as Kenya, Nigeria, Pakistan, and Bangladesh. These populations are also forecast to keep growing rapidly for the next decade, so they have a demographic edge on the competition. For them, the trick is to avoid falling for the fallacy of the "demographic dividend," the idea that population growth pays off automatically in rapid economic growth. It pays off only if political leaders create the economic conditions necessary to attract investment and generate jobs. In the 1960s and '70s, rapid population growth in Africa, China, and India led to famines, high unemployment, and civil strife. Rapid population growth is often a precondition for fast economic growth, but it never guarantees fast growth.

In most countries, before the 2000s, strong population growth was the norm but typically did not produce an economic miracle. In my study, more than 60 percent of the 698 cases had a working-age population growth rate of more than 2 percent, but only a quarter of those population booms led to an economic miracle or an average growth rate of 6 percent or more in the same decade. The countries where a population boom failed to produce an economic miracle include Turkey in every decade between 1960 and 2000, and the Philippines in every decade between 1960 and 2010. Today not even Kenya can assume that its world-leading population growth rate—projected at 3 percent between 2015 and 2020—will automatically make it a world-beating economy.

The Arab world provides a cautionary tale. There between 1985 and 2005 the working-age population grew by an average annual rate of more than 3 percent, or nearly twice as fast as the rest of the world. But no economic dividend resulted. In the early 2010s many Arab countries suffered from cripplingly high youth unemployment rates: more than 40 percent in Iraq and more than 30 percent in Saudi Arabia, Egypt, and Tunisia, where the violence and chaos of the Arab Spring began. In

India, where hopes for the demographic dividend have also been sky high, ten million young people will enter the workforce each year over the next decade, but lately the economy has been creating less than five million jobs annually.

Though discussions of rapid population growth tend to focus on big emerging countries, a rising number of workers is also critical to economic growth in developed countries. In recent decades, the United States has come to see itself as by far the most dynamic and flexible of the developed economies, far more innovative than Europe, far less hidebound than Japan. But much of its recent advantage could be traced to the fact that more young people were entering the workforce. Over the past thirty years, the working-age population has been growing much faster in the United States than in its major industrial rivals: twice as fast as in France and Britain, five times faster than in Germany, and ten times faster than in Japan. That demographic boost helps explain faster U.S. economic growth over the same period. In Germany and Britain, for example, factoring out their slow-growing populations, per capita income has been growing as fast as that of the United States. Over the last thirty years, the U.S. economy expanded at an average rate that was 0.9 percentage points faster than Germany's, and its working-age population also expanded exactly 0.9 percentage points faster. Otherwise this race was a draw.

Population forecasts for the developed world are quite discouraging for the 2015–20 period. Among the ten largest developed economies, the number of working-age people is expected to remain static in France, shrink a little in Spain, and contract at a rapid pace of 0.4 percent a year or more in Italy, Germany, and Japan. The U.S. forecast was less bleak, with a positive population growth rate of 0.2 percent, about the same as those of Britain and Canada. The best news for developed countries was confined unfortunately to smaller ones, led by Singapore and Australia. There the populations are still growing at a good pace, but for the global economy, these countries are too small to make up for weaker growth in all the bigger countries.

Baby Bonuses

The race to fight the population slowdown is already on. Many countries over the past decade have recognized the economic threat and have taken steps to counteract it. In 2014 Denmark revised its high school sex education curriculum, which now warns teenagers about the dangers of waiting too long to have their own children. According to the United Nations, 70 percent of developed countries today have implemented policies to boost their fertility rate, rising from about 30 percent in 1996. At the same time, the number of emerging countries that have active policies to control population growth has leveled off since the 1990s at about 60 percent.

With the birthrate in many countries falling below the replacement level of 2.1, countries that subsidize motherhood are focused mainly on encouraging women to have more than two children, and in some nations the subsidies grow even more generous with the third, fourth, and fifth children. Many nations have tried offering women cash "baby bonuses" and other incentives to have more children, a form of state meddling in the reproductive process that is often ineffective and controversial.

In 1987 Singapore pioneered these efforts, launching a campaign under the slogan "Have three, or more if you can afford it." The range of incentives it offered, including subsidized hospital stays, had little effect on the fertility rate. I was studying in Singapore at the time and can remember people joking about how the subsidies were adding to the lines of expectant Chinese moms looking to schedule C-sections on the highly auspicious date of 8-8-88. Canada introduced a baby bonus that same year, 1988, but withdrew it years later in part because—as other countries have also found—many of the women who responded to direct cash incentives were very poor, and their children added greatly to welfare expenses.[3]

When Australia's treasurer Peter Costello announced his country's first baby bonuses in 2005, he urged women to "lie back and think of the aging population," and more than a few of his compatriots cringed. Six years later Australia cut the bonuses, in part because these incentives did not appear to have much influence on the fertility rate, particularly when weighed against larger changes in society. In most wealthy countries, professional women have been putting off childbirth into their thirties in order to pursue a career—and are having fewer children as a result.

In France, the socialist government of Prime Minister Lionel Jospin tried to address this problem by making its baby bonuses so generous that they would appeal to professional women too. The plan, announced in 2005, was attacked from the right for breaking an already busted budget, and from the left for favoring the rich. Nonetheless the package was approved, including lavish incentives targeted solely at parents to have that golden third child: extra home help subsidies, tax cuts, a 10 percent pension increase, and a 75 percent discount on rail tickets. The parents would also get a monthly allowance of over $400 for a third child, and perhaps most important, if one of them quit work to care for the third child, they would get a stipend of $1,200 a month. That stipend seems likely to decrease the workforce today, in the name of increasing it tomorrow. In response to the critics, Peter Brinn, one of the chief architects of the French plan, defended subsidizing childbirth as "spending on the future." By 2015, however, France too was cutting back significantly on its baby bonuses.

As the magnitude of population decline started to hit home in the emerging world, Chile recently became one of the first emerging countries to offer baby bonuses. Despite its reputation as a conservative Catholic culture with the attendant large families, Chile already has a fertility rate well below the replacement level. In 2013 the government responded to the growing fear of a depopulation bomb by announcing its baby bonus plans. Declaring himself more concerned about the falling birthrate than about natural disasters like the earthquake that hit Chile in February 2010, President Sebastián Piñera announced an escalating onetime payment of $200 for a third child, $300 for a fourth, and $400 for a fifth. "This sudden and precipitous drop in the birthrate represents a serious danger, a serious threat, that will affect what we really want to build as a country," Piñera warned.

Around the same time China—the mother of all population planners—was rethinking its long-standing campaign to control fertility through one-child policies, which have contributed mightily to the country's aging problem. The one-child policy encouraged many parents to abort female fetuses in order to ensure the birth of a male child, resulting in a society where the gender balance is badly skewed. Young men greatly outnumber young women, and many men will find it impossible to find wives. Draconian population controls have had a huge impact on the labor force, which is expected to lose a million workers a year in the coming decades. In late 2015 China finally announced it is ending the one-child policy.

It's hard to predict what distortions aggressive policies encouraging women to have two, three, or more children might produce—something as complex as human fertility cannot be changed in a predictable way. A recent paper by the demographers Hans-Peter Kohler and Thomas Anderson explained why the extent of the baby bust in Europe varies so greatly from country to country. During the Industrial Revolution, women joined the labor force in large numbers, but social norms changed more slowly than the industrial economy. Men were still considered the chief breadwinners, and women were still expected to carry the burden of child rearing and housework. The underlying gender roles started to change in the 1960s, when the culture started to catch up to the economy—but faster in some countries than in others. In France, Britain, and the Scandinavian countries, mothers found it easier to return to work, owing in part to generous childcare services. In more traditional cultures like Germany and Italy, where old conceptions of gender roles ebbed more slowly, more women chose not to have children, and today birthrates are cripplingly low.

The impact of state intervention in the human reproductive process is thus likely to be both slow and unpredictable, due in part to the way cultural lags and sexual biases vary from country to country. China did not intend for its one-child policy to favor males—indeed, it has tried to prevent doctors from revealing the sex of the fetus—but the traditions of a society still built around eldest sons twisted the impact. By 2014, the gender imbalance had reached a new height: 121 male babies were being born for every 100 female babies. On visits to Beijing and Shanghai in the early 2010s, I heard talk that China was reverting to the nineteenth century, when widespread female infanticide created a similar gender imbalance, which by some accounts helped trigger the "testosterone-fueled" carnage of the Taiping Rebellion (1850–64). This story was told half in jest, but the gender imbalance is a real concern. In other countries, the subsidies for more children are likely to have their own sets of unintended consequences. It is hard to see this kind of campaign as a positive sign for any economy.

A more promising approach focuses on trying to bring more people into the active workforce. That means opening doors to people who are physically and mentally capable but are not formally employed. While population shifts gradually, measures to reshape the workforce can have a rapid impact, because you don't have to wait fifteen to twenty years for a woman, a retiree, or an economic migrant to grow up. Providing childcare services can bring women with children back to work. Opening the nation's doors to economic migrants can expand the working aging population virtually overnight. And reversing the twentieth-century campaign that pushed the retirement age down into the fifties in many industrial countries could bring a forgotten generation back to work very quickly. To drill down into likely changes in the size and talent of the labor pool, watch mainly for shifts in the number of senior citizens, women, migrants, and even robots entering the workforce.

Free the Forced Retirees

In recent decades the widening impact of population decline has been magnified by a worldwide decline in the labor force participation rate—

or the share of working-age adults who are in a job or looking for one. There are some major exceptions to this drop-off in workers, including Germany, France, Japan, and the United Kingdom, but the United States is seeing one of the more dramatic declines. In the last fifteen years, the labor force participation rate in the United States has fallen from 67 to 62 percent, much of it coming after the global financial crisis. Without that decline in participation, the U.S. labor force would have had twelve million more workers in 2015. Though some of this shift may be a passing phenomenon, reflecting the millions of unemployed workers who gave up on looking for a job in the frustrating depths of the great recession, the decline in participation would have happened anyway because of aging. In the United States, the labor force participation rate drops from a little over 80 percent for 45-year-olds to less than 30 percent for 65-year-olds, and it is expected to continue falling in most countries as the world ages.

Smarter countries are rethinking the whole idea of a "retirement age," a concept that was unknown before the 1870s. In earlier periods, people worked until their bodies or minds gave out, and they prepared for their dotage by having a lot of children, in the hope that at least one would care for them. Then a railroad company in western Canada asked a seemingly narrow but, as it turned out, portentous question: How old is too old to drive a train safely?[4] The answer back then was 65, which became the official retirement age in many countries. Even as older people remained active into their seventies and eighties, the age limit stuck.

The first government retirement benefits, offered to ease the financial uncertainties of old age, also appeared in the late nineteenth century, in Bismarck's Germany. Back then fertility rates in Europe were well above the replacement level, and life expectancy was much lower, so the working-age population was growing rapidly, in absolute numbers and as compared to the elderly population. With a growing supply of workers to fund a limited number of pensioners, Bismarck's retirement plan—which taxed the young to pay pensions to the old—worked fine.

Circumstances have reversed. Working-age populations are stagnating, but the Bismarckian "pay as you go" retirement plans remain the standard, even though various critics say they have become unsustainable Ponzi schemes. It's not possible to recruit enough young contributors to pay for the pensions of retirees, who have become a bit too comfortable with these plans. While I was visiting Vienna in October 2013, a vibrant Austrian hotel manager told me in a casual chat that, still fit at 58, she was looking forward to her retirement in two years, when she said she would be entitled to public pension benefits nearly equal her last salary. She planned to replace her work with tango dancing, cross-country cycling trips, and backcountry skiing adventures.

Even the richest countries have figured out that they can no longer afford golden years that come so early. To figure out which nations are most vulnerable to aging and its costs, simply compare the number of working-age people between 15 and 64 to the number of dependent people who are older than 64 or younger than 15—also known as the dependency ratio. Changes in the dependency ratio say a lot about an economy's growth potential, by revealing what percent of the population is entering its productive years, saving money, and contributing to the pool of capital available to invest rather than drawing down pension funds. During its postwar economic boom, South Korea's GDP growth rates rose or fell year by year very closely in line with changes in the dependency ratio. China's GDP growth also peaked in 2010, the same year the dependency ratio bottomed out at one dependent for every three workers and started to climb.

This number today holds a lot of drama, particularly in aging regions like Europe, where the size of the working-age population relative to the elderly population has fallen by half since the 1950s and is expected to halve again over the next thirty years. The aging process, which has already hit most advanced countries, is expected to unfold even faster in emerging ones, again because of a sharper fall in fertility rates and a faster rise in life expectancy. Worldwide, the average person today lives nineteen years longer than he or she did in 1960, but in China the average person lives thirty years longer and dies at 75. This progress is remarkable, but it has a cost. Today the share of the Chinese population that is over 65 is on track to double from 7 to 14 percent between 2000 and 2027. By way of contrast, that doubling process took 115 years in France and 69 years in the United States.

Population trends impact an economy mainly by increasing or decreasing the number of available workers, but they have a secondary impact on productivity. In recent years countries with faster-growing populations have also tended to exhibit faster productivity growth. As the dependency ratio declines, with more people entering the workforce and earning an independent living, a country's income increases, and that creates a greater pool of capital, which can be used to invest in ways that further raise productivity. According to the demographer Andrew Mason, this secondary demographic dividend was an important boost to the economic growth rates of East and Southeast Asia, where saving rates are relatively higher and the workforce has been relatively large.[5]

Furthermore, a more experienced labor force also tends to be more productive. The best-positioned countries are those taking steps to keep older people in the workforce and out of the "dependent" population. In 2007, Germany increased the retirement age from 65 to 67 for men and women, a measure that will be phased in gradually. Most other European nations have followed suit, including Poland. Over the next five years, Poland's working-age population is expected to shrink by more than 3 percentage points to 66 percent, the sharpest drop in any large country, while the elderly population continues to boom. Battles over raising the retirement age and other issues unique to a gray society now shape political debate, while Polish entrepreneurs have tried to make an opportunity out of aging. Rest homes that Poles call Houses of Peaceful Elderliness are multiplying all over the country. European countries including Italy and Portugal have already pegged changes in the retirement age to increases in life expectancy, and others are already debating a retirement age of 70 or more. There are holdouts—notably France—but pushing back the retirement age is a big step forward for aging economies, and every additional year that it is pushed back saves billions in pension costs and delays the impact of the depopulation bomb.

It would be a mistake, however, to assume that the state can press all aging workers to stay on the job with the stroke of a pen. In Mexico, the official retirement age is 65, but the typical Mexican man retires at 72. In France, the official retirement age is also 65, but the typical Frenchman actually retires before 60. Changing the official retirement age and the level of pension benefits can encourage people to stay on the job, but it can't produce overnight changes in the work culture. In most countries, the duration of the retirement "golden years" continues to lengthen, weighing on the economy. In the thirty-four industrial countries that belong to the Organization for Economic Cooperation and Development (OECD), from China and South Korea to the United States and Britain, the gap between the age at which the average person retires and the age at which he or she dies is now fifteen years, having increased steadily from two years in 1970.

The costs of paying pensions are mounting to crippling levels, perhaps nowhere more than in Brazil, where the average man retires at 54 and the average woman at 52—earlier than in any OECD member country. Meanwhile the average pension covers 90 percent of the retiree's final salary, compared to an OECD average of 60 percent. Brazil is one of the countries where the growing imbalance between workers and retirees most threatens the shaky edifice of Bismarckian retirement systems. On this front too governments are struggling to keep up with the effects of the depopulation bomb.

What Happened to Women in the Workforce?

The worldwide movement of women into the workforce that energized much of the postwar era has stagnated in the past twenty years, with the average female labor force participation rate stuck at around 50 percent.

Typically women participate in the labor force at a very high rate in poor rural countries, where feeding the family requires all hands to work in the fields. The participation rate then falls as countries industrialize and move into the middle-income class, as some women shift to housework, falling out of the formal labor force. Finally, if the country grows richer still, more families have the resources to send women to college—and from there they often enter the labor force in large numbers.

To get a sense of which economies have the most—or the least—opportunity to generate growth by building up the female labor force, one can compare countries in the same income class. Among rich countries, according to a 2015 study by Citi Research, female labor force participation ranges from nearly 80 percent in Switzerland to 70 percent in Germany and less than 60 percent in the United States and Japan. To its own benefit, Japan is waking up to this fact. Since coming to power in 2012, Prime Minister Shinzo Abe has explicitly recognized the role that women could play to fix Japan's severe aging problem, and he has incorporated "Womenomics" as a central element in his plan to revive the economy. Womenomics includes improving childcare services and parental leave, cutting the "marriage penalty" that taxes a family's second earner at a higher rate, and encouraging Japanese corporations to put more women in executive positions. During the first three years of Abe's term, some eight hundred thousand women entered the workforce, and he claimed his campaign was also pushing more women into corner office jobs.

In Canada, an effort to open doors to women produced quick results. Only 68 percent of Canadian women participated in the workforce in 1990; two decades later that figure had increased to 74 percent, largely on the back of reforms including tax cuts for second earners and new childcare services. An even more dramatic boom in the number of working women came in the Netherlands, where the female labor participation rate has doubled since 1980 to 74 percent today, as a result of expanded parental leave policies and the spread of flexible, part-time working arrangements. In relatively short order, the Netherlands caught up to and raced past the United States, in terms of utilizing the talents of its women.

No matter how aggressive these campaigns get, all countries have a higher male than female participation rate, though this gender gap varies widely by country. The countries with the smallest gender gap, less than 10 percent, include Norway, Sweden, Canada, and Vietnam. Vietnam may seem like an unlikely entry on that list, but these gender gaps are related to political culture, and many socialist or Communist countries, including China, have taken concerted steps to bring women into the workforce. That is true even in Russia, which has a relatively high female labor force participation rate despite Soviet-era laws that close over 450 occupations as "too strenuous for women." Vladimir Putin signed off on these restrictions when he took power in 2000, and Russian courts upheld them as recently as 2009. In a 2014 survey of 143 emerging countries, the World Bank found that 90 percent have at least one law that limits the economic opportunities available to women. These laws include bans or limitations on women owning property, opening a bank account, signing a contract, entering a courtroom, traveling alone, driving, or controlling family finances.[6]

Such restrictions are particularly prevalent in the Middle East and South Asia, the regions with the world's lowest rates of female labor force participation, 26 and 35 percent respectively. The gender gap exceeds 50 points in Pakistan, Iran, Saudi Arabia, and Egypt, and the hurdles to working women often involve a combination of written laws and cultural norms. In a *New Yorker* magazine piece, Peter Hessler profiled a Chinese entrepreneur who opened a cell phone factory in Egypt but had to shut it down within a year partly because his female employees—despite a strong work ethic—were compelled by Egyptian cultural norms to refuse night shifts and to quit once they got married.[7] In larger countries such as India, where fewer than 30 percent of women participate in the labor force, the overall figures also conceal shocking pockets of backwardness. In the Indian state of Bihar, out of a population of 100 million, only 2 percent of women work in formal jobs that are counted as part of the labor force.

The cultural barriers are real but not insurmountable. Latin America, which has a reputation for harboring some of the world's most macho cultures, is also making rapid gains in bringing women into the workforce. Between 1990 and 2013 only five countries increased their female labor force participation rate by more than 10 percentage points, and all were Latin countries. In first place was Colombia, where the share of adult women active in the workforce rose by 26 percentage points, followed by Peru, Chile, Brazil, and Mexico.

The reasons for this boom are complex, but one is that Latin educational systems have opened up to women; in Colombia, Profamilia, a private group founded in the 1970s by wealthy women, has played a major role. Profamilia took on the powerful Catholic Church and lobbied for wider access to contraception, so that women could choose to delay childbirth in favor of a career. The fertility rate has dropped sharply, while the female labor force participation rate has skyrocketed. In many countries, all the leaders need to do to reap the economic boost from working women is to lift existing restrictions, which is a lot easier than providing costly new childcare services or generous parental leave.

Cultures don't change overnight, but laws can. The IMF says that when countries grant women the right to open a bank account, female labor force participation rises substantially over the next seven years.[8] Yet the pool of untapped female talent is still huge. Many countries are starting to recognize how much they stand to gain by opening worksite doors to women. The biggest gains are possible in the countries with the worst aging problems and the lowest female participation rates, including Japan and South Korea. In the United States, women joined the workforce in record numbers for much of the postwar era, but that trend peaked around 2003 and has been ebbing. A possible reason is that the United States combines a particularly high marriage tax penalty with unusually low spending on childcare services. It is also the only industrial country with no national policy guaranteeing some paid leave for new parents.

The OECD recently estimated that eliminating the gender gap— bringing as large a share of adult women into the workforce as men— would lead to an overall increase in GDP of 12 percent in its member nations between 2015 and 2030. The GDP gains would peak close to 20 percent in both Japan and South Korea and more than 20 percent in Italy, where less than 40 percent of women are in the formal labor force. A similar analysis in 2010 by Booz and Company showed that closing the gender gap in emerging countries could yield even larger gains in GDP by 2020, ranging from a 34 percent gain in Egypt to 27 percent in India and 9 percent in Brazil.

The Battle to Attract Migrants

One basic driver of population growth has remained steady in recent decades. Since 1960 the global fertility rate has plummeted, and life expectancy has extended from 50 years to 69 and is still rising, but the rate of migration has stayed pretty much the same. Half a century ago migrants accounted for about 3 percent of the global population, and in 2012 they still accounted for about 3 percent. And for all the fear generated in 2015 by the surge of more than one million refugees into Europe from war-torn Syria, Iraq, and Afghanistan, these surges are likely to last only as long as the localized violence. The more powerful underlying trend is the collapse of working-age population growth in the emerging world, which is already decreasing flows of economic migrants from these countries to the developed world. Between 2005 and 2010 net migration from developing to developed countries totaled 16.4 million people, but from 2010 to 2015 that total fell by nearly five million.

In fact, at least before anti-immigrant movements took off in Europe and the United States in 2015, the competition to attract foreign workers had been heating up. According to the United Nations, the number of countries that had publicly stated plans to try to increase the size of their populations "via immigration" more than doubled to twenty-two in 2013, from ten just three years earlier. To get a sense of which countries are doing well in attracting migrants, watch for which nations have been gaining or losing the most in population, as a result of net migration. Between 2011 and 2015 among the biggest gainers in the developed world were Australia, Canada, the United States, and Germany.

Perhaps the big surprise is Germany, which in 2015 received global attention for a growing backlash against the influx of war refugees that included arson attacks on local refugee centers and neo-Nazis chanting "Heil Hitler." Chancellor Angela Merkel suffered a decline in her popularity ratings that was partly attributable to her policy of opening doors wide to immigrants. However, were it not for a positive boost from net migration, Germany's population would have shrunk after 2011. Between 2011 and 2015, net migration boosted the German population by 1.6 percent—a number that exactly matched the increase in the United States, which is seen as the land of immigrants.

While the inflow of migrants was a big plus for the German economy, it was still relatively small compared to the pace of population decline. Between 2014 and 2015 the number of new arrivals spiked more than eightfold to about one million, but Germany would have to accept even more—about 1.5 million—every year between 2015 and 2030 in order to maintain its current balance of working-age people to retirees. That is not to suggest that Germany can or should simply accept more than a million refugees a year, because the challenges of integrating that many people into the economy quickly are real. It is only to dramatize the scale of Germany's aging problem, in which the imbalance between old and young is unfolding even faster than the refugees were arriving in 2015. This situation is typical for many industrial countries: Even a huge increase in the number of migrants they accept will only partially offset the depopulation bomb.

Outside of the refugee crisis, Canada and Australia have seen even bigger migration-driven boosts to their population than Germany, with total increases of 3.3 and 4.3 percent respectively since 2011. In recent years Australia's population has grown faster than that of any large developed country mainly because it has been open to orderly immigration. Two-thirds of the country's population growth is accounted for by migrants, most of them arriving from India and China. Australia's population is aging and its economic growth slowing, but if it keeps its doors open—which is far from certain in 2015, as an anti-immigrant movement gains momentum—the economic deceleration will be far slower than in most other rich countries.

Japan has been the anti-Australia, closing its doors about as tightly as a modern nation could. Less than 2 percent of its population is foreign born, compared to 30 percent of Australia's. Until recently this insularity was considered a competitive advantage; in the 1980s analysts inside and outside Japan saw the "harmony" of a monotone culture and the absence of ethnic conflict as one reason for its economic rise. Prime Minister Yasuhiro Nakasone and other political leaders publicly embraced the "homogeneous" society as essential to Japan's identity and strength. As recently as 2005, internal affairs minister Taro Aso—who later became deputy prime minister—celebrated the idea of Japan as "one race, one civilization, one language and one culture."

Some high government officials still take that line, but their views have collided with a widening realization in the Abe administration that Japan is going to be one lonely, shrinking civilization if it does not welcome economic migrants. Prime Minister Abe has increased the number of visas available to these new arrivals, and the numbers are picking up. But right now Japan has a net annual gain from migration of about fifty thousand people a year, and it would have to increase that number roughly tenfold to make up for its projected population decline through the year 2030. In other words, Japan would have to become a lot more like Australia.

South Korea is another ethnically uniform culture that once embraced its homogeneity as a source of cohesion in politics and discipline in the workforce. But it has been changing much faster than Japan in the face of a similarly stark decline in its working-age population. The shock of the Asian financial crisis of 1997–98 forced South Korea to rethink its cloistered ways. While there were about a quarter-million immigrants in South Korea before the crisis, since the year 2000 the immigrant population has increased 400 percent to 1.3 million, compared to an increase of just 50 percent in Japan. South Korea's government now promotes multiculturalism as official policy. Immigration services officials boast of their far-reaching efforts to lure talent, and the United Nations has lauded South Korea's system of providing foreigners with work permits in industries facing labor shortages. Though the working-age population is already shrinking, it would have been shrinking four times more rapidly without the influx of migrants. Further, since taking office in 2013, President Park Geun-hye has promised new moves to address the aging problem by attracting young foreigners to work in South Korea.

These campaigns to recruit economic migrants contrast with the disorganized efforts of nearby Thailand, now known as the "Old Man of Southeast Asia" because it is the only country in that region in which the working-age population is expected to shrink over the next five years. Led by a proselytizing bureaucrat who came to be known as Mr. Condom, Thailand in the 1970s pushed a birth control program that was, some now argue, too successful. Cops handed out condoms in traffic, and monks blessed condoms in temples. Mr. Condom—his real name was Mechai Viravaidya—offered free vasectomies at his restaurant chain Cabbages and Condoms and developed an international reputation by bringing fistfuls of condoms to World Bank talks. The fertility rate fell sharply, from 6 children for the average woman in 1970 to below the replacement level in the early 1990s.

Women aren't the answer for Thailand, because its female labor force participation rate is already more than 70 percent—by far the highest among countries at Thailand's income level, owing to the liberal Thai culture. Compared to others in Southeast Asia, this laid-back Buddhist society is also unusually open to foreigners, with nearly four million immigrants comprising more than 5 percent of its population, versus less than 1 percent in the Philippines and Indonesia. It is common in Thailand to meet foreign executives running major companies—something that rarely happens in more nationalist neighbors such as Indonesia or Malaysia. Migrant laborers—mainly fellow Buddhists from Myanmar, Laos, and Cambodia—also move easily in and out of Thailand, but they come as they choose, neither recruited nor discouraged. "It's a classic Thai tale. No conscious policy," a Bangkok-based economist told me during a visit to the city in October 2013. "Technically many of the immigrants are here illegally, but who really cares about the law?" To counter its aging problem, Thailand would need to offer a more deliberate welcome to immigrants.

Among the large emerging nations, the big recent gainers from migration have been Turkey, Malaysia, and South Africa, all of which have become regional magnets for refugees and job seekers. Between 2011 and 2015 inbound migration increased the population of South Africa by 1.1 percent, of Malaysia by 1.5 percent, and of Turkey by a striking 2.5 percent. In 2014, even as right-wing parties across western Europe were screaming for the expulsion of immigrants and refugees, Turkey quietly extended legal status to more than one million refugees, many of them from Syria. At least some Turkish leaders recognized the opportunity to import labor muscle and talent, including the many doctors and other well-educated professionals in the refugee ranks. In 2014, according to World Bank president Jim Yong Kim, a quarter of the new businesses in Turkey were started by Syrians, and the fastest-growing regions of Turkey were those where refugees had settled.[9]

Brain Gain, Brain Drain

As the competition to attract labor heats up, the competition for skilled labor is going to be especially fierce. As of 2014, two-thirds of the OECD member nations had recently implemented, or were in the process of implementing, policies designed to increase high-skilled immigration.

These programs have driven a 70 percent increase in the number of university-educated immigrants living in OECD nations to a total of 35 million over the 2000s. Despite the anti-immigrant upwelling of 2015, that underlying competition to attract foreign talent has continued.

For decades, the United States has benefited from brain gain, which has helped to fuel the entrepreneurial energy of American society. Today immigrants make up 13 percent of the total U.S. population, but they account for 25 percent of the new business owners and 30 percent of the people working in Silicon Valley. Of the top twenty-five U.S. tech companies in 2013, 60 percent were founded by first- or second-generation immigrants. Steve Jobs at Apple: second generation from Syria. Sergey Brin at Google: first generation from Russia. Larry Ellison at Oracle: second generation from Russia. Jeff Bezos at Amazon: second generation from Cuba. While many of these founders with immigrant roots hail from countries mired in war or economic dysfunction, quite a few come from families that left the heavily regulated economies of Europe, including old East Germany (Konstantin Guericke of Symantec), France (Pierre Omidyar of eBay), and Italy (Roger Marino of EMC).

In recent years Silicon Valley tycoons have become increasingly concerned that the United States was closing its doors to highly skilled foreigners, putting the country at a disadvantage in the talent wars. Since 2000 the United States has let in more and more foreigners to study but not to work. The number of student visas rose to nearly half a million over that period, but the number of employment or H1B visas held steady at around 150,000. The United States was sending 350,000 graduates home each year, mostly to India and China, and competitors were circling California, picking off fresh talent.

In 2013 the tech analyst Mary Meeker circulated photos of a billboard that the Canadian government placed on Highway 101, the main artery through Silicon Valley, taking a cheeky jab at President Barack Obama's promise of a foreign policy "Pivot to Asia." The billboard read, "H1B problems? Pivot to Canada." Before a visit to the Bay Area in the summer of 2013, Canada's minister of citizenship, immigration, and multiculturalism, Jason Kenney, said he was going to spread the word that Canada is "open for newcomers" and was "not going to apologize" for poaching talent. "If you guys cannot figure out your immigration system, we're going to invite the best and the brightest to come north of the border," he said.

It would be hard to find a crisper declaration of the global talent war. One way to identify winners is to look for countries where immigrants account for a large and growing share of university grads, which suggests that the nation has been gaining in educated talent. This gain is most dramatic in Britain, Canada, and particularly Australia, where immigrants represent 30 percent of the total population but 40 percent of university grads. That 10 percent gap represents significant brain gain. In the United States and Japan, immigrants represent equal shares of the university-educated population and the general population, so their impact is less powerful. In Germany, the Netherlands, and some other European countries, the immigrant population is less likely to hold degrees than the local population.

These differences are not small. The Chinese and Indian families moving to Australia and Canada tend to bring their high educational standards with them, and their children do as well on standardized high school tests as the locals. In fact, in Australia they do better—the only major industrial country where this is the case. In the United States and Britain, they do somewhat worse. But in many continental European countries, particularly in the north, they do dramatically worse. In Sweden, for example, 20 percent of native students score "below the level required to participate fully in modern society," but 60 percent of first-generation immigrants fall below the benchmark. Similarly glaring disparities are found in Germany, France, Switzerland, and other northern countries, where concerns are growing that migration is feeding the rise of an underclass, further taxing overburdened welfare and pension systems.

There is no question that cultural barriers complicate the process of integrating migrants into an advanced economy, but the same is true of integrating women and the elderly. Moreover, the fear of unskilled migrants is probably overblown. A growing body of research shows that immigration—skilled or not—tends to boost productivity and economic growth. World Bank economist Caglar Ozden recently looked into the often-heard charge that immigrants steal jobs from locals and found little truth to the claim.[10]

In general Ozden found that migrants often take jobs that locals don't want or can't fill. On a visit to Greece in June 2015, when its debt crisis was still raging and concern was high over double-digit youth unemployment, I was struck by how many local business owners nonetheless complained about the work ethic of young Greeks, saying they prefer to live at home on the generous pensions of their mothers, who shield them from grunt jobs. Almost to a man, the business owners said they liked to hire immigrants who were eager to work, a claim that has some support in data showing that in Greece the labor force participation rate is 10 percentage points higher for migrants than for locals.[11] That is the highest gap in Europe, so Greece is perhaps an extreme case, but migrants do often fill unwanted positions.

Ozden also found that unskilled migrants tend either to have no impact on local wages and employment or to increase wages and employment. He draws a parallel with the case of Malaysia, where the large recent influx of foreigners allowed many high-school-educated locals to become junior managers of immigrant laborers rather than be laborers themselves. This resulted in a big boost to economic growth, and the boost from skilled migrants tends to be even larger.

The main human drivers of productivity growth in the United States are scientists, tech professionals, engineers, and mathematicians—fields in which immigrants are already overrepresented. In this way migrants tend to fill jobs locals don't want at both the low end and the high end, whether as maids or math professors. Skilled migrants also spur technological progress by carrying across borders the sort of information that is hard to write down, because they are learned and disseminated through hands-on experience, like the details of making semiconductors. According to Harvard University's *Atlas of Economic Complexity*, the key to driving economic growth is not so much individual experts as the combination of expertise required to make complex products: for example, the mix of experience in batteries, liquid crystals, semiconductors, software, metallurgy, and lean manufacturing required to make a smartphone. The fastest way to secure this array of talent is to import it. The same idea applies to more and more fields in an age when even cooking has become culinary science. On a trip to Peru in January 2014, I was surprised to discover that by some rankings, Lima is home to three of the world's top twenty restaurants, a result of the mixing of Latin and Asian styles that has its roots in the migration of labor from China and Japan back in the nineteenth century.

For many emerging nations, the battle is as much about retaining as attracting talent. In the 2000s, by one estimate, some ninety thousand inventors moved out of China and India, many of them to the United States. That represented potentially dramatic gains for the United Sates and substantial losses for the emerging giants, but there is no systematic way to track these trends. I simply keep my ear to the ground for current evidence of brain drain and its reverse.

Sometimes the headline numbers can be misleading. Between 2011 and 2015 Russia witnessed strong positive net migration due to an influx of hundreds of thousands of job seekers from former Soviet Satellite states, led by Ukraine. But the increasing numbers of talented Russians leaving the country outstripped this influx. More than 180,000 Russians left in 2013, five times more than those who departed in 2009 and close to peaks reached during the banking crisis in 1998. Those leaving were entrepreneurs, writers, scientists, and the sons and daughters of families that could afford to send their children abroad to study, in the hope that they could eventually settle outside Russia. Dinner table conversation among the Russian elite dwelled on how to secure a visa to a desirable foreign country and how to get one's money out with the family.

The Chinese economy was much farther from a crisis situation than Russia's, but my colleagues there reported similar chatter. More than

ninety thousand millionaires left China between 2000 and 2014—by far
the largest outflow in raw numbers for any country. A Barclays Bank
survey in 2014 of two thousand wealthy Asians found that the Chinese
were by far the most likely to be considering emigration, with 47 percent
of them saying they aimed to leave their home country within five years.
Among the Chinese aiming to emigrate, roughly three out of four cited
economic security, a better climate, and better job and school opportunities for their children overseas. Chinese dinner table conversations were
all about the best place to go: the United States or Australia or Canada.
Recent news reports said that tens of thousands of Chinese were looking
to invest in Australia and Canada in order to secure special visas that
allow large investors to move to those countries legally. When smart people are seeking to move out of a country it is a bad sign, and when they
are looking to move out along with their money, it is an even worse sign.

Even as governments battle to attract immigrant talent, popular
backlashes against mixing migrants into society are still common if self-
defeating. Outside insular Japan, the general rule of thumb for most
industrial democracies is that immigrants account for 10 to 15 percent of
the population. Recent polls by Ipsos MORI, the British market research
group, show that the populace in Germany and the United Kingdom
believes the immigrant community is twice that size. The perception
gap is even wider in France and the United States, with polls indicating
that people think the immigrant population is three times bigger than it
really is: American respondents estimated that immigrants account for
32 percent of the population, when the actual figure is 13 percent.

This misperception reflects fear of outsiders and skews political
debate toward limiting immigration rather than welcoming a healthy
mix. In 2015, a front-running candidate for U.S. president, Donald
Trump, promised to force Mexico to pay for an impregnable wall on
the border. But with the working-age population in Mexico poised to
fall as well, Mexicans will have less reason to seek work in the United
States. Trump and his supporters didn't realize it, but in the four years
before 2015, net migration from Mexico had fallen to zero, in part

because construction jobs in the United States had been harder to find. This dynamic, with falling population growth in the emerging world reducing migration to the developed world, is likely to grow stronger in coming years.

Welcome, Robot

Fear of the robotic future is now as strong as fear of migrants and refugees, and it is built on a lack of imagination. In the early nineteenth century, when nine in ten Americans worked in farm jobs, it would have been hard to imagine that this figure would fall to about one in one hundred today and even harder to imagine where all the new jobs would come from. No one could have foreseen the full scale of the employment boom in the manufacturing and services industries. Paradoxically, pessimists today argue that robots will replace manufacturing jobs, and leave humans with no jobs at all, because it is again hard to imagine what comes next.

The pessimists say that the latest tech revolution is different because earlier generations of machines were made as tools for humans to use, but the newest technology is made to think like humans. This transformation is not about robotic arms providing muscle on the assembly line, they say—it's about automatons with artificial intelligence capable of "machine learning" and of, one day, designing the assembly line, all powered by the awesome computing capacity of the cloud and big data. In one of the most widely cited forecasts, the Oxford University researchers Carl Benedikt Frey and Michael Osborne predicted in late 2013 that about 47 percent of U.S. jobs are at risk from automation in the next decade or two.[12] The most common job for American men is driving, and one forecast has driverless smart cars and trucks replacing them all by 2020.

This line of logic parallels many arguments we have heard before. Berkeley's Machine Intelligence Research Institute has tallied up forecasts for when artificial intelligence (AI) will arrive, and the standard prediction today is that it will be upon us in twenty years. But that was also the standard prediction in 1955. The joke in the AI field is that if you say AI is coming in twenty years, you can get investors to fund your work; if you say five years they will remember and expect you to deliver, and if you say one hundred years they won't be interested.

While the robotics revolution could come faster than most previous technology revolutions, it is likely to be gradual enough to complement rather than destroy the human workforce. A huge gap still exists between the size of the world's industrial robot population—about 1.6 million—and the global industrial labor force of about 320 million humans. Most of these industrial robots are currently unintelligent machines, committed to a single task like turning a bolt or painting a car door, and indeed nearly half of them work in the car industry, which is still the single largest employer (of humans) in the United States.

Workplaces evolve to incorporate machines, but people find a way to fit in. Though U.S. banks have replaced a lot of humans with automated tellers, the savings have allowed them to open up a lot more branches, so that in total the number of human tellers actually increased from 500,000 in 1980 to 550,000 in 2010. Addressing the predictions of a jobless future, the Harvard economist Lawrence Katz has remarked, "We never run out of jobs. There is no long-term trend of eliminating work for people."[13]

If automation was displacing humans as fast as implied in recent books like Martin Ford's *The Rise of the Robots*, then we should be seeing the negative impact on jobs already. We're seeing the opposite. Another mystery of the postcrisis era is that while economic growth has been unusually weak, job growth in the major industrial countries (which use by far the most robots) has been relatively strong. In the G-7, the group of seven top industrial countries led by the United States, unemployment has fallen faster than expected in the face of weak economic growth, and faster than during any comparable period since at least the 1970s. Not only that, but the unemployment rate has been falling despite the fact that in Germany, Japan, Britain, and every G-7 country except the United States, the share of working-age people who participate in the labor force has been rising. The job picture has been particularly strong in Germany, Japan, and South Korea—which are also the industrial countries that employ the most robots.

Admittedly, the automaton invasion is in its early stages and picking up speed, but both historical and current evidence suggests humans will come to some agreeable arrangement with these invaders of their own creation. One of the new trends is cobots, industrial robots with swing arms safe enough to work alongside and in cooperation with people, rather than inside cages. The techno-optimists believe robots will be our servants, not our replacements, and will free us for lives of pampered leisure in retirement. Be that as it may, a strong practical argument can be made that the answer to fewer young people is more robots. An alarmed interviewer recently asked the Nobel economist and author Daniel Kahneman about the threat posed by the "rise of the robots" to a heavily industrialized country like China. "You just don't get it," Kahneman responded. "In China, the robots are going to come just in time" to rescue the country from population decline.[14]

In the future, economists may count growth in the working robot population as a positive sign for economic growth, the same way that today they analyze growth in the working-age human population. Whether by design or happy accident, many of the countries with the most rapidly aging populations also have the largest robot populations. According to the International Federation of Robots, the highest density of robots in the world can be found in South Korea, which in 2013 had 437 industrial robots per 10,000 employees, followed by Japan with 323, and Germany with 282. China was way behind with only 14, but on the bright side—arguably—it also had the world's fastest-growing robot population, up by 36,000 in 2013.

I am optimistic on automation in the workplace because I believe that the laws that govern the economic world are similar to those that govern the physical world, in which nothing is ever lost, nothing is gained, and everything is transformed. Over the past twenty-five years, as McKinsey consulting has pointed out, about a third of the new jobs created in the United States were types that did not exist, or barely existed, twenty-five years ago. In the next transformation of the workplace, humans are likely to replace the jobs lost to robots and artificial intelligence with new jobs we can't yet imagine.

All Hands on Deck

As the economic impact of population decline unfolds, some analysts will argue that the smart response to slower population growth is no response. That was the contention of many people in Japan, where the rapid aging of the population was visible as early as the 1960s, when the birthrate first fell below the replacement rate. The do-nothing argument is that the economic impact of population decline doesn't matter, if it doesn't lower per capita incomes. But it is hard for any country to hold that above-it-all pose. The reality of global competition will always intrude. In 2010 China became the world's second-largest economy, passing Japan, which has since mobilized much more aggressively to try to restart economic growth and respond to the challenge that China poses to its political and military position in Asia. A growing population matters for global status and the power that comes with economic might, apart from the greater dynamism and higher productivity that results from new people entering the workforce.

To assess which nations are best or worst positioned to grow, look first at projections for growth or shrinkage in the working-age population, to gauge the potential baseline gain for future economic growth. Just as important, track which countries are doing the most or the least to leverage whatever population gains they will enjoy. Are they opening the workforce to the elderly, to women, to foreigners? Are they taking steps to increase the talent level of the workforce, particularly by attracting highly skilled migrants? In a world facing a future of growing labor shortages, it's all hands—human or automated—on deck.

2

THE CIRCLE OF LIFE

Is the nation ready to back a reformer?

I N RETROSPECT, I MAY HAVE TAKEN THE INVITATION TO OFFER a "frank opinion" on Russia's future a bit too literally. In October 2010 a big Russian bank called to say the prime minister's office was inviting me to address that theme at an upcoming conference in Moscow's World Trade Center. I showed up to find a packed crowd in the large hall, with Vladimir Putin sitting on the podium along with other dignitaries, including then French finance minister Christine Lagarde. When it was my turn to speak, I tried to be frank, recounting how, when Putin took office as president in 2000, his nation was still traumatized by the multiple crises of the late 1990s. Putin's aggressive reforms, including a flat income tax of 13 percent, had helped unleash a halcyon era in which the average Russian income had more than quintupled from $2,000 to $12,000.

Then I turned to the present and future and, as Lagarde shot me a sideways glance, suggested it was not as bright. The challenges of generating economic growth had changed now that Russia was a middle-class country. Russia's economy was losing momentum chiefly because it had failed to diversify away from oil and gas, and it could not rely on a continuing windfall from high oil prices—which had pumped $1.5 trillion into the economy over the previous decade. There is an old saying,

I noted, that a rich country makes rich things, and while Russia needed up-and-coming new industries, it in fact had fewer small and medium-size businesses than most other developing economies.

As I continued, I noticed that Putin was looking stern and taking notes, and I flattered myself that he might have found something useful in my remarks. I did not realize that the conference was being broadcast live on Russian national TV; nor did I expect the frantic messages from my New York office early the next morning, asking, "What have you done?" The Kremlin-controlled coverage of the conference mentioned me as the ungrateful guest who had provided the gathering's only sour note, and it dismissed my remarks as the meanderings of a Wall Street type whose money Russia didn't need anyway. I was happy to be leaving town later that same day.

A few months later, in a public forum back home, I had the opportunity to interview former president George W. Bush. I asked him how Putin had changed since their 2001 meeting, when Bush said he had looked into the Russian president's soul and seen a man with whom he could do business. Bush responded that Putin had been corrupted by success, that he had grown more arrogant as the Russian economy took off. In their first encounter, Russia had been battling its way out of a severe financial crisis in 1998, and Putin had been relentless in his reform efforts, particularly in paring down Russia's debts. But by 2008 he was gloating over the American subprime mortgages that had tilted the world into a financial crisis. Putin the pragmatist had given way to Putin the populist, spending Russia's savings on giveaways like pension increases, and Putin the nationalist, reasserting Russian power in ways that were provoking fears of a new Cold War.

Bush's remarks began to crystallize in my mind a pattern I had seen repeat itself over and over, which is that even the most promising reformers tend to grow stale and arrogant with time, with decisive consequences for their economies. This aging process had eventually caught up to some of the most durable founders of Asia's miracle economies. During the 1970s and '80s in Indonesia, Suharto engineered rapid growth before his increasing proclivity to favor friends and family sparked the 1998 riots that burned Jakarta and ended his rule. In Malaysia, Mahathir Mohamad presided for twenty years over a similar miracle, but in 2003 a revolt within his own party toppled him, too. Even as Bush and I spoke, this same process of decay was unfolding in Turkey, where Prime Minister Recep Tayyip Erdoğan was on the path from pragmatic reform to populist nationalism and was being criticized at home as the "new Putin."

Though Putin is an extreme case, his evolution from reformer to demagogue is, I would argue, following the natural circle of political life, in which a crisis forces a nation to reform, reform leads to growth and good times, and good times encourage an arrogance and complacency that leads to a new crisis. During his first term, Putin listened to reform-minded advisers like economics minister German Gref and finance minister Alexei Kudrin, and pushed tax reform alongside efforts to save windfall oil profits and invest in new industry.

The good times were very good—the Russian economy nearly doubled in size between 2000 and 2010—but they encouraged a sense of complacency among Russians and gave full flower to the arrogance of their leader. Intoxicated by sky-high approval ratings, Putin quit pushing reform and focused on entrenching his hold on power. In 2011 he let Kudrin go, and the same year Russia's economy slowed sharply. It is too simple to say these events represent cause and effect, but the end of reform is one reason for the deep and protracted slowdown in Russia's economy.

The essential question to ask about the impact of politics on the prospects for any economy is this one: Is the nation ready to back a reformer? To answer it, the first step is to figure out which position the nation occupies on the circle of life. Nations are most likely to change for the better when they are struggling to recover from a crisis. When a country's back is against the wall, the general public and the political elites are most likely to accept tough economic reform. On the far side of the circle, nations are most likely to change for the worse in boom times, when the populace is sinking into complacency, too busy enjoying its good fortune to understand that in a competitive global economy, the need to reform is constant.

The second step is to figure out whether the country has a political leader capable of rallying the popular will behind reform. The circle of life captures broad, cyclical swings in the popular will, which have their greatest impact when new leaders have the charisma and good sense to translate a popular desire for change into a concrete reform agenda. The most auspicious moment is the arrival of the right leader, and Putin fit this profile when he assumed power as prime minister of Russia in 1999, then won a resounding election victory in the presidential elections the following year. In a crisis, the nation often demands a change in leadership, so look for the promising reformers among the newcomers: The crisis is likely to give them a strong mandate for change.

The least auspicious periods come under stale leaders, who tend to hang on to power by passing out government largesse as a reward to powerful allies and to a complacent populace. Boom times encourage even genuine reformers to grow arrogant and hang on to power too long, so watch out for stale leaders overstaying their welcome; they foretell a turn for the worse. Indeed, many of the mass political protests that have erupted since the crisis of 2008, from Turkey to Brazil and across the Arab world, were fundamentally revolts against stale leadership.

The circle of life operates in all countries but not always at the same speed. In the poorer nations of the emerging world, growth is much less steady and less predictable than in the richer ones of the developed world, and it is marked by sharp upturns and prolonged downturns. Often the downturns in emerging countries are of such a large magnitude that they can wipe out all or most of the gains made during the boom periods, limiting a nation's progress over time. In fact, many countries have slipped backward repeatedly. The quintupling of the average Russian income between 2000 and 2010 was impressive, yet that gain only returned the average income back to where it was in 1990, before it collapsed in the banking crises of the 1990s. Today the slide has resumed. In 2014, as a new crisis hit Putin's Russia following a collapse in oil prices, the nation's average per capita income fell again, from its peak of $12,000 in 2008 to $8,000.

This is how the circle of life turns, from the ashes of one crisis to the ashes of the next. In bad times, leaders blame foreigners and other forces beyond their control. In good times, they are quick to take credit. Even if the economic gains are generated in part by global forces— like the rising global oil prices that boosted petrostates like Russia after 1998—political leaders tend to see strong growth as confirmation of their own effectiveness. They come to assume along with their acolytes that, under such gifted leadership, their economy is destined to succeed. The Congress Party government of Manmohan Singh, who ruled India for much of the 2000s, came to believe the hype that the country was towering above other emerging nations. Many voters believed it too. The national conversation shifted away from the reforms required to keep growth strong and came to focus instead on how to spend the riches that Indians expected to continue flowing indefinitely from an economy growing at an annual pace of 8 to 9 percent. That shift was a clear harbinger of the sharp slump in growth in the 2010s.

The occasional successes and frequent failures of political leaders are central to the rise and fall of nations, and the circle of life offers a few guidelines for spotting which countries are about to enter a period of rapid growth, and which are about to fall off the growth map.

Any newspaper reader has read dozens of columns ending with the recommendation that this or that country needs "structural reform," which is timeless wisdom in the sense that it can wisely be said of any nation at any time. There is never a moment when a country does not need to repair something "structural," which sometimes refers to "micro" problems with the way business and government operate, and at other times to "macro" problems like high inflation, an overvalued currency or budget and trade deficits. Often there is a pretty reasonable consensus on what the most useful repairs might be. Even in the polarized U.S. political scene today, support seems to be growing for cutting uncompetitive corporate tax rates. In poorer countries the punch list can be so long that where a new leader begins may not matter: cutting peace deals with rebels, building roads, opening to trade, or jailing crooked finance officials.

However, pinpointing when a country is ready to make hard changes is more important than identifying the specific content of the reform. And typically, the public's willingness to back change depends on whether it is feeling the urgency of a crisis or the laziness of fat times. The critical role that popular mood plays in driving the circle of life unfolded vividly in countries from Russia to India and Brazil during the global boom of the 2000s; many nations assumed that high growth would last forever, and the only "reform" question on the table was how to share the coming wealth. The sense that the party would never end was palpable to any visitor to Rio or Moscow or Delhi, where many people came to feel that a prosperous future was their destiny. Thus the potential for change of the kind we are interested in—the tough reforms that can change a nation's direction for the better—would have to await a turn in the circle of life. Unfortunately, all these countries needed a good crisis.

A good crisis raises the probability that a nation will embrace change and new leaders, but it is very hard to say which new leaders will be successful reformers. They are a rare breed, and their efforts always face innumerable challenges, whether from entrenched interests at home or from headwinds in the global economy. Nonetheless, from my own experience on the road, I have a couple of rules about the type of leaders who are most likely to be able to shape popular support for change into a workable reform program. Simply put, the probability of successful, sustained reform is higher under fresh leaders rather than stale leaders, under leaders with a mass base rather than well-credentialed technocrats, and under democratic leaders rather than autocrats. Though China's boom of the last three decades has done much to burnish the reputation of a certain brand of technocratic and autocratic economic leadership, the evidence from other countries doesn't bear out that view.

Fresh Leaders

French president Charles de Gaulle once said, "A great leader emerges from the encounter of will and an exceptional period in history," and this is the basic dynamic linking crises to promising new reformers. The bigger the crisis, the greater the shock to the public, and the more eagerly people will support a fresh leader, even if that change disrupts the old order.

The first big shock to postwar prosperity came in the 1970s, when much of the world felt leaderless in the face of stagflation—stagnant economic growth coupled with high inflation, triggered by a complex of forces including the excess spending of the welfare states and sharp oil price hikes engineered by the OPEC cartel and the petrostates. The widespread sense that their countries were coming apart prepared many nations to accept the idea of radical change and led to the rise of pioneering free market reformers: Margaret Thatcher in Britain, Ronald Reagan in the United States, and Deng Xiaoping in China. As is often the case in crisis periods, the promise of these leaders was often obscured by the gloom of the times; early on many observers dismissed Reagan as an ex-actor, Thatcher as a grocer's daughter, and Deng as a faceless member of China's collective leadership. China circa 1978 was too shell shocked by the recent mob violence of the Cultural Revolution to harbor high expectations for any leader.

The pain caused by any crisis will induce many countries to demand change—but not always to embrace hard reform. Some countries will turn to populists promising easy prosperity and a restoration of national glory, the way Venezuela embraced Hugo Chávez and Argentina turned to Nestor Kirchner after the Latin crises of the 1990s. Others will turn to real reformers, as the United States, Britain, and China turned to Reagan, Thatcher, and Deng in the 1980s.

All three took over countries facing a crisis of national status, following a decade that gave their people reason to fear that they were losing ground to major global rivals. Thatcher and Reagan both campaigned on vows to turn back "socialism" at home and abroad. They also set out to make up for the humiliations of the 1970s, when Britain fell deep into debt and became the first developed nation to seek an IMF bailout. British conservatives worried openly that their overregulated welfare state had shifted to the left of even a socialist state like France. Americans fell into the "malaise" of the Jimmy Carter years and began to fear that they could be subject to oil-price blackmail at the hands of the OPEC cartel. Deng, in turn, unleashed his pragmatic reforms in part because he had visited Singapore and New York and had seen that these capitalist economies were far ahead of his own. Fear of being overtaken—a shared crisis of national status—gave all these countries an urgent motive to reform.

The unusual thing about the Reagan, Thatcher, and Deng generation was how, in wildly different economic settings, they settled on similar reforms to address their crises. The low growth and high inflation of the 1970s was traceable in varying degrees to cumbersome state controls, and the solution pushed by this generation of leaders created a basic template for free market reform. In the United States and Britain, that template included some mix of loosening central control over the economy, cutting taxes and red tape, privatizing state companies, and lifting price controls while supporting the central bank policies that played the critical role in taming inflation. In China, it included freeing peasants to till their own land and opening to foreign trade and investment. Controversy over the legacy of these leaders endures, but their reforms doubtless brought a new dynamism to stagnating economies. As the United States and Britain started to recover in the 1980s, and particularly as China's economy took off, these role models helped to inspire a new generation of reformers.

By the 1990s, under the influence of the new free market orthodoxy, many emerging nations started to open up to outside trade and capital flows, and some were getting themselves in trouble, having borrowed too heavily from foreign creditors. Debt-induced currency crises struck first in Mexico in 1994, spread throughout East and Southeast Asia in

1997–98, then leapfrogged to Russia, Turkey, and Brazil over the next four years. The circle of life was turning, as crisis gave birth to a new upwelling of support for reform. From the bankruptcies and economic debris of 1998 sprang the next generation of new leaders, and a largely unheralded new group of reformers: Kim Dae-jung of South Korea, Luiz Inácio Lula da Silva of Brazil, Erdoğan in Turkey, and Putin in Russia.

It is easy to forget now, as both Putin and Erdoğan cling to power, but this quartet built the foundation of rising government budget and trade surpluses, shrinking debts, and falling inflation that helped to underpin the greatest boom ever to lift the developing world. In the five years before 2010, that boom virtually erased the specter of bad times in poor countries, and 97 percent of emerging economies—107 of the 110 nations for which there is relevant data—were catching up to the United States in terms of their average per capita income. That catch-up rate of 97 percent compares to an average of 42 percent for every previous five-year period going back fifty years. Moreover, the three countries that were falling behind between 2005 and 2010 were small ones: Jamaica, Eritrea, and Niger. Every reasonably large emerging economy was catching up, and the leaders of South Korea, Russia, Turkey, and Brazil contributed more than any other leaders to what became known as "the rise of the rest."[1]

Like the Reagan generation before it, the Kim generation exploited a popular sense of crisis and diminished national status to push reform. I attach Kim Dae-jung's name to this generation because he was arguably the most impressive change agent in the group. Kim had only a vocational education and hailed from the poor southern provinces long neglected by the northern power center around Seoul. A charismatic populist, he became one of the leading dissidents against South Korea's authoritarian regimes of the 1970s and '80s, when he was jailed repeatedly. Kim finally won election at the height of the Asian financial crisis in 1998, scoring the first victory for an opposition leader in postwar Korea. He set about not only balancing the books but also breaking up the secretive ties among politicians, state banks, and leading conglomerates that had allowed and even encouraged Korean companies to run up the massive debts that melted down in the crisis. His government created a new agency with the power to shutter the least stable banks and to compel the others to keep enough reserves on hand to cover their loans. No member of this leadership generation did more to reform the basic structure of his nation's economy, which is one reason South Korea remains economically stronger than Russia, Turkey, or Brazil today.

Still, the accomplishments of Kim's peers were also remarkable, for their time and place. After being appointed to succeed Yeltsin in the wake of the ruble crisis of '98, Putin won the presidential election of 2000 on promises to restore a firm hand to Russia. Under the influence of advisers like Kudrin and Gref, he took big, creative steps in the right direction. He placed a large part of the oil profits in a rainy-day fund, and he cut a deal with Russia's new class of tycoons, allowing them free rein to run their businesses so long as they stayed out of politics. To reduce the opportunities for corruption inherent in a byzantine system of taxes collected by multiple government agencies, he cut the number of taxes from 200 to 16, combined multiple income tax rates into the low flat rate, set up a single collection agency, and fired all the tax police, many of whom were corrupt. The lower tax rates actually raised revenue and helped Putin rebalance the budget. Unlike Kim, he did little to make banks or companies more competitive or to build manufacturing industries, but he did put the national finances on a stable foundation for the first time since the collapse of the Soviet Union.

Two years later Erdoğan took office in Turkey, on the heels of a currency crisis and amid raging hyperinflation. Like Putin, Erdoğan put his economy on a more stable footing, also following the lead of able financial advisers like the economy minister Ali Babacan. Erdoğan too traveled to London and New York, making speeches about integrating his country into the West, saying it was his party's "mission to prove" that the principles of free market democracy "can also be the basics of a Muslim society." He handled his nation's finances with impeccable responsibility, reforming a wasteful pension system, privatizing

troublesome state banks, passing a law to shut down bankrupt companies more smoothly, and vowing to maintain a budget surplus. Whatever criticism Erdoğan and Putin would bring upon themselves later,
the positive impact of their early reforms would be hard to deny: Over
the next decade, the Turks, like the Russians, would see their average
per capita income rise many times over, to more than $10,000. Both
countries would move from the ranks of poor nations to the middle
class, at least for a while.

The type of crisis that opens the door to fresh leaders is the kind
that triggers a change in mindset. It can spring from popular reaction
to a major shock, as in the case of the Asian financial crisis of 1997–98,
which mobilized not only the Koreans but also the Indonesians and other
nations to reform. But it can also spring from slow-burning frustration
with a long-term loss of economic stature. All but one of the reformers
and potential reformers above, from Thatcher in the 1980s to Putin,
emerged in an economy that in the previous decade had been losing
ground to its rivals—losing share in regional or global GDP. The exception is Erdoğan in Turkey, which was not losing ground to its neighbors
only because countries in that region were in even worse slumps.

Some observers will have several objections to this narrative. One is
that Putin and Erdoğan reformed only because they had to, as a condition for getting bailout money from the IMF, so it is a mischaracteriza-
tion to suggest that they were ever genuine reformers. But the point is
that very often crisis can force leaders to reform, whether they believe
in it, or because the population demands it, or because creditors force
their hand. What was clear to anyone visiting Moscow or Istanbul in
the early 2000s, or listening to the hardheaded Turkish and Russian
reformers like Babacan or Kudrin, was that Putin and Erdoğan were
under pressure not only from the IMF but also from their own people and from the painful fallout of a national crisis. Turkey and Russia
were ready to change, and Putin and Erdoğan were the right leaders
to shape reform, because they were popular charismatic figures who
understood the urgency of the moment.

Another natural objection is that Russia and Turkey were swept up in the general emerging-world boom of the 2000s, so the strong growth they enjoyed was no particular credit to Putin or Erdoğan. While good luck in the form of a global boom certainly played a role in their success stories, the economic policies of these leaders need to be contrasted with those followed by Chávez in Venezuela and Kirchner in Argentina. Through the cycle, Russia and Turkey fared far better in economic terms than Venezuela and Argentina, experiencing both more solid growth and much lower inflation.

The same mix of good luck and good policy marked the rise of the last member of this generation, Lula da Silva in Brazil. Elected in 2002, he took over from Henrique Cardoso, who had begun to tame hyperinflation. But it was Lula who had the charisma and street credibility to change Brazil's worldview, and who got credit for the turnaround that followed. The first Brazilian president from the working class, Lula had lost a finger in an industrial accident at the age of nineteen and was described by critics as "blue collar, quasi-illiterate and nine-fingered"; many expected him to resume the generous public spending that had helped fuel hyperinflation the decade before. Among investors, fear of Lula was so high that the prospect of his victory led to sharp falls in the Brazilian currency and the stock market, and this very crisis helped inspire Lula's early reforms.

Lula appointed as his central banker a former head of FleetBoston named Henrique Meirelles, who vowed to whip inflation and did, raising interest rates to more than 25 percent. With the help of the global commodity price boom, Brazil's economic growth accelerated under Lula. Following in the footsteps of great leaders before him, he combined a basic understanding of what his country needed to recover with the popular touch needed to sell hard reform, and thus he helped to extricate his country from an exceptionally difficult moment.

The next worldwide upheaval came in the global financial crisis of 2008. It was the deepest crisis since the 1930s, and any event of that scale was bound to inspire loud demands for change. Indeed, what followed was a popular revolt against seated rulers across the world, conducted in the ballot box and on the streets. In democratic nations, voters turned on their governments. Between 2005 and 2007, citizens of the world's thirty largest democracies, including the twenty largest emerging democracies, had voted to return the ruling party to power in two out of every three national elections. Between 2010 and 2012, as the global slowdown spread to the developing world, the rejection rate doubled, and citizens voted to toss out the ruling party in two out of every three elections. That antigovernment revolt swept out incumbent parties across much of Europe, as well as in Chile, Mexico, and the Philippines, and it later rolled on to sweep out incumbents in India, Indonesia, Italy, and elsewhere. Though it is too soon to judge the newcomers, the next high-impact leaders are likely to rise from reformers elected to address problems highlighted by the events of 2008.

Stale Leaders

Every post-crisis transition is complex, but one strong pattern does emerge: While reform is most likely under bold new leaders, it grows less likely as time passes, as the leader's focus turns to securing a grand legacy or rewarding family and friends. One simple way to think about this rule is that high-impact reform is most likely in a leader's first term, less likely in the second term, and unlikely beyond the second term, when leaders will tend to run out of reform ideas or the popularity to implement them, or both. There are, of course, exceptions—Lee Kuan Yew governed Singapore for more than three decades and never seemed to lose energy for reform—but the general pattern holds.

Staleness overtook many of the most celebrated reformers. Reagan fell victim to the "second term curse," that recurring cycle of scandal, popular fatigue, and congressional opposition that has made it tough for American presidents to push change after their first terms. Though some observers doubt that the curse is real, the noted historian Michael Beschloss has said there is something to it, given that no president has accomplished what he set out to do in his second term, at least not since James Monroe, two centuries ago.

Even Deng, who was subject to neither term limits nor elections, was effectively diminished in influence after about two terms in office. He took power in 1980 and ruled as party and military chief until growing popular demands for political freedoms—to match the economic freedoms he had granted—erupted in the 1989 uprising at Tiananmen Square. After the bloodshed, Deng relinquished his posts as military and party chief but held on to his informal role as "paramount leader," which he used to continue pushing the same mix of economic pragmatism and political repression. Thus a man who was arguably the most important economic reformer of the twentieth century retained his most powerful official roles for only nine years, a striking benchmark for how quickly even the best leaders grow stale. Since then China has also followed a strong tradition of completely overhauling its leadership every ten years.

While Lula and Kim had the good sense not to fight to hold on to power, even Lula began to demonstrate the arrogance and complacency typical of aging regimes. In 2009, when the global financial crisis was devastating many Western nations but not yet the emerging nations, Lula was nearing the end of his second term and began to crow about how well Brazil had weathered the crisis. He lectured the world about how the financial cataclysm of 2008 "was caused by no black man or woman or by no indigenous person or by no poor person. This crisis was fostered and boosted by irrational behavior of some people that are white, blue-eyed."[2] He didn't realize the crisis would hit Brazil and many other emerging nations in the following years, after he stepped down as scheduled on January 1, 2011, in accordance with Brazilian law.

Alas, Erdoğan and Putin did not show the same respect for the legal limits on their power. Both are now in their fourth terms in top leadership posts, which is very rare in major countries, and they are particularly ripe examples of stale leadership. As late as 2006, the willingness of Russian leaders to exercise restraint in spending and to listen to basic advice on how to keep growth alive, including the need to diversify away from oil, was still impressive. Soon thereafter, however, policy shifted as the government began to drain the rainy-day fund it had set up to save oil profits, and to spend heavily on giveaways to please the masses, including large increases in pension payments to a rapidly growing population of senior citizens. That combination threatened to undermine Russia's hard-won budget stability.

Meanwhile in Turkey, critics leveled the charge about Erdoğan as being "the next Putin," increasingly autocratic and uninterested in reform, cracking down on civil liberties and aggressively punishing dissent. After taking power as head of the Islamic AK Party in 2002, he had started well, and until the end of his first term in 2007, Turkey was recognized as one of the leading reformers in the emerging world. Erdoğan was widely praised for opening up opportunities to the pious Muslim majority, who had long been excluded from positions of power. This mainstreaming of the majority set off a growth boom that made Erdoğan popular not only among practicing Muslims but also among some elements of the old, secular "White Turk" elite.

With each election, Erdoğan's legislative majority grew, but so did his arrogance. By the time his third term began in 2011, he was alienating secular Turks by more aggressively enforcing Islamic social mores in crackdowns on nightclubs, alcohol, smoking, drinking, and kissing in public. Like Putin, Erdoğan spent heavily to burnish nationalist pride, in his case pushing projects designed to revive the Islamic greatness that had been Turkey in the Ottoman era, including the world's largest mosque. That further alienated secular Turks. Two years later, Erdoğan's plan to turn a popular Istanbul park into an Ottoman-inspired mall would envelop Turkey in a broad middle-class revolt against aging governments across the emerging world, from Egypt to Brazil.

Writers raced to explain this outburst of unrest in the summer of 2013, and all focused on the middle-class protesters, not the stale regimes they were targeting. A *Washington Post* team identified the "middle-class rage" of societies that "are now demanding more." A *New York Times* writer began his piece in an upscale restaurant in the Istanbul suburbs, where he saw a revolt of "the rising classes" and of the "educated haves" who had benefited most from the regimes they had come to reject. The Stanford political scientist Francis Fukuyama spotted a "middle-class revolution" of tech-savvy youths. These were rich stories, well told, but the growing middle class was not a harbinger of the coming protests. Yes, the middle class was growing in the protest-stricken nations, but it was growing in many other countries as well. Over the previous fifteen years, in twenty-one of the largest emerging nations, the middle-class population had expanded by an average of 18 percentage points as a share of the total population, to a bit more than half.[3]

The protests, however, had erupted in nations where the middle class had grown very fast, such as Russia (up 63 percentage points) and quite slowly, such as South Africa (up 5 percentage points). The biggest protests hit countries where the middle class was expanding at a pace close to the 18 point average: Egypt up 14 points, Brazil 19 points, Turkey 22 points. In short, there was no clear link between growth in the middle class and the rise of middle-class protest.

The stronger link among these protests was their target: Every one of them targeted an aging and complacent regime. The economic boom that lifted the emerging world in the 2000s had convinced many national leaders that they were personally responsible for their nation's success. They started playing tricks of various kinds—dodging term limits, switching offices—to hang on to power. Between 2003 and 2013, among the twenty most important emerging economies, the average tenure of the ruling party doubled from four years to eight years. That was fine with the prospering majority in most of these countries—until economic growth in the emerging world started to slow sharply at the end of the decade.

The first protests erupted in 2011, with the sharp intensification of mine strikes in South Africa. Later that year came protests against Singh's government in India and against Putin in Russia, where some marchers carried posters comparing Putin to notorious dictators-for-life like Muammar el-Qaddafi of Libya and Kim Jong-il of North Korea. By 2013, of the twenty most important emerging economies, seven had seen outbreaks of political unrest: Russia, India, South Africa, Egypt, Turkey, Brazil, and Argentina. And every one of those eruptions came against a regime that had been in power for longer than eight years and had failed to keep pace with the economic challenges of the post-crisis world.

The working assumption has to be that even strong leaders will lose reform momentum, the longer they stay in power. Often the timing depends at least in part on the state of the economy. When Nestor Kirchner took over as president of Argentina in mid-2003, Argentina was struggling to get back on its feet after a four-year period of outright economic depression. Kirchner, a committed populist, nonetheless kept on the reform-minded finance minister Roberto Lavagna, who had helped Argentina tighten its belt to get through the last years of the depression. But once the economic recovery seemed well entrenched in 2005, Kirchner fired Lavagna and lurched back to the left. It was a telling moment, much like Putin letting go of Kudrin in 2011. Beware when presidents start firing the reformers on their staff.

The stock markets clearly sense this process of decay. Since 1988 the major emerging nations have held a total of ninety-one national elections, producing a total of sixty-seven new leaders, including fifteen who lasted two full terms in office. The two termers are by definition a politically successful group, led by the likes of Putin, Erdoğan, Lula, and Singh. But as their tenures wore on, the national stock markets grew increasingly critical of how they handled the economy; as a group, they outperformed the global average for emerging markets by 16 percent in the leader's first term, but in the second term there was virtually no outperformance. Some of the weakest results came under Erdoğan in Turkey, where the stock market lagged behind the emerging-world average by 18 percent during his second term, from 2007 to 2011; Donald Tusk in Poland, which lagged by 6 percent during his second term from

2011 to 2014; and Singh in India, which lagged by 6 percent during his second term from 2009 to 2014.

As regimes age, markets can almost smell the gradual death of reform. Though leadership terms tend to run around four years, they can vary quite widely in duration, particularly in parliamentary systems where the prime minister can call snap elections. To pinpoint the moment when markets tend to turn on seated prime ministers and presidents, I looked again at the ninety-one national elections since 1988 and identified thirty-three leaders who lasted at least five years in power. The results: For these leaders as a group, for the first three and a half years, the median market return tended to rise faster than the emerging-world average—to be exact, they outperformed the average by more than 30 percent in the first forty-one months of the leaders' tenures. Perhaps even more telling, nearly all (90 percent) of that gain against the emerging-world pack came in the first twenty-four months of the new regime. After three and a half years, however, the market started to move sideways. This looks like strong confirmation that the political honeymoon phase—the early years of an administration—is the period when an emerging-world leader is most likely to push through reform with a positive impact on the economy. Markets, of course, tend to go up when investors have reason to expect the economy to pick up pace in the future and for inflation to decline.

It's worth noting that running the same analysis for developed countries revealed no clear connection between stock market returns and aging political leadership. This doesn't mean that leaders don't matter in rich countries, only that politics matters more in emerging ones, where institutions are weaker and new or aging leaders can have a clearer impact on the economy's direction and therefore on the mood of the markets.

It is the rare leader who realizes that the best way to secure a respected place in history is to retire after a good run. Many presidents aspire to die in office and seek to hang on by removing term limits, or by switching from one top leadership post to another, or by installing a relative or crony to serve in their place. In Russia, Putin has dodged term limits by shifting from the president's office to the prime minister's office and back. Erdoğan has embarked on a similar path: Having failed to change the rules so he could run for a fourth term as prime minister, he ran in 2014 for president and won. Upon taking office, he announced that a new $600 million, thousand-room palace that he had commissioned as the new residence of Turkish prime ministers would instead become the new home of the president. Like Putin and many others before him, Erdoğan could have secured an unblemished legacy as one of his nation's greatest postwar leaders—if he had stepped down gracefully after two terms. Instead, he is mired in controversy. In the end, said Ralph Waldo Emerson, every hero becomes a bore.

It is a bad sign for any country when its leader can't give up the trappings of power and views himself as consubstantial with the nation. The Bolivian socialist Evo Morales presided over a reasonably strong economy for two terms, then recently succeeded in changing the constitution to allow himself to run for a third, which is not a good sign. Meanwhile the current leaders of Brazil, Malaysia, South Africa, and Venezuela were all handpicked by their predecessors and often follow similar policies. Others essentially inherited power from a relative or spouse, which is why the ambitious wife of Peruvian president Ollanta Humala came to be seen as his possible successor, and how President Cristina Kirchner of Argentina arrived in her post.

If aging governments are unlikely to offer people hope of economic reform, the reverse is true for young regimes. Consider again the protests in the summer of 2013: At that time eleven of the twenty-one major emerging nations had ruling parties that had been in power for less than eight years, and none of those governments became a target of mass protests. The one debatable case was Egypt, where the Arab Spring toppled two regimes in quick succession, but by 2013 the protests were targeting the military government of former field marshal Abdel Fattah el-Sisi, which was widely seen as a revival of the old Mubarak dictatorship. In short, middle-class protesters across the world were attacking regimes they saw as moribund while often giving new regimes a free pass to prove themselves. And those new regimes counted among them several fresh leaders who were at least trying to push serious economic reform, including in Mexico, the Philippines, and Pakistan. In these countries, the young, the educated, and the newly prosperous middle classes had no reason to tweet their friends and hit the streets. They had reason to believe change for the better was possible under a new leader, and so did anyone watching these nations.

Populist Demagogues, versus Populists Who Get It

Successful leaders often share these two key attributes: popular support among the masses and a clear understanding of economic reform, or at least a willingness to delegate power to experts who do get it. In contrast, populist demagogues who artfully combine populism and nationalism can be politically successful but tend to be a disaster for their countries.

Consider the way Venezuela and neighboring Colombia parted ways under two very different kinds of populists following the financial crises of the 1990s. In 2002 Venezuelans elected Hugo Chávez, a radical populist who scared the business elite for good reason. He pushed an experimental socialism under which Venezuelan incomes have continued a half-century of decline. Meanwhile, in the same year, Colombia elected Álvaro Uribe, a right-wing populist who not only put the books in order but also managed to quell the multiple guerrilla uprisings that had for decades been the chief obstacle to growth in his country. Uribe was hugely popular both at home and abroad; indeed, his first term saw the Colombian stock market rise more than 1,600 percent—the biggest increase for any of the sixty-three first-term leaders in my study of the market reactions to emerging-world elections. However, that vote of global confidence in Colombia's future may have gone to Uribe's head: He tried to amend the constitution not once but twice, winning his bid for a second term but losing his bid for a third, tainting his legacy.

Admittedly, it can be difficult to distinguish between populists who get it and those who don't. When national leaders meet international reporters and global investors, they arrive well prepared to sound sharp, speaking the latest economic jargon. In 2005, on a visit to Brazil, I met the former Rio state governor Anthony Garotinho, who had first made his name as an evangelical radio broadcaster and was now running for the presidency and making waves with his anti-American campaign speeches. In private, Garotinho told me to ignore his campaign talk because in fact he liked Americans a lot and welcomed foreign investors. The next day stories appeared in the Brazilian press about our meeting, which appeared to have been leaked to blunt criticism that he was too much of a provincial maverick to hold national office. He lost anyway, but I was left with a new understanding of how heavily to discount anything charming populists say, in public or private.

Journalists are trained to be wary of getting too close to one's subjects, but the same rule applies to anyone working in the economic field. An entry ticket to the circles of power can easily cloud judgment and skepticism, but over time encounters with presidents and prime ministers can start to meld into one smooth pitch. Politicians this successful tend to be world-class charmers, well prepared to show that they know what needs to be done to reform the economy, much as Putin and Erdoğan had done a decade earlier.

I should have taken a larger dose of skepticism into my March 2013 meeting with the leader of Thailand. The country's economic prospects had not looked so good since the recovery from the Asian financial crisis in the late 1990s, and residents of Bangkok were buzzing over their glamorous prime minister, Yingluck Shinawatra. She had managed to calm the country after street battles between her rural supporters and members of the Bangkok elite, who had run her brother and predecessor as prime minister out of the country on corruption charges. The calm was threatened, however, by rumors that the exiled brother was still calling the shots. So when I had a chance to meet the Thai leader at Phitsanulok Mansion, the prime minister's official residence in downtown Bangkok, I asked about her brother Thaksin. "Do you have a little sister?" she responded coyly. I said I did indeed. "Does she always listen to you?" I was charmed, persuaded that she was her own person and Thailand was indeed changing for the better. Within months, however, she began moving to grant amnesty to her brother, triggering a new revolt and a coup that toppled her in May 2014. The renewed turmoil took a toll on Thailand's economy, and the country's growth rate slumped from 5 percent in early 2013 to 2 percent in 2015.

A particularly auspicious mix of personality traits in a leader is a combination of public charisma and private earnestness. Deng Xiaoping was a visionary reformer and magnetic public personality, yet in private he could also surprise visitors like Henry Kissinger with his capacity for going on about the affairs of the department of metallurgy. India's new prime minister Narendra Modi is a bit like that—shockingly nuts and bolts in the flesh. So is the president of the Philippines, Noynoy Aquino, whose earthy charm helps ordinary Filipino voters overlook the fact that he hails from the landed aristocracy. Aquino eschews visionary speeches and, when I met him in Manila in August 2012, spoke about Manila water projects and local sardine fisheries at such length, I have to admit I left the meeting a bit befuddled. But then it occurred to me that, particularly coming on the heels of a string of flamboyantly corrupt and incompetent leaders that stretched back to Ferdinand Marcos, Aquino was exactly the kind of leader the Philippines needed at the time: a brass tacks reformer. By not trying to dazzle, he ended up persuading me that the Philippines would change for the better.

The global markets often react negatively to the rise of left-wing populists, making no distinction between a reckless populist like Chávez and a smart populist like Lula or Erdoğan in their early years. The markets often take the campaign speeches of radical populists at face value and fail to see the closet pragmatists among them, or they project their own hopes for business-friendly reform onto an election. I've seen many cases in which, in the depths of an economic crisis, the markets bet heavily on the economic reformer to win a coming election, only to be surprised by the victory of a left-wing populist. In 2014, the markets were surprised by the win for the left-wing candidate Dilma Rousseff in Brazil, in part because market analysts lost sight of how often nations facing economic trouble will respond to a mix of nationalism and populism—not to the logic of economic reform. Again, crises raise the likelihood that a new leader can push through tough reform but do not guarantee it. No single rule ever governs a nation's economic prospects, and the circle of life is one part of the mosaic that helps predict the rise and fall of nations.

The False Dawn of the Technocrats

The markets also tend to cheer for technocrats, assuming that leaders with backgrounds in the finance ministry, or the World Bank, or the economics department of a prestigious university will understand the requirements of reform and strong growth. Technocrats rarely succeed in the top job, however, because they tend to lack the political flair to sell reform or even to last very long in office. The European Commission president Jean-Claude Juncker captured the lament of technocrats everywhere when he remarked, "We all know what to do, we just don't know how to get re-elected after we've done it."[4]

During the euro crisis of 2010, several nations turned to technocratic leaders for salvation, and they too took sensible steps but could not hold on to power. When Greece's government collapsed in 2011, parliament turned to the former central bank chief Lucas Papademos as its caretaker prime minister, perhaps figuring that a man who had done seminal academic work on unemployment was right for a country where one in four people were out of work. Papademos gave sensible speeches about how Greece needed to make tough cuts in wages and benefits to become competitive again, but he never intended to stay and left after a year. His fellow caretaker prime minister in the Czech Republic, the former national chief statistician Jan Fischer, also lasted about a year, leaving a nice impression among fellow politicians but not among voters. They gave him 15 percent of the tally in the next presidential election.

At the height of the euro crisis, perhaps the highest hopes for a technocrat greeted Italy's Mario Monti, a trained economist who had served as a university president and as the European commissioner responsible for taxes. In 2011 Italy's stock market jumped up on the news that Monti would take over as prime minister, but he too made all the necessary austerity moves and failed to sell them to the public. A little over a year later, he lost his bid to stay on as prime minister, taking only 10 percent of the vote. It took the 2014 election of a charismatic thirty-nine-year old, Matteo Renzi, to reawaken hopes for reform in Italy.

The list of failed technocrats is equally long in authoritarian states, which have been among the most avid believers in the notion that expert authority knows best. The most prominent case is the Soviet Union, where the pseudo-scientific central plan contributed to the empire's collapse. But a similar decay infected countries heavily influenced by the Soviet model, including not only the satellite dictatorships like East Germany but also some of the large democracies, like India under the Congress Party and Mexico during the seventy-one-year rule of the Institutional Revolutionary Party (PRI).

On the other hand, technocratic advisers can often serve leaders well, if they are giving the right advice and leaders are willing to listen. Vikram Nehru, a former World Bank economist, illustrates the point with the story of Bernard Bell, the bank's point man in Asia during the 1960s, when the bank still projected an all-powerful mystique. Bell advised countries on how to reform to spur growth, offering a menu of ideas that generally required governments to export their way to prosperity by opening the economy to global trade. Not every nation was ready to hear this advice. In India, the popular mood was anticapitalist and anti-American, and on a trip to Delhi around 1965, Bell's comments were leaked to a national paper, which ran a story the next day with a headline to the effect "Bernie Bell Go to Hell." Later, Indira Gandhi would capitalize on this nationalist mood to rule India. For close to a decade, she nationalized banks and strategic industries like coal and produced India's worst decade of growth in the postindependence era. Peter Hazlehurst, a correspondent for *The Times* of London, captured Indira Gandhi's ill-fated populism this way: "She is a little left of self-interest."[5]

Soon after his trip to Delhi, Bell offered pretty much the same advice to the newly self-installed leader of Indonesia, General Suharto, and got the opposite response. Suharto was so impressed, says Nehru, he called World Bank chief Robert McNamara and asked him to appoint Bell as the bank's representative in Jakarta. Bell served in Jakarta from 1968 to 1972 and, along with a circle of U.S.-educated Indonesian technocrats who came to be known as the "Berkeley Mafia," helped transform the impoverished country into a mini-Asian miracle over the next two decades.

The best way for technocrats to be successful is therefore as staff members of an authoritarian regime like Suharto's, which can command rather than rally popular support. Chile was a successful technocracy in the 1970s, when the dictatorship of General Augusto Pinochet put the task of economic reforms in the hands of the "Chicago Boys," eight Chilean economists from the University of Chicago. They managed to bring hyperinflation and public spending and debt under control with a reasonably limited amount of economic pain—albeit with brutal suppression of political opposition. Korea and Taiwan were also economically successful technocracies in their early authoritarian years, as were Singapore and China.

But technocrats can cause more harm than good to the economy when they try to push reforms that sound smart in theory but ignore local sentiment. In Argentina during the 1990s, President Carlos Menem tried to replicate the success of the Chicago Boys by appointing his own U.S.-educated experts. They imposed an experimental system of currency controls that helped stabilize the Argentine peso and restore growth for a while but eventually led to mounting public debts and the outright depression that began in 1998. Argentina entered a four-year period that saw the economy contract by nearly 30 percent, and in 2002 it defaulted on $82 billion of debt—then the largest sovereign debt default on record. That experience left behind a populace deeply suspicious of technocrats bearing ideas for economic reform.

Argentina thus seemed to join an unusual class of nations, those that have been in decline for many years but have enough residual wealth to pretend they don't really feel the pinch of crises. In recent times, this class has also included Japan and Italy, both with rapidly aging populations and economies that are losing ground to their peers, yet are still relatively wealthy and relatively free of debts to foreigners—who might force them to reform. When I arrived in Buenos Aires in April 2015, the economy was contracting and had the highest inflation rate of any major country, officially reported at 30 percent. Expecting to find a capital in crisis, I found instead a raucous party in the hotel and restaurants spilling into the streets late on a Wednesday night. Argentines told me there was little sense of crisis and the public appetite for change was marginal—many people had bitter memories of the late 1990s depression and still blamed it on Argentina's last attempt at major reforms.

Even at the central bank, officials gave me a presentation that ignored both the current recession and Argentina's long fall from the ranks of developed nations, focusing instead on how much better things were compared to 2002, the depths of the depression. In a country this hardened to crises, it appeared that even the long-term decline in national status was not enough to induce Argentines to embrace change. Though Argentines once saw Buenos Aires as the Paris of South America, I heard them comparing their country favorably to smaller neighbors like Paraguay. Yet even in Argentina, nothing is permanent. By late 2015, the surprise election success of a reform-minded leader, Mauricio Macri, appeared to signal that Argentines might finally have had enough of stagnation.

China is the very different case of a successful technocracy that may be growing too confident in the ability of its technocrats to control economic growth. For years, China reported much less volatile economic growth than other developing nations, creating suspicion that it was manipulating the numbers to make the economy look like a smoothly running machine, and to foster social harmony. For a long time, I thought that suspicion was overblown. When Deng Xiaoping took power in 1979, one of the first things he told his underlings was that he wanted honest data—not the inflated numbers they had been feeding Mao to stroke his ego. Even in 1990, after the fallout from the events in Tiananmen Square, the Deng regime reported growth of less than 4 percent, way below the official target of 8 percent. And as recently as 2003, Deng's handpicked and equally pragmatic successors were openly criticizing provincial leaders for overstating local growth numbers in an attempt to advance their careers. That is, of course, how technocracy is supposed to work—objectively.

Increasingly, though, China's government has twisted that ideal, manipulating numbers to fit a political mission. In a cable revealed in 2010 by WikiLeaks, Chinese premier Li Keqiang was quoted acknowledging that official GDP numbers are "man made," and saying that he looks to more reliable numbers—on bank loans, rail cargo, and electricity consumption—to get a fix on the actual growth rate. Independent economists then started tracking these numbers as the "LKQ Index," which has shown in recent years that actual growth is falling well below the official target. Yet from mid-2012 onward, the authorities reported growth rates that came within a few decimal points of the official target of 7 percent not only every year but every quarter.

This level of precision is not plausible, even for economic engineers who had been as successful to date as Beijing's. With an average income of about $10,000, China has reached the stage of development at which even the previous "miracle economies" of East Asia began to slow, from a rate near double digits to 5 to 6 percent. Beijing appears to be fixated on hitting a growth target that is no longer realistic for a middle-income country. In July 2013 a top Chinese official declared that the leadership would not "tolerate" a growth rate below a "floor" of 7 percent, as if it were possible to banish downturns in an $8 trillion economy. In an attempt to prevent this natural slowdown, Beijing has resorted to increasingly aggressive manipulations. Most dangerously, it has unleashed a flood of more than $20 trillion in credit since 2008, and that flood now threatens to swamp the economy.

The underlying motivation is the technocratic, political obsession with hitting a growth target that no longer makes sense. That target seems to have come from a back-of-the-envelope calculation of how fast China needs to grow to double its GDP by 2020—an ambition with no basis in economics and reminiscent of the man-made targets that guided the Soviet Union's effort to catch up to the West. We all know how that attempt ended. It is simply not possible to engineer endless runs of fast growth, with no downturns in the business cycle, and that lesson applies equally to the technocrats in Beijing.

Bullets versus Ballots

Following the spectacular three-decade boom in China, there is a strong tendency to believe that autocracies are better than democracies at generating long runs of growth, a myth that may be built not so much on the rise of China as on coverage of the rise of China. The New York University development expert William Easterly has analyzed coverage in *The New York Times* between 1960 and 2008 and found that the paper ran some 63,000 stories on autocratic governments, a staggering 40,000 on their successes, and just 6,000 on their failures. These were not all China stories, but the overreporting of autocratic triumphs may well have reinforced the general impression that Chinese authoritarian capitalism is a model worth emulating for developing countries, particularly at the early stages of development.

Autocrats sometimes do succeed. Authoritarian rulers can often ignore or overrun opposition from the legislature, the courts, or private lobbies, and that power allows visionary leaders to accomplish a lot more than democratic rivals. Autocratic leaders—from President Park Chung-hee, who ruled South Korea for much of the 1960s and '70s, to Chiang

Kai-shek and his son, who ruled Taiwan from 1949 through 1978—have produced enduring economic miracles. Autocrats can suppress special interest lobbies and any opposition to breakneck development, because the threat of the bullet keeps people in line. They can steer the population's pool of savings toward growth industries, and they can ignore popular demands for wage hikes so those industries become and remain globally competitive. Perhaps above all, they can commandeer land to build highways and ports and other basic building blocks of a modern economy, in a way no democracy can match.

However, because autocrats face few checks and balances and no opposition at the ballot box, they can veer off in the wrong direction with no one to tell them otherwise, and they can also hang on to power indefinitely, more often than not with bad results for economy. The threat of stale leadership looms larger in authoritarian nations than in democracies, which give people the opportunity to choose fresh leaders in fair elections every four to six years. For every long run of 10 percent growth produced by a Deng Xiaoping, as Easterly has pointed out, there were several long periods of stagnation under a Castro in Cuba, a Kim in North Korea, or a Mugabe in Zimbabwe. Stale leaders tend to do the most long-term economic damage in authoritarian countries, which have much less fluid mechanisms for responding to popular demands for change or for bringing in fresh leaders.[6] Once an autocratic regime is forced to hold elections, it loses its power to force rapid growth, but it gains an incentive to let growth rise naturally by, for example, respecting property rights and breaking up state monopolies.

Both democratic and authoritarian systems have advantages and disadvantages in the race to generate strong growth, and neither has a clear lead. I've studied the record for each of the last three decades, and during that period there were 124 cases in which a nation posted GDP growth faster than 5 percent for a full decade. Of those strong growth spells, 64 came under the rule of a democratic regime, and 60 under an authoritarian regime. So there is no reason to assume autocratic regimes have generally brighter growth prospects—despite the widespread admiration for Chinese-style command capitalism.

Moreover, those averages conceal the big flaw in authoritarian regimes, which is that they are much more likely to produce extreme results, meaning wilder swings between periods of very high and very low growth. In the postwar period, cases of both superfast and super-slow growth have been generated mainly under authoritarian governments.* The most accurate records go back to 1950 for 150 countries, and they show 43 cases of superfast growth, in which the economy grew at an average annual rate of 7 percent or more for a full decade. In 35 of those 43 cases, the economy was run by an authoritarian government. These cases include some of the "miracle economies" (like Korea, Taiwan, and China) that managed to keep rapid growth alive for several decades. But it also includes many vanishing acts that grew superfast one decade only to disappear the next, including Venezuela, which vanished in the 1960s, Iran in the 1970s, and Syria and Iraq in the 1980s.

Nations ruled by autocrats are also much more prone to long slumps. In the same group of 150 countries going back to 1950, there have been 138 cases of extreme slow growth, in which a nation posted an average annual GDP growth rate of less than 3 percent for a decade. And 100 of those 138 cases unfolded in nations under authoritarian regimes, ranging from Ghana in the 1950s and '60s to Uganda in the 1980s, Saudi Arabia and Romania in the 1980s, and Nigeria in the 1990s. Overall, since 1950 authoritarian regimes were at the controls in three out of every four nations that posted growth of more than 7 percent, or of less than 3 percent, for a full decade.

The nightmare scenario for any country comes when the economy flip-flops between boom and bust, with years of superhigh growth followed by outright recessions. And it turns out this nightmare is shockingly common. Again looking back to 1950, I found 36 countries that

---

* To calculate whether a country was governed by an autocratic regime during this period, I relied on a standard measure for distinguishing authoritarian versus democratic regimes, the Polity IV database. Put out by the Virginia-based Center for Systemic Peace, it assesses regimes year by year.

have seen at least nine individual years of growth faster than 7 percent *and nine individual years of negative growth,* scattered over this sixty-five-year period. In short, these countries have spent a good part of the postwar era in a state of boom and bust so violent, it has been almost impossible for ordinary citizens to lead normal lives. Two things stand out on this list: first that 34 of these 36 countries were in the emerging world—testimony to the link between weak institutions in the emerging world and volatile growth. The exceptions were Iceland and Greece, and by some measures Greece has recently fallen back into the "emerging" category. Second, 27 of these 36 countries were governed by an authoritarian regime for most of this sixty-five-year period. In short, a large majority of these roller-coaster economies were governed by autocrats, and the result was long-term stagnation.

For example, since 1950 consistently autocratic countries including Iran, Ethiopia, Iraq, Jordan, Syria, Cambodia, and Nigeria have spent fifteen years or more growing faster than 7 percent. Yet at best they have seen their per capita incomes increase by a factor of two or three, and only Iran and Jordan have average incomes above $4,500, because those boom years were wiped out by nearly as many bust years. Even Iran has attained an average per capita income of just $11,000, because twenty-three years of superfast growth have been largely offset by nine scattered years of negative growth.

In some of the worst cases, one suffering country has gone through extreme booms and busts under the same long-seated ruler. Jordan is a constitutional monarchy, ruled for the last sixty-two years by just two Hashemite kings, Hussein and Abdullah, and more than half have been years of extreme high or low growth. Worse still was President Robert Mugabe, the independence hero turned albatross of Zimbabwe. He has been in power for thirty-five years, with more than half of those years whipsawed by superfast or superslow growth. Under Mugabe the economic life of Zimbabwe has been almost unimaginably chaotic, with ten straight years of negative growth through 2008, followed by a deceptively dramatic rebound off of a floor that can only be described as below rock bottom. All told, Zimbabwe is poorer today than when Mugabe took office.

That is not, however, the most neck-snapping economic performance by an autocrat. Hafez al-Assad ran Syria for thirty years, until 2000, and nearly two-thirds of those years were marked by extreme high or low growth, with most of the good years concentrated in the oil boom of the 1970s and '80s. The prize for most dizzying economic leader of recent decades goes to Saddam Hussein, who ran Iraq for twenty-five years through 2003, with more than three-quarters of those years marked by extreme growth, punctuated by a series of wars and some of the wildest swings on record. Iraq's economic growth rate spiked to 40 percent in 1993 and 1996 but collapsed to negative 20 percent in between. This is the authoritarian roller-coaster effect at work.

Of course, characters like Mugabe and Saddam Hussein are among the most notorious autocrats of recent decades, but the same story has also unfolded in less infamous regimes, albeit with somewhat less dramatic booms and busts. In Brazil, for example, the military toppled an increasingly left-leaning government in a 1964 coup and moved quickly to restart the economy by cutting red tape, creating a central bank, working to lower budget deficits, and cutting taxes for exporters. The economic growth rate accelerated from less than 5 percent to double digits until the first oil price shock hit in 1974, and the military government—increasingly embattled by its violent crackdown on critics at home and abroad—tried to command a continued boom. It started borrowing heavily, piling up foreign debts it could no longer pay, when the second oil shock hit in 1979. The economy slid into recession and runaway inflation by the time the junta agreed to new elections in 1984. In some respects, the country never recovered from the meddling instincts of the later military government, and its per capita income relative to the United States is at the same level as it was in the 1970s.

In contrast, democracies dominate the list of countries that since 1950 have registered the fewest years of extreme growth. Together, for example, Sweden, France, Belgium, and Norway have posted only one year of growth faster than 7 percent. That came in France in 1960. However, since 1950, these four European democracies have all seen their per capita incomes increase five- to sixfold to a minimum of more than $30,000, in part because they rarely suffered full years of negative growth. France saw the most years of negative growth, with seven, while Norway saw the least, with two. This is the stabilizing effect of democracy at work, and it has extended to emerging countries like Colombia and South Africa, which also score high for democratic governance and register few years of extreme growth.

The record of extreme booms and busts should give pause to any nation that ever yearned for the firm hand of an autocrat. In recent decades, many economically troubled nations have looked to a strongman to restore prosperity. In the long run, however, stable and enduring growth is more likely under a democrat, who lacks the power to engineer spectacular runs of success or failure. Even autocrats who produce long periods of strong growth often become, in the end, predatory defenders of the status quo, trampling on property rights to enrich their own clique, discouraging anyone who is not a friend of the big boss from taking any stake in the economy. This is why so many democratic countries have adopted term limits, in order to prevent regimes from growing stale and corrupt.

This is also one widely overlooked reason why China continued to function so well after Deng Xiaoping left office, two decades ago. While Deng was no democrat, he understood the problem of stale leadership and instituted the age and term limits that now prevent even the top Chinese leaders from hanging on for life. Two five-year terms, and they're done. That separates Beijing from other autocracies that are trying to copy its model but are not obeying its rules, like Vietnam. In 2015 Prime Minister Nguyen Tan Dung was sixty-five, and behind the scenes the age limit for starting a new high-level job was raised to sixty-seven, just old enough to disqualify nearly all his main rivals but not Dung himself. He was said to be trying to shift into the post of Communist

Party general secretary. Dung had already been in power ten years, and with his rivals out of the way, a local source said, the new post—should he attain it—could make him the most powerful and enduring leader Vietnam had seen in "several hundred years."

Back to the Circle of Life

The circle of life is a rule of politics, not science. It tells you that the likely timing and direction of change depends in part on where a country stands on the circle of crisis, reform, boom, and decay. Like any other life-form, the world economy follows cycles of decay and regeneration, its energies scattering and lying formless for a time, only to gather again into new shapes. The political lives of modern economies follow a similar cycle, exploding in crisis only to re-form and revive before dying out once again. This circle of life helps explain why so few developing economies manage to grow fast and long enough to enter the ranks of the developed economies. It also helps put into perspective why those that make the leap are called "miracle" economies: They have defied the natural complacency and decay that kills most long booms.

Many years can pass between the onset of a crisis and the arrival of a leader with the potential to push transformative economic reform, and even that arrival only raises the probability of strong growth. Many other factors will play a role in determining whether a new leader achieves reform, and whether that reform leads to strong growth. Strange gaps can appear, particularly when global conditions make it hard for any economy to take off.

Even in the worst periods of global stagnation and unrest, the circle of life will always continue to turn, however slowly, transforming the ashes of crises into the seeds of reform. During 2011 the series of revolts that came to be known as the Arab Spring started in Tunisia, triggered by the self-immolation of a street vendor who had been denied official permits by a corrupt bureaucracy. Discontent over the Arab world's long-term economic dysfunction helped to spread the fire of revolt against aging dictators from Tunisia through Egypt and all the way to Syria. Soon, however, the "spring" came to be seen as a false dawn, as toppled autocrats were replaced by new autocrats, as in Egypt, or with civil war and pure chaos, as in Syria and Libya and Yemen. Hope that this crisis would lead to a flowering of democracy, free market reform, and economic prosperity turned into hopelessness for the fate of the region, with the intriguing exception of Tunisia. In late 2014 Tunisia completed the region's first peaceful, post-Spring transfer of power, to a new president promising to focus on reforming the economy.

The Arab Spring was an extreme case of the rule—big crises will always give birth to major new reformers, though not all will manage to make reform stick. As George Mason University professor Jack Goldstone argued in a 2011 article for *Foreign Affairs*, the Arab Spring revolts targeted a particularly corrupt brand of "sultans" who, unlike rival monarchs, lacked any public legitimacy and ruled strictly by fear and by favoring cronies. The dictatorship run by the Mubaraks in Egypt or the Assads in Syria and the Ben Alis of Tunisia follow a line of "sultanistic regimes" that included the Ceausescus in Romania, the Duvaliers in Haiti, the Marcoses in the Philippines, and the Suhartos in Indonesia. These family dictators were loathed as usurpers, and their kind of regime tends to leave a vacuum of power when it falls. The resulting chaos can delay the formation of a stable new regime for a half a decade—longer if a civil war breaks out, argued Goldstone. In that light, Tunisia's move to a relatively stable new government came unusually fast. The rest of the Arab world is following the more normal pattern and in fact may need a good deal more than half a decade to begin repairing the social fabric.

The stages in the circle of life are well understood. The fact that crisis and revolt can force even reluctant elites to reform has been clear at least since the early critiques of Marx, who thought capitalist societies would collapse in a series of increasingly violent attempts to defend the upper classes. Instead, facing the economic depressions of the late nineteenth and early twentieth centuries, political leaders proved capable of reforming liberal capitalism, deflecting popular revolt with the creation of the welfare state, starting in Germany and Britain. The link between boom times and political complacency is equally well documented, for example, in the cases of modern Japan and Europe, which are often described as too comfortably rich to push tough reform. What is far less well recognized is that even in more normal periods, the circle of life turns, constantly shaping and reshaping economies for the better or worse.

The former Indonesian finance minister Muhamad Chatib Basri has come close to capturing the full circle in a favorite saying: "Bad times make for good policy, and good times make for bad policy." In his own country, Basri told me, this cycle has played out repeatedly, including during his tenure as finance minister under Susilo Bambang Yudhoyono, popularly known as SBY, who was president from 2004 to 2014. In his first term SBY helped stabilize Indonesia after the political uncertainty of the early post-Suharto years, but in his second term he grew complacent, even in the face of mounting government deficits. Basri says he urged SBY repeatedly to address the problem by cutting spending on energy subsidies; the president responded by making minor cuts when Indonesia faced a budding currency crisis in the summer of 2013, then quit reforming when the crisis passed later that year. Pressed to follow through on the subsidy cuts, according to Basri, the president responded, "Why? The country is now doing fine."

The circle turns erratically, even in democracies where elections are regularly scheduled. Nations may wallow in complacency for years, which helps explain why the "lost decades" that have gripped Japan and many nations in Latin America often lasted longer than a decade. On the other hand, particularly strong-willed leaders or nations have been known to keep pushing reform for many decades, but these have been limited to the rare "miracle" cases including Korea, Taiwan, and Japan before its lost decades began in 1990.

The credit crisis of 2008 was deep enough to create popular support for reformers, and indeed many powerful candidates emerged in the subsequent elections. Many took office only after the global slowdown spread from the rich nations to the emerging ones after 2010, reflecting the widening impact of the crisis. In December 2012, Enrique Peña Nieto came to power promising to bust up the monopolies that have long strangled Mexico's economy. The same month Shinzo Abe took office and electrified Japan watchers with a sweeping plan to end the stagnation that has engulfed his nation for a generation. The next year Nawaz Sharif took over in Islamabad pushing reform and turned Pakistan into the world's hottest stock market of 2013. Renzi won the Italian election the next February. The following month Narendra Modi won his landslide victory, raising sky-high expectations that he could turn India into the next China by growing the economy at a near-double-digit pace.

It is too early to say whether any member of this new generation will become a Thatcher or a Kim, in part because good policy has to combine with good luck to produce a successful reformer. No matter what the new reformers get right on the policy front, they need many other factors to fall into place to produce a run of strong growth. And as of 2015, all the new leaders face the bad luck of trying to revive their national economies amid the weakest global economic recovery in postwar history.

The evidence on balance shows that politics matters for economic growth, and the fortunes of a nation are likely to turn for the better when a new leader rises in the wake of a crisis, and conversely a nation is likely to be worse off when a stale leader is in office.

3

GOOD BILLIONAIRES, BAD BILLIONAIRES

Is inequality threatening growth?

THE GROWING GAP BETWEEN THE SUPERRICH AND THE REST became a hot-button issue worldwide by 2015, but no national leader was fighting to redistribute wealth as aggressively as President Michelle Bachelet of Chile. When I arrived in Santiago that April, her supporters were promising to "take a bulldozer" to the model of lean government and low taxes that had made Chile the richest but also one of the most unequal societies in Latin America. And Bachelet was delivering. Taking cues from a student protest movement that undermined her predecessor Sebastián Piñera, she was proposing a bigger government with higher spending to help the poor, and higher corporate taxes to pay for free university education. Fearing more government intervention, corporate executives I spoke to were so rattled by Bachelet's populist rhetoric that they had dramatically cut back their investments in Chile. As investment collapsed, GDP growth slowed to less than 3 percent from an average of near 6 percent during Piñera's term. I thought it would be interesting to get a view on where this all-out war on inequality would lead by talking to Piñera, one of Chile's richest men—a billionaire who made his fortune in the credit card business.

He had retreated to a modest office from which he manages his wealth, tucked away in a nondescript Santiago tower and strikingly devoid of the bodyguards and security systems that surround many Latin American tycoons. If Piñera did not seem worried about his safety, he did seem agitated about Bachelet's policy direction. To fight inequality, he said, a country needs to pursue two goals—redistributing the pie while growing it at the same time—and during his tenure Chile had done both. Inequality had in fact fallen,* he argued, but not fast enough to quell the protests. Now Bachelet was demonstrating how a single-minded focus on redistributing wealth during good times can kill strong growth and make everyone poorer for it. "The long history of Latin America," Piñera told me, "is that when times are good, countries turn to the left, and when times are bad, they turn to the right."

This pattern is familiar, even beyond Latin America. All too often in the emerging world, the backlash against an entrenched class of well-connected tycoons has brought to power a populist firebrand who pursues redistributive policies that can burn down the economy. In the extreme cases, populist demagogues seize private businesses and farms for the state, ban foreign investors from entering the country, raise taxes to choking levels in the name of helping the poor, ramp up the size of government, and spend heavily on wasteful subsidies, particularly for cheap fuel. This basic menu of growth-killing policies has shaped the agenda of populists in many deeply unequal societies, including postcolonial cases such as Robert Mugabe of Zimbabwe, Kenneth Kaunda of Zambia, Julius Nyerere of Tanzania, Kim Il-sung of North Korea, Sheikh Mujibur Rahman of Bangladesh, and Zulfiqar Ali Bhutto of Pakistan.

The African cases are particularly notorious: During more than three decades in power, Mugabe grew ever more aggressive in redistributing property from the old white elite to the black majority, but all too often the beneficiaries were his cronies. In 2000 he started displacing white

---

* Piñera served from 2010 to early 2014, and World Bank data show that Chile's score on the Gini index of inequality fell from 52 in 2009 to 50.45 in 2013.

farmers with new black owners, who in many cases did not know how to farm. That led to a collapse in agricultural production and turned a food-exporting nation into a net importer. Unemployment spiked to more than 90 percent, and hyperinflation broke out, with prices doubling every twenty-four hours, a process that so thoroughly destroyed the value of the local currency that it soon cost billions of Zimbabwe dollars to buy an egg, and 35 quadrillion to buy one U.S. dollar. Finally in 2015 Mugabe scrapped the Zimbabwe dollar, and now a mish-mash of foreign currencies, from the U.S. dollar to the South African rand, circulates in his country.

Mugabe's regime is almost a corrupt parody of how a focus on redistribution without growth can destroy trust in the local economy, but a similar process has occurred in many countries, on every continent. In Pakistan, Zulfiqar Ali Bhutto formed his People's Party in the 1960s and got his chance to rule after the military's humiliating 1971 defeat in war with India. He set to work delivering on his promises to redress inequality, placing caps on how much land private citizens could own and nationalizing industries from finance and energy to manufacturing. The result was corruption, hyperinflation, and a declining standard of living.

This same impulse to use state power to redistribute wealth has, in milder forms, animated more recent leaders, including Joseph Estrada of the Philippines in the late 1990s, Thaksin Shinawatra of Thailand during the 2000s, and, more recently, Michelle Bachelet. Estrada swept to power in 1998 with the backing of rural voters who felt left behind by privatization policies that had boosted growth, but mainly in the cities. Estrada took the usual leveling steps—handing out land to tenant farmers, increasing welfare spending—which drove up government debt and deficits, fueled inflation, and helped trigger the protests that toppled him after three years in office.

Arguably, self-destructive populism has been most pronounced in Central and South America, driven by high levels of inequality with roots in the colonial era. In this region, European elites managed to consolidate their political and economic power, rather than losing it, after these nations achieved independence. That concentration of power and wealth provoked the rise of populists promising radical redistribution, starting with Fidel Castro in Cuba in the late 1950s. It continued with Juan Velasco of Peru starting in the late 1960s, Luis Echeverría Álvarez of Mexico in the 1970s, Daniel Ortega of Nicaragua in the 1980s, Hugo Chávez of Venezuela in the late 1990s, and Nestor Kirchner of Argentina in the 2000s. Echeverría, for example, took over from an administration that had focused on developing new industries, which widened the income gap between cities and the countryside (as the early stage of industrialization often has). Echeverría then set about trying to close the gap by raising food subsidies, restricting foreign investment, redistributing land to peasants, and nationalizing mines and power plants. This onslaught scared off foreign investors, encouraged Mexicans to move money abroad, and led to a balance of payments crisis, energy shortages, rising unemployment and inflation, and slower growth. When protests broke out, tourists fled the country too.

These are the destructive "turns to the left" that Piñera had in mind, and he was agitated because this periodic backlash had finally reached his country. Chile had been an exception to the normal rhythms of Latin populism since the 1970s, when the regime of dictator Augusto Pinochet demonstrated that opening to foreign trade and investment, cutting red tape, keeping debt and deficits under control to contain inflation, and privatizing state enterprises and pensions could unleash high and stable growth. Having taken power following a coup, Pinochet implemented brutal measures to suppress opposition leaders, which alienated many Chileans. His bloody reign finally came to an end in 1990, after seventeen years. Nonetheless, Pinochet's economic legacy endured, though some critics argued that his policies had sown the seeds for a rise in inequality. For the next twenty years, while Chileans kept right-wing parties associated with the Pinochet regime out of power and elected left-of-center leaders, they all continued to follow policies of financial stability. That includes Bachelet during her first term from 2006 to

2010. Even after she came back to power in 2014, Bachelet at least did not break the habits of budget discipline established by Pinochet, proposing both higher spending to help the poor and higher taxes to pay for it.

It was Bachelet's populist rhetoric that scared off the investment dollars Chile needed to develop new sources of growth. The country's average income had reached a solidly middle-class level of $15,000, but to drive growth, the economy still relied on simple commodity exports such as copper, at a time when global copper prices were slumping. By discouraging investment, which Chile needs to move beyond commodities, Bachelet was inadvertently preventing economic progress—in a predictable response to the popular clamor for wealth redistribution.

The basic question: Is inequality threatening the economy? This is one of those issues that need to be addressed more by political art than by economic science. Inequality starts to threaten growth in part when the population turns suspicious of the way wealth is being created. If an entrepreneur is creating new products that benefit the consumer or building manufacturing plants and putting people to work, that form of wealth creation tends to be widely accepted. However, if a tycoon is making a fortune by cozying up to politicians and landing contracts from the government, or worse by capitalizing on Daddy's contacts, then resentment surfaces, and the nation's focus turns to redistributing rather than creating wealth.

The most rigorous statistical measures of inequality can offer a useful snapshot of the big picture, but they are updated too infrequently to provide the necessary warning signs of fast-shifting popular sentiment. The most common measure of income inequality, the Gini coefficient, scores a nation from one to zero: One represents a totally unequal society in which one person gets all the income, and zero represents a completely egalitarian society in which everyone has the same income. But the Gini score is derived from official data by academics, using a variety of methods, published on no particular schedule and for no consistent sample of countries. There is no more current source for cross-country comparisons than the World Bank, and as of mid-2015 its most recent Gini scores for Chile came from 2011, for the United States from 2010, for Russia from 2009, for Egypt from 2008, and for France from 2005. The long shelf life of Gini scores renders them useless as a current indicator of which nations are most threatened by rising inequality.

My approach to monitoring trends in inequality starts and ends with keeping an ear to the ground, because I know of no data that will clearly signal shifts in a nation's attitudes toward wealth. But I do use a careful read of the *Forbes* billionaire list as one tool to identify the outliers: countries where the scale and sources of the largest fortunes are most likely to trigger tensions over inequality, and to retard growth in the economy. To identify countries in which tycoons are taking an unusually large and growing share of the pie, I calculate the scale of billionaire wealth relative to the size of the economy. To identify countries in which the tycoon class is becoming an entrenched elite, I estimate the share of inherited wealth in the billionaire ranks. Most important, I track the wealth of "bad billionaires" in industries long associated with corruption, such as oil or mining or real estate. It is the rise of an entrenched class of bad billionaires in traditionally corruption-prone and unproductive industries that is most likely to choke off growth and to feed the popular anger on which populist demagogues thrive. I also listen closely to how the public is talking about the nation's leading tycoons, because it is often the popular perception of inequality, even more than the reality, that shapes the political reaction and economic policy.

To skeptics who find issues like wealth inequality or an approach like reading billionaire lists too soft to take seriously, I would argue that this is an increasingly vital sign. Some world leaders still tend to dismiss vices like inequality, and the corruption that often feeds it, as timeless and inevitable sins that are common to all countries, particularly poor ones in the chaotic early stages of development. But this is a cop-out. Developing societies do tend to be more unequal than rich ones, but it is increasingly unclear that their inequality problem will naturally disappear.

The belief that inequality fades over time had been the working assumption since the 1950s, when the economist Simon Kuznets pointed out that countries tend to grow more unequal in the early stages of development, as some poor farmers move to better-paying factory jobs in the cities, and less unequal in the later stages, as the urban middle class grows. Today, however, inequality appears to be rising at all stages of development: in poor, middle-class, and rich countries. One reason for the widening threat of inequality is that the period of intense globalization before 2008 tended to depress blue-collar wages. It became much easier to shift factory jobs to low-wage countries, while continuing advances in technology and automation were replacing jobs that had earlier lifted many people into the middle class. As inequality spreads within countries, at every level of development, it is increasingly important to monitor the wealth gaps in all countries, all the time.

Conflicts over inequality have been around for decades but have recently metastasized into a global confrontation, affecting large swaths of the developed and developing worlds. All over the globe, political leaders have taken up the battle against inequality and started pushing hard for redistribution, from Korea and Sweden to Chile and the United States. In Washington, Democrats have gone on the march against inequality, and even the normally staid head of the Federal Reserve Bank, Janet Yellen, promised in 2014 to run the central bank in the service of "Main Street and not Wall Street."

It's not often that one sees central bankers on the ramparts, but Yellen's promise overlooked the role the Fed itself was playing in turbocharging the rise of billionaires worldwide. The rise in inequality had been particularly dramatic for measures of wealth rather than income, and the Fed had been instrumental in fueling wealth on Wall Street not Main Street. To boost growth following the global financial crisis of 2008, the Fed pumped record amounts of money into the U.S. economy through multiple rounds of "quantitative easing," which involved buying bonds on the public markets. The hope was that this infusion of capital would promote a strong recovery and job growth. Instead, the United

States experienced its weakest recovery of the postwar era, coupled with an unprecedented period of financial speculation.

Much of the Fed's easy money was diverted into purchases of stocks, luxury homes, and other financial assets, as well as into financial engineering (like share buybacks) designed to further increase the price of those assets. Everyone who owned stocks or bonds got richer, but since the wealthiest people own the lion's share of these assets, they got richer the fastest. When other central banks matched the Fed's easy money policies, they helped to feed the growing wealth gap in their own countries, too. In a 2014 study of 46 major countries, the research arm of the bank Credit Suisse found that before 2007, wealth inequality was on the rise in only 12 of those countries; after 2007, that number more than doubled to 35, from China and India to Britain and Italy.[1]

The easy money experiments began in 2008, and by the time quantitative easing ended in 2014, the richest 1 percent of the world's population had increased its share of global wealth from 44 to 48 percent of the total, which had risen to $263 trillion. A 2014 study by the Pew Research Center found that "the wealth gap between America's high income group and everyone else has reached record levels since the Great Recession of 2007–2009," with wealth rising for upper-income families and stagnating for the middle- and lower-income groups.[2] The high-income families were 3.4 times wealthier than middle-income families in 1983, and while that gap widened gradually over the next quarter century to 4.5 times wealthier in 2007, it widened rapidly to 6.6 times wealthier in 2013. The poor were not getting poorer, but the wealth of the rich, and particularly the superrich, was growing faster. The 0.01 percent was doing even better than the 1 percent, with billionaires leaving millionaires in the dust. Between 2009 and 2014, despite the weak global economy, the number of billionaires worldwide rose from 1,011 to 1,826. During that five-year period, Piñera was focused on his day job as Chile's president, but global markets lifted his net worth by $400 million to $2.6 billion, according to *Forbes*.[3]

A healthy economy should be creating wealth, even pockets of great wealth, but the central question is one of balance. The process of growth and wealth creation is more likely to remain popular if the largest pockets of wealth do not come to dominate the economy. Chile had only twelve billionaires in 2015, but they controlled fortunes worth 15 percent of the economy—one of the highest shares in the world. In that light, the eruption of self-defeating battles over inequality even in a former bastion of moderation like Chile should have been less surprising.

Reading the Billionaire Lists

Billionaire watching is exploding as an industry, alongside the growing billionaire class. *Forbes* has published its annual World Billionaires List since the 1980s. The number of billionaires has doubled in the last five years and tripled in the last ten, making this list a large and increasingly relevant sample. Nations such as China and Russia, which had no billionaires two decades ago, now have a significant class of the ultrawealthy. This explosion has spawned a cottage industry of *Forbes* copycats, which produce a steady stream of titillating reports on the superrich.

There's the *Bloomberg* Billionaires Index and the Billionaire Census, while others track a specific range of the superwealthy, like the Hurun Report out of China and the Global Wealth Report from Credit Suisse Research. Several of these sources including *Forbes* and *Bloomberg* now update their rankings in real time, using live market data. There are books spinning off the data, too, including *Plutocrats* by Chrystia Freeland and *Billionaires* by Darrell M. West. The mushrooming of the billionaire-watchers reflects our conflicted times since they appeal both to voyeurs of the upper crust and to critics of wealth inequality.

Some of this information caters to luxury goods marketers or to those keeping score for their own tribe: The University of Pennsylvania, it turns out, produces more billionaires than Yale, Harvard, Princeton, or any other school, and so on. All these lists are limited by the fact that their calculations are derived largely from public information, particularly stock and property holdings, so the real-time indexes of billionaire wealth mainly reflect what the market is doing that moment. It is no doubt striking that multibillionaires like Bill Gates and Carlos Slim routinely see their fortunes fluctuate by hundreds of millions on any given day, but it signifies nothing in particular. Only in the broader year-to-year changes does the information get interesting.

Lately some of this billionaire data has surfaced in serious economic discussions. In his generally admiring review of Thomas Piketty's 2013 international best seller on inequality, *Capital in the Twenty-First Century*, former U.S. Treasury secretary Lawrence Summers questioned the French author's claims about the enduring power of inherited wealth in the United States by pointing to the high degree of churn among American billionaires. Summers highlighted the fact that only one out of every 10 names on the original *Forbes* list in 1982 were still on the list in 2012. The author and venture capitalist Peter Thiel also incorporated billionaire lists into his entertaining lament about the stagnant state of technological innovation. Scanning the *Forbes* global list of the ninety-two people who were worth more than $10 billion in 2012, Thiel found only eleven tech industry figures in the group, all of them names he considered distressingly familiar, such as Gates, Ellison, and Zuckerberg. By way of comparison, he found twice as many names that made their bundle mainly by "mining natural resources," a group Thiel ridiculed as "basically cases of technological failure, because commodities are inelastic goods, and farmers make a fortune when there's a famine."

Summers, Thiel, and others are on to something. But these lists need to be read in a structured way to reveal even anecdotally telling data about the scale of billionaire wealth, whether it is coming from productive industries, and the extent to which the tycoon class faces real competition. It is natural and healthy for a growing economy to generate wealth, so long as the tycoons are not in control of an outsize share of the nation's wealth, are not congealing into a stagnant elite bound by family ties, and are emerging in innovative and productive industries rather than those where political connections often decide who will be a billionaire.

Scale: Shockingly Large Billionaire Shares of the Wealth

I first started to read the billionaire lists around 2010, inspired by a turn for the worse in India, where one scandal after another was exposing the corrupt ways of an old elite, which had wormed itself ever more deeply into parliament, into the world of Bollywood movies, and into the commanding heights of industry. Just a few years prior, leading business tycoons were among the nation's most trusted figures, admired for building successful companies that burnished India's global image. But the scandals started destroying that trust, exposing collusion between leading business figures and politicians. They were caught manipulating auctions for wireless spectrum, angling for ownership stakes in a new cricket league, and rigging real estate transactions, among other unsavory deals. More and more new tycoons seemed to be rising not on merit but on political connections, and many Indians were disgusted by the brazenness of these machinations. In Mumbai, CEOs complained to me that the first question now for any investment decision was about which officials had to be bribed to get the deal done.

To check the popular impression of the increasingly stagnant and dominant elite, I did a quick scan of the 2010 billionaire list and found that the top ten Indian tycoons controlled wealth equal to 12 percent of GDP—compared to only 1 percent in China. Moreover, nine of India's top ten were holdovers from 2006 compared to zero in China, and this stagnation was relatively new; on India's 2006 list, only five billionaires had been holdovers from 2001. A cover story I wrote for *Newsweek International* in September 2010 argued that the rise of crony capitalism was "India's fatal flaw," and it was greeted with great skepticism in Delhi's political circles. Top officials told me that corruption is normal when a young economy is taking off, citing the robber barons who ruled America in the nineteenth century. But as economic growth fell by almost half in the years that followed, many of the same officials came to acknowledge that an abnormally high level of corruption and inequality* was one of the main factors in the slowdown.

Rising crony capitalism steers money and deals to undeserving hands, but it also sets off a chain reaction in the political system. India's courts after 2010 started to sense the popular outrage, and in a policy akin to killing a few chickens to scare the monkeys, they took strict action against some high-profile targets. The judges began denying bail to accused businessmen, holding them in jail for months before formal charges were filed; they began pressuring agents of the Central Bureau of Investigation (CBI) to push forward with corruption charges and questioned their probity if they dropped a case. By 2012, the crackdown was widening, and at parties in the lavish "farmhouses" that wealthy Indians keep as second homes on the outskirts of Delhi, it sometimes seemed that every other guest was either out on bail or about to go to jail.

At this point it was not clear which was worse: crony capitalism or the backlash. Bureaucrats grew fearful of attaching their name to any policy or even approving any permit that might look pro-business, lest they be tarred as corrupt themselves. Businessmen started avoiding deals that might require government approval, which in India is an expansive list. Investment ground to a halt, and the atmosphere of suspicion lingered for years. India's finance minister Arun Jaitley, a lawyer himself, lamented in 2015 that government investigators were operating by "the golden rule that I must somehow make the case, and it is good luck of the accused to get a fair trial." This culture of investigative "overkill," he warned, has "hindered the whole process of economic decision-making." India needed to grow rapidly to address poverty and inequality, but the rise of crony capitalism and the subsequent attempt to restrain it had instead impeded growth.

---

* Inequality was rising in India: the richest 20 percent of the population earned 44.2 percent of the income in 2011, up from 42.3 percent in 2004.

It's difficult to clearly define when the scale of billionaire wealth threatens to throw an economy out of balance, but comparing each country to its peers throws the outliers into stark relief. Total billionaire wealth in the past few years has averaged about 10 percent of GDP both in emerging countries and in developed countries. So if billionaire fortunes are more than 5 percentage points above that average, as is the case today in Russia, Taiwan, Malaysia, and Chile, that seems threatening. India is still high at 14 percent, or 4 points above the average, but trends are shifting for the better.

Since I started reading billionaire lists, the results in Russia have always told a grim tale. After the fall of Communism in the late 1980s, the Russian state sold off what had been communally owned companies to well-connected private businessmen, creating a new class of oligarchs. Russia now has more than one hundred billionaires, the third most in the world after the United States and China. Despite the 2014 collapse in the Russian stock market and real estate values, Russian billionaires still control fortunes equal to 16 percent of GDP, and their spending habits helped turn Moscow into an open-air showroom for Bugatti and Bentley. In recent years they have responded to economic troubles at home by taking money abroad. The fertilizer tycoon Dmitry Rybolovlev reportedly spent more than $2 billion on art, including $100 million on paintings by Rothko and Modigliani, and his daughter Ekaterina purchased a Greek island for $153 million and a New York apartment for $88 million. The steel magnate Roman Abramovich was said to be angling to buy up a block on Manhattan's Upper East Side, one multimillion-dollar brownstone at a time.

The scale of billionaire wealth in Russia was unrivaled in the emerging world before 2014, but that is changing. Chile, Taiwan, and Malaysia are now just as top heavy with billionaire fortunes. Billionaire wealth in Malaysia amounts to 15 percent of GDP, despite a long-standing campaign to spread the wealth from the old Chinese business elite to the ethnic Malay majority. Taiwan is also a surprise, in a bad way, since it has often been cast alongside South Korea as a nation that

managed to produce a decades-long run of high growth with no spike
in inequality. But Taiwan's billionaires today control wealth equal to 16
percent of GDP, the same level as their Russian counterparts, and more
than three times the share controlled by their South Korean peers. For
the scale of its billionaire wealth, Taiwan's elite is starting to look disproportionately large.

The developed nations also have their share of bloated billionaire
elites, though none more unexpected than Sweden. Despite its lingering
reputation as a society of committed socialists, Sweden turned sharply
to the right after a major financial crisis in the early 1990s. It cut many
taxes and lowered support payments for the poor and unemployed. Sweden's economy has since grown more steadily than most of its developing world peers, but so has inequality. Billionaires now control wealth
equal to 21 percent of GDP, up from 17 percent in 2010. There are
twenty-three Swedish billionaires, but the scale of their wealth is astonishing, even by Russian standards, and helps explain a recent political shift back to the left. The Social Democrats won the 2014 election,
promising to impose higher taxes on the rich and to reduce inequality
to levels last seen in the 1990s.

The billionaire class in the United States did not look terribly
bloated until recently, despite the country's long-standing reputation
for a particularly brutal form of winner-takes-all capitalism. For years,
U.S. billionaires had controlled fortunes equal to roughly 10 percent
of GDP, close to the global average. That share increased to 13 percent
in 2013 and 15 percent in 2014, driven in part by the rise of Silicon
Valley tycoons and by easy money pouring out of the Fed. As we have
seen, since 2009 the Fed's experimental monetary policies helped fuel
a simultaneous boom in all the major financial asset prices—stocks,
bonds, and real estate. Since the top 1 percent of Americans control
50 percent of the financial wealth, they gain most when these asset
prices boom.

On the flip side, it is normally a healthy sign when the scale of a
nation's billionaire fortunes is below the global average of 10 percent

of GDP. It seems fair to say, for example, that the countries where billionaire wealth is 5 percent of GDP or less, such as Poland, South Korea, and Australia, may enjoy a certain foundation of political stability; their elites do not form as large a target for social unrest and political agitation.

Post-Communist Poland is a particularly interesting case, with only five Polish billionaires. As a group, there is something charmingly anti-Abramovich about them; they are almost incapable of flashy self-promotion. One, the banking magnate Leszek Czarnecki, holds a world record in underwater cave diving, which is about as far from surface displays of wealth as you can possibly get. Darius Milek, who made his billion manufacturing shoes that he piles up in big bins and sells out of street kiosks fashioned from metal shipping containers, readily concedes that all his customers really care about is price. That's why he doesn't bother with shoe boxes. The superrich Polish elite is emerging as the low-glitz opposite of the Russian elite, anchored by at least half a dozen self-made entrepreneurs who are building their wealth toward a billion with a grinding work ethic. Marek Piechocki, whose fast fashion company is bursting out of the old Gdansk warehouse where it started twenty years ago, is pretty typical. He seems to be always at work, and for years he was known for driving the same old car and showing up at meetings in the same old suit.

The Poles' neighbors in the Czech Republic, another eastern European country that has avoided billionaire bloat since divorcing the Soviet Union, share a similar style. When I met Andrej Babiš, an agribusiness billionaire who was serving as Czech finance minister, in Prague in May 2014, I was struck by how little this tycoon-turned-populist politician had to say about the economic strengths of his country, which was by most accounts a bright spot in troubled Europe. Most finance ministers spend a lot of effort promoting their country to investors, but not Babiš. Instead, he delivered a darkly comical rant against political infighting in Prague and "a corruption matrix that has been building" since the fall of Communism. This seemed a bit over the top, yet it is what you want to see in the national elite: no excess, no complacency, and a certain sense of urgency even in relatively good times.

Then there are anomalies like Japan, where the share of GDP held by billionaires—2 percent—is unusually low for a rich country. One cannot help but suspect this is a symptom of the economy's chronic incapacity to create significant wealth. Some academic research shows that growth typically tends to slow when inequality is very high but also when it is very low.[4] While it seems a bit odd to argue that any billionaire class is too small for a nation's good, that may be the case in Japan, and some Japanese seem to realize this. They have a word, *akubyodo*, which translates as "bad egalitarianism" and is used by critics to describe a corporate and political culture that rewards seniority more than merit and risk-taking. Everyone gets credit for staying in a job, but no one gets rewarded for standing out. Rising Japanese billionaires like Hiroshi Mikitani, an e-commerce magnate known for adopting ideas from American corporate culture and criticizing his countrymen for their lack of English proficiency, get a lot of media attention precisely because they are so unusual. It's not a good sign when dynamism is seen as offbeat.

Quality: The Good versus Bad Billionaires

Though new faces on the billionaire list can be a favorable sign for the economy, this holds true only if they are good billionaires, emerging outside what economists call "rent-seeking industries." These industries include construction, real estate, gambling, mining, steel, aluminum and other metals, oil, gas, and other commodity industries that mainly involve digging natural resources out of the ground. The competition in these sectors is often focused on securing access to a greater share of the national wealth in natural resources, not on growing the wealth in fresh, innovative ways. Major players spend a lot of time trying to win over regulators and politicians to secure ownership of a limited resource and the right to extract the maximum possible rent from that resource, by bribery if necessary. To make a rough qualitative judgment about the sources of great fortunes, I compare the total wealth of tycoons in these corruption-prone businesses to the total wealth of billionaires in the country. This yields the share of the wealth generated by "bad billionaires."

The bad billionaire calculation no doubt does a disservice to the many honest real estate and oil tycoons, but even in nations where these industries are clean, they tend to make weak contributions to steady economic growth, either because they are relatively unproductive or because they tie a nation's growth to the volatile swings of commodity prices. The assumption is that the rest of the billionaires make a greater contribution, but I reserve the label of "good billionaire" for tycoons in industries that are known to make the most productive contributions to economic growth or that make popular consumer products like smartphones or cars. These "good" industries include technology, manufacturing, pharmaceuticals, telecoms and retail, e-commerce, and entertainment, and they are least likely to generate popular national backlashes against wealth creation.* To be clear, I don't see the results here as hard data, in the way, for example, that credit or investment growth or current account numbers are hard data; reading the billionaire lists in a systematic way serves instead as a loose filter, turning up a form of anecdotally telling evidence for whether nations are generating wealth mainly in clean industries that attract public admiration or in dirty industries most likely to stir popular anger.

The balance of power between good and bad billionaires can change fast, and globally this balance has shifted three times within the last fifteen years. At the height of the dot-com boom in 2000, tech billionaires outnumbered energy billionaires three to one worldwide. A decade later the rise in prices for oil and other commodities flipped the balance, with energy tycoons outnumbering tech magnates three to one.

---

* In a few cases, I counted tycoons in good industries as bad billionaires, based on well-documented ties to political corruption.

By 2012, the downturn in commodity prices was shifting the balance again, and tech billionaires outnumbered energy billionaires by about 1.5 to one, or 126 to 78 worldwide.

The revival of the good billionaires has continued since and has even spread to economies more closely associated with corruption than tech innovation. In 2010 India was mired in controversy over the rise of crony capitalism and corrupt tycoons, but that began to change over the next five years. Between 2010 and 2015 India saw one of the world's sharpest gains in the clout of good billionaires, who saw their total fortunes rise by 22 percentage points to 53 percent of total billionaire wealth. India's 2015 billionaire list is filled with new faces, and most of them are in productive industries like pharmaceuticals, education, and consumer goods. Since 2010 Dilip Shanghvi, who is the founder of Sun Pharmaceuticals and perhaps the most unassuming and least flashy billionaire I have ever met, has shot from number thirteen on India's list to number two.

These trends may have taken the edge off the anticorporate, antigrowth sentiment that had been building in Delhi over the prior decade. An Indian brokerage firm called Ambit started tracking the fate of crony capitalists through its "connected companies index," which monitors seventy-five firms that operate in rent-seeking industries and are believed to have benefited significantly from close ties to government officials. The stock prices for these companies have collapsed with the growing backlash against political influence peddling and the public's intense focus on corrupt deals. Between mid-2010 and mid-2015, India's stock market rose 50 percent, while the connected companies' index lost half its value, a sign that crony capitalism was in decline, along with the luster of making money on rising commodity prices. Only a few years ago the scions of Indian commodity billionaires were piling into the family businesses, but now I hear some of them say they are keener on hot tech start-ups.

The commodity tycoons seem to be slipping a bit in Brazil too, along with global prices for its commodity exports. Brazilian entrepreneurs have earned a reputation for managing to carve out competitive businesses in good industries like consumer and media, despite having to deal with a government prone to overregulation. This is true, but the niche carved out by good billionaires is still relatively small, and they account for 36 percent of total billionaire wealth, one of the lower shares among big emerging countries. They occupy an isolated space that brings to mind a term coined by the Brazilian economist Edmar Bacha, who described his country as "Belindia," one part prosperous and small like Belgium, the other vast and backward like India.

China has been generating new billionaires at a rapid pace for years, but until recently there appeared to be a ceiling on the scale of their wealth. Until 2013 no Chinese tycoon had ever built a fortune worth more than $10 billion, and several who had approached that mark had landed in jail on corruption charges. Authorities may in fact have been enforcing an unwritten rule against ten-figure fortunes, perhaps fearful that some magnate might grow rich enough to fund political challenges to Communist Party rule. Even now, some billionaires continue to live in fear of what in China is referred to as "the original sin"—many Chinese tycoons made their first bucket of gold by cutting a deal to stretch some obscure rule, and knowledge of that deal is used against them at will by the authorities.

But the $10 billion ceiling was broken in 2013 when Zong Qinghou shot out of nowhere to become China's richest man, at least briefly, as a 75 percent jump in the market value of his bottled water and tea company lifted his fortune to near $12 billion. Soon thereafter the combination of a global tech boom and the vertical ascent of the Shanghai stock market helped boost the fortunes of six tycoons above the $10 billion mark by the end of 2014, with three of them crossing $15 billion. All three were founders or leaders of Internet companies: Jack Ma of Alibaba, Robin Li of Baidu, and Ma Huateng of Tencent. Despite the fact that the state has been interfering more directly in the economy in recent years, these new billionaires are rising in the most liberalized and competitive private sector businesses, not "old money" sectors like telecoms, banking, or traditional manufacturing, where state companies still dominate. Several of the newcomers are in their forties and are less beholden than older tycoons to political connections, and more dependent on the opinion of global markets, since their companies are often listed in New York. By early 2015, according to the Hurun Report, new Chinese billionaires were emerging at the rate of five a week, and by October China had surpassed the United States for most billionaires in the world, by 596 to 537. Ma had been replaced at the top by Wang Jianlin, a real estate and entertainment impresario whose net worth had mushroomed to $34 billion.

The return of the good billionaires is hardly universal, however. Few new or good billionaires are to be found in nations where an aging regime has turned away from reform and cultivated a class of politically connected tycoons. Two of these regimes are in Putin's Russia and Erdoğan's Turkey. The billionaire class in Turkey controls a rising share of the economy, and the share of wealth that comes from rent-seeking industries has spiked. Nine out of every ten Turkish billionaires live in Istanbul, long the commercial center of the country. Even billionaires who hail from the heartland of Anatolia tend to relocate to Istanbul, to be closer to the action.

But no city rivals the concentration of wealth and power in Moscow. In Russia, 85 of the country's 104 billionaires live in Moscow, which remains unrivaled as the world capital of bad billionaires. The global decline in prices for oil, steel, and other commodities has sapped the wealth of Russian oligarchs in recent years, but they continue to dominate the economy. Nearly 70 percent of Russian billionaire wealth comes from politically connected industries, by far the largest share in the world. These imbalances make Russia a prime candidate for a political backlash against inequality, and in fact the conspicuous consumption of the super-rich is matched by their heavy security. Abramovich, the steel magnate, recently bought a $450 million yacht with a missile detection system.

Under Putin, the government has often exploited popular unease with these billionaires in the most cynical way, protecting the oligarchs who stay in favor, while making an occasional propaganda show of humbling those who trample the proletariat. In one case, back in 2009, Putin traveled to the industrial town of Pikalyovo to force the aluminum billionaire Oleg Deripaska and other tycoons to settle a dispute with local workers over unpaid wages. After signing the agreement, the humbled magnate wandered off with the pen, and as gleefully recounted in the state media, Putin called him back to return the pen, while lecturing Deripaska about his "trivial greed." This was likely all for show, since Deripaska and Putin are still believed to be close allies.

Popular resentment against the billionaire class is also palpable in Mexico, where the tycoons are famous for growing rich on monopolies. They have almost exclusive control over industries ranging from telephones to concrete, and television to tortillas, which earn monopoly profits for their owners while driving up prices. The resulting anger helps explain why the Mexican rich live in fear of kidnappings for ransom, and the superrich live behind high walls and heavy security. The contrast to the high profile of many billionaires in Asia, where they are often treated as national icons, could not be sharper.

On a November 2014 trip to Mexico City, I was taken aback early one morning when I walked down from my hotel room and found the corridors peppered with silent men in dark suits and earpieces. They also dotted the sunny courtyard where I was meeting a Mexican journalist over breakfast, and I asked him what was going on. The men in suits were the security force for one of Mexico's top billionaires. A commodity tycoon, he stays so far from the limelight that the local newspapers had only recently gotten their first picture of him when he arrived for a meeting with President Enrique Peña Nieto. When billionaires feel compelled to lie that low, something may be wrong with a nation's system of wealth creation.

Family Ties

Bad billionaires often arise through family empires, particularly in the emerging world, where weaker institutions make it easier for old families to cultivate corrupt political ties. To identify nations where blood ties are most likely to be reducing competition and churn, I use *Forbes* data that distinguishes between "self-made" and "inherited" billionaire fortunes.

Among ten of the top developed economies in 2015, the inherited share of billionaire wealth topped out at over 65 percent in Sweden, Germany, and France, and it fell to a bit more than 30 percent in the United States and Britain and to 14 percent in Japan. Among ten of the largest emerging economies, the range was even wider, from more than 80 percent in South Korea to more than 50 percent in India, Indonesia, and Turkey, down to 1 percent in China and 0 percent in Russia. Though I would argue that in general heavy concentrations of family wealth are a bad sign for an economy, one has to be careful to drill down into the sources of family wealth.

In many countries, new billionaires often arise within older companies and have seen their wealth building toward the billionaire mark for many years, in some cases for many generations. In these cases, blood ties may not be the enemy of clean and open corporate governance, particularly in cases where the family has stepped back to play an ownership and oversight role in a publicly traded company, leaving the management of the company in professional hands. This can be a strong combination because the family keeps the company focused on the long term, and the market keeps it open to scrutiny. This, for example, is the model in Germany, were billionaire families control some of the world's most productive companies, including many of the *Mittelstand* companies that drive the flourishing manufactured export sector and are more a source of pride than resentment.

This also seems to be the case in Italy and France, which have seen quite a few new names appearing on recent billionaire lists. Many of these new entrants derive their wealth from old family companies and have risen slowly from the multimillionaire ranks to the billionaire lists. Since 2010, twenty-eight new billionaires have emerged in Italy, with more than half coming from the fashion and luxury goods industries. Two of Italy's new billionaires were Alberto and Marina Prada, from the Prada fashion house, established in 1913. Italy also saw new billionaires emerge from Dolce & Gabbana and Bulgari. Though France's billionaires tend to come from industries that are not typically associated with political corruption, they do tend to come from companies with old family roots, like Chanel and LVMH. *Forbes* puts two-thirds of French billionaire wealth in the "inherited" categories, and as in Italy, much new wealth is arising from old companies. Pierre Castel, who is new to France's billionaire list in 2015, built his fortune in a wine company founded in 1949. The stocks of companies in the luxury goods industries have been bid up sharply in recent years, based on booming sales in emerging markets, particularly in China. These new billionaires are capitalizing on the competitive advantage France and Italy have in producing fine handcrafted goods, which is part of their national identity.

For all the talk in recent years of the economic rise of a new Asia, many of its leading tycoons still emerge from within family companies and conglomerates, and here their reputation is decidedly mixed. In South Korea many of the tycoons derive their fortunes from family holdings in large companies like Samsung and Hyundai and count as good billionaires in the sense that their money comes from productive industries. On the other hand, stocks in these companies continue to sell at a discount compared to peers in other countries, due in part to lingering doubts related to their corporate governance or treatment of minority shareholders. There is also growing public concern that South Korea's commercial life is ruled by a self-perpetuating elite bound by blood ties. Despite the fact that South Korean billionaires control wealth of very limited scale relative to the size of the economy, and operate almost entirely outside the rent-seeking industries, the dominance of family fortunes in the billionaire class helps explain why in recent years inequality has surfaced as a political issue in Seoul.

A similar political backlash is starting to percolate in Taiwan, where the scale of billionaire wealth is not only much higher than in South Korea, but family connections also play a strong role. Inherited wealth accounts for 44 percent of the billionaire fortunes, and half of the twenty-eight billionaires in Taiwan are related to at least one other person on the list. The Wei family alone has four members in the billionaire class. The perception that Taiwan's formerly egalitarian society is developing an increasingly entrenched family elite has helped the opposition make inroads against the ruling KMT party by blaming it for rising inequality. The KMT has responded by taking steps to rein in the elite—including the passage in 2014 of a "rich man's tax" targeted at nearly ten thousand of the nation's wealthiest residents, with their tax rate increasing from 40 to 45 percent.

In countries like Taiwan, growing resentment of the billionaire class is compounded by the advanced age of the leading tycoons. In 2015, the average age of billionaires worldwide was close to 63, in both rich and poor countries. The countries with the youngest billionaires were Vietnam, the Czech Republic and China, where the average age was 53. Meanwhile, many of the oldest billionaires were found in the same countries where tycoons control a disproportionately large share of the economy and derive much of their wealth from inherited fortunes: The average age was 74 in Malaysia, 68 in Chile, and 67 in Taiwan. Taiwan's youngest billionaire was 46 years old, compared to 34 in China and 25 in the United States, reinforcing the impression of an older family-based elite.

New billionaires whose companies rise quickly out of nowhere—such as twenty-five-year-old Evan Spiegel of Snapchat—are the global exceptions, emerging as they do from hothouse environments like Silicon Valley. Indeed, the United States and China are quite unusual in terms of the number of billionaires they have generated from the ranks of young solo entrepreneurs, unaided by family ties.

The absence of inherited wealth should be a good sign, demonstrating that new business can compete with entrenched ones. In some countries, including Britain and the United States, that appears to be the case. Though critics like Thiel cite the familiar names of Gates, Ellison, and Zuckerberg as symbols of a stagnating upper-class, these figures did not inherit their wealth; they are self-made entrepreneurs. Zuckerberg is twenty-nine. By the standards of most countries, they are fresh faces. Though there are six members of the Walton family on the U.S. billionaire list, including four of the top twelve, they are quite unusual and together they account for $171 billion or nearly a fifth of the inherited billionaire wealth in the United States. Minus these Walton fortunes, the inherited share of U.S. billionaire wealth falls from 34 to 29 percent. Though the Waltons' company has stirred political controversy for paying low wages and driving small retailers out of business, there is no denying that through the smart application of technology to tasks like managing retail distribution and inventory, it has boosted productivity across the United States and global retail industries. The Waltons are an interesting case of sometimes controversial good billionaires.[5]

It's very hard, in contrast, to make a positive case for the apparently negligible role of family ties in China and Russia. In these countries, the fact that little inherited wealth is found on the billionaire list likely owes less to a competitive economy than to the relatively recent Communist-era campaigns to smash "bourgeois" families and confiscate their wealth. The reason that the data aggregators at *Forbes* magazine could find almost no inherited wealth in China and Russia may simply be that the tycoon class is of recent vintage and has not yet had time to pass on wealth to a second generation, or that many older members are careful to cloak their wealth. In China, alongside the new tech entrepreneurs, there is a rising class of well-connected Communist Party "princelings," many of whom may not count on the billionaire list because their net worth is in the hundreds of millions, or because they are hiding their wealth from a widening official crackdown on corruption.

Since taking office in late 2012, President Xi Jinping has been pressing well-publicized corruption cases even against some of the highest-ranking members of the Communist Party, and fear has spread among the Chinese elite. Many of these investigations are targeting not only high officials but also the business interests of their wives, siblings, and children. Cobb Mixer, a former undersecretary of the U.S. Treasury and a China expert, told me that this fear is changing the informal greetings elite Chinese use with one another. In the 1980s one common greeting was "Have you eaten yet?"—a reference to the famines China suffered during the 1960s and '70s. Since Xi took office in 2012 and started his crackdown, Mixer said, the new greeting is, "Have you been in yet?"—the word *in* refers to jail. By early 2015, more than 400,000 party members have been reprimanded and more than 200,000 prosecuted. Increasingly, the crackdown looks like a genuine effort to change the working culture of the party and cleanse it of corruption. That is a good sign for China.

Country	Total billionaire wealth/GDP	Bad billionaires wealth/total billionaire wealth	Inherited billionaires' wealth/total billionaire wealth
Brazil	8%	5%	43%
China	5%	27%	1%
India	14%	31%	61%
Indonesia	7%	12%	62%
Mexico	11%	71%	38%
Poland	2%	44%	0%
Russia	16%	67%	0%
South Korea	5%	4%	83%
Taiwan	16%	23%	44%
Turkey	6%	22%	57%
EM Average	9%	31%	39%

Country	Total billionaire wealth/GDP	Bad billionaires' wealth/total billionaire wealth	Inherited billionaires' wealth/total billionaire wealth
Australia	5%	45%	41%
Canada	8%	11%	47%
France	9%	5%	67%
Germany	11%	1%	73%
Italy	7%	3%	51%
Japan	2%	9%	14%
Sweden	21%	5%	77%
Switzerland	15%	29%	62%
United Kingdom	6%	25%	32%
United States	15%	10%	34%
DM Average	10%	14%	50%

Source: Forbes Billionaires List, March 2015

Why Bad Billionaires Matter Most

The rubric of good versus bad billionaires is the most important part of this rule, because even if the superrich control an unusually large share of the wealth, and leading families face little competition, they can make a positive contribution to growth if their wealth is concentrated in productive companies. They are also much more likely to be revered if they are getting rich by developing new smartphone apps rather than by milking their political connections.

Often, in emerging nations as in developed ones, a low share of bad billionaires can make up for weak scores on the other metrics. In South Korea, one reason the dominant industrial families are not a larger source of controversy is the patriotic storyline South Koreans learn from a young age, about how their proud nation overcame adversity (including the lack of oil and other natural resources) to become a leading industrial power. The aura of the top industrial families has diminished in recent years, but it remains a fact that very little billionaire wealth—just 5 percent—comes from corruption-prone industries, and it helps that they do not display their affluence in a garish way. Also, enough new blood is coming up to give entrepreneurs hope of competing. South Korea has a number of rising billionaires, including self-made cosmetics tycoon Suh Kyung-bae, who has tapped a growing global fascination with Korean style, and online gaming entrepreneur Kwon Hyuk Bin, whose game Crossfire was a blockbuster hit in China.

In Taiwan, too, the large scale and large inherited share of billionaire wealth is mitigated by the fact that so many of them are in productive tech industries. A large portion of Taiwan's billionaire wealth—77 percent—is created in productive companies, which tend to be concentrated in the manufacturing and assembly of parts for global computer brands. Some of the largest supply parts for iPhones and other Apple products. They operate in a highly entrepreneurial economy, in which intense competition has kept most companies in the small and medium-size class. The scale of billionaire fortunes in Taiwan also tends to be relatively modest (by billionaire standards). Worldwide in 2015 the average fortune of the roughly eighteen hundred billionaires is $3.9 billion, and in Taiwan it is $2 billion. Like their Korean peers, Taiwanese billionaires keep a relatively low profile but typically do not live in fear for their security.

In developed countries, too, a weak class of bad billionaires can reduce the likelihood of a political backlash against wealth creation and growth. Among the largest developed economies, bad billionaires control the smallest shares of billionaire wealth in Italy (3 percent) and Germany (1 percent). The economies of Germany and Italy don't have much in common, but they do share this almost complete absence of major fortunes tied to rent-seeking industries. German billionaire wealth comes from a particularly broad range of productive businesses, from ball bearings to BMW, shipping to software, consumer goods to Google. One of the earliest investors in Google was a far-sighted German, Andreas von Bechtolsheim. Though many of the new German billionaires on the 2015 list came from older companies, at least three others arose in a tech incubator, which has become a somewhat controversial global force by cloning American Internet businesses from Europe to India and Indonesia. The three Samwer brothers, Alexander, Marc, and Oliver, became billionaires when they took the Berlin-based incubator Rocket Internet public in late 2014.

In Sweden, the rise of good billionaires has, I suspect, also taken some edge off the emerging backlash against inequality there, despite the fact that these fortunes are so large and so much of their wealth is inherited. Sweden has the worst scores among developed nations for both the scale and the inherited share of billionaire wealth, but it ranks third for quality. Only 5 percent of Swedish billionaire wealth originates in traditional rent-seeking industries, and much of it is created at globally competitive companies, including H&M in fashion and Ikea in furniture retailing. These companies make most of their revenue abroad, and they are pulling money into Sweden—not battling for a greater share of domestic resources. Nonetheless, the overwhelming size and deep family roots of billionaire fortunes could still be a drag on Sweden's growth, particularly if their sheer scale provokes a public backlash against wealth creation.

The analysis is similar for the United States, where the traditional lines between good and bad billionaires are growing murky. Many of the top ten tycoons have been around for a couple of decades, but the companies they own—Microsoft, Berkshire Hathaway, Oracle, and Walmart—would make any economy more globally competitive. Below the top ten, a new changing of the guard appears to be under way. Many names connected to hot tech companies of the 1990s, like Jerry Yang of Yahoo!, have faded away, while those connected to hot new mobile Internet apps—including Jack Dorsey of Twitter, Eric Lefkofsky of Groupon, and Jan Koum of WhatsApp—have risen up to the billionaire list in recent years. Though Silicon Valley has seen protests over the growing disparity between techies and low-paid service workers, on the national stage tech tycoons are treated as celebrities. The billionaire entrepreneur Elon Musk, whose interests range from electric supercars to space tourism, is celebrated in scholarly reviews on how he is "changing the world."

There are many billionaire folk heroes from Silicon Valley, largely because consumers love the services they provide. WhatsApp gained seven hundred million followers in its first six years in business, which is more than Christianity gained in its first nineteen centuries, as *Forbes* magazine has pointed out. This rapid adoption is increasingly typical of new technology: More than forty years passed between the invention of electricity and the moment it reached a quarter of the U.S. population, and that lag has been shrinking ever since, to thirty years for radio, fifteen years for the PC, seven years for the World Wide Web, and just three years for Facebook. That is why Mark Zuckerberg, character flaws and all, is a popular icon and the subject of a full-length Hollywood feature film about his life. According to a 2011 study by Facebook, the theory that there are only "six degrees of separation" between any two people on earth no longer holds. Now, owing to social media, there are only 4.7 degrees of separation, and for that many Americans thank their Internet billionaires.

In American culture today, it is hard to point to any iconic bad billionaire. There is no modern equivalent of John D. Rockefeller or the other early-twentieth-century robber barons. Even when companies like Microsoft and Google have been vilified as death stars seeking to dominate the tech universe, outside certain rabid techie circles their billionaire founders have remained generally popular figures. In fact, the leading American billionaires, Bill Gates and Warren Buffett, have been out front in anticipating a backlash against great wealth, publicly urging their peers to bequeath their fortunes to philanthropy (as Rockefeller did, late in life) and arguing for high inheritance taxes to forestall the rise of a family-based plutocracy. One would expect the iconic bad billionaires to arise from rent-seeking industries like oil and gas, the way Rockefeller earned his reputation building Standard Oil. But in the United States the real source of new oil wealth has been the technology for extracting oil and gas from previously unreachable reserves trapped in shale rock formations. Thus many of these new U.S. resource tycoons do not fit neatly into the group Thiel described as cases of "technological failure."

How Inequality Kills Growth

The worldwide rise in inequality has produced a torrent of new research into its causes and consequences, and whatever one's ideology, it is hard to dispute the growing view that low levels of inequality fuel long runs of strong economic growth, and that high or rapidly rising inequality can prematurely snuff out growth.[6]

The main line of argument starts with the observation that as incomes rise, the rich tend to spend a smaller share of their additional income—and save more of it—than the poor and middle class do. The rich already buy all the basics, from food to gas, that they want and have little room to increase spending on these consumer staples when their wealth rises. On the other hand, when the poor and middle class have more cash on hand, they will spend more on clothes or food, or on better cuts of beef, or on gas for that weekend trip they had been denying themselves. The way economists put it is that the rich have a lower "marginal propensity to consume" as incomes rise. As a result, during periods when the rich control a growing share of the national income, growth in total consumer spending tends to slow, holding back the economy's growth rate.

A second line of argument touches the central theme of this book: spotting change. Among its most persuasive proponents are the IMF researchers Andrew Berg and Jonathan Ostry, who draw a clear link between the level of inequality and the inevitable "hills, valleys and plateaus of growth." They show that, in the postwar period, Latin America has enjoyed spells of rapid growth as frequently as the more highly touted economies of Asia. The big difference is that in Latin America the growth spells have tended to be shorter and much more likely to come to a premature end in violent "hard landings" that set the economy back many years, measured against the basic goal of catching up to incomes in the developed world. Why the violent endings? Berg and Ostry found the clearest explanatory link was to the high level of inequality in Latin America: "Inequality may impede growth at least in part *because* it calls forth efforts to redistribute that themselves undercut growth. . . . In such a situation, even if inequality is bad for growth, taxes and transfers may be precisely the wrong remedy."

The authors were not saying that popular demands for redistribution always retard growth; it is a question of balance, one that echoes a point former president Piñera made when I met him in Santiago. He said, "You have to attack inequality with both sides of the scissors," referring to the need to find a way to invest that will both encourage the economy to grow and spread the wealth.

The biggest threat to growth arises when an emerging nation has already committed to heavy spending on redistribution through social welfare programs, as both Brazil and India had in recent years, and then decides to spend more. Tossing more money at the problem of poverty can throw budgets out of balance, create an unwieldy state, and ultimately backfire by derailing the growth necessary to pay for social welfare. Berg and Ostry also found that lower income equality is closely tied to long growth spells, in part because it gives the poor the financial means they need to get ahead by investing in education or by starting small businesses.

High levels of inequality can instead magnify the impact of the financial crises that arise in the closing stages of strong growth spells. When a boom period reaches a manic stage, a high concentration of wealth at the top can encourage the rich to take a portion of their bulging fortunes and indulge in risky forms of financial speculation, in the kinds of conspicuous consumption that whip up social resentment, and then to ship a large share of the national wealth offshore when the inevitable crisis arrives.

Once a crisis starts, politicians must decide who will suffer the brunt of the losses, and the festering anger can make it much harder for creditors and debtors to reach agreement. As the Eurozone nations struggled to resolve the debt crisis in Greece, one of the basic hurdles was that neither Greece's creditors nor its own citizens were eager to help bail out the government of a deeply unequal society in which the rich have barely paid taxes in decades. By 2015, the backlash was palpable, and fear bloomed in the Greek economy. Leaving a hotel in the island of Santorini that summer, the general manager and his staff repeatedly warned me to carry my bill and credit card slip; customs officials were now randomly checking travelers for proof that hotels were not accepting cash, the preferred payment method of tax dodgers.

Bad Billionaires and the Meddling State

Bad billionaires are the sour cream rising to the top of corrupt societies. It is possible to sound out which societies are most corrupt using the annual surveys conducted by Transparency International (TI), which asks frequent travelers to rate countries from zero (perfectly clean) to 100 (completely corrupt). Since corruption is typically most severe among the poorest countries and tends to decline as countries grow richer, the best way to judge the level of corruption in a country is by comparing it to nations with similar average income. A 2012 study by Renaissance Capital found that fifteen countries, including Poland, Britain, and Singapore, are less corrupt than their peers, with TI scores 10 to 20 points lower than the average for their income level. Another six countries, including Chile and Rwanda, are much less corrupt than their peers, with TI scores 20 to 30 points lower than the average for countries at their income levels. On the darker side, twenty-five countries, led by Russia and Saudi Arabia, are more corrupt than normal for their income level, and unsurprisingly, these countries tend to be dominated by rent-seeking industries, particularly oil. Of the twenty-five countries that ranked as more corrupt than the average for their per capita income category, eighteen are oil exporters. That does not mean all oil tycoons are bad billionaires, but it does confirm that oil states tend to be havens for bad billionaires.

A strong link also exists between high levels of corruption and high levels of inequality, both of which can kill growth. Bad billionaires often seek to accrue an ever-greater share of the national wealth, and they thrive on rising corruption. Ned Davis Research has shown that countries that rank worst among their peers on the TI corruption surveys, such as Venezuela, Russia, Egypt, and Mexico, tend also to be the most unequal. Countries that rank best on the corruption surveys, including South Korea, Hungary, Poland, and the Czech Republic, are typically more equal than their peers.

Furthermore, inequality is strongly linked to corruption found in the black economy, where owners conduct their business in cash and off the books, to evade taxes. Researchers at the Organization for Economic Cooperation and Development have found that countries with large black economies also tend to be the most unequal and that this is no accident. Jobs in the black economy are often poorly paid, with no benefits, on dead-end career paths. Bad billionaires are the kings of this shady realm, which is large. It accounts for 8 percent of GDP in the United States and over 10 percent of GDP in many European countries, including Britain, Germany, and France. The black economy is also more than 25 percent of GDP in a range of developed and emerging countries, from Italy and Poland to Mexico and Turkey. At the extreme, it comprises more than 35 percent of GDP in five emerging nations: Brazil, the Philippines, Russia, Thailand, and Peru.

Large black economies can breed social resentment, since the art of dodging taxes is often most refined among the rich. In India, the government manages to collect income taxes equal to only 3 percent of GDP, and the size of the black economy is estimated to account for around 30 percent of GDP. This is one reason India suffers from chronic government deficits. The culture of avoiding taxes starts at the top: In a vast population with more than 250,000 millionaires, only 42,000 individuals report incomes of $150,000 or more, as economist Tushar Poddar has pointed out. He argues that tax dodging at the top creates a strong disincentive for any Indian citizen to pay up, in turn perpetuating tax evasion.

The habits of the billionaire class matter greatly because they tend to set the tone for the wider business culture. In India, many of the top tycoons command sprawling empires that often include at least one but often all four of the following businesses: a local hospital, a school, a hotel, and a local newspaper. One of India's top newspaper publishers recently pointed out to me that this rule of four now often holds true even for local kingpins in relatively small towns. The reason is simple. Most people understand it is wrong to take cash bribes, but few in India see much of a problem in accepting gifts in kind, even one as valuable as free medical treatment for a family member, free schooling for a child, free hotel banquet facilities for a niece's wedding, or favorable coverage for one's business or political ambitions in the local rag.

These ancillary businesses are seen as unprofitable but necessary investments for cultivating contacts among politicians and bureaucrats, who often repay their benefactors by granting special licenses or other favors. Backdoor deals of this kind entrench the power of insiders and increase inequality, while funneling money into unproductive industries. India has a bewildering array of publications, most too small to be economically viable. Of more than 13,000 dailies and 86,000 magazines, fewer than forty have more than 100,000 readers. Bad billionaires may not own most of these publications, but they set the tone of a business culture in which it is seen as quite routine to own a newspaper for the purpose of peddling influence.

Governments that can't control or tax their dodgy tycoons are also hamstrung in their ability to invest in ways that help address inequality, such as building roads and airports. In short, bad billionaires tend to feed a vicious cycle of corruption, rising inequality, and slow growth.

The Rise of the Billionaire Rule

The billionaire rule is growing in importance, because inequality has been rising all over the world, from the United States and Britain to China and India, due mainly to massive gains for the very rich. While in many nations all income classes are making gains, the rich are gaining much faster than the poor and the middle classes. Income and wealth gaps are growing, even as the number of people living in poverty falls, and the global middle class is expanding in size. As a result, the poor are more likely to rub shoulders with the middle class, and both are more likely to live in the shadows cast by a fast-growing global billionaire class. Inequality and the tensions it can cause are rising in importance as a political issue and threat to growth.

I am wary of countries where crony capitalism and bad billionaires are on the rise because they can reflect a deeper dysfunction: a business culture in which entrepreneurs become brazen after a run of success, a political culture in which officials grow complacent after a long period in power, a system in which cumbersome or nonexistent rules virtually invite corrupt behavior. I am also on the lookout for positive turns in countries that are responding to growing inequities by repairing the system: for example, by writing land acquisition laws that fairly balance the interests of farmers and developers, or holding auctions for public goods like oil fields or wireless spectrum in a transparent manner that rules out backroom deals. Mexico's auction in 2015 to sell offshore oil rights was considered underwhelming because it drew relatively low bids, but it was a success for the system because it was conducted live on national TV, which made crony deal-making unlikely, if not impossible. In this kind of changing environment, which can be detected only by observation and not in data, good billionaires can rise and help trigger a process of wealth creation that spreads its fruits more broadly.

The billionaire class is a useful bellwether for the economy as a whole. As the number of billionaires rises, the data are getting more significant over time, as a statistical sample and an analytical tool for spotting countries where the balance of wealth is skewing too sharply to the super rich. Measuring changes in the scale, rate of turnover, and sources of billionaire wealth can help to provide some insight into whether an economy is creating the kind of productive wealth that will help it grow in the future.

It's a bad sign if the billionaire class owns a bloated share of the economy, becomes an entrenched and inbred elite, and produces its wealth mainly from politically connected industries. A healthy economy needs an evolving cast of productive tycoons, not a fixed cast of corrupt tycoons. Creative destruction drives strong growth in a capitalist society, and because bad billionaires have everything to gain from the status quo, they are enemies of wider prosperity and lightning rods for social movements pushing predictable demands for redistributing rather than growing the economic pie.

4

PERILS OF THE STATE

*Is the government meddling
more or less?*

I WAS SURPRISED BACK IN 2011 WHEN THE BUZZ AT DAVOS, THE annual summit for the global elite, was about the "Beijing Consensus." The phrase captured the belief that China would overtake the United States not only as the world's largest economy but also as the world's leading economic model. At that time, the United States was struggling to recover from the credit meltdown that had triggered the global financial crisis three years earlier; U.S. unemployment was still high, and instead of taking action the government seemed paralyzed by partisan bickering between Democrats and Republicans. *Gridlock* had become Washington's defining term. Meanwhile China's government had responded to the "American-made" crisis by rolling into action as only a single-party dictatorship can. It had ordered massive new spending and lending that pushed China's growth rate back up to near double digits in 2010, a year when the United States barely grew at all. Talk of the new Beijing Consensus implied that many countries had come to see the virtues of an active, authoritarian hand guiding the economy, and that this new view was displacing the old Washington Consensus, in support of freedom in markets, trade, and politics. "The Rise of State Capitalism" was the theme of a number of new books and magazine covers in 2011.

I watched all this with great skepticism. For one thing, it was mainly the European and American political and business elites who were marveling about China, not their peers in emerging nations. A year before, in the Egyptian seaside town of Sharm el-Sheikh, I had met with Gamal Mubarak, son of his country's soon-to-be-deposed dictator. When I asked him whether his country would back off from the nascent liberalization process that his government was belatedly undertaking, he responded that the future was still in liberalizing the economy, along the lines of the Washington Consensus, because his country had learned from hard experience that state control doesn't work.

In India, my home country, the talk in business circles was not about the Beijing Consensus, either. It was about the growing power of the middlemen who hold court in the Tea Lounge of the Taj Mansingh, an iconic hotel in the heart of Delhi, the national capital. Long known as the place where rich couples are introduced to each other by their families for a prospective match, the Tea Lounge was now a hot spot to meet the kind of fixer who could clear away government obstacles and delay. At one table sat the middleman who could resolve delays in land purchases from the state; at another sat the go-to guy for cases stuck in the backlogged courts; at another sat the fixer who could speed the approval of state bank loans. These characters were widely seen as products of an overindulged bureaucracy and a classic symptom of the problems traditionally associated with state capitalism. The evolution of a place such as the Tea Lounge into a kind of shadow cabinet office was a symptom of the rot in the system, which would soon discredit the then ruling government of Manmohan Singh.

The admiration for state capitalism began to fade only after many of the global elite had lost some $2 trillion in bets on its rise. The total value of emerging stock markets dropped from $11 trillion in 2008 to about $9 trillion in 2013, and *all that $2 trillion loss came out of state companies*. Meanwhile the global market value of private companies held steady during that period. The Davos crowd was not all talk—many strategic investors had been putting their money on the Beijing Consensus, in the form of large purchases of stocks in state-run companies in China and in other large emerging nations such as Russia and Brazil. The resilience of China's economy and the increasingly popular idea that its all-seeing state could "command" strong economic growth had a huge impact on investor psychology. In 2008 there were five state firms among the world's ten most valuable companies, up from none in 2003. China's largest oil company, PetroChina, was number one, having displaced ExxonMobil. Surely this was further proof that China's command economy could be more profitable than America's free market economy?

The story didn't play out that way. Many global investors had gotten too excited about the potential for state capitalism in the general exuberance for all emerging economies, which had boomed after 2003. Stock markets moved upward with the economic boom, and by the end of the decade, investors were no longer making careful distinctions between weak and strong countries or state versus private companies. This was a mistake for which many people would pay dearly.

Following the global financial crisis in 2008, many emerging nations, including China, had started using state companies as tools to dispense jobs or cheap subsidies, in an effort to protect their people from the slowdown in global growth. Impressed by China's pumped-up economic growth, investors failed to see at first what this effort to manage growth was doing to the profitability of state-owned companies. There were some exceptions, with a few well-run state banks and other state companies in nations like Indonesia and Poland, but in general the profitability of these companies was low, and management was often in the hands of political cronies. China had been praised for avoiding the massive debts that had tripped up the U.S. economy, but now it was directing state banks to provide easy credit to state companies, which were visibly failing to put the money to good use: Their profitability (measured as return on equity) fell from 10 percent in 2009 to 6 percent by late 2013. Ironically, by the time the media hype over state capitalism was peaking at Davos in 2011, the market value of state companies around the world had already started to plummet.

State companies had accounted for 30 percent of the total value in emerging stock markets worldwide in 2008, but over the next five years their share was cut in half. By late 2013, there were, once again, no state companies in the global top ten: PetroChina had slipped from number one to number fourteen. The American technology firm Apple had meanwhile taken the top spot. If the global market ever intended to endorse the competitive virtues of state capitalism, it had since withdrawn that endorsement.

The question to ask for any economy is this: Is the state meddling more or less? In general, and particularly in a period like the current one, when many governments have been intervening so aggressively, less is better. Government attempts to manage economic growth come in many and varied forms, but I watch three basic trends: changes in the level of government spending as a share of GDP, coupled with an assessment of whether that spending is going to productive ends; the misuse of state companies and banks to achieve essentially political goals; and the extent to which the government allows private companies room to grow.

When Spending Becomes a Problem

How much government spending is too much? This is a tricky subject always, and especially amid today's ideological wars. The reality is that the state is the only investor large enough to build infrastructure like roads and bridges, and that in some emerging nations the state is in fact too weak—collecting too little in taxes—to invest adequately in these basics. However, the size of any government needs to be manageable so that it can be focused on a few key tasks. When the state is spending too lavishly on free food or subsidized gas or on running loss-making hotels and airlines, the whole economy will be poorer in the long run. I have to admit that my own views have been shaped by growing up in India, a country where the lingering socialist influence still creates many glaring examples of state intervention gone wrong: for example, a public school system in which teacher absenteeism runs as high as 45 percent in some states, because candidates often pay to obtain tenured positions, then don't bother showing up, taking a second job in private schools instead. Similar scandals infect a public health network that provides free treatment, but too often in rat-infested clinics without real doctors and with cleaning boys left to administer injections. On an issue that stirs such strong political convictions, objectively identifying which nations are getting the balance right can be tough.

There is also no clear answer to what is right. I begin by looking for the extreme outliers, the countries where state spending habits appear most out of balance and thus are most likely to threaten growth. The normal postwar pattern has been that as a country grows wealthier, spending by the government has tended to grow as a share of the economy. So to spot potential outliers, I identify which national governments are spending much more (or much less) as a share of their economy than other nations at the same income level. The worst possible sign comes when a relatively fat state is getting fatter, compared to its peers. Among the top twenty developed economies, the rotund king of this class is France.

The French government spends an annual sum equal to 57 percent of GDP, more than any other nation in the world, barring the possible exception of Communist throwback states like North Korea. France's spending level is 18 percentage points above the norm* for developed nations, the biggest gap in the developed or developing world. The other wealthy countries in which state spending dominates the economy— amounting to more than half of annual GDP—are Sweden, Finland, Belgium, Denmark, and Italy.

In France, however, the heavy taxes that support this outsize state have become such a burden that many businesses and businesspeople

---

* The norm here is defined using a simple regression, comparing government spending as a share of GDP to GDP per capita. Government spending data is from the IMF, which includes national, state, and local government and defines spending broadly to include everything from the public payroll to welfare payments.

say they are giving up and leaving the country. The tradition of the strong French state goes back centuries, and the French are unrivaled producers of jokes about government bumbling. Georges Clemenceau, an early-twentieth-century French president, described France as "a very fertile country: you plant bureaucrats and taxes grow." A few decades later the comedian Michel Coluche quipped that if there was a tax on stupidity, the state would pay for itself. And a modern writer, Frédéric Dard, remarked, "It's when you are paying your taxes that you realize you can't afford the salary you earn."

Of course, France is under intense pressure to change, as many of its neighbors have been since the crisis of 2008. Greece used to be one of the countries where state spending accounted for more than half of GDP, but since the crisis of 2008 it has seen that share of its nation's GDP fall by 4 percentage points, to 47 percent—in large part because its creditors forced Athens to make painful cuts in civil service jobs and salaries. Greece continues to move in a promising direction, narrowing the size of its giant state, albeit to levels that are still way above the norm for its income level and fat by any measure.

Greece combined the bloated spending habits of a France with a level of tax dodging more typical of a developing nation. The culture of tax avoidance and welfare fraud that it fostered made it difficult if not impossible to fund its generous welfare state, which is what pushed the country so deep into debt. The Greek journalist James Angelos documented this dysfunctional culture in *The Full Catastrophe*, describing, for example, one Greek island where 2 percent of the population (nearly ten times the European average) were claiming to be blind, in order to collect welfare benefits for their visual disability, in cahoots with local officials and hospitals. Depending on who was doing the counting, Greece was spending somewhere between 16 and 18 percent of GDP on public pensions, the highest share in Europe and a huge drain on its limited resources.

Still, the recent downsizing of even the Greek state demonstrates how the government is not in all cases evolving into the all-powerful creature that some fear. There are countervailing forces in play. If the state is spending way too much on giveaways, it tends to be forced back in line by global markets, as we recently saw in Europe. Former U.S. Treasury official Roger Altman has pointed out that if Germany had not pushed Greece and other European nations to make painful spending cuts in response to the debt crisis, they would have had to make those cuts anyway, because global markets were charging interest rates as high as 40 percent to extend more loans to these governments. Spending less was the only way to make those debts manageable.[1]

The recent European financial crisis led to two recessions in a space of less than six years, an unusual double crisis that might mark a turning point on the continent. Prior crises had already started to erode the welfare state, and that trend may continue. The Scandinavian countries such as Sweden and Finland cut back their welfare states after financial crises in the 1990s. Since then Sweden has seen state spending fall from 68 percent of GDP to 48 percent of GDP, and the government has emphasized lowering corporate tax rates to stimulate growth, while keeping personal tax rates relatively high to fund social services. Germany has also made changes to its spending habits, lowering social benefits in the early 2000s by reducing payments to those unwilling to look for work or enroll in training programs. Germany still shows up as a relatively big spender, with the government accounting for 44 percent of GDP, but that figure has moved down by close to 3 percentage points over the last decade. Other European nations are so scarred from the recent public debt crisis that they will be under pressure to keep the welfare state in check.

The lighter spenders in the developed world included the United States, Austria, and Australia, with government spending amounting to between 35 and 40 percent of GDP. Switzerland was even lower at 32 percent, which is in part an illusion, because its pension and healthcare systems are managed by agencies that are not counted as part of the government. Nonetheless, Switzerland's government is quite lean, with relatively few public employees, and it collects taxes that amount to only

27 percent of GDP—second lowest among developed countries (after the United States) and nothing compared to France, which collects 45 percent. The streamlined Swiss state is in part a product of a political system that gives a lot of power to local cantons and to voters. Many major issues have to be decided by public referendum, which gives Swiss voters the right to veto any hike in a tax rate of just 27 percent, one of Europe's lowest.

Emerging Big Spenders

Among the twenty largest emerging nations, the biggest state spender today is Brazil, where spending by local, regional, and national governments amounts to 41 percent of GDP, or 9 percentage points more than is normal for a nation with an average per capita income of $12,000. In fact, Brazil's spending habits are much closer to those of European welfare states than those of fellow emerging economies. The second biggest spenders are Argentina and Poland, where government spending is also more than 40 percent of GDP and 8 percentage points above the norm for their income levels, followed by Saudi Arabia (7 percentage points out of line), Russia, and Turkey (5 percentage points above the norm).

In emerging countries, however, some of these numbers have to be taken with a grain of salt: Russia officially reports that state spending amounts to 36 percent of the economy, but even top government officials have privately said that the state share of the economy is closer to 50 percent, up from 30 percent in 2000, which would make it a bigger spender than Brazil. The confusion is indicative of the post-Soviet fog that still shrouds the Russian state in secrecy; meanwhile in Poland the government reports a figure for state spending that is credible, 42 percent of the economy in 2014, having fallen from 45 percent five years before. So the real direction of change is positive for Poland and worrisome for Russia.

Brazil's state expenditures are both high and rising, distorting the economy in a number of ways. When millions of Brazilians joined street

protests across the country in 2013, their central complaint was that
the state takes more and more in taxes but delivers less in public services. To check the validity of that complaint, the Brazilian Institute
of Planning and Taxation, a consulting firm, compared Brazil's record
of collecting taxes and delivering services against thirty other major
countries. It found that Brazil collected taxes equal to 35 percent of
GDP, the heaviest burden among emerging nations, but ranked dead
last in terms of how much tax collection delivered in public services, as
evidenced by its substandard hospitals, inadequate grade schools, and
the lousy bus services that ignited the mass protests. Brazil's spending
poses a huge burden on locals because of both the size of the tax bills
and the complexity of the tax code. Roberto Setubal, CEO of Brazil's
largest private bank, Unibanco Itaú, once told me it takes longer to fill
out taxes in Brazil than in any other country because the forms demand
so much information, including a complete profit and loss statement
from every individual.

At the other end of the scale stand the large emerging countries where
state spending is unusually light, a group that includes Mexico, Taiwan,
and above all South Korea. In both Taiwan and South Korea, government spending accounts for a low 22 percent share of the economy—15
percentage points under the norm for countries at their income level.
However, in South Korea that share had grown 3 percentage points since
2008, and more important, it was growing in ways that made a productive contribution. For example, to help overcome one of South Korea's
big economic obstacles, which is that relatively few women participate
in the workforce, the government has been investing in childcare centers to help new mothers get back to the office—a move that by some
estimates could add a full percentage point to GDP growth. Taiwan is
taking similar steps to build a welfare state that works: In 1995 it had
no public healthcare system, and it now has one that covers nearly 100
percent of the population and costs just 7 percent of GDP compared to
18 percent for the mixed and still spotty public and private coverage in
the United States.

In general, the governments of emerging Asian countries tend to be relatively small, partly because even the rich Asian countries like Japan have been slow to build a welfare state. Only 30 percent of Asia's population is covered by a pension plan, compared to more than 90 percent in Europe. Interestingly, the widely held generalization that Latin governments are somehow prone to overspending is not borne out by the current numbers. Along with the government in Mexico, those in the Andean countries of Colombia, Peru, and Chile all look relatively undersized. Chile is the most undersized of this group, with government spending amounting to 25 percent of GDP, 8 percentage points below the norm for its income group. It is only the governments of the Atlantic coast—in Brazil, Venezuela, and Argentina—that tend to bloat.

The Dark Side of a Too-Small Government

The state needs to be spending at least enough to provide the essential conditions of civilized commerce, including building basic infrastructure and mechanisms to contain corruption, monopolies, and crime. One clear sign that a state is falling short is when it cannot even collect taxes, a failure that tends to expose both a general incompetence on the part of administrators and a popular disdain for the state. Mexico, for example, collects taxes equal to about 14 percent of GDP. That is quite low for a middle-class country, and lack of revenue is making it hard for the government to maintain law and order or suppress the corrupting influence of drug cartels. Mexico spends just 0.6 percent of GDP on the military, the second lowest level among large emerging countries, ahead of only Nigeria at 0.5 percent. Underpaid Mexican police and prosecutors have often been caught colluding with cartel kingpins, undermining public confidence in the state itself.

Mexico is also far from the most bumbling of states in this respect. In Pakistan, Nigeria, and Egypt, the state manages to maintain only a thin veneer of formal authority, which may help explain the strange sense of fragility you get visiting these places. In Nigeria, state spending amounts to just 12 percent of GDP, which helps explain why so much of the basic infrastructure seems to have been improvised by private citizens and companies, with patchwork roads and jerry-rigged power generators in basements. In Pakistan, a nation of 180 million people, fewer than four million are registered with the tax authority, and fewer than one million actually file taxes. The whole system is so riddled with exemptions and favors, one almost feels the whole edifice of state authority could just blow apart at any moment, in some giant upwelling of the underserved and alienated majority.

When the state is this weak, the economy runs on a paper-thin foundation and becomes particularly susceptible to the debilitating threat of civil war, with various sections of the society feeling excluded. In 2009 the U.S. Agency for International Development (USAID) studied conflicts in sixty-two nations between 1974 and 1997 and found that a typical civil war lasted fifteen years and reduced national GDP by around 30 percent. Even after peace arrived, it took a decade on average just to recover the prewar levels of income, and in four cases out of ten, violence erupted anew within a decade. In 2011 South Sudan became the world's youngest country after breaking from Sudan, but by 2013 a power- and oil-sharing agreement between the two dominant tribes had devolved into a new civil war. Fragility can be tenaciously durable.

The flip side of the underfunded state is the black economy, where people do business off the books in order to evade taxes. The black economy is the ultimate expression of public disdain for the state, reinforcing not only its fragility but also its inefficiency. Jobs in this untaxed netherworld tend to be poorly paid and often dead-end career paths without benefits, and employers in this realm get the kind of productivity they pay for. The black economy can be shockingly large—running anywhere from 8 percent of GDP in Switzerland and the United States to more than 30 percent in Pakistan, Venezuela, Russia, and Egypt.

It also spills over into other forms of dysfunction. Tax dodgers tend to avoid banks, which reduces the pool of savings available for investment and creates an alternative and far less efficient channel for allocating capital. A 2015 story by the *Bloomberg* writer Ahmed Feteha explained that many Egyptians throw fake weddings as a way to raise capital from their network of friends and relatives. One groom, who had just raised $16,000 in a "wedding" party that his bride did not even attend, explained, "Some people hold weddings to celebrate, others do it as a business," or a way to raise money without going to the bank or paying taxes.[2]

As a result of these weaknesses, states can sometimes feel sudden pressure to raise revenue, which also leads to perverse outcomes. Indonesia's democracy was less than two decades old when President Joko Widodo took office in 2014. The economy was slowing and desperately needed new investment in its crumbling roads and bridges. Widodo saw the obvious problem in a nation where total tax collections amount to just 12 percent of GDP, one of the lowest levels in Asia. According to some of his advisers, he tried to fix this problem by calling in the tax collectors and asking them by how much they could raise collections. "100 percent!" some of the agents boasted, hoping to impress. Widodo cut the target to 50 percent, and the finance ministry cut it to a more humble 30 percent, a hike his advisers later admitted was still way too much for one year. In order to hit the target, tax agents resorted to such means as staking out car dealerships and real estate sales offices to collect on the spot. Not surprisingly, car, motorbike, and property sales slumped. Businessmen deferred their investment plants, and the economy slowed further. For the long run, Widodo had the right idea, but the way he put it in play didn't work. When changing any policy, the state has to take into account how it will affect business sentiment, as an abrupt shift can hurt the animal spirits in an economy.

Misreading the Lessons of China

Many historians have pointed out that most of the Asian miracle economies were governed, in their early years, by authoritarian, controlling states. But there is a nuance to this story. In *How Asia Works*,

Joe Studwell writes that no nation, going back to Tudor England in the sixteenth century, produced competitive industrial companies without significant help and protection from the state in the initial stages. Tudor England was followed by the United States, France, and Germany. Then Germany inspired Japan, Japan inspired Korea, with Taiwan and China soon to follow. Studwell added that all these successfully activist states pursued "industrial policy" in a way that cleverly exploited market forces. In South Korea, for example, Park Chung-hee took office in 1960 and used the levers of the state to redistribute land from aristocrats to peasants, creating a broad new class of productive landowners. Rather than just favoring certain business allies, he also set up a competition among leading tycoons that would ultimately produce a few national industrial champions, companies like Samsung that made South Korea a leading export power.

However, no new important emerging nation has achieved this kind of success—growing rapidly thanks largely to the guiding hand of an activist state—in recent decades. Of course, many will respond, what about China? As the Nobel Prize–winning economist Ronald Coase has pointed out, the conventional story about China gets the narrative wrong. China started on the road to becoming an industrial super-power only after the all-encompassing state started to interfere less in the economy. Around 1980 the Chinese government began to ease its grip, one step at a time and always in response to pressure from below. Initially, peasants demanded to sell more of their own produce, then villages sought to run their own local enterprises, and finally individuals pressed for the right to own and run those enterprises.[3]

Since the early 1980s, the output of private companies in China has risen by 300 times, or five times faster than the output of state companies, according to Deutsche Bank research. As a result, the share of GDP produced by state companies has fallen from about 70 percent in the early 1980s to about 30 percent now, with most of that shift coming as market reforms picked up pace in the 1980s and '90s.[4]

This broad trend greatly reduced the power of the Chinese state as an employer and market trendsetter, at least until recent years. In the three decades before 1980, state companies accounted for 70 percent of urban employment, but that share had fallen steadily to just 20 percent by 2010. As the journalist and author Evan Osnos writes in *Age of Ambition*, between 1993 and 2005, Chinese state enterprises eliminated a staggering 73 million jobs, cutting loose all those workers to find some other source of income.

Private industry has proven to be much more dynamic, and by the late 2000s it accounted for more than 90 percent of the production in light industries like textiles, furniture, and food processing. Consider even the trend in investment—spending on new plants, equipment, and infrastructure—which has been the main driver of China's boom in recent years. Just a decade ago state companies accounted for more than 55 percent of the investment in China, but that share had fallen to about 30 percent in 2014.

China's successes were less a tribute to "command capitalism" than to Beijing's steady free market reform. Ironically, the government's recent post-crisis activism—which provoked so much talk about the Beijing Consensus—represented at least a partial reversal of its formerly successful habits. After 2008, Chinese technocrats became increasingly obsessed with hitting unrealistic growth targets, based on the entirely political calculation of what it would take to double the size of the economy by 2020. For Beijing, the path of least resistance was to direct new public spending and state bank lending to big state-owned companies, which began to regain some of the clout they had lost. Private companies saw a slight drop in their share of industrial output and are no longer making inroads in heavy industries like mining or steel. Private companies were still growing faster than state companies in the 2010s, but only 4 percentage points faster, down from 12 percentage points faster a decade earlier.

The fact that other Asian miracle economies developed with the help of an activist state also misses a key point: The leaders of these countries had no qualms about using state power to steer funds to favored companies, but the states themselves were not particularly large. In general, government spending accounted for a relatively small share of GDP, and it still does today. Taiwan and South Korea emerge from a tradition of disciplined state spending, which helps explain why—unlike France—they produce relatively few jokes about high taxes and incompetent bureaucracy.

Lately the size of the state has been growing quickly across many nations; in the emerging world, government spending now amounts to 31 percent of GDP, on average, up from less than 24 percent in 1994. While this is in part natural, since government has grown with national wealth for all countries in the postwar era, my sense is that most countries are getting less economic bang for their government buck. Much of the economic expansion in emerging economies in the 2010s has come from a rushed attempt by governments to spend their way out of the global slowdown, and these hasty efforts too often lead to massive waste. So the key factor to look for—at least in the current global scene—is states that are just meddling less.

Spend in Haste, Repent at Leisure

Particularly when a ruling regime has been in power for many years, states tend to overspend more when the economy is facing a crisis or a downturn. The incumbent rulers start scrambling to protect themselves and use the levers of the state to promote their own popularity by attempting to generate growth at any cost. They spend heavily on make-work projects, or they order state companies to create jobs or to keep prices artificially low, in an attempt to protect their citizens from the pain of the downturn.

This creeping inclination to spend heavily in hard times was very visible after the crisis of 2008. The collapse in housing and stock market prices came as a shock to American and European consumers, who started importing less from China and other emerging economies. To compensate, many emerging-world governments began spending heavily to encourage consumer spending at home. Many rich countries also tried to dampen the impact of the Great Recession with public spending, but their outlays would be dwarfed by those of emerging nations. Over the next two years, among the world's twenty major economies, the governments of developed nations spent a sum equal to 4.2 percent of their GDP on various projects aimed at combating the recession. Their counterparts in the big emerging nations spent more than half again as much, 6.9 percent of GDP, and they outspent rich nations for a simple reason: They could afford to, at least for a time.

Unlike the governments of the developed world, those of the emerging world went into the crisis of 2008 with generally low levels of public debt, large reserves of foreign currency, and strong government budget surpluses or at least relatively small budget deficits. Having money to burn, they burned it, and the initial result was a great jet flame of growth. After bottoming out at just 3 percent in mid-2009, the average GDP growth rate among the major emerging economies rebounded to more than 8 percent in 2010. With that apparent success, a rousing cheer bubbled up from supporters of strong government. The International Labor Organization teamed up with the European Union on a report in late 2011 lauding the contribution of heavy government stimulus spending to a "spectacular" recovery in Asia and to one nearly as impressive in Latin America.

Alas, by that point, the flameout was already under way. China's official growth rate slumped by more than a third between 2011 and 2014, Brazil's by a factor of ten, and the average GDP growth rate for the emerging countries had returned to around 3.5 percent, about the same rate as in the 1990s, when growth was disrupted by multiple crises. The big difference in the late 1990s was that most emerging nations had no money to burn, no lenders they could turn to, and thus they could not borrow to pump up growth. They were pressured instead to reform, clean bad debts out of the system, take steps to control spending, contain inflation, and (in a few cases) make companies more competitive. That cleansing set them up for the unprecedented boom of the 2000s.

After 2008, however, the governments of the emerging world started to borrow from the future to produce that brief flash of growth in 2010. And they paid for it dearly. By 2014, the government budget surpluses of 2007 had melted into an average deficit equivalent to 2 percent of GDP, which was creating real worries. Burned so often in the past by crises fed in part by government overspending, emerging nations had come to accept that a budget deficit equal to 3 percent of GDP or more was often a warning sign of serious budget problems to come. Indeed Indonesia, after its violent financial meltdown in 1998, adopted a law that allows parliament to impeach the president if the deficit goes above 3 percent of GDP. Along with Mexico, Russia, South Korea, India, and South Africa, Indonesia was one of many big emerging nations in which the budget started to run out of control after 2008.

Mexico was a particularly interesting example: It had not run up a government budget deficit in all the years since it suffered the peso crisis in 1994. In fact, it had run nearly zero deficits right up to 2008, when it raised government salaries and launched new public investments to fight the recession. Five years later the deficit was at a multidecade high of 4 percent of GDP, but its growth rate was stuck at a low 2 percent rate, like many of its peers. Mexico's state abandoned spending discipline in a desperate effort to fight the Great Recession, and the effort failed.

This tale of two crises offers a stark contrast: Following the meltdown of 1998, the governments of the emerging world cut back on government deficits and debt, meddling less in private business. Five years later these countries had low debt burdens and were thus poised for an unprecedented boom. After the crisis of 2008, however, governments in many emerging nations were piling up new debts, intervening more in a failing attempt to stimulate growth, and putting their economies in a position to register weak-to-mediocre growth in the following five years.

When the state tries to roll out spending projects too quickly, much of the spending goes to waste. After 2008 the explosion of big government spending contributed to a serious decline in productivity across the emerging world. In Russia, South Africa, Brazil, India, and China, a critical measure of productivity known as the incremental capital output ratio (ICOR) rose sharply after 2008, which was a very bad sign. It meant that these countries had to borrow a lot more capital to produce the same amount of economic growth, in part because so much of the capital was going to wasteful state projects or government giveaways.

What this ratio shows is that before 2007, it took one dollar of new debt to generate one dollar of GDP growth in the emerging world, including in China. Five years after the global crisis, it took two dollars of new debt to generate one dollar of GDP growth in the emerging world, and in China it took four dollars of new debt to generate a dollar of GDP growth. The evidence for these diminishing returns was everywhere. In Russia, Brazil, India, and especially China, private companies had been cutting investment even as the state had been investing more, and this shift from private to public investment had produced more and more waste. Among the world's twenty largest economies, Russia was one of the biggest spenders, laying out the equivalent of 10 percent of GDP on stimulus in 2008 and 2009 alone, much of it for new bailouts of big state firms. But it got the worst result, an 8 percent contraction in output. China was the biggest spender—laying out the equivalent of 12 percent of GDP—and fittingly generated the most damning examples of government intervention gone wrong.[5]

Government researchers in China issued a report in late 2014 concluding that their country had generated $6.8 trillion in wasted investment since the stimulus campaign began. In some recent years, the reports said, nearly half of all the money invested in China had gone to waste, much of it concentrated in industries that were the main target of the stimulus campaign, including cars and steel. On my visits to China, locals regaled me with tales of dubious public investments. The government, for example, had just finished construction on a $350 million bridge over China's southern border, but on opening day the bridge ended on a dirt ramp leading to an empty field in a vacant new industrial trade zone in North Korea.

Even John Maynard Keynes, the intellectual father of government stimulus campaigns, would likely have been surprised by the scale and duration of many recent spending efforts. His advice focused on emergency spending to ease the pain of a recession, not on open-ended attempts to generate perpetual growth. That is effectively what many emerging nations, spoiled by the boom years of the 2000s, had been trying to achieve with their big spending as the global recovery limped along after 2008.

By 2014, a strange disconnect began to appear in the global conversation. Leading voices in the developed world were calling for more stimulus in Germany and the United States, while at the same time prominent officials in the emerging world were admitting that they had been spending too much for too long. In May Chinese premier Li Keqiang gave a speech in which he said that "if we rely on stimulus to grow from government policy, not only is it not sustainable, but it also creates new problems and risks."[6] In November, the former Indian finance minister P. Chidambaram was more specific, admitting that by launching the stimulus campaign in 2009 and pushing it for so long, his government had "lost control of the economy," resulting in a higher government deficit, rising inflation, and slower growth.[7] And in a conversation with me that same month, the president of Mexico's central bank, Agustín Carstens, said bluntly that "fiscal and monetary policy cannot create growth" in the long run. Few emerging-world leaders would seriously dispute this conclusion, perhaps because so many of them have also seen the damage that heavy-handed socialist regimes can cause.

In all these countries, from India to Brazil, the state tried to manage the economy in a way that did nothing to promote growth in the future, so all they achieved was to delay the pain. In these cases, the spending campaigns produced just a temporary reprieve from the global slowdown, and growth in the future will be slower as a result of the debts rung up to pay for stimulus. This is what it means to say states are "borrowing from the future."

This problem raises an interesting question: Why can't governments spend to stimulate growth in the short term and simultaneously push reform—for example, by cutting regulations or selling loss-making state-owned companies—to increase productivity and growth in the long term? They could, but in practice they seem unable to work toward both goals at the same time. Perhaps this is because stimulus campaigns are motivated by an impulse to protect people from the free market, and reform campaigns are motivated by a desire to free people to compete in the market. Unfortunately, the worthy impulse to protect people— say, by raising food or energy subsidies—often leaves the government without the resources to make necessary investments in a more competitive economy. In 2015, many emerging nations find themselves in this predicament—with a long list of desperately needed infrastructure projects that the government can no longer afford. And once politicians dole out subsidies, they find it very hard to take them back.

The Political Abuse of State Banks

Across the emerging world, state banks are a major impediment to the smooth functioning of the credit system. In the wake of the global financial crisis, government stimulus in emerging nations would have totaled much more than the figure cited above—near 7 percent of GDP—if that figure included all the surreptitious moves that governments use to try to manipulate growth, including massive lending by state banks.

Despite several waves of free market reform in emerging economies over recent decades, the state still runs a large number of banks in many countries. If you want a loan, you ask the government. On average, state banks control 32 percent of all banking assets in the twenty largest emerging nations. That figure is 40 percent or more in Thailand, Indonesia, Brazil, and China (where the line between state and private banks is murky and the actual number is likely much higher). It is 50 percent or more in Taiwan, Hungary, Russia, and Malaysia and a striking 75 percent in India. In Russia, where twenty years after the fall of Communism, capitalism is still stymied by the difficulty of obtaining even a simple loan to start a small business or buy a house, nearly one-third of the anemic credit industry is controlled by just one bank, which is in turn run by Russia's central bank.

Spend a lot of time in the field, and it is all too easy to find evidence that the state is not a competent banker. Even in Chile, the Latin American nation most committed to private-sector capitalism, I am always struck by the number of employees at the offices of the remaining state banks who seem to be aimlessly milling about, on the job but underemployed. More than enough people are available to provide separate escorts from the front door to the security desk, the security desk to the upper floors, the upper floors to the executive offices. It takes half an hour to get through this gauntlet of civil servants, in part because there are so many of them.

State banks' efforts to mobilize lending have a disturbing tendency to backfire, worsening economic downturns. By 2014, in many emerging nations, more than 10 percent of total bank loans had gone bad—meaning the borrower had not made a payment in months. In most cases, including in Brazil, India, and Russia, the bad loan problem was concentrated in the state banks—which had been ordered to dole out more credit to favored companies as part of the stimulus campaign. These accumulated burdens were a big reason that in 2015 the IMF and other forecasters are belatedly lowering their long-term growth forecasts for the emerging world.

Brazil offers a good case study of how the political abuse of state banks can distort an economy. After President Dilma Rousseff took office in 2010, she started to fight the global slowdown by pressuring private banks to lend more, sometimes virtually ordering them to do so in public. Many private banks did not obey, however, on the grounds that the slowdown was already making it hard for their existing customers to repay loans. Facing this resistance, Rousseff turned to pressuring state banks to open the credit spigot.

The result was one country, two banking systems. The private banks were sensibly cutting back on new loans and working to contain the damage from bad loans. Meanwhile state banks were rushing to lend and in the process were racking up many more bad loans. BNDES, the largest state development bank in the world, with $200 billion in assets, was doling out cheap loans to virtually any company that asked, including well-run companies that could have qualified for market-rate loans. Between 2008 and 2014 state bank lending grew at a rate of 20 to 30 percent a year, and the state banks' share of total lending in Brazil rose from 34 to 58 percent, an expansion matched by few if any other emerging markets.

The result was a rapid run-up in debt, of the kind that often signals even slower economic growth in the coming years, when those bad debts clog the entire banking system. By late 2014, Brazil was headed into recession, exactly the outcome that President Rousseff's attempt to pump up bank lending was supposed to avoid.

In India too, major problems were associated with the excessive role played by state banks. Politicians there have long been known to call up managers at state banks to direct them to extend loans to their donors and cronies. Some of the largest state banks have frequent turnover in the chairman's position, as one political appointee replaces another, and every new chairman can be relied on to announce that under his predecessor the bank had been hiding bad loans. So the bad loan totals would suddenly spike, and then the new chairman would report steady progress in correcting his predecessor's mistakes—until he too was ousted in favor of some other political favorite, who revealed a hidden stash of bad loans. All this has thrown doubt on the scale of the bad loan problem, but by 2014 it was clear the figure was cripplingly high. In all, roughly 15 percent of state bank loans had gone bad. They were running out of the capital they needed to make new loans, and weak credit growth was the biggest constraint on Indian economic growth as a new government took office in Delhi that year.

In contrast, the private banks in India tend to be independent not only of the state but also of control by large tycoons or conglomerates, which is quite unusual in the emerging world. By 2014, less than 4 percent of private bank loans had gone bad. Private banks were in solid financial shape and had been increasing the size of their loan portfolios by 20 to 30 percent a year, as state banks were forced to cut back. This critical difference between private and state banks was no secret, certainly not to the stock markets: Between 2010 and 2014 the total market value of private banks rose by about $30 billion, while the total value of state banks fell by about $30 billion. This was the markets' way of voting on which banks are well run and which are not.

The problem with state interference in the credit system is not only its scale, but also its timing. Governments are not well equipped to anticipate rapidly shifting market conditions, and this was glaringly true in the case of China. When two of my colleagues flew over to see how the economy was faring in 2014, they found the gleaming new malls of Beijing so empty in the middle of the week that they sent another colleague back to check whether they were equally empty on weekends. They were. Because the state banks had made so much money available to encourage an increase in consumer spending, the real estate developers were tossing up new malls at a breakneck pace. But they were doing so at a time when Chinese consumers were moving to online retailers. That's where all the increase in consumer traffic was. The added irony was that, for all the money the Chinese state had poured into building new highways, one of the main obstacles for online retailers was that lousy local roads still made it difficult to deliver goods to the consumer's doorstep. The lesson here is that when the state lends in haste, it will repent at leisure.

When State Companies Become Political Tools

If a state is inclined to mobilize its banks to achieve essentially political ends, it is likely to use other state companies the same way. One standard tactic to look out for is the use of state oil, gas, or electric companies to suppress prices, in a misguided effort to prevent high inflation. This only leads to less new investment in the mispriced sectors, which exacerbates shortages over time and makes for more wasteful consumption. In Brazil, the government of President Rousseff deployed the state oil company, Petrobras, to fight inflation, a particularly dreaded threat in a nation with bitter recent memories of hyperinflation. Between 2010 and 2014, the inflation rate had crept up from 4 percent to around 7 percent, even as growth slowed. The government refused repeated requests from company executives to hike the heavily subsidized pump price of gasoline at a time when global oil prices would have justified a sharp increase. This badly hurt the profitability of Petrobras and encouraged excessive fuel consumption in Brazil.

State-owned companies are also viewed by some politicians as mainly job-creating machines. A rough rule of thumb is that on average, in both developed and emerging countries, jobs in the government and in state-owned companies combined amount to about 20 percent of all employment, based on data from the International Labor Organization (ILO). Countries with government employment well above that mark look bloated. Interestingly, in the East Asian economies such as Japan, Korea, and Taiwan—known for running relatively efficient governments—the share of government jobs in total employment is below 10 percent; South Korea is at the extreme end of the spectrum, with less than 5 percent of jobs in the public sector. On the flip side, the nations at the top of the ILO list are major oil exporters—Norway, Saudi Arabia, and Russia—where the state accounts for more than 33 percent of all jobs. Norway may seem like a surprise on this list, but it has a penchant for state capitalism much like the other oil exporters, and the government accounts for more than half of GDP.

Since the global financial crisis hit in 2008, Russia has been using state companies as safe havens for job creation in the downturn, expanding the already bloated 400,000-person payroll at Gazprom, the gas giant and one of the largest Russian state companies, if not the largest employer. The national railway alone employs more than one million people. In China, where it is often difficult to figure out where the state ends and the private sector begins, estimates of the state's share of total employment are around 30 percent, which is a relatively high number, and it has been inching higher since 2008, though it is down considerably over the last three decades. Streamlining the behemoth state-owned enterprises is cited by economists covering China as one of the top priorities for Xi Jinping's administration. The nation's state tobacco company alone employs half a million people and accounts for 43 percent of cigarette sales worldwide. The company is larger than its next five global rivals combined and accounts for 7 percent of Chinese government revenue. As *Bloomberg News* pointed out in a 2015 profile, China's financial dependence on cigarettes perhaps explains why the state tobacco company is allowed to sponsor elementary schools, where its banners proclaim, "Tobacco helps you become talented."

There Is No Free Gas

Perhaps the most self-defeating aspect of the government's involvement in the economy is energy subsidies, which play a major role in encouraging waste and draining national treasuries. In the Middle East and North Africa as well as parts of Central Asia, many governments spend more on providing their people with cheap fuel than on schools or healthcare. In these regions, annual spending on energy subsidies amounts to more than 8 percent of GDP, a cripplingly large share. In six countries—Uzbekistan, Turkmenistan, Iraq, Iran, Saudi Arabia, and Egypt—energy subsidies account for more than 10 percent of the economy. Uzbekistan spends more just to subsidize cheap energy—28 percent of GDP—than the United States spends on the military or on social security.

Few economists in any political camp would defend this spending choice. Energy subsidies keep fuel prices irrationally cheap, encouraging people to burn too much fuel and spew more of the carbon emissions that contribute to global warming. Cheap prices strangle local energy suppliers, discouraging investment and causing shortages, which fuel inflation. They also encourage smuggling and are the reason why even in an orderly country like Canada, profiteers are smuggling in gas from the United States, where low taxes underpin low gas prices. Fuel subsidies also tend to widen income and wealth inequality in poor countries, because states that subsidize energy have little choice but to subsidize it for everyone, despite the fact that those benefits go to support the privileged class of car owners. According to the IMF, in emerging economies, more than 40 percent of the $600 billion in annual energy subsidies worldwide goes to the richest 20 percent of the population. The same cannot be said of food subsidies, which at least help those in extreme poverty survive and remain active in the workforce.

Yet energy subsidies remain widely popular, particularly in oil-rich regions where much of the population seems to see oil the way most nations view water—as a natural bounty that should be free to locals. And if one country is rich in oil, the neighbors will tend to expect free gas too. Oil-poor Egypt spends as heavily on energy subsidies as oil-rich Saudi Arabia, just over 10 percent of GDP, even though pretty much everyone recognizes that artificially cheap energy encourages citizens to waste it.

In India, after 2008, the cost of energy subsidies was rising so sharply that by 2013, the largest state energy company, ONGC, was spending more than twice as much on subsidies as it was earning in profits. Though India has the fourth-largest coal reserves in the world, it was forced to import more and more coal during this period, because of delays in approving land purchases and issuing permits, and because the state failed to protect mines from attack by the radical Maoist gangs known as Naxalites.

Of late, an increasing number of countries have started talking about cutting energy subsidies—a strong positive sign for many deeply dysfunctional economies. The military leader of Egypt, Abdel Fattah el-Sisi, began to roll back the subsidies that left citizens paying just eighty cents a gallon for gas and warned them that more painful sacrifices would be necessary. Under President Susilo Bambang Yudhoyono, Indonesia started to cut fuel subsidies, and his successor, Joko Widodo, has continued to reduce them. The subsidies had been pushing the Indonesian budget deficit up toward 3 percent of GDP—putting their regimes at risk under the law that allows parliament to impeach the president for running a high deficit. Similar discussions over cutting subsidies were under way in Ukraine. Even a radical populist like President Nicolás Maduro of Venezuela—where fuel subsidies amount to more than 8 percent of GDP—seemed to recognize the resulting absurdities. Preparing his followers for a possible increase in gasoline prices, Maduro pointed out that his government's heavy energy subsidies make a full tank of gasoline cheaper than a bottle of mineral water. Maduro's comments suggested that he recognized the scale of the subsidy problem but did not necessarily indicate that he was going to interfere less in the economy, because he was proposing to take money out of energy subsidies and put it into a welfare fund that pays for other giveaways.

The debate over "guns versus butter" started before World War II and found its most famous proponent in President Dwight Eisenhower, the general and war hero who argued that heavy spending on America's "military-industrial complex" would threaten its ability to produce civilian goods. Today, the debate has shifted to *roads versus butter* and the argument that every dollar a government spends subsidizing free food or energy is a dollar it cannot spend building roads or other infrastructure, which boost future growth in a way that freebies cannot.

The Fifty Shades of Meddling in Private Companies

What's needed is a sensible Leviathan that spends its limited resources in a strategic way and acts consistently and predictably, based on a clear economic rationale. The government ought to create stable conditions in which entrepreneurial types—whether in the state sector or in the private sector—dare to invest. It needs to create a rule of law.

Even in an era when it is hard to find a successful activist state, competently building competitive industries, state interventions in the economy differ hugely in quality. In short, some states are much more adept than others at regulating and spending in a way that allows private enterprise to flourish. Consider the contrasting cases of Russia and Poland, both of which shook off Communism in the late 1980s but kept a large government, though in two very different styles. Poland is evolving in line with the strong-state tradition of continental European powers like Germany, developing an open model in which the state supports the private economy with the help of clear rules. Russia is regressing, aggressively expanding the state at the expense of the private economy, based on rules that shift with the whims of politicians and their friends. Erratically enforced laws are as big an obstacle to growth as pure lawlessness.

Russia's strategy has been to use the power of the state to build government companies at the expense of the private sector. The largest of the state oil companies, Rosneft, spent tens of billions buying out smaller energy companies, including the once highly efficient arm of a British joint venture, TNK-BP. This takeover of one of the most profitable international oil companies by a national government behemoth was described by many analysts as a disturbing sign of the times in Russia, with economic growth slowing sharply. As the 2010s roll on, the trend has spread to other industries, with state-run banks pushing out foreign rivals and a state umbrella company venturing into armaments, pharmaceuticals, and other industries.

A few islands of private-sector vitality remain in Russia, in industries such as high tech. The old Kremlin political elite, many of whom started their careers in the Soviet era, were content to leave younger members of the wider Moscow elite free to innovate in technology. The Russian tech industry is gaining momentum, making Russia one of the few nations in which local companies have been able to hold their own against popular American search and social networking sites. For a while, Putin and his team at the Kremlin left the Internet sector free to thrive, largely unregulated and unprotected, even at a time when Chinese Internet companies were prospering with the assistance of state barriers against foreign competition.

By 2014, however, that was changing. The Kremlin began requiring that foreign IT companies operating in Russia had to locate their

servers in Russia, thus making it easier for the state to monitor traffic. That April Russia's biggest celebrity entrepreneur, Pavel Durov, fled
the country after waking up one morning to find that nearly half the
shares of his social networking site—sometimes described as the Russian Facebook—had been transferred into the hands of allies of Putin.
This seems to be something of a trend in the Internet age. When a tech
start-up first gains a foothold in an emerging country, politicians see it
as a ticket to national riches and, fearful of killing a golden goose that
they don't really understand, leave it alone, at least until it grows big
enough to matter.

In Poland, state companies are still important players in industries
from copper mining to banking, but in contrast to the situation in Russia, none of them have been swallowing up private rivals with encouragement from the presidential suite. Instead, Poland is pushing its state
companies to reform, to become more like competitive private companies. Even in unionized industries like mining, state companies have
brought in professional management, cut payrolls, and raised profits,
transforming themselves into legitimate global competitors. As former
Communist-era monopolies, these firms inherited much of the large
market share they still control at home today, but the state no longer
defends their position by undermining private entrepreneurs. The Por-
tuguese tycoon Luís Amaral paid $30 million for a Polish food retailer
in 2003 and turned it into a multibillion-dollar operation, in part by
selling food wholesale to mom and pop stores, helping them compete
against hypermarkets. Amaral says that in more than a decade of building his business in Poland, "I never spoke to a Polish official once."

That wouldn't happen in Russia, where old state companies still
maintain bloated payrolls for political reasons, and regulations are
revised with an eye to rewarding politically connected oligarchs. This
kind of backroom deal with the state always has a tendency to discourage any business activity outside the "in" crowd. As a result, small and
independent business is a dying breed in Russia. On a recent flight to
Moscow, my colleagues sat next to a Russian entrepreneur who is start-

ing an organic winery but does not plan to sell in Russia, because he wants to remain independent and avoid attracting government attention. The number of companies listed on the Moscow stock exchange exploded from fewer than 50 in 2002 to 600 in 2008 but has since slowly dwindled to fewer than 500. This is hardly a natural or inevitable result of the global financial crisis, because in Poland, where the government has created more fertile ground for entrepreneurs, the number of listed companies has continued to mushroom, from 200 in 2002, to 450 in 2008, and to around 900 today.

The Brazilian state has been imposing dense regulations for so long, the country has developed an unusual entrepreneurial subculture devoted to exploiting loopholes in the law or helping others exploit them. For example, a revamp of regulations in 2002 led to an explosion in dentistry, such that Brazil now has more dental schools and more dentists per capita than the United States or Europe, and it is also one of the few if not only countries that have insurance companies that offer only dental insurance. Many other kinds of service companies are found only in Brazil, such as a big car rental company that rents only to corporate clients and makes its money selling one-year-old cars, and firms offering credit card payment services that owe their existence to regulations governing access to credit card terminals. These businesses are creative but are innovating in order to dodge or exploit government rules, so they provide services that would serve no purpose outside Brazil. This is the opposite of a society in which competitive global companies flourish under the rule of sensible laws.

Another way to judge how well the state is managing the private sector is to watch for good versus bad privatizations. Following the financial crises that rocked the emerging world in the 1990s, the sale of state companies to private owners became a popular solution to the inefficiencies that had helped trigger these crises. Back then, privatization generally meant the sale of a majority stake, so that new owners had the power to push for real change. That was what some observers call "true" or good privatization, but that approach has fallen out of fashion.

With the exception of a few smaller countries, like Romania, most governments in the emerging world are now willing to part only with minority stakes. Whether complete or partial, not all privatizations yield good results. India, for example, has adopted a de facto policy of what I can only describe as privatization by malign neglect: The political class can't bring itself to sell off old state companies, or to reform them either. Instead, it simply watches as private companies slowly drive the state behemoths into irrelevance. Thirty years ago state-owned Air India was basically the only way for Indians to fly, but the rise of agile private airlines, including Jet and Indigo, has reduced its share of flights to less than 25 percent. The same goes for telecommunications, where former state monopolies like MTNL and BSNL have been allowed to slowly wither in the face of more nimble private telecom companies, and together they now account for less than 30 million of India's 900 million telecom subscribers.

For the government to protect these state behemoths is hard, given the consumer demand for better services. Back in the 1980s, when India's telecom sector had no private operators, it would typically take a consumer more than a year to get a new phone connection, the phone line would be of poor quality, and it would often go dead until a local technician was bribed to come and fix it. Similarly, flying was a luxury, owing to the high cost of tickets on state-owned airlines, and three-to-four-hour delays on any route were common. Consumer anger finally forced the government to open these sectors to private competition.

The state would have done a lot better to simply sell off these companies when they were still valuable, but now it is losing money on them hand over fist, and they are worth a pittance. This approach—refusing either to privatize or to protect state monopolies—is the worst possible combination for the government's finances.

A Sensible Role for the State

Though it is easy to sketch in broad strokes, the connection between economic reform and faster growth is so devilishly complex in the details that when researchers go looking for data supporting the connection, they often don't find it. But that doesn't mean it doesn't exist; it just means that, given how many different factors influence growth, no single act of the state will stand out in fancy statistical correlations. Anyone who has experience on the ground in emerging nations will tell you, however, that when the state is investing wisely and moving toward creating predictable and stable rules, good things are more likely to happen.

When commentators talk about "structural reform" in emerging countries, they are generally talking about writing and enforcing sensible rules, following the basic lessons of Econ 101. These lessons say that an economy's output is the simple sum of basic inputs, including land, labor, and capital. So what "structural reform" often entails is the creation of an efficient legal regime governing the purchase of land to build factories, the lending of capital to finance the construction of those factories, and the hiring and firing of workers to staff them. In Indonesia, a recent increase in public investment was made possible by the passage of a law that speeds the acquisition of land for everything from police stations to power plants and youth sports camps by setting deadlines of days or weeks for every step in a process that used to drag on for years.

Though it is politically incorrect to say so, some cultures seem more eager than others to embrace sensible rules governing land, labor, and capital. In the early 1990s, for example, only a handful of nations had a law requiring the government to restrain itself by achieving a balanced budget, and now more than thirty emerging-world governments operate under these self-imposed constraints. But not all take these limits equally seriously. In 2015 the battle over how to resolve Greece's debt crisis was in part a culture war pitting those like Germany, who thought Athens should be punished for breaking the spending rules of the Eurozone, against those, including the Greeks themselves, who felt they should be forgiven. In Indonesia, the budget law is honored in spirit, and the economy slowed in 2014 and 2015 partly because the Widodo government took the painful step of cutting spending to keep its deficit under the legal cap.

The opposite of a rule-based system is one based on the deals cut between political bosses and their clients, which can be even more complex. In 2015 a new left-wing government in Greece trumpeted the arrest of a prominent businessman on tax evasion charges as a major blow to the system of *diaploki*, or collusive ties between the old ruling parties and prominent business families, particularly in the energy and construction industries. But the Greek journalist Yannis Palaiologos pointed out that *diaploki* did not serve "just a few fat cats" but extended to political clients throughout society, offering cushy protections to lawyers, pharmacists, truck drivers, state bank and utility employees, and even the youth wings of political parties. Clientelism in this wider sense remained "an important part of the sad story of Greece," because while the political party Syriza was busting a few tycoons, it was restoring protections for its preferred clients. The widespread sense that some citizens were getting special treatment continued to "erode the fabric of trust in Greek society" and undermine the economy.[8] The same could have been said for many "clientelist" societies from India to South Africa.

India may be the world's largest democracy, but it still has a relatively loose respect for the whole idea of following rules. Even an etiquette-obsessed sport like golf is played in a nonstop stream of boisterous chatter and under free-flowing rules that are often debated hole by hole, depending on how favorably the ball drops. In the 2000s, India drafted a fiscal responsibility law capping the budget, but it was shelved when it threatened to block the government's desire to ramp up spending in response to the crisis of 2008. This kind of uncertainty can produce perverse outcomes, especially in developing countries, where institutions are not yet well established and the rules are still evolving. In assessing the touch of the state, the question to ask is whether the government is interfering more or less.

My checklist for what to watch for starts with taking a read on government spending as a share of GDP, to spot the real outliers, and checking on whether the spending is going to productive investment or giveaways. I also watch whether the government is using state companies and banks as tools to artificially pump up growth and contain inflation, and whether it is choking or encouraging private businesses. In recent years many countries have been raising the government share of the economy to bloated proportions, steering bank loans to the unproductive and undeserving, promoting the interests of big state companies, subsidizing cheap gas for the rich and middle class, and enforcing insensible rules in an unpredictable way that make it difficult for private companies to thrive. Many states are now managing the economy in ways that do more to retard than to promote growth. As a result, surveys in several countries show that trust in the government to do the right thing is running at very low levels and probably fueling the rise of fringe parties and radical leaders. Less meddling and more focused government spending would make for better economic and political outcomes.

5

THE GEOGRAPHIC SWEET SPOT

Is the nation making the most of its location?

FOR CENTURIES, DUBAI HAD BEEN A DESERT TRADING CENTER with a buccaneering spirit, surrounded by white coral sands and peopled by pearl merchants and gold smugglers. Only in 2002 did the tiny emirate allow foreigners to buy land for the first time and give them substantial incentive to do so. The ruling family of Sheikh Mohammed bin Rashid Al Maktoum offered foreign buyers a free resident permit, low taxes, and cheap loans, and they came in droves. The population exploded from half a million to two million, as skyscrapers, marinas, and man-made islands shaped like palm trees materialized almost overnight, along with a cosmopolitan culture of soulless extravagance. The previously obscure emirate became famous for public architecture as spectacle—a hotel shaped like a sail, the world's biggest mall—but its private homes are just as prone to over-the-top display. I was told about a former clerk in the Indian embassy who made it big trading white goods and built himself a house with a blue spaceship on the roof. Another subcontinental émigré built a waterfall in his home emblazoned with the YSL logo, as a gift for a wife who likes Yves Saint Laurent.

When the global debt bubble burst in 2008, I thought the white sands were shifting out from under this desert boomtown. The crisis exposed Dubai for building its public and private showplaces on $120 billion in loans, in an economy with an annual GDP of $80 billion. In early 2009 Sheikh Mohammed publicly promised that his emirate could pay its debts, but it missed its next payment just two weeks later. The market crashed, and the economy slid into a deep downturn. Traveling often through Dubai, I was skeptical that it could recover anytime soon, but I underestimated its capacity to adapt.

One of seven emirates or royal principalities that make up the United Arab Emirates, Dubai has a history of prospering when its neighbors are in turmoil, indeed in part because its neighbors are often in turmoil. It thrived amid the two U.S. wars in Iraq, and following the terror attacks of 9/11, and again after the Arab Spring revolts of 2011. As the revolts spread in the Arab world, Dubai rebounded sharply from its debt problems. Investors from all over the world started pulling money out of Egypt, Libya, and Syria and pouring it into Dubai. While many Middle Eastern economies were stalling due to political unrest, Dubai was posting growth rates several percentage points faster than the emerging-world average. The port city attracted job seekers from around the world, and its population grew at an annual pace close to 10 percent. The hotels that had gone vacant in 2009 were full again by 2013. Travelers arriving by air nearly doubled in five years to 65 million, making Dubai International one of the world's five busiest airports.

Doubters like me had wondered whether the Maktoums could find customers for the world's largest mall and tenants for the world's tallest building, but it turned out they could. Importantly, the economy was also driven less and less by big construction projects; as a share of GDP, construction had fallen from more than 30 percent in 2008 to 20 percent. The transport, trade, and tourism industries housed in those new skyscrapers were fueling growth. That's not to say Sheikh Maktoum had lost his taste for the dramatic, announcing $130 billion in new mega-projects in 2012, including a new $100 billion city to be named after himself, with a forty-acre swimming pool that would be, of course, the world's largest. The announcements triggered worries that Dubai was again ringing up extravagant debts. For those skeptics, a local developer hung a thirty-story banner on one of his downtown buildings with the message, "Keep Calm, There is No Bubble."

By 2013, I was less concerned about the bubble threat than I was curious to know what made Dubai so resilient. The basic answer is that Dubai had built an open house in a closed neighborhood. Surrounded by oil states that produce fabulous wealth but are mired in civil strife and the internecine warfare among Muslim sects, Dubai alone keeps its doors wide upon to all comers. Many people in the region have a stake in ensuring nothing happens to undermine the safe haven status of Dubai, a place where Taliban rebel leaders, Somali pirates, and Kurdish guerrillas can gather to cut deals or trade guns so long as they keep their heads down and don't disturb the local peace, as author James Rickards describes the scene in *Currency Wars*. Rickards compares modern Dubai to the wartime Casablanca enshrined in the Hollywood movie: "neutral turf" where combatants in the surrounding wars can "meet, recruit and betray one another without immediate fear of arrest."[1]

Dubai is an extreme example of a geographic sweet spot, a place that makes the most of its geographic location. Geography matters for growth: Today Poland and Mexico have a big potential advantage in global competition thanks to their location on the border of the vast commercial markets of western Europe and the United States. Vietnam and Bangladesh are taking advantage of their position on existing trade routes between China and the West to take away some of the export manufacturing business that had been done mainly in China. (For a map of the current geographic sweet spots and global shipping routes, see p. 402.) But geography is not destiny; the potential advantage of proximity to the United States or China will ebb and flow with the strength of those economies, and many countries on or near major trade routes and rich markets will not take the steps necessary to prosper from their position. Morocco is taking advantage of its location, a short hop across the Mediterranean from southern Europe, to develop export industries, but nearby on the same coast Libya and Sudan are crumbling politically and economically.

Nations that qualify as geographic sweet spots combine the pure luck of an advantageous location with the good sense to make the most of it by opening their doors to the world, particularly to their neighbors, and also making sure that even their own most remote provinces are entering the global mainstream. Mexico, for example, is developing vibrant second cities not only along the U.S. border but throughout the country.

Dubai could have fallen victim to the political and economic dysfunctions that plague the Middle East, but instead it has managed to turn itself into the commercial hub of a region that sits on 60 percent of the world's known oil reserves. On a map of global shipping routes showing critical chokepoints—from the Malacca Strait to the Panama Canal and the Strait of Hormuz—Dubai is perched like a cashier overseeing the flow of oil out of troubled oil states such as Iraq and Iran. Dubai has in fact prospered more than its oil-rich neighbors by turning itself into their regional headquarters for shipping as well as travel, information technology, and financial services.

In Dubai the state is unobtrusive, but everything is monitored, often by surveillance camera. If you speed on Sheikh Zayed Road, the main drag, you'll rarely see a police officer, but you will get a ticket in the mail. And should a joyride end in a crash, the cops turn up instantly, sometimes in the Lamborghinis that belong to the police fleet. This high-tech and well-financed state presence may help explain why Dubai has so far not been the target of a successful terror plot, although it has disrupted several in recent years. Minorities feel safe because tolerance is also enforced with vigor: Dubai is home to more than one hundred nationalities, from Pakistani laborers to British soccer celebrities, as well as to Christian churches, a Hindu temple, a new Sikh *gurdwara*, and to Shiite mosques, which are unheard of in other Sunni-dominated Gulf countries.

Though other Gulf states, including Saudi Arabia, Bahrain, and Qatar, also compete for a share of trade and investment in the Middle East, these conservative societies have not yet opened fully to foreign money and foreign ways, perhaps in part because they are rich in oil and gas while Dubai is not. Dubai's only choice was to become Casablanca. Whatever the reason, the differences are glaring. Saudi Arabia is erecting the world's tallest building, trying to steal that title from Dubai's neofuturistic Burj Khalifa. But will outsiders flock to a country so insular it still has a hard time accepting foreign tourists, particularly unveiled women? In 2013 Saudi Arabia attracted few visitors, mainly the five million Muslims who make the annual pilgrimage to Mecca, compared to the 65 million people who visited tiny Dubai. By creating a peaceful and liberal oasis, Dubai is attracting flows of money from all over the world, including its conservative neighbors. Incoming flights from the Saudi capital of Riyadh are full of Saudi women who shed their veils midflight, ready to enjoy the world's largest malls, beachfronts, and all that Dubai has to offer.

Even before it began to emerge as a global crossroads in the 2000s, Dubai avoided the internal battles within the Middle East, including the violent Shiite-Sunni divide. After Iran's 1979 revolution turned the country into a Shiite theocracy, the Sunni monarchies of the Gulf region, including Saudi Arabia and most of the United Arab Emirates, shunned the religious government in Tehran commercially and politically. Only the Emirate of Dubai kept its doors open. After Iran was accused of developing nuclear weapons in the mid-2000s and much of the world joined in slapping economic sanctions on Tehran, Dubai became the largest hole in the sanctions regime. When all the big global banks pulled out of Tehran, Dubai kept commerce flowing through the *hawala* system, an informal network for money transfers. Over the decades Dubai has become home to the largest Iranian expat community outside the United States, with 450,000 residents and branches of ten thousand Iranian businesses, all linked to Iran by two hundred flights a week.

Dubai's secret is openness to everyone, but the luck of a location near Iran could be a huge boost in coming years. Asked what explains Dubai's economic resilience, Rahul Sharma, a former editor of the locally published *Khaleej Times*, suggested an answer could be found in a walk along Dubai Creek, which has been expanded into a man-made river. Along its wharves, crews load sleek dhows with tires, refrigerators, washing machines, and all manner of cargo, much of it bound for Iran. Karim Sadjadpour, an associate at the Carnegie Endowment for International Peace, says Dubai's success is in part a result of Iran's failures and isolation, as most of the emirate's trade with Iran consists of re-exporting goods from countries that won't do business with Tehran. As the Iranian government moved in 2015 toward cutting a deal to lift the sanctions, there was talk that Dubai might build on its old ties and proximity to the Persian kingdom to emerge as a "Hong Kong of Iran." The reference is to the 1980s, when Beijing was emerging from isolation, and freewheeling Hong Kong was prospering as China's key link to the outside world. Hong Kong is another good example of how the luck of location can combine with good policy to produce economic booms.

These cases illustrate a basic question for any economy: Is it making the most of its geographic location? To spot likely winners, I track which countries are doing the most to exploit their location by opening doors to trade and investment with the world and with their neighbors, and to balance growth in the major cities with the provincial regions. Dubai is a city-state of just 2.2 million people and has no provinces of its own, but its aggressive cultivation of ties to its neighbors and lately to the world shows that even a desert location short on local talent can be transformed into a geographic sweet spot.

Ties to the World

The pressure on countries to make the most of their locations and attract a larger share of global trade is only likely to increase in the coming years. Though we live in a more interconnected world than we did a decade ago, the general perception that we live in an *increasingly* interconnected global economy no longer holds, in some crucial respects. Trade is one of them. The growth rate of global trade flows has slowed quite abruptly. From 1990 to 2008 the global economy grew rapidly, but trade grew 2 to 2.5 times faster. Then came the global financial crisis, nations turned inward, and since then global trade has been growing more slowly than the global economy. As a result, between 1990 and 2008, global trade expanded from less than 40 percent of GDP to almost 60 percent, but since then it has retreated a bit.

For a number of reasons, this stagnation in global trade may not be just a temporary disruption. One is a major shift in China, which imported vast quantities of commodities, industrial parts, and equipment as it became the assembly plant for the world. Lately, China has been importing less, as its economy slows sharply and as it makes more of the parts it needs at home, which has a depressing effect on global trade.

Another reason is a turn for the worse in geopolitics. For much of the postwar era, the nations of the world conducted increasingly successful negotiations to cut import tariffs. In the United States, for example, at the height of the protectionist wars that helped prolong the Depression of the 1930s, the average tariff on imported goods hit 60 percent, but it fell steadily to 5 percent in 1980, where it remains today. The steady success of these tariff-cutting negotiations helped set the stage for the ensuing boom in global trade. By the early 1980s, as free market ideas spread to the emerging world, developing countries began to cut their import tariffs, which fell on average from a high of nearly 40 percent then to less than 10 percent by 2010.

At this point, international negotiators had moved on to target more complex and sometimes "invisible" trade barriers, like safety regulations that block imports and state subsidies that give local exporters an unfair advantage. These issues proved too tough for diplomats to resolve. The last round of global trade talks was launched in 2001 at a summit in Doha, Qatar, and was supposed to finish in 2005 but went off the rails in 2008 amid the tensions of the global financial crisis. The dispute was multifaceted, but the core of it involved clashes between the United States and India over Indian demands for the right to protect farmers with a special tariff in the event of another crisis, and between the United States and Europe, which accused each other of unfairly subsidizing farmers. Ten years beyond its 2005 deadline, the Doha round is technically alive but dead in the water.

The old consensus born in good times—that more free trade is better for all countries—has been deeply shaken in the post-crisis slow-growth world. In November 2008, amid fears that the global financial crisis would trigger a revival of 1930s-style trade wars, the leaders of the G-20 nations publicly renounced trade controls. Then they began quietly rolling out what the trade expert Simon Evenett calls "stealth protection measures," such as subsidies for export industries; since 2008, Evenett has counted more than fifteen hundred such measures instituted by G-20 countries.

During hard times, nations often turn inward and bar foreign businesses from competing in their home market. This is one of those times. As talks on broad global trade deals came to a standstill, the United States and China started to build rival alliances on the regional level. China was working to bring together sixteen Pacific nations that count for half the world's population in its Regional Comprehensive Economic Partnership, while the U.S. response involved seeking partnerships on both major oceans. In late 2015 the United States crossed the line first, sealing a deal with the eleven other prospective members of the Trans-Pacific Partnership, which the U.S. administration openly promoted as a way to prevent China from "making the rules" in global commerce. China was expected to respond by pushing harder to finish its own regional deal in the Pacific, while the U.S. administration still had to persuade congressional opponents and key U.S. allies to get on board. In Asia, major players like South Korea stayed out of the American partnership. In Europe, a loose grouping of right-wing populists and trade unions lobbied against the Washington-sponsored Transatlantic Trade and Investment Partnership, on the grounds that rules brokered by the United States would favor its own interests.

To get a handle on which countries are likely to thrive in export competition, the first thing I check is how open they are to global trade. Among the largest emerging nations, trade including both exports and imports amounts to 70 percent of GDP on average, and countries that are above average are led by major export manufacturers. At the top are countries with trade accounting for more than 100 percent of GDP— which is possible since most of their consumption is imports and most of their national income comes from exports: the Czech Republic, Vietnam, Malaysia, and Thailand.

Though economies that rely heavily on exports face a hard time growing when global trade is slowing, as it has been recently, the benefits of high export income are such that in the long run, when the trade picture stabilizes, open trade powers will be more competitive than closed economies. In a 2015 response to the antitrade lobby in Europe, the Swedish industrialists Antonia Ax:son Johnson and Stefan Persson pointed out that before their country opened to foreign trade under the liberalizing hand of finance minister Johan Gripenstedt in the 1860s, Sweden was poor and not only by European standards.[2] It was poorer than the Congo. After that phase of opening and reform, Sweden entered what it now remembers as the "100 Years of Growth."

The most closed economies, with trade at less than 50 percent of GDP, fall into two groups. One is a cluster of very populous countries like China, India, and Indonesia that rely less on trade simply because their domestic markets are so large. The other group includes oil- and commodity-driven economies like Nigeria, Argentina, Iran, and Peru, which have a history of protecting themselves from foreign competition and relying on high commodity price swings to generate growth. The more closed they remain, the smaller their share of newly limited global trade flows. On a list of thirty of the largest emerging countries, the most closed by a significant margin is the heavily populated commodity economy of Brazil.

In Brazil, trade has been stuck for decades at around 20 percent of GDP, the lowest level of any country outside deliberately isolated outliers like North Korea. Though Brazil is a leading exporter of soybeans, corn, sugar, coffee, beef, poultry, and other agricultural commodities and has been hyped as a breadbasket to the world, it has been resisting opening to the world for a long time. Its 20 percent trade share of GDP is smaller than more populous countries like China and India, and smaller even than populous commodity economies like Russia and Indonesia, all of which have a trade share of GDP that is close to or above 40 percent.

Unlike Brazil, some of these big emerging nations have also been pushing to open wider to trade. In 2000 Brazil had three free trade agreements; now it has five, all with small economies like Egypt, Israel, and the Palestinian Authority. Over the same period, the number of agreements cut by India went from zero to eighteen and by China from zero to nineteen, including agreements with major economies all over the world.

Taking full advantage of geography to carve out a commercial sweet spot is important for a nation's long-term growth prospects. Export sales earn the foreign income that allows a nation to import whatever its population wants to consume, to invest in new factories and roads, and to do so without falling into the pathology of rising foreign debts and recurring currency crises. It is no accident that during their long runs of strong economic growth, the postwar Asian "miracles" in Japan, South Korea, Taiwan, and Singapore also sustained average annual manu-facturing export growth of more than 10 percent. A nation's chances of economic success are greatly improved by prowess in manufactur-ing goods for export, which highlights the importance of location. Any nation that wants to thrive as an export power has a huge advantage if it starts with a base close to trade routes that connect the richest custom-ers to the most competitive suppliers.

It Is Partly the Luck of Location

Economic growth has followed existing trade routes since well before the modern era. In the sixteenth century the nations of western Europe suddenly started to grow faster than their rivals in Asia and Latin Amer-ica; for the first time in history, the inhabitants of one region clearly distanced themselves from all others in terms of average income. In a 2005 article titled "The Rise of Europe," the development experts Daron Acemoglu, Simon Johnson and James Robinson set out to explain this continental boom and found that the answer was a combination of geography and a readiness to exploit it.[3] Between 1500 and 1850, they argued, the boom in Europe was driven mainly by nations with two key advantages: port cities on major Atlantic trade routes, and monarchies that respected private property rights and granted merchants the most latitude to exploit growing trade channels. Thus the economies that led the sixteenth-century boom in Europe were Britain and the Netherlands, driven by early respect for property rights and the thriving Atlantic ports of London and Amsterdam.

In recent years it became fashionable to argue that location no longer matters, because the Internet makes it possible to provide services from anywhere. But physical goods still make up the bulk of global trade flows, and location still matters for companies that want to be close to their customers and suppliers. Worldwide, flows of goods amount to about $18 trillion a year, significantly greater than flows of both services and capital, which account for about $4 trillion each. So for the foreseeable future at least, the exports that matter most to economic growth are exports of manufactured goods like those loading onto the dhows of Dubai. In 2015 the Hong Kong–based economist Jonathan Anderson put together a "heat map" of the world's hottest economies by plotting the location of countries that have seen manufactured exports grow significantly as a share of GDP since 1995. He found fourteen countries, confined mainly to two regions: Southeast Asia led by Vietnam and Cambodia, and eastern Europe led by Poland, the Czech Republic, and Hungary.

Why these few nations, in these regions? The common link was location. These manufacturing export success stories unfolded next to the big consumer markets of Europe and the United States, or "on the same shipping lanes that Japan and the original Asian tigers" used to transport goods to markets such as the United States. Vietnam is replacing

China as a base for making sneakers for export to the West. Poland is prospering as a platform for German companies to make cars for export to western Europe. To a smaller extent, Mexico and Central America have also seen an increase in manufactured exports as a share of their economy, owing in part to their geographic proximity to the United States. Mexico is a good example of why proximity matters, because while its wages have been falling of late relative to China's, its biggest gains date back further and have come from lower transport costs to the United States, particularly for heavy items that are expensive to ship, like cars.

Geography also helps to explain the recent comeback story of Vietnam. In the late 2000s, Vietnam was widely hyped as the next China, on the strength of its large population of cheap labor and its reform-minded Communist government. I was skeptical of this story. Vietnam's ruling Communist Party was nowhere near as competent as China's, its population was one-tenth as large, and its institutions were not prepared to make good use of the billions of foreign dollars that flowed into the country before the global financial crisis. Vietnam indulged in a classic credit binge, on a scale that would normally signal a sharp slowdown in the economic growth rate. But Vietnam managed to minimize the downturn; its economy did slow from nearly 8 percent before the crisis to 5 percent, but this was still one of the fastest growth rates in the post-crisis world.

The strongest explanation for Vietnam's resilience was that the government was getting a number of things right to exploit its position on key east-west trade routes. While the Communist Party was still dodging key reforms such as the privatization of bloated state companies, it was aggressively courting outside trade and investment. After striking a major trade deal with the United States in 2000, Vietnam joined the World Trade Organization in 2007 and benefited greatly as export manufacturers started looking for alternatives to China's rising wages. At a time when global trade was growing slower than the world economy for the first time in a generation, Vietnam was one of the few emerging countries that was increasing its share of global exports, which had quintupled to 1 percent since 2000. That 1 percent may not sound like much, but it is five times Vietnam's share of global GDP, showing that in trade competition Vietnam is punching way above its weight. In 2015, Vietnam has surpassed its much richer and more developed neighbors like Thailand and Malaysia as Southeast Asia's leading exporter to the United States.

In surveys, Japanese firms cited Vietnam ahead of Thailand and Indonesia as their preferred site for new Asian plants, drawn in by a cheap currency, reasonably inexpensive labor, and a rapidly improving transportation network. Once known for designing road and port projects aimed at pleasing local Communist Party officials rather than serving global trade routes, Vietnam has been correcting those mistakes. Work is in full swing on new metro lines in Ho Chi Minh City as well as on new roads and bridges all over the country, including the rural north. Samsung plans to build a $3 billion smartphone plant in northern Thai Nguyen province, alongside the $2 billion plant it opened in 2014. Smartphones have become the nation's leading export product, an impressive step forward for a country with an average per capita income below $2,000. Vietnam is building an old-school manufacturing powerhouse, reminiscent of Japan in the 1960s, and is turning itself into a new geographic sweet spot. In 2015 Vietnam is positioned to gain more than any other member of the U.S.-sponsored Trans-Pacific Partnership, with one estimate projecting that the trade deal could boost Vietnam's GDP by more than 10 percent over the next decade.[4]

Ties to the Neighbors

As progress on global trade deals evaporates amid renewed superpower rivalries, some smaller nations are shifting focus to building regional trading communities and common markets. This trend flows from an obvious fact—it is natural for any nation to trade most heavily with its neighbors. Postwar economic success stories have tended to appear in regional clusters, from East Asia to the Persian Gulf and southern Europe. Lately new clusters have begun to appear on the west coast of Latin America, the east coast of Africa, and possibly in South Asia as well. As Ax:son Johnson and Persson pointed out in defense of the Transatlantic Trade and Investment Partnership, these regional trade alliances, once formed, can develop a positive momentum of their own. The European Union began with six members; it now counts twenty-eight. The Association of Southeast Asian Nations began with five members; it now has ten.

The most compelling model is East Asia, because its rapid rise was driven in significant part by trade among its member states. The growth of trade within the region helps explain why many of its economies posted long runs of growth faster than 6 percent. China, Japan, Taiwan, and South Korea were all willing to leave behind wartime grudges and cut business deals, and now they are thrashing out big trade deals too. In 2015 China signed a landmark free trade agreement with South Korea that was expected to inspire copycat deals across East Asia.

The impact of regional trade deals could be even larger in the least well-connected neighborhoods. Around 70 percent of exports from European countries go to neighbors on the same continent, and in East Asia and North America, the figure is 50 percent. At the opposite end of the spectrum, in Latin America, the figure is 20 percent, in Africa it is 12 percent, and in South Asia just 5 percent. So the Latin, African, and South Asian nations have the most room for new trade ties to drive growth.

Strong leadership has historically played a key role in helping some regions take off. Asia's postwar boom began in Japan, spread to a second tier of economies led by South Korea and Taiwan, then to a third tier led by Thailand and Indonesia, and a fourth led by China. A Japanese economist called this the "flying geese" model of development. As Japan rose up the development ladder to make ever more sophisticated products, the second tier learned from its example and slipped into the industries Japan had vacated, followed themselves by the third tier, and so on.

The boom in intraregional trade that helped lift the nations of Northeast Asia out of poverty has since spread to the Southeast, where trade among Indonesia, Malaysia, Thailand, and the Philippines has grown significantly. Meanwhile trade between the Southeast Asian economies and China has exploded, rising by an average of 20 percent a year for the last twenty years. A leading Asian Development Bank official once told me that in the late 1980s Thai prime minister Chatichai Choonhavan began turning the former battleground states of Indochina into a marketplace by reaching out to Vietnam, Laos, and Cambodia, and persuading them to drop their Communist guard, to start cutting trade deals, and to build roads and other transport ties. Those regional connections quickly evolved into a network "as dense as the wiring on a computer chip," the official said.

Southeast Asia saw one of the strongest regional trade booms ever recorded, and yet it was still not quite powerful enough to leap the fence to South Asia, which includes India, Pakistan, Bangladesh, and Sri Lanka. Isolation, lawlessness, and the lingering bitterness produced by regional wars have made it difficult to lower the hostility at border crossings in South Asia, and trade within this region has stagnated at just 5 percent of its total trade with the world. In very few regions are neighboring states as distant from one another as they are in South Asia, and so far no leader has stepped forward to start opening these doors in a steady, disciplined way.

When I met Sri Lankan president Mahinda Rajapaksa in August 2013 in Temple Trees, the graceful official residence in downtown Colombo, his country was being courted aggressively as a trade and investment partner by China and India, both of which were attracted by its strategic location on key east-west trade routes. China in particular was pouring in money, including $15 billion for a "new city" on reclaimed land not far from Temple Trees. The president seemed unconcerned that despite the inflow of capital, Sri Lanka was running up foreign debts and a sizable current account deficit. When I asked how he planned to finance this deficit at a time when global banks were increasingly reluctant to lend to emerging nations, Rajapaksa responded with a wink and a thumbs-up, "We have China!"

He appeared to be betting too heavily on limitless benefits that can flow to a globally attractive location, while also downplaying the importance of his neighbors in India. When he found out where I was from, he explained, "India is like a relative, but China is like a friend. And relatives are more stingy than friends." Two years later, after a sharp economic slowdown, he was out of office and under investigation for sweetheart deals with Chinese contractors. Sri Lanka's new government, under President Maithripala Sirisena, has been looking to aggressively expand trade and investment links with India and to have the island nation serve as a bridge between India and Pakistan, but regional trade has still been slow to increase.

Africa's budding trade unions have been looking to the formation of the European Community in the 1950s for ideas to attract investment flows to their member nations, many of which are small and difficult to reach: Fifteen African nations are landlocked. Building cell towers in nations of the African interior like the Democratic Republic of Congo can be twice as expensive as it is in coastal states like Kenya, owing to the poor state of the roads and the power grids. Even Kenya, long seen as the jewel of East Africa, has its problems. It takes on average nineteen days to ship goods in from Singapore, 4,500 miles away, but twenty days to truck the same goods 300 miles down the road from the port at Mombasa to the capital in Nairobi. And Kenya has a $60 billion economy; in the many African nations where GDP is under $10 billion, outsiders often see even less reason to bother trying to surmount these obstacles.

The most promising effort to jump-start trade has been made by the East African Community (EAC), founded in 2000 by Kenya, Tanzania, and Uganda, and later expanded to include Rwanda and Burundi. This community aims to gain leverage in global trade negotiations through numbers and to begin laying the regional network of infrastructure— roads, rails, ports—required to accelerate commerce. At a time when the hype for "Africa Rising" is giving way to recognition that Africa is fragmenting into hot and cold economies, the EAC has become a pocket of resilience. Between 2010 and 2014 the number of African countries growing at a pace faster than 6 percent fell from twenty-five to twelve, and the number growing at 6 percent with relatively low inflation was just six. Of these six, three were the founding members of the EAC, where exports had risen 30 percent over the previous five years, while export growth for the rest of Africa was flat. The strongest exporter in the EAC was Rwanda, which is landlocked and recently scarred by tribal violence. It has prospered both as a result of smoother regional customs clearing systems and its own efforts to build better roads and learn from other economies that rose from politically tense and isolated locations, like Singapore.

In contrast to the EAC, many new trade groups on the continent are struggling to make progress. To cite one prominent case, the countries of West Africa have been trying since 1975 to found a union known by its acronym ECOWAS, built around the anchor state of Nigeria. But wars and chaos have limited its accomplishments to what has been called "organizational matters such as the drafting of protocols and the conduct of studies."[5] A regional passport that was supposed to ease travel has done nothing to prevent the harassment and delays that travelers face at border checkpoints.

It turns out that the splintering of a continent into faltering and successful regional trade regimes is not that unusual. A similar divide is widening in South America. On the Atlantic coast there is an old alliance led by Brazil, which has traditionally been hostile to free trade, while on the Pacific coast there is a new alliance led by Chile that has been embracing free trade. The core of the old alliance is Mercosur, a trade group founded in 1991 that links Brazil, Argentina, Venezuela, and smaller allies like Bolivia and Paraguay in what has been described as "an anti-gringo talking shop."[6] Their long-standing hostility to free trade helps explain why, among the world's fifty busiest ports, only one is located on the ten-thousand-mile coastline of South America, at Santos in Brazil.

Mercosur's leaders have pursued growth strategies based on heavy populist spending and state intervention, and they have not welcomed free trade. Within Mercosur, trade has declined as a contributor to growth in its member economies over the twenty-five years since its inception, and commentators have written off small, landlocked members like Bolivia and Paraguay as too isolated from global trade routes to prosper.

As Mercosur was failing to gain traction, Mexico was looking in the opposite direction, politically and geographically. In the early 1990s it joined the North American Free Trade Agreement, and since then exports to the United States have increased from 6 percent of Mexican GDP to 24 percent. Despite that success, Mexico could not interest the Mercosur partners in wider trade deals, so in the 2010s it turned its attention to joining the new Pacific Alliance with the Andean states of Chile, Colombia, and Peru.

In an *Atlantic* magazine piece called "The Most Important Alliance You've Never Heard Of," the former Venezuelan minister of trade and industry Moisés Naím wrote that within twenty months of its founding in 2013, the Pacific Alliance achieved more than Mercosur had in two decades.[7] Its members pushed integration not only through trade but also by creating a regional stock exchange and privatized pensions systems, establishing a common market for the movement of people as well as money, and developing ambitious plans to improve road and rail links. The alliance quickly eliminated 92 percent of the tariffs among its four member states, scrapping visa requirements for business and tourists traveling within the region, and focusing their pronouncements on practical progress rather than bashing the United States.

Chile played the lead role in the Pacific Alliance, in a way reminiscent of the role Japan played as a leader of the "flying geese." Essential elements of the economic reforms introduced in Chile during the 1970s would spread in the 1990s to Peru under President Alberto Fujimori, and in the next decade to Colombia under President Álvaro Uribe. Now the Pacific Alliance tightens those long-standing ties. The richest of the three Andean members, Chile, has also become a major investor in the other two, pouring $2.3 billion into Peru and Colombia in 2011, up from $70 million in 2004. That's not to say the prospects for all three nations are equal, but a shared commitment to making the most of a location well off the major global trade routes is positive for all involved.

Geography Is Not Destiny

With sufficient political will and the right policies, nations can redraw the map of global trade routes to their own advantage. In the early twentieth century, the major global trade routes crisscrossed the Atlantic, but after World War II Japan and China managed to carve out a new route anchored at one end on their own coasts. Within a generation the Asian powers used cheap labor to more than make up for the cost of shipping goods all the way from the Pacific to Europe and the United States. Asia is thus reclaiming its status as the world's "economic center of gravity," according to McKinsey & Company.

By pinpointing the location that is most central to global economic activity, McKinsey produced a map showing how this "center" has shifted over time. It started out in central China a thousand years ago, shifted gradually to North America by 1960, and has since been moving back toward Asia. The most striking point is that the center of gravity moved farther between 2000 and 2010 than it had in the previous fifty years, moving rapidly over the North Pole and back down toward China, a vivid demonstration that global trade patterns can and do change.

As Peter Zeihan points out in his 2014 book *The Accidental Superpower*, the United States has more "prime port property" than the entire Asian coast from Lahore to Vladivostok.[8] And yet China has managed to prosper on the northern end of that inhospitable coast. Under strong leaders starting with Deng Xiaoping in the early 1980s, it carved out its own geographic destiny. China dredged rivers and harbors to create six of the world's ten busiest ports, all of them man-made. The same is true of Dubai: The port at Jebel Ali is entirely man-made and is now the world's seventh busiest, deep enough to host U.S. aircraft carriers and large enough to handle new supersize container ships that are causing traffic jams at American ports, which are too shallow to unload such large vessels at the docks.

More recently, with wages rising sharply in China, less sophisticated industries including textiles, toys, and shoes are on the move, seeking cheaper supplies of labor. They are not necessarily going to the countries with the cheapest labor, which in any event counts for only 5 percent of export production costs in emerging nations, on average.[9] Instead of choosing nations with the lowest wages, such as Bolivia or Egypt or Nigeria, manufacturers are choosing countries such as Vietnam, Cambodia, and Bangladesh for a combination of reasons. They have lower wages than China, are located on existing Pacific trade routes, and have a policy of opening doors to outsiders. The current east-west shipping routes run right through the Indian Ocean, closer to southern India than to Bangladesh, but Bangladesh is attracting much more textile production than India because it offers fewer bureaucratic hurdles.

After leaving the Indian Ocean, the major shipping routes run into the Red Sea, then through the Suez Canal and into the Mediterranean. There they pass along the coasts of many North African states that are in chaos or struggling (Libya, Sudan, Algeria) and precious few that are emerging as trading powers. One success is Morocco, which is among the first African countries to draw serious interest from major Western companies looking to build export-manufacturing plants. A relatively placid kingdom, Morocco's appeal lies in its new free trade zones, a stable currency, cheap labor, and competent leadership. European companies are building not just simple toy and textile factories there but advanced industries such as aeronautics and automobiles. Renault recently opened a car factory in Morocco, which is expected to attract more factories given its proximity to the rich markets of Europe.

In the period before 2008, when global trade was still growing faster than the world economy, the map of shipping routes was morphing into a spaghetti bowl of ever thicker strands, not only between China and the

West. Many connections among poor countries were emerging for the first time. The rise of commerce among developing nations—including those in the southern hemisphere that have never been close to the economic center of gravity—has come to be known as "South-South trade." The share of South-South trade in total world exports has doubled to more than 25 percent over the last twenty years, and the share of developing world exports that goes to other developing nations has risen from just over 40 percent to near 60 percent.

Opportunities to carve out new global trade routes, particularly those connecting the South to the South, are therefore numerous. Many major highway arteries that have been talked about since the nineteenth century still exist mainly as grand ideas. British colonizers first imagined a Trans-African Highway, but plans for this Cairo-to-Cape Town route were never fully executed. Many of the stretches that were built are decaying into impassable potholes or are teeming with bandits and other road hazards; it is mainly extreme tourists in road-warrior vehicles, not traders, who do the full Cairo–to–Cape Town run. The death rate on highways in Africa is eight to fifty times higher than in developed countries, and the World Bank estimates that bad roads lower productivity in Africa by 40 percent. The highways connecting Central and South America are a similar semipermeable tangle of more or less finished roads, broken in the middle by the dreaded Darien Gap, sixty miles of dense rain forest that has long thwarted travelers seeking to cross the Panama-Colombia border.

China is at the forefront of a campaign to reshape the geographic destinies of remote nations, spending billions on new trade routes through some of the world's less-tracked regions. For example, Beijing is supporting a $60 billion plan to build the first major east-west highway connecting the Atlantic and Pacific coasts of South America, running twelve hundred miles and crossing the Andes to link Brazil to Peru. This one megaproject would not be enough to make either Brazil or Peru a rich nation, but it will help connect their more remote regions to the world. For China's part, these projects open up access to supplies of oil and other natural resources and serve to demonstrate its growing global influence.

In 2013 Chinese president Xi Jinping issued the first in a series of announcements unveiling his plans for a New Silk Road. This was a deliberate evocation of the Old Silk Road, which tied China to the West at the height of its economic power under the Mongol emperor Genghis Khan and his successors in the thirteenth and fourteenth centuries. The original "road" was actually a vast and ever-changing network of land and sea routes, cutting through western China and central Asia. The new route aims to connect central China to its border provinces, and the border provinces to seaports in China and beyond, including ports that China is helping to build from Gwadar and Karachi in Pakistan to Chittagong in Bangladesh, Kyaukpyu in Myanmar, and Colombo and Hambantota in Sri Lanka. China plans to raise some $300 billion in funding, a massive sum that nonetheless falls short of the demand for new transport links in these regions, which the Asian Development Bank and others put in the trillions of dollars.

China seems to understand well the basic rule that a nation makes the most of its location by opening itself to the world and to its neighbors, and by making sure its own provinces participate in the opening. As nations continue to grow, development will normally spread along the coast and, eventually, to inland cities as well. As Japan emerged as a new trading power in the postwar era, for example, the port in Tokyo grew into a superport region circling Tokyo Bay; it now encompasses dock facilities in the neighboring cities of Yokohama and Kawasaki as well. Encouraging the regional spread of growth has always been part of China's plan. At a World Bank forum in the 1980s, the Indian planning commission official Manmohan Singh, who later became prime minister, asked a Communist Party official whether China's move to create coastal zones with special subsidies for industrialists would run the risk of increasing the wealth gap between city and countryside. "I certainly hope so," the official responded. The idea was that the coast would take off first, and the rest of the country would benefit later.

Perhaps the most overlooked part of China's New Silk Road plan is the one that was unveiled in early 2015, focusing on "domestic silk roads." Fanning out from the center of the country, these new road and rail corridors would turn western Xinjiang province into a travel hub for Central and South Asia; southwestern Guangxi and Yunnan into hubs for Southeast Asia and the Mekong region; and Inner Mongolia and Heilongjiang into hubs for traveling north to Russia. Ultimately many of these roads would link up to the New Silk Road ports from Pakistan to Myanmar, completing the link among China's provinces, its neighbors, and partners as far away as the Baltics and Brazil. When complete, the network could bring long-forgotten outposts of the Silk Road, like the western city of Urumqi, back onto global routes for the first time since the Mongol era.

Though not nearly as grand in scale, a similar internal transformation is unfolding in Colombia, which is also working to reconnect its entire nation to the world. The most populous Andean nation, with nearly 50 million people, Colombia has a much larger domestic market than Peru (30 million) or Chile (10 million), and in 2015 it is close to winding down a decades-long insurgency by finalizing a peace deal with the last of the rebel armies. The potential end of hostilities raises the possibility of reopening long-isolated parts of the country and drawing more investors and visitors. Since it is closer to the major North American markets than its southern counterparts, Chile and Peru, Colombia's geographic potential is unsurpassed in the region. In 2012 President Manuel Santos signed a major new free trade agreement with the United States, which his Atlantic rivals like Venezuela dismissed as more consorting with the gringos.

No nation is too remote to reconnect to global trade routes, not even Colombia, which former president Alfonso López Michelsen once described as the Tibet of South America—lovely but inaccessible. Its three largest cities, Bogotá, Cali, and Medellín, are inland Shangri-Las cut off from the coast by three mountain ranges and isolated by the long guerrilla war. Building roads in the steep Colombian mountains can cost $30 million per kilometer, roughly twenty five times more than in rural areas of the United States, which is why 90 percent of the country's roads are unpaved. President Santos has in recent years set up a new agency to cut through the remaining obstacles to road building—now more likely to be posed by bureaucrats than by insurgents. Colombia also has a $55 billion plan to build new roads and ports and to take advantage of being the only South American nation with coasts facing both the Atlantic and the Pacific. The spending plan aims to double the speed of truck traffic, which now crawls at an average 30 to 40 kilometers per hour. The new highways could add a full percentage point to Colombia's GDP annual growth rate, in part by reconnecting the big three inland cities to the coasts and to the world.

Second Cities

To make the most of any geographical advantage, leaders also have to bring their own most backward provinces into the global commercial flow, a point that became apparent to me on recent visits to Thailand, the country that lies in the geographic heart of Southeast Asia. Over the past decade the Thai economy has been undermined by conflict between political parties representing the Bangkok elite on one side and the impoverished provinces on the other. When I visited Bangkok in 2010, the urban-rural conflict was erupting in street violence, and local experts told me that the disaffection of the northern countryside could be traced to the top-heavy structure of a society centered in the capital. They said one number summed up the entire conflict: The ten-million-plus population of central Bangkok is more than ten times larger than the population of the country's second-largest city, Chiang Mai.

A ratio that lopsided is abnormal in any country with a sizable population. In smaller countries, it's common for the citizenry to be concentrated in the capital, but in midsize countries with a population of 20 million to 100 million, as well as in large countries of more than 100 million or meganations of more than 1 billion, it is unusual. A look at twenty of the major midsize emerging nations shows that in most, the population of the largest city outnumbers that of the second city by roughly three to one. That rough benchmark holds today for fifteen major emerging countries in this midsize population class, ranging from Poland, Turkey, Colombia, and Saudi Arabia to Kenya, Morocco, Vietnam, and Iran. The three-to-one ratio held in the past and still holds today for the urban centers of the "Asian miracle" economies, including Tokyo and Osaka in Japan, Seoul and Busan in South Korea, and Taipei and Kaohsiung in Taiwan. My sense is that any midsize emerging nation where this ratio is significantly more than three to one faces a risk of Thai-style political instability driven by regional conflict, and this imbalance is a drag on growth. When one overlooked part of the population is stuck in backward towns and villages, they are more likely to rebel against the privileges of the capital elite.

Today only five major midsize emerging economies stand in clear violation of the three-to-one rule: Thailand, Malaysia, Chile, Argentina, and Peru. Though Bangkok accounts for about 15 percent of Thailand's 68 million people, it accounts for 40 percent of GDP. The capital city is where the king holds court alongside a revolving cast of civilian and military rulers, and where most of the clashes between the rural and urban political parties have taken place in recent years. Peru's population is even more imbalanced: The eight million residents of Lima outnumber residents of Arequipa, the second city, by a factor of twelve. That fact helps explain why Peru is still struggling to stamp out the last embers of the Shining Path, a rural insurgency that started to burn out in the early 1990s. Chile is also deeply lopsided: Santiago is seven times more populous than the second city, Valparaiso, and many Chilean businessmen told me on a recent trip that they increasingly prefer to invest in neighboring Colombia, where growth is spread across the country and is filtering into the second cities.

Colombia is the only Andean nation that is showing signs of more balanced internal growth. Bogotá's 9.8 million people number less than three times that of Medellín, and both Medellín and the third major city, Cali, are growing at a healthy pace. The recent transformation of

Medellín from the murder capital of the world to model city is one of the more dramatic examples of how a country can promote economic growth by freeing up its provinces. In the 1990s Colombia decided to enlist mayors in its battle against narco-traffickers, giving local officials more control over their own budgets and police forces. Medellín began to turn around under a shaggy-haired, jeans-wearing mathematician-turned-mayor named Sergio Fajardo, who took steps to bring the city's most remote and drug-infested slums into the commercial mainstream. Medellín built a lift system of gondolas to reach slums that cling to the hillsides surrounding the city, making it possible for slum residents to find jobs and classes downtown. Since 1991 the city's annual murder rate has fallen from 380 per 100,000 residents to 30. The mansion where local drug kingpin Pablo Escobar was shot dead by police is now a stop on a popular tourist bus line, and Medellín bustles with an optimism that contrasts dramatically with the frustration and fatalism of many Latin American cities.

Another second-city boom is unfolding in Vietnam, thanks largely to its manufacturing prowess. Historically, the southern region around Ho Chi Minh City, formerly Saigon, was the wealthiest and most entrepreneurial part of the country, owing to its ties to the Khmer Empire and later to the United States. But it was the northern region around Hanoi, with historic ties to more insular Chinese empires, that won the civil war in 1975 and still calls the shots. The Hanoi government has wisely buried the hatchet and is now promoting investment all over the country. In 2014 the world's two fastest-growing ports were both in Vietnam, one in the south in Ho Chi Minh City and the other in the north, in the city of Haiphong. Between them, on the central coast, the old American naval base at Da Nang has tripled in population to nearly a million since the war and has been described by some as the emerging Singapore of Vietnam, with a bustling port and a streamlined local government. The city's symbol is a new highway bridge over the Han River, built in the shape of a dragon with a mouth that breathes real fire.

The three-to-one rule also holds in the developed world, where seven countries have a midsize population between 20 and 100 million, and in five of them the ratio between the population of the largest and the second largest cities is roughly three to one. They are Canada, Australia, Italy, Spain, and Germany. In the United Kingdom, London has ten million people and is four times larger than Manchester, and that gap has been growing in recent decades. Residents of Manchester and other second cities have long complained that national policies and media attention are too focused on London, which generates 20 percent of the country's GDP. The British government is trying to address this problem by devolving more power to the regions in a bid to create more vibrant cities.

The one clear violation of the three-to-one ratio is in France. Paris's population of ten million is seven times larger than that of the second city, Lyon. The Paris region accounts for an outsize 30 percent of the economy, reflecting the French tradition of centralizing power. National policies have long been drafted to favor the capital, which is one factor contributing to stagnation in the economy. In the 1960s and '70s, the national government started a campaign to build new towns, but their growth was hampered by the weakness and fragmentation of local political authorities. In 2014 French lawmakers voted to redraw the political map of France by reducing the number of domestic regions from twenty-two to thirteen in order to cut down the bureaucracy, trim costs, and consolidate power. One way a turnaround in the economic prospects of France will likely manifest itself is in the emergence of large cities other than Paris.

By virtue of their size, countries with a population of more than 100 million will have many large cities, and so the relative size of the second city does not tell me much about the country. To get a sense of which countries in that cohort have dynamically growing regions leading to more balanced growth, I look at the broader rise of second-tier cities—meaning cities with more than a million people. The broad rise of second-tier cities is particularly important for the largest countries because, due to their size, they should be able to generate a number of rapidly growing urban areas. This part of the rule—tracking the rise of second-tier cities—therefore applies mainly to countries in the next two size categories, those with more than 100 million people and those with more than one billion people.

Eight emerging countries have populations of more than 100 million but less than a billion, ranging from the Philippines with 101 million to Indonesia with 255 million. As countries develop, they naturally generate more second-tier cities, so it is also important to compare countries to peers at a similar income level. In the class of countries with an average per capita income around $10,000 and a population over 100 million, Russia is the laggard. Over the last three decades it has seen only two cities grow to a population size of one to five million, compared to ten in Brazil, one of the more dynamic stories in in this class. The most dynamic is Mexico, which has also produced ten cities of more than a million people since 1985, in a national population little more than half of Brazil's. Mexico is also the only country in this size and income category where many second-tier cities are growing faster than the capital. In recent decades Mexico City has actually lost ground to second-tier cities in share of the total population, which is highly unusual. In 1985 fewer than 10 percent of Mexicans lived in cities with between one million and five million people, but now that figure is 21 percent.

The flowering of second-tier cities in Mexico is intimately connected to the manufacturing centers producing cars and other exports bound for the United States. Among the fastest-growing Mexican cities with populations of more than a million, three are in states on the U.S. border: Tijuana, Juárez, and Mexicali. The northern boomtown of Monterrey has doubled in population to 4.5 million over the last thirty years and become a center of manufacturing innovation that is spreading across the country. In central Mexico, Querétaro is a jack-of-all-trades, making everything from wine to appliances and trucks, as well as offering services from call centers to logistics. León, once known as the city of shoes and leather, was hard hit by Chinese competition but responded by shifting to agro-industry, chemicals, and cars. Aguascalientes is home to Toyota's most modern manufacturing plant outside Japan. Farther south the city of Puebla has a large Volkswagen plant. The flourishing of these export-manufacturing cities all over the country is a sign of strong regional balance in economic growth.

Until recently the anti-Mexico among the large emerging nations was the Philippines, where the influence of a twentieth-century plantation society has created a remarkable split in the population between the capital and the countryside. Currently 13 percent of Filipinos live in Manila, a proportion that has not changed since 1985 and is more than the share of people living in all other Philippine cities combined. This unique "missing middle" is quite astonishing even for a relatively undeveloped country—the Philippines' average income is less than $3,000. However, signs of life have emerged in second cities like Cebu and Bacolod, which have seen their populations grow by 25 percent since 2000 and are starting to attract some of the call centers and IT service companies that have become an important pillar of the economy.

In the developed world, there are only two countries with more than 100 million people, and they have vastly different track records for developing second-tier cities. Since 1985 fifteen cities in the United States have grown to have more than one million people, while in Japan the comparable number is one, Hamamatsu, an industrial city about 160 miles southwest of Tokyo, which grew in part by absorbing surrounding towns in 2005. There are some mitigating excuses for Japan, including the fact that its national population is smaller than that of the United States, and its growth has slowed much more sharply. Still, the tendency of Japanese policy makers to keep doing what they have long been doing, including in the provinces, has fueled the lack of regional dynamism. The major cities of Tokyo, Osaka, and Nagoya have been dominant for decades, and complaints about the urban-rural divide are an evergreen political issue despite many billions spent on subsidizing shrinking rural towns whose elderly residents prefer not to move.

The United States, by contrast, is the only rich country in the world that has seen massive internal migration, with a postwar shift of more than 15 percent of the population from the old industrial areas of the Northeast and Midwest to the South and West. They have followed the flow of companies and jobs, which have moved to younger states with lower tax rates, less heavily unionized workforces, and sunny environments made tolerable for summer office work by the spread of air conditioning since World War II. Of the fifteen U.S. cities that have risen into the million-plus category, thirteen are in the South or in the West, from Jacksonville, "the city where Florida begins," to Sacramento, the capital of California. The single biggest urban population boom came in Las Vegas, which over the last three decades has mushroomed from a Nevada desert gambling town of half a million into a global tourist destination of 2.5 million.

The next population class, meganations with more than a billion people, consists of only two entries, China and India. And here China is winning the race to build second cities, hands down. China has a remarkably large number of cities that started out with fewer than a quarter-million people three decades ago and mushroomed into metropolises of more than one million, and in some cases much more. In all, there are nineteen such boom cities in China, led by Shenzhen with more than ten million and the neighboring city of Dongguan with more than seven million. In a sense, the mass migration to the southwestern United States has an even larger echo in China, where the move has been from inland provinces to the southeastern coast.

Over the same time period in India, only two towns of under a quarter-million have emerged as cities of more than one million—Mallapuram and Kollam in Kerala state—and their emergence is due largely to a redrawing of the local administrative map. If it were not for a widening of their boundaries in 2011, these two cities' populations would still fall well short of the one million mark.

Of course, one reason for China's lead is that its economy has grown much faster than India's, and industrialization encourages urbanization. But even with that caveat in mind, India has also done less to develop second cities. China created dynamic special economic zones to encourage growth in southeastern coastal provinces, led by Guangdong and Fujian, where many of the fastest-growing cities emerged. One of the surprises about China's top-down approach to development is how much freedom Beijing granted to its lesser cities to take advantage of their location, even to commandeer land or funnel bank loans into building projects. This was authoritarian-style development but with power dispersed to the local level. Shenzhen was a Pearl River fishing village before 1979, when Beijing turned the area into one of China's first experiments in opening to foreign trade and investment. The resulting boom lifted neighboring Dongguan and Zhuhai, which along with Shenzhen are three of China's fastest-growing cities. In fourth place is Yiwu, an inland city in Zhejiang province that has prospered as the eastern terminus of the longest cargo railway line in the world, connecting China to Madrid.

In contrast, India is a large and slow-moving democracy, where local opposition can block land development and the state still reserves huge swaths of urban land for itself. As former World Bank China director Yukon Huang has pointed out, the sprawling urban estates reserved for civil servant housing and military cantonments are a legacy of colonial rule. In my experience, no capital in the emerging world has a neighborhood anything like Lutyens Delhi, named after the British architect who designed the administrative area of India's capital city. This area includes a "bungalow zone" of hundreds of homes on more than twenty-five square kilometers owned almost entirely by the government and surrounded by verdant parklands and laced with wide tree-lined roads. Top officials jockey with one another for residences in this urban oasis, some of which are valued at upward of $50 million. In the emerging world, the only comparable government enclaves I know of are also in India, in the hearts of second-tier cities like Patna and Bareilly.

India tried to create special economic zones on the China model, but these zones have restrictive rules on the use of land and labor, so they have done little to create jobs or build urban populations. India's outdated building codes discourage development in downtown areas and drive up prices, which is one reason average urban land prices are now twice as high in India as in China, according to the Global Property Guide. Though the once all-powerful government in Delhi has in recent decades ceded significant spending authority to chief ministers in India's twenty-nine states, that power has not filtered down to the mayoral level, and it shows. Smaller cities struggle to grow, and when rural Indians do move to urban areas, they tend to choose the four megacities, with populations of over ten million: Mumbai, Delhi, Kolkata, and Bangalore. If China is a nation of boom cities, India is a land of creaking megacities, surrounded by small towns and not enough vibrant second cities.

The Service Cities

The rise of cities along trade routes that carry hard goods is today accompanied by the rise of cities at the center of various service industries. When the Internet first started to revolutionize communications in the 1990s, experts thought it would allow people to do most service jobs just about anywhere, dispersing these businesses to all corners of every country and making location irrelevant. That dispersal is happening for lower to midlevel service jobs, but as the Columbia University urbanologist Saskia Sassen has pointed out, the headquarters of service industries from finance to insurance and law are actually concentrating in a network of about fifty "global cities." These service cities are led by New York and London but are cropping up from Shanghai to Buenos Aires.

Today the Internet is making geography irrelevant neither for manufacturing industries nor for service industries. People still meet face to face in order to manage and build service companies that provide everything from Internet search engines to cargo logistics, and new companies in these industries typically set up in the same town to tap the same expert talent pool. The result is the rise of cities with a cluster of companies and talent in a specific service niche. In South Korea,

Busan continues to thrive as the nation's leading port and as a regional hub for port and logistics service companies. In the Philippines, Manila has been rising for some time as a major global provider of back office services, and now that business is spilling over into its satellite cities, including Quezon and Caloocan. Dubai continues to build on its dual role as a major port moving oil and other goods and a service hub for the Middle East. The key to the success of these locations is that they create a place where people want not only to work but also to live, in the way, say, that Swiss cities like Zurich and Geneva combine striking efficiency with stunning beauty and have turned a landlocked and mountainous country into a geographic sweet spot.

In Poland, second cities such as Krakow, Gdansk, and Wroclaw are emerging as competitive centers for global services and manufacturing industries, with companies that are starting to break into Western markets for the first time. Many of these companies are still run by the founders, who tell similar stories of setting up shop after the collapse of Communism in the late 1980s, then fighting their way through hard times before reaching a critical mass—many of them have annual sales of nearly one billion dollars—where they feel comfortable enough to break out of Poland and start moving into Germany, next door. These companies range from manufacturers in fast fashion and shoes to providers of novel services like debt collection, a profession still undeveloped in western Europe. In late 2014 a Wroclaw entrepreneur said that with bad loans rising across the Eurozone in the wake of the region's debt crisis, the continent's secretive banks had started looking for a discreet partner to help retire the problem quietly. That's why he set up a Polish agency to collect debts in Germany. The Polish CEO said his agency takes a "soft approach" to this abrasive profession, which he expects will ease his move across the border. The firm has been opening offices in Germany and hiring German-speaking Poles to collect debts by phone.

To carve out a geographic sweet spot, a country needs to open its doors on three fronts: to trade with its neighbors, the wider world as well as its own provinces and second cities. Poland is perhaps the leading example of a European nation firing on all three fronts, while in Asia the leader is China, with countries like Vietnam and Bangladesh close on its tail. In Latin America the leading examples are Mexico and, of late, Colombia. Its 2012 free trade deal with the United States was the first of its kind in South America; it is part of one of the more promising new regional trade alliances along with its Andean neighbors and Mexico, and it has encouraged the transformation of Medellín from murder capital to model second city. In Africa, Morocco and Rwanda are carving out export success stories in very rough neighborhoods.

Location still matters. Economic growth has long tended to flower along the trade routes that carry manufactured goods; now it is flourishing in service industry capitals as well, and this trend may be gaining momentum in a period of deglobalization. In recent years, as growth in global trade leveled off and global capital flows have fallen sharply, the process of globalization nonetheless has accelerated in two important categories. The number of international travelers and tourists has continued to rise rapidly, and Internet communications have continued to explode, which could open up new opportunities for countries that can exploit these trends. The Israeli historian and author Yuval Harari has argued that the future for the world may be visible in the habits of the American millennial generation, which is less inclined to spend money on traditional "stuff" like furniture or clothes than on "experiences," from real-world travel, restaurants, and sports to the virtual kind available everywhere on smartphones. The craving for experiences, Harari and others predict, will only pick up speed if automation leaves humans with less work and more time to fill. This could be a growth opportunity for countries that can turn themselves into tech, travel, and entertainment hubs, but it is a limited opportunity so far.

Geography is never enough to produce strong growth on its own, unless a country takes the right steps to turn its fortuitously located ports and cities into commercially attractive magnets. The luck of location can change too: Both Poland and Mexico are on the border of large and rich markets, but lately Mexico has been luckier than Poland, because the United States has been growing much faster than Europe. Trade routes are not written in stone, and the advantages or disadvantages of location can be reshaped by good policies. Not so long ago China was itself still pitied as the poor and backward "Middle Kingdom," isolated in the "remote Far East," before it took the steps necessary to carve out a new geographic sweet spot.

6

FACTORIES FIRST

*Is investment rising or falling
as a share of the economy?*

HIGH UP IN ONE OF THE GLASS TOWERS OF SANTA FE, A pristine suburb of Mexico City that was purpose-built for big business, I sat in a corner office with expansive views of a scene that transported me out of the emerging world. To my right, I could see helicopters dropping executives off on the rooftop of a neighboring corporate megalith, while my hosts described to me the tableau to my left, an enclave of multimillion-dollar homes known to locals as Narnia, after the fantasy realm in the C. S. Lewis novels. Formally called Bosques de Santa Fe, it is a gated community with separate pathways and entrances for the help, designed for billionaires and those who would like to be seen as billionaires. Above all, Narnia appeals to superwealthy families seeking to escape the crime and traffic in the streets of Mexico City, an hour away. This scene, from the autumn of 2014, was my most recent glimpse of how in some nations the rich are trying almost to secede from reality, particularly when the state is not investing enough in the basic facilities and security of a modern economy.

For most visitors, such breakdowns in the functions of government will appear in the form of endless lines at the airline ticket counter,

overflowing trains with people squatting on the top, or underpaid traffic police hitting people up for bribes, as is happening in Mexico. Other
telltale signs will be only slightly more subtle, showing up in freelance
attempts to plug these gaps in the public networks or to bypass the
public sphere entirely. Private gated communities are spreading across
Latin America, and the whirring of helicopters over Santa Fe brought
to my mind a similar scene in Brazil, where a network of private heli-
pads links the rooftops of corporate headquarters in São Paulo, allowing
executives to evade the endless traffic on the streets below. In Nigeria and many other African countries, private companies insure themselves against frequent failures in the public power grid by buying large
generators—and massive oil tanks to fuel them—in order to keep the
lights on and the elevators running when daily blackouts hit. Quora, the
question-and-answer Web forum, lists unusual jobs that are unique to
certain nations, many of which have evolved to address gaps in public
service networks. One such job is designed to overcome the lack of ferry
services in remote river villages of Vietnam, where students and teach-
ers on the way to school will cross the river by hopping into a big plastic
bag and enlisting a strong man to carry them across the current.

Two kinds of spending drive any economy—consumption and
investment—and while in most economies people and governments
spend more on consumption, investment is the more important driver
of growth and business cycles. Investment spending is usually more volatile than consumption spending, and it helps create the new businesses
and jobs that put money in consumers' pockets. It includes investment
by both the government and private business in construction of roads,
railways, and the like, in plants and equipment from office machines to
drill presses, and in buildings from schools to private homes. The basic
question for a nation's economic prospects: Is investment rising or falling as a share of the economy? When it is rising, growth is much more
likely to accelerate.

Over time I've come to see that there is a rough sweet spot for the
level of investment, measured as a share of GDP. Looking at my list

of the fifty-six highly successful postwar economies in which growth exceeded 6 percent for a decade or more, I found that on average these countries were investing about 25 percent of GDP during the course of the boom. Often growth picks up as investment accelerates. So any emerging country aiming to grow rapidly is generally in a strong position to do so when investment is high and rising—roughly between 25 and 35 percent of GDP. They are in a weak position to grow when investment is low and falling—roughly 20 percent of GDP or less.

It is hard to determine whether investment is going to rise or fall, and that judgment can only be made subjectively, by looking at the scale and promise of public investment plans and by considering whether the state is encouraging private companies to invest. In Mexico and Brazil, investment has stagnated at around 20 percent of GDP or less for many years—and the proliferation of secure private communities and private transportation networks testifies to the fact that many locals have given up on waiting for the government to act, and invest on their own to fill the gaps.

Strong growth in investment is almost always a good sign, but the stronger it gets, the more important it is to track where the spending is going. The second part of this rule aims to distinguish between good and bad investment binges. The best kinds unfold when companies get excited about some new innovation and funnel money into creating new technology, new roads and ports, or especially new factories. Of the three main economic sectors—agriculture, services, and manufacturing—manufacturing has been the ticket out of poverty for most emerging countries. Even at a time when robots threaten to replace humans on the assembly line, no other kind of business has the proven ability to play the booster role for job creation and economic growth that manufacturing has in the past.

The most successful postwar development stories, starting with Japan in the 1960s, all began by manufacturing simple goods, such as clothing, for export to rich nations. As farmers moved off the land out of agriculture and into more productive factory jobs in urban areas, the factories started investing in upgrades to make more profitable exports, moving up from clothing to steel, then from steel to flatscreen TVs or cars or chemicals.

Then comes a major shift. As factories pop up around cities, service businesses from restaurants to insurance companies emerge to cater to the growing industrial middle class. Manufacturing starts to give way to services, and investment levels off and starts to shrink as a share of the economy, because services require much less investment in plants and equipment than factories do. In the top developed economies today, investment as a share of GDP averages barely 20 percent, ranging from 17 percent in Italy to 20 percent in the United States and 26 percent in Australia. The share of investment that goes to manufacturing also tends to decline as a nation grows richer; the manufacturing share of GDP typically rises steadily before peaking somewhere between 20 and 35 percent, when the nation's average per capita income reaches about $10,000 in purchasing power–parity terms. That natural decline, however, does not mean factories are not important to richer countries.

As a nation develops, investment and manufacturing both account for a shrinking share of the economy, but they both continue to play an outsize role in driving growth. Manufacturing now accounts for less than 18 percent of global GDP, down from more than 24 percent in 1980, but it remains a key driver of innovation. In manufacturing economies at all levels of development, according to the McKinsey Global Institute, the manufacturing industries account for nearly 80 percent of private-sector research and development and 40 percent of growth in productivity, which is really the key to stable growth in the future. When workers are turning out more widgets per hour, their employer can raise their wages without raising the price it charges for widgets, which allows the economy to grow without inflation.

Today many developing countries have come to recognize how important it is for them to boost productivity by investing in factories first, if they want growth without the crippling side effects of inflation. It is no accident that emerging nations with the strongest records of investment growth also boast some of the world's strongest manufacturing sectors. Of the top five nations ranked by investment as a share of GDP in 2014, four were also among the top five by manufacturing as a share of GDP: China, South Korea, Malaysia, and Indonesia. Outside the lucky cases of small countries that hit the lottery by discovering oil or natural gas, most nations have found it impossible to even begin the process of breaking out from poverty without building manufacturing industries as an initial step.

In this decade investment growth has stalled in much of the emerging world, as governments and businesses ran out of ways to raise funds after the global financial crisis in 2008–9. In developing countries the annual rate of growth in investment fell by more than a third, to about 1.7 percent. Outside the major exception of China, the rate collapsed from 10 percent in 2010 to zero in 2014. In much of the world, thus, investment vanished as a contributor to economic growth, and in countries ranging from Brazil to Russia, the Czech Republic, Egypt, India, South Korea, Mexico, Poland, and Taiwan, it fell as a share of GDP. In some of these economies, particularly the commodity-driven ones like Russia and Brazil, falling investment was gutting what factories a country did have, retarding the whole process of industrialization and development.

In the key emerging nations, the share of manufacturing in the economy currently ranges from 10 percent of GDP in Chile to more than 30 percent in China; the commodity-driven economies of Russia and Brazil are in the low teens, near the bottom of the list. In Africa, despite the celebrations over its economic revival in the 2000s, manufacturing was actually shrinking as a share of GDP, continuing a decline from 18 percent in 1975 to 11 percent in 2014. Some of the largest African economies, including Nigeria and South Africa, were actually deindustrializing, slipping backward down the development ladder.

While rising investment usually augurs well for economic growth, any strength taken too far can become a weakness. The trick is to stop short of overdoing it, which is why the ideal level of investment is capped at roughly 35 percent of GDP. Beyond that level, excess looms. In the postwar period, only ten countries have seen investment top 40 percent of GDP, a group that includes South Korea in the 1970s and Thailand and Malaysia in the 1990s. Only two of these countries, Norway in the late 1970s and Jordan in the late 2000s, escaped a major slowdown after. This is a critical element of this rule, because the historic pattern shows that investment flows in cycles, and once it hits a peak at more than 30 percent of GDP and begins to fall, economic growth slows by a third on average over the next five years. And if investment peaks at more than 40 percent of GDP, growth slows even more sharply, by about half in the five years following the peak. The reasons for this slowdown go back to the basic nature of the economic cycles, which is that as a period of strong growth advances, people get complacent and sloppy, and more money goes to increasingly unproductive investments. The economy slows because the contribution from productivity falls.

This signal has been flashing a bright warning to China in the 2010s. Despite the global slowdown in investment, China was still caught up in the extraordinary momentum of perhaps the biggest investment boom the world had ever seen. Between 2002 and 2014 investment rose from 37 percent of GDP to 47 percent, a level never before attained by a large economy. China's devotion to investing in heavy industry was such that each year it was pouring more than twice as much cement-per-citizen as any other country in the world, including the United States. By many measures, China was pushing the strength of investment in industry too far, as more and more of the investment started to flow toward unproductive targets, and once it started to fall, it was likely to continue falling for some time. The record of previous Asian miracles showed that trends in investment spending tend to be "monophasic," meaning that once trends turn, the same conditions persist for many years.

The Virtuous Cycle of Manufacturing

For all the danger signs China now faces, it has to be noted that it took a very long time for these risks to emerge. China's industrialization process started from an extremely low base, and for three decades the investment went into factories, roads, bridges, and other productive assets. Only when the boom was entering its fourth decade did the government and private companies target more frivolous investment projects. Indeed, this is often the case: When good investment binges start in manufacturing, they tend to become self-propelling for many years. The Harvard economist Dani Rodrik calls manufacturing the "automatic escalator" of development, because once a country finds a niche in global manufacturing, productivity often seems to start rising automatically.[1]

The early steps have always involved manufacturing goods for sale to foreigners, not to locals. In a study of 150 emerging nations looking back fifty years, the Emerging Advisors Group, a Hong Kong–based economic research firm, found that the single most powerful driver of economic booms was sustained growth in exports, especially of manufactured products. Exporting simple manufactured goods not only increases income and consumption at home, it generates foreign revenues that allow the country to import the machinery and materials needed to improve its factories—without running up huge foreign bills and debts.

In short, in the case of manufacturing, one good investment binge seems to lead to another. Building factories generates funds for upgrading them, which then increases pressure to invest in improving roads, bridges, railroads, ports, power grids, and water systems—the infrastructure that allows a country to move manufactured goods from its factories onto the global export market. In the nineteenth century, the United States saw two huge railroad spending booms, followed by two quick busts, but the booms nonetheless left behind much of the basic network that helped make the country the world's leading industrial power a few decades later.

Today various international authorities have estimated that the emerging world needs many trillions of dollars in investment on these kinds of transport and communications networks. Among those nations, Thailand and Colombia have plans to spend tens of billions of dollars on projects that could transform their landscape, the way the construction of a nationwide highway system after World War II radically shrank travel times in the United States and Germany. The same could be said for much of China's boom, which built, among much else, a network of highways that is the envy of many much richer nations. Only in the 2000s did the money start to find its way into projects that President Xi Jinping criticized in October 2014 as "weird architecture," including buildings designed to mimic the shape of a bird's nest, an ice cube, a doughnut, a fantastical Chinese landscape painting, giant trousers, and so on.

Once an economy starts down the manufacturing path, its momentum can carry it in the right direction for some time. When the ratio of investment to GDP surpasses 30 percent, it tends to stick at that level for a long time—nine years on average for the postwar cases I have studied. The reason for this stickiness is that many of these nations seemed to show a strong leadership commitment to investment, particularly to investment in manufacturing, which can begin a virtuous circle.

There are of course a few exceptions. The Soviet Union invested massively in factories, but when it fell, Russia had little to show for it. Investment peaked at 35 percent of GDP in the early 1980s, but much of that money was directed by the state into ill-conceived one-industry towns, from the timber mills of Vydrino to the paper mills of Baikalsk and the mines of Pikalyovo. These state-sponsored industries quickly proved incapable of competing with modern global rivals after the Soviet Union collapsed in 1989. What was left was a rump Russian state with increasingly idle and empty industrial towns and no export-manufacturing base to speak of.

The modern outlier is India, where investment as a share of the economy exceeded 30 percent of GDP over the course of the 2000s, but little of that money went into factories. Indian manufacturing had been stagnant for decades at around 15 percent of GDP. The stagnation stems from the failures of the state to build functioning ports and power plants or to create an environment in which the rules governing labor, land, and capital are designed and enforced in a way that encourages entrepreneurs to invest, particularly in factories. India has disappointed on both counts: creating labor-friendly rules and workable land-acquisition norms.

Between 1989 and 2010 India generated about ten million new jobs in manufacturing, but according to the World Bank economist Ejaz Ghani, nearly all those jobs were created in enterprises that are small and informal and thus better suited to dodge India's bureaucracy and its extremely restrictive rules regarding firing workers.[2] It is commonly said in India that the labor laws are so onerous that it is practically impossible to comply with even half of them without violating the other half. Ghani points out that this proliferation of small shops came despite reforms that were supposed to make it easier for entrepreneurs to build larger factories and export their wares. Informal shops, many of them one-man operations, now account for 39 percent of India's manufacturing workforce, up from 19 percent in 1989, and they are simply too small to compete in global markets.

During visits to New York in the 1990s, I remember being struck by the fact that so many of the manhole covers on the streets of Manhattan were imprinted with the label "Made in India." I took a certain encouragement from that, thinking that perhaps it was an early sign of manufacturing progress to come, but that hope never panned out. The Indian software entrepreneur Jaithirth Rao wrote in January 2014 that a friend scanned his office for something made in India and found that "the carpet is from China, the furniture is from Malaysia, the light fixtures are from China, the glass partition is from all places, Jebel Ali in the Middle East and so on."[3] Even statues of the Hindu elephant god Ganesh, which are found all over India, Rao went on to add, are now imported from China.

That common products like carpets and lighting would be produced in China is perhaps understandable, given its economies of scale and the worldwide market for these items, but I was stunned recently to hear from the head of one of India's largest conglomerates that something as quintessentially Indian as *agarbatti*—the incense sticks that perfume most religious and social occasions—are now manufactured mainly in Vietnam.

After Narendra Modi became prime minister in 2014, he launched a "Make in India" campaign. But there was still a basic problem: His aides, at least initially, were not talking about building simple factories first, in industries like toys or textiles, of the kind that can employ many millions of people and jump-start an industrial middle class. They were talking about advanced factories in industries like solar-powered appliances and military weapons, which require the highly skilled workers not yet found in abundance among India's vast population of the rural underemployed. India was attempting to skip over a step in the development process, not for the first time.

The Service Escalator

During its boom years, before the global financial crisis, India was growing in large part on the strength of investment in technology service industries, not manufacturing. This gave birth to a cottage industry of Indian economists trying to prove, in optimistic hindsight, that this approach would work as a development strategy. In a globalizing world, they argued, more and more services could be delivered over the Internet. One might still need a local beautician for a perm, or a landscaper to cut the lawn, but the Internet would make it possible to replace any number of local service agents, from the lawyer to the insurance broker, from the radiologist to the techie to fix your Internet connection. Instead of growing richer by exporting ever more advanced manufactured products, India could grow rich by exporting the services demanded in this new information age.

These arguments began to gain traction early in the 2010s in new research on the "service escalator." A 2014 working paper from the World Bank made the case that the old growth escalator in manufacturing was already giving way to a new one in service industries, which can range from taxi rides, haircuts, and restaurant meals to medical care.[4] The report argued, in this hopeful vein, that while manufacturing is in retreat as a share of the global economy and is producing fewer jobs, services are still growing, contributing more to growth in output and jobs for nations rich and poor. It said that the old beliefs that service jobs tend to be ill paid and unproductive no longer apply to even poor nations such as Ethiopia, where labor productivity is rising faster in services than in other sectors—particularly as more modern services like mobile phone networks catch on. Its message was that not only Ethiopia but all of Africa could avoid the specter of "jobless industrialization" by creating jobs in services instead.

The case for the new service escalator is an encouraging and logical vision, and one almost hopes it is correct. So often forecasters extrapolate depressing trends into a vision of a depressed future, and this is exactly what was happening in discussions of the decline of manufacturing and the rise of automation. Prognosticators had spun these trends into forecasts for a future in which people cede good factory jobs to machines, leading to mass unemployment. Of course, predictions like these had been advanced since the dawn of industrialization, and had repeatedly been proven wrong. While one sewing machine could replace many seamstresses in the textile industry, the spread of the technology created new jobs for sewing machine operators in other industries, from furniture to toys and eventually to upholstered car seats. In times of job destruction, we should be looking not for a catastrophic ending but for the next transformation, because that is the normal cycle.

The next turn may now be visible in the way the process of deglobalization is unfolding. Though global trade has slowed, and global capital flows have retreated, the flow of travelers, tourists, and Internet communications has continued to explode, and all of these fuel service industries. Moreover, the share of people whose mobile phone is "smart" has risen from less than 20 percent to 75 percent in just the last five years, so services are expanding their reach by going mobile.

However, for now, one basic problem with the idea of the service escalator is that in the emerging world most of the new service jobs are still in very traditional ventures, not in creating virtual realities or high-end travel experiences. Consider the ubiquitous curbside tire repair stalls from Lagos to Delhi, or what might be called the barbershop in a box. In small Indian villages, many entrepreneurs will cut your hair for a pittance in what looks like a large plywood coffin, tipped up on one end. It would take a bold tourist to venture inside. When farmers move from the fields into service jobs such as these, it is not a means to generate export earnings or provide a boost to national economic development.

The trend that got some Indian economists so excited was the arrival of modern services, which in India meant information technology (IT) services that by the late 1990s had made cities such as Bangalore and Pune internationally famous boomtowns and home to rising corporate giants including Infosys and TCS. It was hoped that, just as Korea moved up from manufacturing textiles to manufacturing kitchen appliances, India could move up from selling simple back-office services—the roadside repairs of the IT sector—to more advanced and profitable consulting and software services. But this vision has limitations. A decade on, India's tech sector is still providing relatively simple IT services, mainly the same back-office operations it started with, and the number of new jobs it is creating is relatively small.

In India, only about two million people work in IT services, or less than 1 percent of the workforce. Smaller copycat IT service booms have occurred in the neighboring countries of Pakistan and Sri Lanka, but those have produced jobs only in the tens of thousands. The same applies to the Philippines, where employment in the booming call center industry exploded from zero to more than 350,000 employees in the 2000s, but that still represents a tiny fraction of the workforce. So far the rise of these service industries has not been big enough to drive the mass modernization of rural farm economies. In the Asian miracle economies of Japan and South Korea, as much as a quarter of the population migrated from farm to factory during their long periods of rapid growth. At the peak of its manufacturing prowess in the early postwar years, America employed one-third of its labor force in factories.

People can move quickly from working in the fields to working on an assembly line, because both rely for the most part on manual labor. The leap from the farm to the modern service sector is much tougher, since those jobs often require more advanced skills, including the ability to operate a computer. The workers who have moved into IT service jobs in the Philippines and India have generally come from a pool of relatively better-educated members of the urban middle class, who speak English and have at least some facility with computers. Finding jobs for the underemployed middle class is important, but there are limits to how deeply it can transform the economy, because it is a relatively small part of the population. For now, the rule is still factories first, not services first.

It's Tough to Get on the Escalator

The evolving challenge for countries such as India is that it is tougher and tougher to get into the manufacturing game or to stay in it. Since China launched its manufacturing drive three decades ago, the number of would-be manufacturing powers has mushroomed and now includes contenders from Vietnam to Bangladesh. It has become harder and harder for established export manufacturers just to hold on to their customers, in part because the entire sector has been shrinking worldwide.

It had become increasingly difficult to compete in international manufacturing even before the crisis of 2008, which subsequently made the field even tougher. In the boom years of the past decade, exports out of the big emerging economies had been growing at an annual pace of 20 to 30 percent, and that pace peaked near 40 percent in 2008 and again in 2010. But then global trade slowed, and export growth in these nations turned negative between 2010 and 2014. With competition intensifying as the manufacturing sector shrank, rich countries began moving more quickly to block the tricks (subsidizing exports, undervaluing currencies, and reverse-engineering Western technology) that the East Asian nations used to become export powerhouses back in the 1960s and '70s.

The other obstacle is automation. The current wave of new technology is not creating machines that can do one thing well, like sew a stitch; it is creating increasingly smart robots that seem capable of doing just about anything—driving a car, playing chess, running faster than Usain Bolt, finding the box of needles in an Amazon warehouse and moving it to the shipping dock. Because modern factories employ more and more robots but fewer people, it will be more difficult for upcoming nations to move 25 percent of their labor force from farms to factories, the way the Asian miracle economies did. The digital revolution is now revolutionizing the factory floor, as 3D printers make it possible to conjure up products as varied as building materials, athletic shoes, designer lamps, and turbine blades without a human hand to aid in the production or assembly of the parts.

Worse, for emerging nations, is the fact that developed nations led by the United States are far ahead in these advanced manufacturing techniques. The United States itself is undergoing a mini-manufacturing revival driven by the discovery of cheap shale gas, which is bringing down power costs, and by a shrinking gap between U.S. manufacturing wages and those of its competitors, including China. The United States is now a major customer for goods manufactured in the emerging world as well as a rival to emerging-world manufacturers. By 2015 there were even stories about a few U.S. companies making a comeback in simple industries like clothes and sneakers.

As a result, emerging countries can no longer ride the manufacturing escalator for as long as they did just a decade ago. This makes clear how remarkable are the rare nations that have managed to defy these trends, and have continued to build on a large manufacturing base. Most notably, the South Korean industrial juggernaut continues to roll, with manufacturing continuing to increase in recent years to 28 percent of GDP, among the highest shares for any large economy, even as its average per capita income has risen above $20,000. Only six other developed nations have manufacturing sectors that account for nearly 20 percent of GDP or more—Singapore, Germany, Japan, Austria, Switzerland, and Liechtenstein.

Germany in particular has shown remarkable success expanding as a manufacturing export power, even when it was already a rich country. Exports have expanded to 46 percent of GDP from 26 percent in 1995, driven in part by the well-known Hartz reforms, which have gutted the power of unions and restrained labor costs. This move has been attacked as a "beggar thy neighbor policy" by fellow members of the Eurozone, who now share a continental currency with Germany and can no longer respond to falling German labor costs by allowing their own national currencies to fall. But Germany has also pushed reform in many other ways: It has a core of medium-size industrial companies known as the *Mittelstand*, whose family owners are known for thinking in the long term, and they have made smart strategic use of the abundant supply of cheap, well-educated labor that opened up to them after the fall of the Berlin Wall. Many have invested in new factories in Poland and the Czech Republic, as well as in the United States and China, effectively exporting the German industrial model. 2010 was the first year in which German car companies made more cars abroad than at home, helping to forge what is arguably the leading global industrial power. According to the International Cluster Competitiveness Project at Harvard Business School, in the top 51 global industries, German companies hold a top three position in 27, more than any other country including the United States, in second with 21, and China, in third with 19.

The Stabilizing Effect of Factories

The harder it gets for nations to climb onto the manufacturing ladder, the more clearly the success stories stand out. The clearest measure of a country's ability to enter the virtuous circle of manufacturing is its share of the global market for manufactured exports and particularly the recent change in that share. Few countries have lately seen a significant improvement by this measure: The exceptions are led by China, Thailand, and South Korea, where in recent years the strong manufacturing base has continued to push the economy forward at an annual growth rate of 3 to 4 percent, even though it has been carrying a huge burden in household debt, equal to 150 percent of GDP.

However, the most interesting demonstration of how manufacturing insulates an economy from other threats is Thailand. At the height of the Asian currency crisis in late 1997, I traveled to Thailand at the invitation of local businessmen who insisted that the economy was much more stable than it appeared. Yes, the housing market was melting down in Bangkok, but they wanted to show me the other side of the country, the manufacturing base. I flew over from India, and the contrast to India's potholed roads and back-alley craft shops was startling. My hosts swept us from the airport straight out on to the new Chonburi motorway toward the eastern seaboard—a brief drive along a four-lane speed tunnel that fed not one but a series of deepwater ports, anchored by the towering loading cranes of the port at Laem Chabang. About one hundred kilometers from Bangkok began a stretch of what can only be described as industrial plants in paradise, with auto factories, petrochemical refineries, and shipbuilding docks sprinkled among gentle green pagoda-dotted hills that rolled down to white sand beaches. Few Westerners had heard of this factory-beach scene, but the Japanese were already there in force, particularly as investors and customers for the auto plants, and the coastal village of Pattaya had sprouted a go-go bar district catering to them.

Today this coast is a popular tourist and retirement destination for Europeans, as well as home for many of Thailand's best-paid workers. But back then it was a largely hidden monument to the country's muscle in export manufacturing. I was stunned to find this seaboard buzzing with manufacturing activity in a country that still had an average income of $3,000, and it was strong proof of what Thailand could be expected to achieve despite—or perhaps even because of—the Asian crisis. As the Thai currency collapsed, it lowered the price of exports from these eastern seaboard factories and propelled the country toward a recovery.

This is just one striking case of how strong manufacturing can provide stabilizing ballast amid storms that would normally sink an economy. Even today Thailand gets attention in the global headlines less as a manufacturing powerhouse than as a prolific incubator of political chaos and coups. It has one of the world's most volatile political systems, having suffered thirteen coups and a further six coup attempts since the 1930s, including the May 2014 putsch that toppled Prime Minister Yingluck Shinawatra. The generals have since largely removed both Shinawatra and her once-voluble rural supporters from public view, growth has slowed, and Thailand's democracy hangs in the balance. Yet before the last coup, Thailand had sustained an economic growth rate of around 4 percent for a decade even when protesters blocked the international airport or the army took over parliament.

Before 2014, Thailand's economic stability was grounded in the fifth-highest investment rate (30 percent of GDP) and second-largest manufacturing sector (also near 30 percent of GDP) among large economies. In recent years not even China has seen its manufacturing industries grow faster. Thailand is one of the very few major emerging economies that have increased their share of global exports in the past few years, including its shipments of steel, machinery, and cars. These growth industries have given Thailand one of the lowest unemployment rates in Asia, under 3 percent on average over the past decade. An unusually large proportion of Thai adults are gainfully employed, and that has long been a stabilizing factor for the economy. Alas, no trend is permanent. The coup leaders who toppled Shinawatra seem more focused on political "reform" to make sure she and her supporters don't make a comeback than on keeping alive her plan to invest billions of dollars in new transport links to keep the export-manufacturing machine humming.

The Rare Tech Booms

The next form of a good investment binge, after manufacturing, is technology, but past records show that such booms have been confined for the most part to the leading industrial nations and in recent years particularly to the United States. They are exceedingly rare in the emerging world. India has made important inroads into IT services and in other specialized businesses like pharmaceuticals, but in a limited way. The leading emerging-world exceptions are Taiwan and South Korea. Both these countries have invested heavily in research and development—more than 3 percent of GDP a year over the past decade—in order to create technology industries from scratch. By contrast, Chile—also widely seen as an economic success—spends less than 1 percent of GDP a year on research and development and as a result is likely to struggle to grow now that its average income is a relatively high $15,000.

South Korea, the most broadband-connected country in the world, has been creating globally competitive technology companies in a broad range of industries, from cars to consumer electronics. Taiwan's companies tend to be smaller and are quick to respond to new global trends. During a March 2014 visit to Taipei, I talked to the chairman of a large bank who traced this flexibility to the country's long history of foreign invasion, arguing that the people of Taiwan have been forced to adapt to many cultures and have learned to be open-minded. Known for making components for PC makers, mobile handsets, and other consumer electronics, Taiwan's companies have moved into fast-growing tech sectors such as consumer electronics for cars and "athleisure," in which fashion and sportswear companies combine to produce trendy athletic wear that can be worn outside the gym.

The only other country that began developing broad strength in technology while it was still emerging is the even smaller and more unusual case of Israel, which was recently reclassified as a developed market. It is home to the second-most start-up companies in the world after the United States and spends nearly 4 percent of GDP on R&D.

Several large U.S. corporations, such as Microsoft and Cisco, set up their first overseas R&D facilities in Israel, and the country is a magnet for venture capitalists. Israeli companies are developing video that puts the viewer inside a three-dimensional, 360-degree virtual world, creating smartphone hardware that can monitor your vital signs without attaching probes to your body, and putting the country's deep military expertise to use in building cybersecurity systems. Israel is a legitimate technology export power, deriving 40 percent of its GDP from exports and half of its export income from tech and life sciences.

In recent years trend-spotters have cited new Silicon Valleys or alleys or deserts popping up in one emerging-world city after another, from Nairobi to Santiago, but often these are micro-investment booms, consisting of only a few individual start-ups in one small neighborhood. They rarely amount to much in the end. Another possible exception is unfolding in Mexico. The northern border city of Monterrey has been importing technology ever since it brought in the nation's first ice factory from the United States in the nineteenth century. That led to the first beer company, which evolved into the FEMSA conglomerate, now at the heart of the city's transformation. An early scion of the family that founded FEMSA went to MIT and later with his alma mater's help set up its Mexican counterpart, the Monterrey Institute of Technology. Mexico's MIT now plays a role similar to that played by Stanford University in Silicon Valley, a cornerstone of a local culture that celebrates engineering, entrepreneurship, and aggressive innovation. In the 2000s, when drug lords began moving into Monterrey suburbs and warring among themselves, local companies mobilized, pushing to replace the often-corrupt federal police with a better-paid local force, which played the key role in driving out the gang leaders.

Today Monterrey is the quiet home to a striking array of companies that are applying high technology to the improvement of everything from lightweight aluminum auto parts to white cheese, tortilla-based prepared meals, and even cement. The late CEO Lorenzo Zambrano brought his Stanford training to the task of turning Cemex into the world's most advanced cement company, transforming its signature product into what he liked to call, in Silicon Valley argot, a tech-based "solution." Cemex has nine research labs, focused on everything from improving its business processes to developing stronger ready-mix concrete. In Colombia, the company has convinced the government to buy more expensive new cement that lasts longer, which ends up saving the country money on repaving its mountainous road network. Mexico's central government recognizes the potential of Monterrey's entrepreneurial culture to transform an economy still dominated by state monopolies, and it has contributed to some $400 million in new investments that have poured into the city's research facilities since 2009.

The idea of a good binge may sound a bit like an oxymoron, but these binges are healthy because even if they lead to a crash, the country involved doesn't emerge from the hangover with an empty wallet. It finds itself stronger than it was before the binge, with new canals or rail lines or fiber optic cables or semiconductor fabrication plants or globally competitive cement factories, which will help the economy grow as it recovers. In short, as the French economist Louis Gave has argued, an investment binge can be judged by what it leaves behind.

In 2001 the conventional wisdom was that tech investment bubbles fuel mainly junk companies, so no one was surprised that year when the collapse of the dot-com bubble led to multiple spectacular flame-outs, like Pets.com. Subsequently, the Harvard Business School professors Ramana Nanda and Matthew Rhodes-Kropf found that, compared to stock bubbles in other kinds of companies, tech bubbles are likely to fund more start-ups that fail but also more that go on to become extremely successful (judged by how much money they attract when they go public) and innovative (judged by how many patents they win).[5] For every few dozen companies like Pets.com that went under in 2001, there was a pioneering survivor like Google or Amazon that would help make the United States much more productive. In fact, the tech boom of the 1990s helped to drive the U.S. productivity growth rate up from 2 percent in the 1980s to near 3 percent, the highest rate since the postwar recovery period of the 1950s.[6] A productivity boom of this scale is not that unusual in poor countries—where just building roads can greatly increase productivity—but it is rare in advanced economies.

For a while, as the Internet mania gained steam, the huge investment in fiber optic cables to run faster connections looked like the biggest bubble of all. But it left behind the cables that have made high-speed broadband connections a reality, as the useful life for fiber optics is fifteen to twenty years. Emerging countries including South Korea and Taiwan pushed broadband even faster at the height of the binge, and they now rank among the world's most wired nations. As Louis Gave points out, even though the tech boom imploded, it left consumers with the ability to make phone calls and transfer data more cheaply, as well as to make use of call centers and other cost-effective services located in countries such as India or the Philippines, thus contributing to higher growth and improved standards of living in both rich and poor countries.

Something analogous happened during the early postwar period in Japan and South Korea, where the governments steered money into building world-class companies. Some of those, like Daewoo in South Korea and Sogo in Japan, were gutted in ensuing crises. Others survived to become globally competitive brands in technology industries, like Hyundai and Samsung. The hangover from a binge on good investments in factories or technology tends to increase productivity for years after the boom has ended.

Still, for an emerging nation, even technology cannot play the same catalytic role as manufacturing because no country has figured out how to leapfrog the stage of building basic factories that make simple goods such as clothing, and that require only relatively simple skills that can be mastered by workers coming straight off the farm. It takes time to train those workers for jobs in more advanced factories or in more modern service industries. Tech booms also originate and remain centered in the leading technology powers, including Britain in the nineteenth century or the United States today.

The Bad Binges: Real Estate

The worst kinds of investment binges leave behind little of productive value, in part because they are not prompted by some hot new technology or innovation. Often the trigger that sends investors rushing into a bad binge is a chance to capitalize on spiking prices for a coveted asset, such as housing, or a natural resource, such as copper or iron ore. Home construction may accelerate for a bit, which is not necessarily a bad thing, particularly in a poor country that needs more housing. But real estate investment binges typically have a limited long-term return: A house will provide a home to one family but will not provide a steady boost to economic output or increase productivity. And since so many people dream of buying that perfect home or fantasy second home, the real estate market seems particularly prone to irrational manias.

The quality of an investment binge—whether it is good or bad for the economy—also depends heavily on how businesses pay for it. If they aggressively borrow money, whether from banks or through other forms of debt like bonds, the usual outcome when the bubble bursts is a drawn-out mess. As businesses try to renegotiate their debts and banks are forced to write off the bad loans, the credit system is paralyzed, and the economy slows down for years. But if businesses instead raise money for their investments by selling equity on the capital markets, the market sorts out the mess much faster. Stock prices fall, and owners are forced to take the hit, no fuss and no negotiation. The best way to fund a binge is by foreign direct investment, which often flows to emerging markets in the form of foreigners building or buying direct stakes in new factories or other businesses. As owners, they tie themselves to the fate of these projects for the long haul. This very stable source of financing can't flee easily in a crisis.

Nations often move from good binges to bad ones and back. In the United States, for example, the dot-com boom of the late 1990s is now recognized as a classic good binge. Financed mainly by the stock market and venture capitalists, the boom ended with a sudden collapse in the value of those shares, but there was no long debate about who should take the pain. Consequently the U.S. economy suffered the shallowest recession in its postwar history in 2001. But the subsequent boom in the U.S. housing market was a bad binge financed largely by debt. The collapse of the real estate boom in 2008 led to a global crisis, the sharpest recession in postwar history, and an agonizingly slow recovery, as banks and their customers struggled to pay down the debt and return to a sense of normalcy.

Real estate binges are often pumped up by borrowing and, as a result, tend to end in a serious economic slowdown. Some of the most famous economic miracles ended with the implosion of a debt-fueled property bubble, including Japan in 1989 and Taiwan in the early 1990s. The general rule is that what goes up must come down, but a recent report on eighteen of the worst housing price busts since 1970 showed that all of them struck only after real estate construction investment reached an average of about 5 percent of GDP. In the United States, for example, real estate investment peaked at about 6 percent of GDP in 2005, three years before the implosion. In Spain, it peaked at 12 percent of GDP in 2008, two years before the implosion. In China, it peaked at around 10 percent in 2012, and prices in many cities have been weakening over the past couple of years. That suggests a rough benchmark for when a real estate investment binge reaches a manic stage—when it reaches about 5 percent of GDP.

Bad Binges: The Curse of Commodities

Another kind of bad binge flows from the well-known "curse" of natural resources. Most emerging countries that invest heavily in the production of raw materials are unable to grow rapidly for any long stretch of time, whether it is Nigeria in oil, Brazil in soybeans, or South Africa in gold. No other investment target inspires such consistently high hopes and deep disappointments. And so far in the 2010s, nearly one-third of all global investment has flowed into commodity industries, a level similar to the one-third share that went into technology during the dot-com craze of the late 1990s. Between 2005 and 2014, there was a 600 percent increase in the capital expenditures for oil and mining companies, and now these supplies are flooding the global market even as demand in China and other countries continues to slow. By 2015, it has become clear that this binge is going to end in tears.

To demonstrate the self-defeating pattern of commodity investment binges, I looked at the growth in the average real income of eighteen large oil-exporting nations since the year they started producing oil. Income in twelve of the eighteen countries has fallen when compared with average U.S. income. In one country—Syria—the average income has remained stuck at 9 percent of the U.S. average, exactly the same as when it started producing oil in 1968 and incomes are now collapsing with the outbreak of civil war. Three others—Ecuador, Colombia, and Tunisia—have seen only marginal relative gains. In short, the average income has stagnated or fallen behind in 90 percent of these oil-rich countries. The discovery of oil has stunted development, which is why it has come to be seen as a curse.

The way the curse works is that the production of oil sets off a scramble among elites to secure shares of the profits rather than invest to build roads, power plants and factories. In oil-exporting countries, the leadership becomes decreasingly reliant on revenue from taxpayers, then less inclined to listen to them as voters; instead it quiets their rumblings by spending a part of its oil revenue on subsidized gas, cheap food, and other unproductive freebies. Meanwhile other industries suffer. Foreigners pump in money to buy the oil, which drives up the value of the currency, in turn making it difficult for local factories—what few exist—to export their goods. The oil windfall tends to undermine every local industry other than oil.

This is the classic "Dutch disease," a term inspired by the collapse of manufacturing in the Netherlands after it discovered North Sea oil in 1959. Despite the developed-world origins of the term, the affliction has hit poor countries hardest. Over the past decade, this disease has struck in Brazil, Russia, South Africa, and much of the rest of Africa. For the most part, only countries that were reasonably well off (and well diversified) before they discovered their resource wealth, such as Norway and Canada, have invested commodity profits wisely enough to avoid seeing their development blocked by the rise and fall of commodity prices.

For richer commodity countries, the new resource is not the only source of wealth and so does not become an irresistible lure to corruption. Stronger growth follows a commodity boom if a nation manages either to save the windfall in a rainy day fund, which it can use to counter cyclical collapses in commodity prices, or to invest in industries that turn petrol into petrochemicals, or iron ore into steel, or rough diamond rocks into polished stones. Since discovering diamonds in the 1960s, Botswana managed, in partnership with the De Beers diamond company, not only to turn revenues from this coveted gem into a source of steadily rising per capita income but also to diversify into other industries. But Botswana is one of the rare exceptions to the "curse."

This highlights the limits of the widely hyped "renaissance" in Africa, where many economies grew rapidly in the last decade. Investment rose from 15 to 22 percent of GDP on average across the continent, but much of the money flowed into services and commodity industries. The economies that picked up speed, including Angola, Sierra Leone, Nigeria, Chad, and Mozambique, did so in large part due to rising prices for their most important commodity exports. To the extent that they attracted foreign investment, it came mainly from China and went largely into oil fields and coal or iron ore mines. Manufacturing shrank as a share of Africa's exports, and millions of Africans actually moved backward, out of industrial jobs and into less productive work in informal shops.

So while heavy investment in manufacturing stabilized societies such as Thailand and South Korea, heavy investment in commodities proved deeply destabilizing in an economy like Nigeria. With its 175 million people, Nigeria is the largest economy in West Africa, but it has been falling steadily behind the rest of the world since it started pumping oil in 1958. Nigeria's average income has declined from about 8 percent to about 4 percent of the U.S. average income, while tens of billions of dollars in oil wealth have disappeared into the pockets of government ministers. Former president Goodluck Jonathan was seen as a clean departure from a string of billionaire kleptocrats when he took over as president in 2010, but he proved too weak to stop the thievery. A top Nigerian bank executive told one of my colleagues that when Jonathan's successor Muhammadu Buhari took office in 2015 and tried to clean house, he sent the names of thirty-six candidates for cabinet posts to be vetted by the government's Economic and Financial Crimes Commission. The commission responded before the day was out, rejecting thirty-three of the names as corrupt.

In *The Looting Machine*, Tom Burgis details the decay, noting, for instance, that locals refer to the Power Holding Company of Nigeria, or PHCN, as "Please Have Candles Nearby." Burgis says the high cost of power is one of the main reasons that, over the last quarter-century, all but 25 of Nigeria's 175 textile mills shut down, wiping out all but 25,000 of the 350,000 manufacturing jobs that the mills once provided.[7] The business of making Nigeria's classic fabrics, with their bold colors and shiny finishes, has shifted mainly to China, where over the same period entrepreneurs have opened sixteen large factories devoted to producing textiles stamped "Made in Nigeria." Nigerians still favor their classic designs, but vendors on the streets of Lagos and Kaduna make no effort to conceal that most of the garments come from China, smuggled in to dodge an import ban on textiles. Burgis shows how smuggling kingpins, including a shadowy figure named Mangal, have added to the corruption of the economy.

Africa's richest man, Aliko Dangote, who has interests in everything from food processing to cement manufacturing, told me in July 2015 that in his home state of Kano in Nigeria, twenty million people get by on forty megawatts of power, which in a developed country is the standard capacity for a town of forty thousand. Without a steady supply of power, very few businesses, local or foreign, dared to invest in factories, and manufacturing today accounts for less than 5 percent of Nigeria's GDP, the fourth lowest in all Africa, right below war-torn Ethiopia.

The result is that oil economies such as Nigeria are far more vulnerable to outside shocks than are manufacturing economies. During a meeting in October 2015, the former Nigerian finance minister, Ngozi Okonjo-Iweala, told me that the nation's overdependence on one commodity, referred to as "monoculture," had long troubled Nigerian policy makers, but they just seemed unable to steer the country in a different direction. In 2015, when once again falling oil prices drained the already pilfered treasury, the central bank was forced to devalue the currency, since Nigeria had saved little of the oil windfall and had hardly any foreign exchange reserves. In a manufacturing economy like Thailand, such a move makes it easier to sell the country's manufactured exports and helps stabilize the economy. But a currency collapse in Nigeria provides no significant boost to manufacturing exports because, for the most part, they don't exist.

There is one caveat to the curse of oil, which is that commodities can be a blessing in the short term, even for less diversified countries. The long-term "miracles" are all manufacturing economies, but on my list of fifty-six countries that saw at least a decade of very rapid growth, twenty-four are commodity economies, including Brazil and Indonesia. This is not surprising. The two-hundred-year history of commodity prices is that, in inflation-adjusted terms, the average price of commodities is unchanged. Upswings tend to last for a decade but then prices drop like a rock and stay low for around two decades, taking a number of steel- or oil- or soybean-driven economies up with them, unless the leadership has taken steps to break the curse.

Consider the roller-coaster trajectory of Saudi Arabia, where average income doubled to $20,000 as oil prices shot up in the 1970s and early '80s, but halved to $10,000 as oil prices retreated in the 1990s, then more than doubled in the next decade to $25,000 as oil prices resumed their climb. When oil prices plateaued in the early 2010s and then fell sharply in 2014, so did average Saudi incomes. Brazil, Argentina, Colombia, Nigeria, and Peru have experienced a very similar ride since 1960, seeing their average incomes rise and fall with prices for their main commodity exports. Now they may face another period of stagnation. Based on the historical pattern, in which commodity prices tend to rise for a decade then fall for two, the fact that prices started to falter in 2011 suggests that commodity economies now face another extended period of stagnation.

If manufacturing binges tend to fuel other good binges, in infrastructure or technology, commodity investment binges tend to fuel equally bad binges in commercial or residential real estate. This makes it all the more important to look under the hood of any investment binge, to see where the money is going. I lost track of this point during the recent boom in the Andean region, where over the last decade investment was rising steadily to 27 percent of GDP in Peru, and 25 percent in Colombia by 2013. This put both countries right in the investment sweet spot, a rare success particularly given that after 2008 investment was shrinking in much of the world.

But in fact, large swaths of the investment were going to commodity projects—oil in Colombia, copper and gold in Peru—and into real estate projects inspired by optimistic forecasts for the prices of oil, copper, and gold. When those commodity prices faltered one by one, the price drop threatened to lead to cancellations and delays of the new investment projects and the associated real estate developments. By 2014, home price increases were decelerating sharply in Colombia.

There is one case in which a commodity investment can qualify as a good binge, and that is when the investment uses new technology for extracting the commodity from the ground. The most recent example is the oil and gas binge in the United States, inspired by the new technology for drawing these energy sources from shale rock. In 2015, as the oil price has fallen below $50, many of the new shale companies can no longer make a go of it and are going bust. That has led to the loss of tens of thousands of jobs in the shale boomtowns of Canada and the American

Midwest and sent tremors through the junk bond markets, which had been major supporters of the shale investment boom.

But if the value of a binge is measured by what it leaves behind, this one left behind a brand-new industry that had put pressure on older players to lower oil prices, providing cheap energy that made the U.S. economy much more competitive. The industry took advantage of record low interest rates by ramping up debt and spending around a third of a trillion dollars on drilling new wells, digging twenty thousand in just the last five years, and multiplying the number of rigs operating in the United States eightfold to sixteen hundred. It built a reservoir of new expertise that rapidly improved the ability of these rigs to fracture shale and extract oil from the fragments, and the technology spread as far as Australia. In 2015 many of the U.S. rigs have gone idle, but they are still there, ready for when demand returns and they are needed again. Just as the dot-com era investment in fiber optics and other technologies did a decade earlier, the shale bubble has created a new and valuable industrial infrastructure that can be used long after the boom is over.

When Good Binges Go Bad

When investment rises steadily as a share of GDP for many years, it often begins to shift from good targets to bad ones. In the late stages of a good boom, the number of opportunities to invest in high-return factories or technologies will diminish before the optimism does. That's when people turn to investing or speculating in houses, in stocks, or in commodities like oil and gold, and the binge starts to go bad.

This general decay of good investment trends into bad ones has led to many a real estate bubble, including those that popped across Europe and the United States in the 2000s and the one that threatens China in the mid-2010s. While the U.S. housing collapse helped trigger the global financial crisis, China's bubble was by many measures more severe, and the spectacle of good money chasing bad was just as clear. Investment in real estate rose from 6 percent of China's GDP in 2008 to 10 percent five years later, and by 2013, the price of land in China had risen 500 percent since 2000. In major cities, prices for preowned homes were rising much faster than average incomes, feeding middle-class resentment of those who could afford a house and creating a disillusioned generation of involuntary bachelors whose inability to buy a home rendered them unsuitable in the eyes of potential brides.

China faced the flammable double threat of bubbles in credit and investment, two cycles that often move in tandem. Since investments are often funded by borrowed money, a rapid expansion in credit often accompanies a healthy pace of growth in investment, and a turn for the worse hits both at the same time. China's investments were deteriorating on both counts in the 2010s, with more of the financing coming from debt, and more of the investment going to unproductive targets like real estate. By 2014, the property market had hit a rough patch, with prices falling in major cities and work coming to a halt on mega-development projects across the nation.

China's sheer size tends to produce larger-than-life tales, and the word *ghost town* fails to capture the full scale and chutzpah of its vacant megaprojects. One such project was coming up outside Tianjin, a big city about two and half hours southwest of Beijing. Tianjin's planners dreamed of building a financial district to rival New York. Called Yuji-apu, the officials boasted that it would cover an area three times larger than the Wall Street financial district, and the original sketches of the skyline included what one writer called twin towers, "uncannily similar" to those destroyed in the 9/11 terror attack. But work on this mock-up of Manhattan slowed nearly to a halt by the summer of 2014. The twin towers had dwindled to one, which stood there finished but empty and cordoned off, as did the replica of Rockefeller Center.

It is not yet clear how the China story will end, but this process of decay in the quality of a binge—from good investments in factories or roads to questionable ones in real estate megaprojects—often results in a meltdown of some kind. Thailand is a classic case, because its long record of strong investment—in the roads and factories that transformed its eastern seaboard—got derailed in the late 1990s. The optimism of the preceding boom inspired many Thais to begin borrowing heavily to buy real estate, creating a bubble that when pricked helped trigger the Asian financial crisis of 1997–98.

The same story unfolded in Malaysia, where at the peak of its boom in 1995, investment reached 43 percent of GDP, the second-highest level ever recorded in a large economy, behind only China today. Guided by the authoritarian and increasingly megalomaniacal hand of its then prime minister, Mahathir Mohamad, some of the investment proved useful in the end. The vast new international airport that Malaysia opened at the height of the Asian Financial Crisis in 1998, which was criticized as another example of vainglorious overspending, is no longer too big for current demand. But much of the investment unleashed by Mahathir went into grand visions—including a new tech city called Cyberjaya, and a new government administrative district called Putrajaya—that were in the end just unnecessary real estate projects. Built on the outskirts of Kuala Lumpur, the capital, Putrajaya featured a prime ministerial palace designed to be Islam's answer to Versailles. Twenty years on, that new city is home to just a quarter of the 320,000 people it was originally designed to house. Binges motivated by nationalist or personal pride rarely pan out quite the way they are planned.

The Opposite of a Binge Is the Blahs

Of course, the worst-case scenario is little investment growth. If investment is way too low as a share of GDP—around 20 percent or less—and stays low for a long period, it is likely to leave the economy full of potholes and other glaring gaps. During the global boom of the last decade, money was pouring into emerging countries, and many, including India and Egypt, used the funds to invest in new or expanded airports, which made the old ones stand out even more. The dilapidated state of the airports in Kuwait City and Nairobi were symptomatic of the investment malaise in Kuwait and Kenya, but the most striking case was Brazil.

There most airports are relics of the 1950s and '60s, resembling long sheds lining a runway. I have had to allow three hours to reach Guarulhos International Airport in São Paulo from the city center and another two hours to check in. Yet Guarulhos languished untouched through the investment boom of the 2000s before a new terminal finally became functional just a few days in advance of the soccer World Cup in June of 2014.

The damage inflicted by weak investment is the opposite of the damaged one by binges—a story not of excess but of stagnation and errors of omission. Countries that invest too little leave roads unpaved, schools unbuilt, the police ill-equipped, and factories suspended in the blueprint stage. That is true today even in some promising countries, like Mexico and the Philippines. But at least those two nations have active plans to pump up investment. The situation is most dire in countries where investment is under 20 percent of GDP, and there is little sign that the government can rally the confidence or find the funding to change the situation. That is the predicament of Russia, Brazil, and South Africa.

This link between weak investment and weak growth is very clear because unfortunately it is so common. The number of success stories—countries that maintained a high rate of investment and thus generated strong GDP growth for a decade or more—is very low. The number of failures is very high, so the sample size is large enough to show an obvious pattern. In the postwar era, if the average rate of investment remained below 20 percent of GDP for a decade, the nation had a 60 percent chance of growing at a paltry rate of less than 3 percent over the course of that decade. These are the nations in which one is most likely to encounter the spectacle of citizens and businesses building private answers to public problems—artful dodges around weak public networks of roads, power lines, or communications.

In African markets including Nigeria, city dwellers often string up their own power lines to effectively steal electricity from the national grid, which simultaneously weakens the state utility and undermines the resources available to the government to set up its own power lines. Africa is now a continent where many people are connected via cell phones, even to mobile banking services, but traveling between neighboring countries via road or rail is still extremely cumbersome.

This is a symptom of weak investment, and it matters. Crippling traffic jams in the major cities are a warning that the supply network is too weak, which is very dangerous to the economy. When it rains in São Paulo or Mumbai, traffic screeches to a halt because the sewers overflow. If a nation's supply chain is built on shoddy road, rail, and sewer lines, supply cannot keep up with demand, which drives up prices. In this way, weak investment is a critical source of inflation—a cancer that has often killed growth in emerging nations.

Investment is the critical spending driver of growth, and a high and rising level of investment is more often than not a good sign. But high and rapidly rising investment can go to waste, so one has to watch carefully where the money is going. The quick rule of thumb is that the best investment binges are those that go toward manufacturing, technology, and infrastructure, including roads, power grids, and water systems. The worst binges tend to be in the property sector—which provide little enduring boost to the economy and often leave countries dangerously in debt—and in commodities, which tend to have a corrupting influence on the economy.

Although a case can be made that services will come to rival manufacturing as a catalyst for sustained growth; that day has yet to arrive. For now the rule is still factories first.

7

THE PRICE OF ONIONS

Is inflation high or low?

THE RELEASE OF A GOVERNMENT'S BUDGET IS A NONEVENT in many countries, but not in some former colonies of Britain such as India, where it is publicly dissected as an annual expression of the government's vision for the future. Back in February 2011, I was on an NDTV news show in Delhi analyzing the latest budget when my fellow guest Kaushik Basu, then the Indian government's chief economic adviser, launched into what I felt was genuinely dangerous advice. At a time when the rising prices of onions and other food items had become a flammable political issue, Basu defended Prime Minister Manmohan Singh by saying that India shouldn't fuss too much about inflation, because rapidly rising prices are perfectly normal for a young and fast-growing economy. When I called this out as one of the biggest myths in economics because most long booms have in fact been accompanied by low inflation, Basu shot back that fast-growing economies like South Korea and China started out with high inflation. Before we could go on our host, the legendary Prannoy Roy, stepped in to suggest we wrestle over the price of onions outside of prime time.

Afterward I could not help but think of the American senator Daniel Patrick Moynihan, also a former ambassador to India, who once had quipped that there are some mistakes only a Ph.D. can make. In India, where the top ranks of policy makers groan with economic doctorates—Singh has one from Oxford, and Basu has one from the London School of Economics—I have often heard that high inflation is to be expected in a developing economy. The thinking is that when a young economy is growing fast, its people will have more money to spend, and with more money chasing the available goods, prices will rise.

This view follows from the standard classroom lessons, which teach that consumer price inflation can be driven by positive demand shocks such as consumer euphoria or excessive government spending, or by negative supply shocks like a sudden rise in oil prices. In practice, however, a young economy is most vulnerable to demand-driven inflation when if it has invested too little in its supply networks. The supply network includes everything from power plants and factories to warehouses, and the communication and transport systems that connect them to consumers. If these supply channels fall short of meeting demand, consumer prices start rising.

High inflation is always a bad sign, and low inflation is often a good sign. In general, an economy is in a sweet spot when inflation is low and GDP growth is high, especially when growth has recently started to take off—because the absence of inflationary pressures may suggest it is the beginning of a long run. If GDP growth is picking up but inflation is rising with it, the boom can't last long because at some point—sooner rather than later—the central bank will have to respond by raising interest rates, in order to dampen demand and subdue inflation. This increase in borrowing costs may also choke off growth. The worst case, however, is high inflation with low or falling growth, because in these conditions the central bank will still have to raise rates to control inflation, effectively putting the brakes on an economy already at risk of stalling. This can lead to stagflation, an extended period of low growth and high inflation.

The question to keep in mind: Is inflation high or low? And one way you can tell whether consumer price inflation is high or low is by comparing the rate in any one country to the recent average for its peer group. As of 2015, the recent average for emerging countries is about 6 percent, and the average for developed countries is about 2 percent.

Between 2009 and 2014, India's well-credentialed political elite had reason to explain away the ominous signs of inflation because the rising price of essential food items such as onions was threatening to end their political careers. Singh's government was in its second five-year term, with prices rising at an average pace of about 10 percent, one of the worst bouts of inflation in India's postindependence history. For decades, India had not ranked particularly poorly on the list of nations with the highest inflation rates, typically finishing each decade with an average ranking somewhere between 60 and 65 out of the 153 emerging nations for which data is available. But in Singh's last five years, India's inflation rate was running twice as high as the emerging-world average, and its ranking had fallen from the low 60s to 144th, right between Timor-Leste and Sierra Leone. Though Basu had insisted during our TV discussion that Singh was handling the inflation challenge "very sophisticatedly," this ranking did not put India in very sophisticated company, and it raised obvious risks both for the economy and for the government.

Rulers have often been toppled when the poor rose up against high prices for food. One of the seminal events that ended British rule in India was Gandhi's Salt March against imperial taxes that were driving up the price of that staple seasoning. In a poor country such as India, basics like salt and onions are pillars of national identity, ingredients without which comfort meals, including daal and kebabs, would "lose their self-respect," as the essayist Nilanjana Roy once put it. Large price increases for onions, ghee (Indian butter), and potatoes also contributed mightily to national parliamentary election defeats for the long-dominant Congress Party in 1989 and 1996. Singh and his advisers were themselves haunted by what Roy called "the ghost of the Great Onion Crisis of 2010," when onion prices doubled in a week and forced the government to ban onion exports—and to start importing from India's archrival Pakistan.

Yet technocrats like Singh by nature operate in partial isolation from any groundswell of public opinion, and he failed to comprehend the degree of public anger. In December 2013 I set out with a group of friends in Indian journalism to track election campaigns in the Indian states of Madhya Pradesh and Rajasthan. In the multihued states of India, it is unusual to find two that share an opinion, but this time we were surprised to hear the same chorus everywhere. From the badlands of Bhind in northern Madhya Pradesh to the colorful bazaars of Pushkar in central Rajasthan, the neighborhood barber, the local carpenter, and the small farmer would angrily reel off to the exact rupee the increase in prices for potatoes, ghee, and, yes, onions over the last five years. Talk of inflation trumped other pressing issues, such as corruption and unemployment. In their speeches, politicians from the opposition parties would quip that there was a time when you could go to the market with a pocketful of cash and return with a bagful of goods, but now you would need a bagful of cash to buy just a pocketful of goods. The ruling Congress Party not only lost those state elections but also suffered a landslide defeat six months later in the national elections. The polls showed that inflation played a major role in its downfall.

When Basu, who is now chief economist at the World Bank, jousted with me on TV in 2011, he had cited the opposite risks. His main concern was fighting too hard in the battle against consumer price inflation, because that would require government spending restraint and tighter money, which if overdone would lead to the shuttering of factories and the loss of jobs. Responding to my suggestion that long, healthy booms were always accompanied by low inflation, he had tossed out the case of China in the late 1970s, when its long boom was in its infancy and inflation was running at around 25 percent, and of South Korea in the late 1960s and '70s, when inflation and growth were both running hot. To check my instinct that this argument misinterprets the basic link between inflation and high growth, I went back and examined the historical record.

The Cancer That Kills Growth

I found that in the postwar era, low inflation has been a hallmark of every long run of strong economic growth. Nations that post long runs of strong growth are almost always investing a large share of their national income, and that investment creates the strong supply networks that keep inflation low. China, Japan, South Korea, and indeed all the Asian miracles followed this model: Heavy investment drove economic growth while inflation was kept in check. On my list of the fifty-six nations that, since 1960, have posted runs of GDP growth faster than 6 percent for at least a decade, nearly three out of four had inflation rates lower than the emerging-world average over the course of their runs. This pattern held even in less celebrated booms like Kenya's in the 1970s and '80s or Romania's between 1971 and 1984, when inflation averaged just over 2 percent, or 18 percentage points below the emerging-world average during that period.

The miracle economies like South Korea, Taiwan, Singapore, and China, which saw booms lasting three decades or more, rarely saw inflation accelerate to a pace faster than the emerging-world average. Singapore's boom lasted from 1961 to 2002, and during that period inflation averaged less than 3 percent, while inflation in the emerging world averaged more than 40 percent. Although in some of the Asian miracle economies inflation was high at the start of the boom, it fell during the course of the boom. Moreover, one of the signs heralding the end of these booms was a flare-up in inflation, like sparks from a sputtering engine. In China, the double-digit GDP growth of the last thirty years was accompanied by an average inflation rate of around 5 percent, including an average rate of around 2 percent over the decade ending in 2010. China saw a brief surge in inflation in 2011, and economic growth in the People's Republic has been slumping steadily since then.

A high rate of inflation is a cancer that kills growth, attacking the living organism of the economy through several channels. Inflation discourages savings, because it erodes the value of money sitting in the bank or in bonds, in turn shrinking the pool of money available to invest. Eventually, high inflation will force the central bank to take action by increasing the price of money through higher interest rates, which will make it more expensive for businesses to expand and for consumers to buy homes and cars; as a result, the growth boom will stall. When inflation is very high—say, in the double digits—it also tends to be volatile, dropping suddenly or accelerating into hyperinflation, adding new hurdles to growth in the economy. In an environment where prices are prone to wild swings, businesses find it difficult to get financing for their projects and also can't be confident of the likely return on their investments. If businesses are afraid to build new supply networks or improve old ones, those networks continue to fall short of meeting demand, which keeps driving up prices. The economy then becomes permanently inflation prone.

A classic case of an inflation-prone economy is Brazil, where investment has stagnated for decades at around 20 percent of GDP, a level way below the sweet spot (of 25 to 35 percent) for an emerging country. The government has consistently invested too little in everything from roads to schools to airports. Whenever economic activity starts to pick up, companies quickly face supply bottlenecks. They begin competing for access to the limited supply of transport, communication, and other services and to secure limited supplies of plywood, cement, and other materials. Hotel owners have to compete even for well-trained cleaning staff. Due to the lack of supply to meet demand, prices and wages begin to rise at a very early stage in the economic cycle. Since Brazilians are accustomed to this pattern, they are conditioned to expect large price increases in a recovery, and the workers are quick to demand higher wages.

This is the opposite of what happens in an economy headed for a long boom. The thirteen best-known postwar miracle economies were typically investing the equivalent of 30 percent of GDP every year during their long booms, and high growth was accompanied by low inflation. This combination made it possible for these countries to sustain their booms for two or more decades. In China, where investment peaked at close to 50 percent of GDP, and much of it was until recently flowing into new roads, phone networks, and factories, it is still almost impossible to hit the limits of the supply network. When China's economy starts to pick up, businesses can simply put half-idle factories and empty roads back on a full schedule. The supply network is more than capable of meeting consumer demand, so there is no upward pressure on prices.

The contrast between China and Brazil is striking. Though both China and Brazil face growing consumer demand from a rising middle class, China's extensive and, in many cases, overbuilt supply networks made it possible, for much of the past three decades, for the economy to grow at 10 percent without triggering inflation. In Brazil, inflation is a problem at a GDP growth rate of 4 percent or even less, which forces the central bank to increase interest rates and restrain economic growth. For all its progress in pulling people up into the middle class, Brazil has inadvertently built a disappointing low-growth, high-inflation economy—the opposite of China's high-growth, low-inflation miracle economy of recent decades.

Victory in the War on Inflation

The general rule—high consumer price inflation is a bad sign—is particularly useful for spotting outliers in a world where most countries have won the war on inflation. In the 1970s the OPEC embargo sent oil prices skyrocketing. Food prices rose sharply too. As workers came to expect spiking prices at the gas pump and grocery store, they began demanding regular wage hikes to meet their basic needs, which pushed companies to hike prices for all kinds of consumer goods. The vicious "wage-price" spiral began, driving the inflation rate into the double digits in rich countries like the United States, and stagflation set in.

Many Americans will remember how President Gerald Ford tried to talk his countrymen out of this inflationary mindset by urging them, through his widely lampooned lapel buttons, to "WIN" or Whip Inflation Now. But they will also remember how Washington did ultimately whip double-digit inflation, owing to the neck-snapping interest rate hikes imposed by Fed chief Paul Volcker in the early 1980s (a move that was nearly matched at the time by the Bank of England). The U.S. economy fell into a painful recession, but this turned out to be a small price to pay, because it led to a long period of strong growth with little or no inflation.

Ultimately, the great majority of countries won the victory over runaway inflation. In developed nations, according to the IMF, the average annual rate of consumer price inflation peaked at more than 15 percent in 1974 and more than 12 percent in 1981, before falling sharply over the course of the following decade. Since 1991 it has averaged around 2 percent.

The rapid calming of consumer prices was even more transformative in the emerging world, where the average annual inflation rate peaked at a staggering 87 percent in 1994, a year when nations like Brazil, Russia, and Turkey had inflation rates well into the triple digits. Then the emerging-world average began dropping steadily, to 20 percent in 1996 and about 6 percent in 2002. It has hovered around 6 percent ever since.

It's hard to overstate what beating consumer price inflation can do for political and economic stability. There is never one cause of a social revolt, but food prices in particular have played a role in many. Though the revolutions of 1848 are often attributed to the spread of democratic ideas in Europe, recent research has argued that the main catalyst was a spike in food prices, which led to the emergence of more liberal regimes in what are now Germany, Austria, Hungary, and Romania.[1] In more recent decades Latin America has been a cauldron of inflation-driven regime change. Between 1946 and 1983 in Latin America, according to Martin Paldam, of the Aarhus University in Denmark, there were 15 cases in which a civilian government fell to the military (or vice versa).

In thirteen of these cases the government's collapse was preceded by a surge in consumer price inflation to 20 percent or more.[2] These regime changes hit countries from Mexico to Chile and Brazil to Argentina and Paraguay. Rising prices for wheat and other grains also contributed to the 1989 fall of the Communist regime in the Soviet Union.

After the 1990s as inflation fell in most emerging nations, it continued to flare up here and there, often with crippling consequences for the powers that be. The University of Minnesota economist Marc Bellemare has found a strong link between prices of grain, cereals, and other foods and the incidence of protests, riots, and strikes in many areas of the world between 1990 and 2011.[3] Inflation helped topple regimes in Brazil and Turkey in the late 1990s, and it was one of the forces that led to the collapse of the Yeltsin government in Russia: Consumer prices were rising at an annual pace of 36 percent during his last year in power, 1999. In 2008 the World Bank president Robert Zoellick noted that world food prices had risen 80 percent over the previous three years, and he warned that at least thirty-three countries faced a heightened risk of social unrest as a result.[4] Though the protest didn't appear immediately, food prices were widely seen as a major driver of the demonstrations and revolts that broke out worldwide in 2011, including the Arab Spring.

The widespread victory over consumer price inflation has only made inflation more useful in spotting dysfunctional economies. A world of inflation-driven price chaos and uncertainty has given way to an inflation-flattened world in which the outliers are easily exposed. Today any country stands out when its consumer price inflation rate is running significantly hotter than its peers. In the emerging world, with inflation running at an average rate of around 6 percent, the major outliers in 2015 are Argentina at 30 percent, Russia at 16 percent, Nigeria at 9 percent, and Turkey at 8 percent. In the developed world, however, with inflation running around 2 percent and dipping lower as the year wore on, the situation was very different. There the fear was not inflation but its opposite, deflation or falling prices, which also can have drawbacks.

How Victory Was Won, and Sustained

Before turning to deflation, it's worth examining how the war on inflation was won, because the weapons used in that victory remain vital to
preventing its return.

In part, the victory was a product of opening to global trade. In the
1980s, the '90s, and deep into the 2000s, booming global trade fueled
explosive growth in international transport, communication, and financial networks. Starting in 1980, the share of imports and exports in
global GDP rose steadily from 35 to 60 percent in 2008, when it stopped
growing and even retreated a bit due to the shock of the financial crisis.
Still, we live in a much more globalized world than we did before 2008,
and the integration of cheap labor from China and other big emerging
nations continues to put heavy downward pressure on both wages and
consumer prices around the world. It is now difficult for local prices to
rise quickly, because if they do, local wholesalers are no longer yoked
to local suppliers. They can shop around overseas for cheaper suppliers
of clothes or hammers or TV sets. For similar reasons, it is difficult for
local wages to soar because producers can shut factories at home and
contract production out to countries with lower wages. These are market forces, largely beyond the control of political leaders.

National leaders did, however, get a few things right. In the late
1990s and 2000s, a new generation of leaders brought a new ethos of
government spending responsibility and accountability to the emerging world. They began investing more wisely, including in supply networks, and stealing less. They also granted central banks more political
independence, which they need to fend off easy-money populists. This
movement got little public notice or support. There were no public
movements to "Free the Central Banks!" Yet no single act could have
done more to control basic prices for the man on the street. And now
central bank independence has become an important measure of a
national commitment to containing inflation.

For much of the postwar era, in the political battles over central banks and easy money, the cause of fighting inflation often lost. Even in many emerging countries where the central bank was nominally independent—and the central bankers well understood the threat of inflation—they were not independent enough to resist public or private political pressure to keep interest rates and borrowing costs low. But the crises of the 1970s showed political leaders how painful inflation can be, particularly for poor- and middle-class voters, who are hit hardest by rising prices for basic staples. Those crises turned many politicians into anti-inflation warriors.

The global revolution that freed central banks to target inflation began in tiny New Zealand. As described by the journalist Neil Irwin, it was triggered by a kiwi fruit farmer turned central banker named Don Brash, who had seen his uncle's life savings wiped out by inflation in the 1970s and '80s. New Zealand passed a law in 1989 granting its central bank independence from the political process and directing it to set a target for inflation. Unions screamed that the move could destroy jobs if large businesses were not able to borrow at cheap rates. Manufacturers called it "undemocratic." One real estate developer demanded to know Brash's weight so he could test a rope to hang him on. But the measure passed. New Zealand's central bank became the first in the world to explicitly declare that fighting inflation would be its number-one priority, and within two years its inflation rate fell from near 8 percent to 2 percent.[5]

Inflation targets are effective if the central bank manages to prove to the public that it is serious—that it is prepared to increase the price of money and induce the pain necessary to control inflation. This proof has the effect of anchoring inflation expectations, meaning that people no longer fear prices will spiral out of control, so businesses can plan for the future and workers don't feel compelled to demand high wage raises, just to keep up with rising consumer prices. This is the confidence Brash inspired.

This success story quickly spread in central banking circles. Canada was next to adopt an inflation targeting strategy, in 1991, followed by Sweden and Britain. Many of the central banks chose a 2 percent target to allow for some flexibility even though genuine price stability would imply zero inflation. Citigroup estimates that fifty-eight countries (including the Eurozone members as one country) accounting for 92 percent of global GDP now have some sort of an inflation target. The qualification "some sort" is meant to cover banks like the U.S. Federal Reserve, which has a dual mandate to target both stable prices and maximum employment.

When I began my career in the mid-1990s, I was struck early on by how quickly central bankers in the emerging world had come to embrace the new anti-inflation gospel. Having seen the damage inflation did to their own countries in the prior two decades, and the recent success of Volcker's anti-inflation fight in the United States, they found religion. Meetings with them were intense affairs, and one dared not venture any levity in the presence of central bankers like Henrique Meirelles of Brazil or Guillermo Ortiz Martínez of Mexico, for the same reason that one suppresses giggles in the pew. Many of these leaders had the zeal of converts. South Africa's Tito Mboweni had been a left-wing radical with posters of Lenin on his office wall, but as a central banker, he became a conservative anti-inflation hawk, preaching the virtues of sound money even when faced with angry attacks from the left wing of his own party, the ruling African National Congress. After all the suffering inflation had caused, there was really no other way for a central banker to think.

Many of them had studied at universities in the United States during the decades when inflation was an area of intense research. India's C. Rangarajan went to the University of Pennsylvania, as had the most impressively stolid figure of this generation, Zeti Akhtar Aziz, who is still in charge of Malaysia's Bank Negara. Many central bankers were inspired by Volcker's victory and also spoke with awe of the long inflation-fighting record of postwar Germany's Bundesbank. If the pressure to match that victory made them dour, it also gave them a sense of belonging to a guardian priesthood, standing between the public and the ravages of rising prices. They all believed that a low and stable inflation rate was the best foundation for growth and that there was no trade-off between inflation and growth in the long term. Former Malaysian central bank governor Jaffer Hussein told me before the Asian financial crisis in 1997, "Good bankers, like good tea, are best appreciated when they are in hot water."

Chile was the pioneer of inflation targeting among the emerging nations, adopting a target in 1991. Many of its peers, including Brazil, Turkey, Russia, and South Korea, would follow, and though rising global competition and other factors clearly played a major role, targeting inflation helped the emerging world beat it. After Mexico adopted a target in 2001, the inflation rate went down from an average of 20 percent to around 4 percent. Indonesia's has come down from 14 percent to about 5 percent since it adopted its target in 2005. Even in Brazil, where inflation was running at an average rate of more than 700 percent in the decade before the central bank adopted a target in 1999, it had fallen to 4 percent by 2006.

This struggle is far from over, however. Though most central banks in major countries have adopted an inflation target, and many in the emerging world have been granted legal "independence," that freedom is not always honored in practice. The world's central bankers and finance ministers meet every year at an IMF-sponsored summit, and at the 2015 gathering in Lima, Peru, the hallway chatter was full of complaints from emerging-world central bankers about political interference. This came as something of a surprise to bank officials from South Africa, because they don't suffer from this kind of pressure themselves. Central bank watchers count South Africa as having one of the few central banks in the emerging world that exercises genuine independence, along with those in Chile, Poland, the Czech Republic, and perhaps a few others. The rest operate in a gray area. Most are officially committed to target inflation yet are still informally obliged to answer the phone when the president's office calls asking for easy money.

How Turkey Won the War, for a While

The war on inflation played out in different ways in different countries, but the onset of inflation in the emerging world derived from a common set of pathologies. These cases are worth a closer look, because they illustrate how leaders who don't understand basic economics, coupled with states that meddle too much and invest too little, can inadvertently nurture inflation.

One of the more dramatic examples comes from Turkey, where these flaws combined to push the inflation rate up to high double digits before the economy collapsed in 2001. Before that crisis, inflation was all but baked into the Turkish political and economic system. Parliament had been dominated for decades by shifting coalitions of secular parties, opposed by even weaker and more fragile coalitions of Islamist parties. Religious or not, all these parties shared a penchant for populist spending promises. At election time, they would vie to one-up each other in guaranteeing voters more government jobs or more generous subsidies. At one giddy point in the early 1990s, a candidate promised every Turkish family "two keys for every household"—one for a house and one for a car.

To promote a sense of security in a nation that was both on the front line of the cold war contest between the United States and Russia, and engaged in a bitter dispute with Greece over control of Cyprus, these populists increased military spending to more than 5 percent of GDP by 1975. Turkey was the poorest country in NATO but one of its heaviest military spenders. The leadership also embarked on a series of building schemes that were more grandiose than productive, including the Southeastern Anatolia Project, a network of dams and canals that was started in the 1970s and hasn't been completed despite an expenditure of some $30 billion to date.

These aren't the efficient investments that help a country grow with low inflation, and many politicians would pay the price at the polls. By the 1990s, Turkey was averaging one new government every nine months. The instability of these wobbly regimes was in turn a major contributor to an inflation-prone economy. Though unions were weakening steadily in the 1980s and '90s, wages were rising rapidly as each new government promised not only more state jobs but also retroactive raises for those who already held state jobs.

To pay for government spending on fat wages, grand projects, and guns, the state turned to its own banks and companies. Turkey's central bank was printing money to lend to the government, which was ordering state banks to lend to bloated state companies, which would inflate prices (outside of election seasons, of course) in order to raise revenue to help cover the government's mounting debts. The government's heavy borrowing and high inflation made it difficult for private companies to get long-term financing—even though many private conglomerates also ran their own banks.

In this uncertain environment, bankers raised interest rates into the triple digits, a level that would normally discourage borrowing and rein in inflation. But in Turkey, sky-high rates had the opposite effect: Companies found they could raise prices to pay back the rising interest on their existing loans. The country's inflation rate averaged 75 percent in the 1980s, 50 percent in the 1990s, and as the crisis of 2001 peaked that February, inflation hit 70 percent. The Turkish lira lost almost half its value overnight. Turkey was in the grips of a vicious cycle in which rising inflation would undercut the value of the lira, making imports more expensive and further driving up both prices and expectations of inflation.

As money fled the country, Turkey had to seek an emergency loan from the IMF, which demanded reform. To comply, the government brought in a new economic team under the former World Bank staffer Kemal Derviş, who began a major overhaul. The central bank was made officially independent, insulating it from political pressure to fund government spending sprees. A bank regulator was established to restrain insider lending practices. The government also shut many of the shakiest banks and injected new capital equal to 30 percent of GDP into the survivors to stabilize their books. State companies, which had been setting prices based on what the government needed to fund its deficit, were sold off to private entrepreneurs, who began setting prices based on market demand. To take payroll decisions away from politicians, councils were created that brought together business and labor to negotiate fair job and wage increases. To everyone's surprise, the councils worked.

Inflation began to ease by the time national elections were held in 2002, but weary Turks took the opportunity to toss out the secular parties that had dominated politics since World War I and usher in the moderate Islamist leader Recep Tayyip Erdoğan. He had just seen inflation topple his predecessor and seemed to recognize that rising prices could kill his regime too. He moved aggressively to rein in state spending: The government deficit, which amounted to about 14 percent of GDP when he took office, fell steadily to a low of 1 percent of GDP in 2011. Continuing the work of his predecessor, Erdoğan sold off more state-owned firms, including telecommunications, sugar, and tobacco companies. By 2004, inflation was in single digits for the first time in thirty years, and the newly stable economy was at the start of a boom that would nearly triple the average income of Turks to $10,500 by 2012. Once again a long run of strong growth was accompanied by a gradual fall in inflation, which bottomed out at 4 percent in 2011.

Then, true to the normal pattern, decay set in. In 2011 Erdoğan won a third term in a landslide victory and showed signs of getting complacent about the economy. Reform stalled, and investment in Turkey slowed. In his early years, the sale of Turkish state companies had attracted foreign investors, and the sharp fall in inflation and interest rates had encouraged Turks to increase their investments at home. But investment was still running at less than 20 percent of GDP, and as Erdoğan got complacent, the quality of public investments took a turn for the worse. His government started investing heavily in new megaprojects, many with an increasingly religious tilt and no clear payoff to the economy. The government's budget deficit widened again, tripling to more than 2 percent of GDP by 2014. And from a low of 4 percent in 2011, the average annual inflation rate doubled to 8 percent over the next four years, well above the emerging-world average and a clear sign of trouble for the economy.

India Belatedly Joins the Fight

India was the only big country suffering from double-digit inflation in the five years after the 2008 global financial crisis, an outbreak that says a lot about what went wrong under then prime minister Manmohan Singh.

Singh took office in 2004, and over the next ten years India's investment rate rose from about 25 percent to more than 35 percent of GDP. That should have been a good sign, but it fed a false sense of confidence among the country's economic elite. Now that India was investing heavily, like China, many leading Indians figured they were also building the next high-growth, low-inflation economy. This rosy vision of India as the next China did seem plausible before 2008, when India's GDP growth was running at 9 percent, with inflation contained at around 5 percent. During most of Singh's first term, inflation was very well behaved.

The second term, starting in 2009, was different. Trying to prevent the economy from slowing as the global financial crisis spread, the Singh government raised public spending at an unsustainable annual pace of 18 percent over the next five years. Increases in investment were mainly driven by the government, which was meddling in increasingly clumsy ways. Private companies were investing less and less, due to growing fears of corruption and increasing uncertainty about the rules of play. Between 2011 and 2013 private investment fell by 4 percentage points to 22 percent of GDP, a drop that would amount to more than $72 billion a year.

State bureaucrats were interfering more not only at the central bank but by issuing new rules one day only to dilute or rewrite them the next. In one particularly striking case, after losing a legal battle to collect tax from the British telecom giant Vodafone for its purchase of a Dutch company with a subsidiary in India, the Singh government in its pique pushed through a law saying that any company, foreign or domestic, would be liable for tax on any purchase of companies with assets on Indian soil—and that this tax would apply to any purchase going back to 1961. The resulting hullaballoo forced the government to back down, but that reversal only left potential investors more unsure about the predictability of the government's next moves.

Rather than investing in ways to help contain inflation, India was spending in ways that made its economy exceptionally vulnerable to inflation. Trying to protect people from the effects of the global downturn, it threw money at populist schemes that tend to push up both wages and prices, including an expensive scheme to guarantee at least one hundred days of paid work to every poor rural household, and another to bolster farmers' incomes by buying wheat and rice at artificially high prices. These programs encouraged Indians to stay in their villages rather than move to factory jobs in the cities, making the economy less productive and more vulnerable to inflation.

It did not help that India was the only major country in the world where the central bank had yet to adopt an inflation target and was still under political pressure to keep interest rates low.

Though India was hoping to be the next China, its government was building another Brazil, a low-growth, high-inflation economy. Between 2009 and 2013 India's key economic numbers flipped for the worse: GDP growth fell by nearly half, to 5 percent, and inflation doubled to 10 percent. As Indian workers came to expect higher prices, they demanded higher wages, and the central bank began to issue open warnings about the threat of a wage-price spiral.

This is a particularly dangerous cycle. Once the spiral begins, it is likely to spin for a few years before the central bank can contain it. Fortunately for India, it got a new central bank chief in 2013, Raghuram Rajan, who immediately made clear he understood that fighting inflation was the bank's top priority. And then in 2014, it got a new prime minister who, despite the populist pressure for the central bank to cut interest rates, seemed to back Rajan's plan to move cautiously with an eye to anchoring inflation expectations. By the next year, the threat was contained, with the plunge in global oil prices also helping India's cause.

Good and Bad Deflation

Inflation is now widely seen as an inevitable part of life, like death and taxes. But before the 1930s inflation was not the norm. According to historical records from the Global Financial Database, which go back to the thirteenth century, the global average annual inflation rate between 1210 and the 1930s was only 1 percent. At the start of this period, price records were available for only Britain and Sweden, but over time more data became available, and by the 1970s this "global" average covered 103 countries. This long-term global inflation rate is not only surprisingly low, at just 1 percent over more than seven centuries. It is even more striking for what the average conceals: sharp and frequent swings between periods of inflation and periods of falling prices, or deflation. Those swings ceased after 1933, when periods of global deflation disappeared and were replaced by an unbroken and unprecedented string of inflation that has lasted more than eighty years. In many countries, inflation has been as inevitable as death for only one lifetime. Before that, deflation was just as common.

The unshakable persistence of global inflation in the second half of the twentieth century has many explanations. The growth of the banking industry and the wider availability of credit, with consequently more money chasing the available goods, probably played a major role in driving up prices. Another is that the end of the gold standard in the 1970s made it easier for central banks to print money. The result was that, as periods of worldwide deflation disappeared after 1933, the average global inflation rate rose, peaking at 18 percent in 1974, then falling sharply over the course of the following decades to around 2 percent by 2015.

To reconstruct the path of inflation and deflation before modern record-keeping began in the twentieth century, investigators reconstruct price changes from sources as varied as government surveys, farm ledgers, doctors' office records, and even nineteenth-century sales catalogs from Sears, Roebuck and Montgomery Ward, the American department stores. The measurement of price changes likely gets a bit less accurate as researchers push the story back toward the Dark Ages, but the basic pattern of a widespread disappearance of deflation in most countries after the 1930s has been confirmed by many sources. A recent Deutsche Bank analysis of the Global Financial Database showed that before 1930, it was common for more than half of all countries in this sample to be experiencing deflation in any given year. After 1930 it was rare for even one country in ten to be experiencing deflation. And in the postwar period, only two economies have experienced an extended period of deflation—defined as one lasting at least three years. Those are the little-known case of Hong Kong—which experienced deflation for seven years, between 1998 and 2005—and the infamous case of Japan.[6]

It is the Japan case that has given deflation a particularly bad name. Japan's experience helps explain why the world took such a scare when deflation appeared to be rearing its head after the crisis of 2008. The world seemed to face a combination of deflationary threats similar to what had undone Japan, including heavy debt, which depresses consumer demand, and supply overcapacity. By 2015, with inflation falling to an average rate close to zero in the developed nations, the fear was that much of the world could fall into the kind of classic deflationary spiral that gripped Japan after its bubble burst in 1990.

When deflation sets in, prices don't just rise more slowly, they actually fall. Consumers start to delay purchases, waiting for the price of the TV or cell phone they want to become even cheaper. As consumer demand stagnates, growth slows, which adds to the downward pressure on prices. Like other Asian miracle economies, including South Korea, Japan had also overinvested at the height of the boom in the 1980s, creating an oversupply of everything—factories, office space, apartments—that had the effect of depressing price increases when growth slowed. But of the postwar miracles, only Japan fell into an extended period of outright deflation: Consumer prices fell steadily for more than two decades after the boom ended in 1990, and economic growth sputtered along at 1 percent during this period.

The bad deflationary spiral can be very hard to stop. As prices fall, people come to expect prices to fall further, and the only way for officials to get consumers to start spending again and halt the deflationary spiral is for the central banks to somehow flush enough money into the economy to persuade the public that prices and markets are going to rise again. That is what Japan's central bank struggled to achieve for years during its war on deflation.

Another reason bad deflation is so hard to stop is the effect that falling prices have on debtors. As prices fall, every dollar or yen or renminbi is effectively worth more, but the totals that debtors owe remain the same. The perverse result is that hard-pressed borrowers are forced to pay down loans in an increasingly valuable currency. As the American economist Irving Fisher put it at the height of the Great Depression, "The more debtors pay, the more they owe."[7] The deflationary spirals that struck much later in Japan and Hong Kong were similarly sustained by strong currencies and mounting debt burdens.

The problem with worrying too much about the lessons of Japan, however, is that not all deflationary cycles follow this scenario. There are plenty of cases of good deflation too. In *The Great Wave*, the Brandeis University historian David Hackett Fischer traced the records for the United States and various European countries as far back as the eleventh century and found long "waves" of time in which prices were either stable or falling, and numerous instances in which the deflationary periods were accompanied by a high rate of economic growth.[8] In these long periods of good deflation, the fall in prices was driven not by a self-reinforcing shock to consumer demand, but by a positive shock to supply.

These long periods of good deflation all date from before the 1930s, and they were driven by technological or institutional innovations that lowered the cost of producing and distributing consumer goods, driving down the price of those goods for long periods of time. Often, in fact, these bouts of good deflation have coincided with beneficial investment binges in new technologies like the steam engine, the car, or the Internet.

To cite just a few cases of good deflation: In seventeenth-century Holland, a new opening to trade and innovations in finance sparked a golden age of inflation-free growth that tripled the size of the economy over the course of that century. A similar period unfolded during the Industrial Revolution in late eighteenth- and nineteenth-century England, where technological breakthroughs such as the steam engine, railroads, and electricity were steadily lowering the costs of making everything from flour—which could now be ground in mechanized mills—to clothing. During this era, consumer prices in England fell by half, while industrial output rose sevenfold. Falling consumer prices in this era were interrupted only by heavy state spending on the Napoleonic, Crimean, and Franco-Prussian wars.

Good deflation broke out in the United States during the early 1920s, when the economy was expanding at a near 4 percent pace annually, and the invention of new labor-saving devices such as the car and the truck were driving down prices for consumer goods such as food, apparel, and home furnishings. In more recent times, though deflation in general has largely disappeared at the global and national level, there have been powerful examples of good deflation in specific industries, including in the tech sector, where the innovations coming out of Silicon Valley were by the mid-1990s reducing the prices consumers paid for increasingly powerful and mobile computing power. That too was having a restraining effect on overall consumer prices.

The takeaway here is that, while low inflation is often a good sign and high inflation is almost always a bad sign, there is no simple deflation rule. One can't say that deflation in prices for consumer products is in itself a good or bad sign. Nothing highlights this fact better than the long boom that the United States enjoyed between the late 1870s and the outbreak of World War I in 1914. During the first half of this period, deflation averaged 3 percent a year, and during the second half, inflation averaged 3 percent a year. Throughout that time GDP growth averaged a robust 3 percent a year.

Though deflation has largely vanished from the global big picture, it is still relevant because it continues to surface in isolated pockets. True, as we've seen, the postwar era has seen only one multiyear period of deflation in a large economy, Japan. It has seen no worldwide bouts of deflation lasting even a single year, as demonstrated by the Deutsche Bank study. But single-year bouts of deflation have been quite common in individual countries. And again, there is no reason to believe these brief, isolated bouts of deflation will have a negative impact on economic growth.

This was the unexpected finding of a study that the Bank for International Settlements (BIS) unveiled in early 2015, amid growing global fears of deflation and the Japan scenario. The bank looked at the experience of thirty-eight countries in the postwar period and found that long bouts of consumer price deflation were indeed rare, but short ones lasting a year were not. Put together, these thirty-eight countries had experienced more than one hundred deflationary years in total. On average, GDP growth was actually a bit higher during deflationary years, at 3.2 percent, than during inflationary years, at 2.7 percent. The years in which deflation was accompanied by strong growth occurred in countries rich and poor, from Thailand in 1970 to the Netherlands in 1987, China in 1998, Japan in 2000, and Switzerland in 2013. The slight growth advantage in deflationary years was not statistically significant, and the BIS researchers confirmed that there is no clear evidence that consumer price deflation is bad—or good—for economic growth.[9] The impact depends on what is driving deflation.

The obvious question then is: Can you tell when consumer price deflation is the good, supply-driven kind, or the bad, demand-driven kind? The honest answer is that this is an extremely difficult task, which requires parsing conflicting forces of supply and demand. The point here is simply that since deflation became a bad word, there has been a bias toward assuming that any hint of deflation is bad for the economy, and that is not borne out by historical evidence. In 2015, for example, consumer demand was weak around the world, and debts were rising in China and other emerging countries—both signs of bad deflation.

But there were also signs of good deflation. For example, one of the most important contributors to the falling inflation rate was the collapse in the price of oil, which has a ripple effect across all consumer goods. The oil price dropped from $110 a barrel in mid-2014 to $50 in early 2015, but it did so for a mix of reasons: the negative impact of slumping demand, particularly in China, but also the positive impact of the new shale oil technologies and discoveries, which suddenly revived production out of the United States. The deflationary force looming over the world included elements of both good and bad deflation. Despite the mixed signals, many voices began to argue that it was time for the world to abandon the fight against the old and clear threat of inflation in order to target the new and debatable threat of deflation.

Consumer Prices Aren't the Whole Story

This argument ignored how much the world has changed in recent decades. The old waves of inflation and deflation have been replaced in the postwar world by steady—but also increasingly contained—inflation. Consumer prices are generally less volatile than they once were, and compared to other kinds of prices, they are also relatively less important as signals of sharp turns in the economy. Today changes in asset prices, particularly prices for stocks and houses, are just as important, because there is an increasingly clear link between real estate and stock market busts and economic downturns.

The rising importance of asset prices is rooted in the recent period of rapid globalization, before 2008. As a result of rising global trade and technological progress over the last three decades, producers can shop around the world for the lowest-wage factories in which to make consumer goods. And consumers can shop around the Internet for the lowest price on everything from T-shirts to chainsaws. These forces tend to stabilize consumer prices.

But globalization has had an opposite effect on asset prices, by opening up local markets to a vastly larger pool of potential buyers from abroad. With more buyers bidding for assets such as stocks and houses, prices tend to rise and to be less stable. Today foreigners are the main owners of stocks in Korea's largest companies, including Samsung and Hyundai. And foreign buyers are one of the main drivers of escalating prices for high-end real estate in cities like Miami, New York, and London. These forces tend to destabilize asset prices and lead to more frequent boom-bust cycles, with a boom in asset prices often signaling a coming economic crash.

Every major economic shock in recent decades has been preceded by an asset bubble. Prices for housing and stocks both spiked before Japan's meltdown in 1990 and before the Asian financial crisis of 1997–98. The stock market mania of the late 1990s in the United States signaled the coming stock market crash of 2000–1, and a brief global recession followed. In the ensuing recovery, America led a booming world economy that saw prices for both houses and stocks skyrocket, until both those markets crashed again in 2008. The world economy suffered a recession then and has been struggling to recover ever since.

Often a crash in prices of houses or stocks will depress the economy, because when those asset prices fall sharply, the result is a real decline in wealth. When people feel less wealthy, they spend less, resulting in lower demand and a fall in consumer prices as well. In other words, asset price crashes can trigger bouts of bad consumer price deflation.

This is what happened in Japan, where the real estate and stock market bubbles of the 1980s collapsed in 1990 and led to the long fall in both asset and consumer prices. It is also what happened in the United States during the Roaring Twenties, when the runaway optimism of the age drove up stock prices by 250 percent between 1920 and the peak in 1929. Then the market crashed and was followed by consumer price deflation in the early years of the Great Depression.

The key question for our purposes: When do rising asset prices reach the bubble stage and start to threaten economic growth?

One rule of thumb is that the bigger the run-up in home or stock prices, the more likely a crash. History shows that many long runs of economic growth ended in a house price bust, so the real estate market is worth especially close watching. In general, if for an extended period of time home prices grow at a faster annual rate than the economy, be on the alert. In a 2011 paper looking into potential causes of the global debt crisis, the IMF studied seventy-six cases of extreme financial distress across forty countries and found several key indicators that seem to rise before these meltdowns, including home prices. While home prices typically rise by about 2 percent a year, that pace speeds up to between 10 and 12 percent in the two years before a period of financial distress. [10]

The increasingly common threat posed by real estate bubbles was dramatized in a 2015 paper by Òscar Jordà, Moritz Schularick, and Alan M. Taylor, who researched 170 years of data for seventeen countries and demonstrated how the impact of housing bubbles has grown and spread.[11] Before World War II, only seven of fifty-two recessions followed the collapse of a bubble in the stock market or the housing market. This link has tightened dramatically since World War II, with forty out of sixty-two recessions—nearly two-thirds—following on the heels of a collapse in the housing or the stock market.

The paper offered a number of benchmarks for understanding the likely fallout from these bubbles. In general, housing bubbles took longer to reach a peak than stock market bubbles, largely because stock prices are more volatile than home prices. Housing bubbles were much less common than stock price bubbles, but when they did occur, they were much more likely to be followed by a recession. And once prices for either houses or stocks rise sharply* above their long-term trend, a subsequent drop in prices of 15 percent or more signals that the economy is due to face significant pain.

---

* Defined by Jordà, Schularick, and Taylor as at least one standard deviation.

But—and this is important—that pain will be much more severe if borrowing fueled the bubble. Debt magnifies these recessions. When a recession follows a bubble that is not fueled by debt, five years later the economy will be 1 to 1.5 percent smaller than it would have been, if the bubble had never occurred. However, if the bubble is debt driven, the losses are worse. In the case of a stock market bubble fueled by debt—meaning investors were borrowing heavily to buy stock—the economy five years later will be 4 percent below its previous trend. A debt-fueled housing market bubble will have an even uglier endgame, with the economy shrinking as much as 9 percent compared with where it otherwise would have been, five years on.

The need to keep an eye on asset price inflation is particularly important in 2015, when many economists are warning that the world faced the opposite concern: Japan-style deflation. In response to the falling rate of consumer price inflation, they say, central banks including the U.S. Federal Reserve should keep interest rates at near-zero levels, to avoid falling into a deflationary spiral from which it could be very hard to escape. To skeptics, who respond that inflation is still the main threat, these economists argue—along with leading central bankers—that the glacial rise in consumer prices proves there is no inflation.

But there is an inflation risk, if one recognizes the threat of asset price inflation. Going back two hundred years, no major central bank had ever set short-term interest rates at zero, before the Fed did it in the 2000s, and other central banks around the world followed. These easy money policies fueled a wave of borrowing to buy financial assets, and today the United States is in the midst of an unusual synchronized boom in prices for the three major asset classes of stocks, bonds, and housing. The easy money advocates argue, correctly, that stock prices hit higher peaks in 2000, and home prices hit higher peaks in 2007, but this misses the bigger picture.

In the past fifty years, valuations of U.S. stocks surpassed current levels less than 10 percent of the time, and prices for bonds and housing are now at similar historic highs. A composite valuation for the three major financial assets in America—stocks, bonds, and houses—is at a fifty-year high. In short, if one considers all these markets, this bubble has reached heights well above those hit during the bubbles of 2000 and 2007, both of which led to recessions. Yet the Fed's argument back in 2000 and 2007 was the same as it is now: The absence of consumer price inflation means there is no inflation risk to the economy.

The Fed now leads a global culture of central bankers who see their job as stabilizing prices, but for consumer goods only, come what may in the asset markets. This needs to change. Today the high level of trade and money flows—compared to the early postwar period—tends to restrain consumer prices but magnify asset prices, so central banks need to take responsibility for both. It's time to recognize that sharp shifts in prices of stocks and houses can foreshadow imminent turns in the economy.

The general rule is that low consumer price inflation is an indispensable buttress of steady growth. Any period of high growth may be doomed if it is accompanied by rapidly rising inflation. High growth is far more durable if consumer prices are rising slowly or even if they are falling as the result of a positive supply shock or good deflation. However, deflation in asset prices is almost always a negative sign for the economy and is usually preceded by a rapid run-up in the price of houses and stocks. In today's globalized world, in which cross-border trade and money flows often tend to restrain consumer prices but magnify asset prices, watching the price of stocks and houses is as important as tracking the price of onions.

8

CHEAP IS GOOD

Does the country feel cheap or expensive?

Not long after the turn of the decade, when Brazil was still one of the world's most hyped economies, I started hearing stories about travelers from Rio flying into Manhattan and renting shipping containers to use as shopping bags. This extravagance was a troubling side effect of the value of the Brazilian currency, the real, which was at a forty-year high against the dollar in inflation-adjusted terms. Wealthy business people and socialites from São Paulo and Rio were coming to Manhattan to shop, see a show, and maybe buy an Upper East Side apartment for future visits; to them, in effect, anything available for purchase in New York felt as if it were on sale for a massive discount. The city's hotels were hiring Portuguese-speaking concierges in order to handle the influx of Brazilian customers. The check-in lines at New York's John F. Kennedy International Airport moved extra slowly for flights back to Rio and São Paulo, clogged by shoppers paying multiple extra fees for bags stuffed with fresh purchases. Though average incomes in the United States were still five times higher than in Brazil, the Brazilian elite felt as if they were the kings and queens of New York.

Brazil's economy had been thrown out of balance by its overpriced currency. The country is a major exporter of raw materials like iron ore and soybeans, and global prices for these commodities were rising fast in the early 2000s. The boom in commodity prices was inflating the value not only of the Brazilian real but also of currencies in other commodity-exporting nations from South Africa to Russia. Though a strong currency made Manhattan feel like one big bargain basement for traveling elites from these countries, it also made cities such as São Paulo and Moscow feel painfully expensive to visitors. They had to trade their own currencies for very expensive reals or rubles before buying anything: a cup of coffee, stock in a company, or even a factory.

This is a critical question for understanding a nation's economic prospects: Does the country feel cheap or expensive? If the country has an overpriced currency, it will encourage both locals and foreigners to move money out of the country, eventually sapping domestic economic growth. A currency that feels cheap will draw money into the economy, through exports, tourism, and other channels, boosting its growth.

This rule continues to elude many political leaders, who are quick to celebrate a strong currency as the byproduct of a strong economy, which is drawing in money from all over the world. That is true—right up to the point when the country starts attracting speculative "hot money" looking to make a quick profit from gains in the currency. Local and foreign speculators will start buying assets like stocks or bonds not because they believe in the strength of the national economy or its companies, but because they believe the rising currency will increase the value of those assets, at least temporarily. For a while this bet is a self-fulfilling prophecy, as hot money adds to upward pressure on the value of the currency. This in turn tends to undermine exports and to discourage companies from making long-term investments, which soon enough hurts the overall prospects of the economy.

The country will be poised to grow not when the currency starts falling but when it has stabilized again at a cheaper and more competitive value. In many countries, nonetheless, the tendency to equate currency strength with a bright economic future persists. These misunderstandings are not as violent as they were in the twelfth century, when King Henry I ruled England. In 1124, alarmed by the falling value of the English sterling and suspecting a conspiracy, he chose to address the problem by summoning nearly one hundred royal money changers to the palace at Winchester and, in what historian Nicholas Mayhew described as "a very public occasion designed to bolster confidence," subjected the entire lot to castration or, for the luckier ones, amputation of the right hand.[1] Today the understanding of why currencies move the way they do, and what to do about it, has advanced a bit but perhaps not as much as you might expect.

Why Cheap Is Just a Feeling

Framing the key question about a currency in terms of how cheap it "feels" may sound vague, but there is no better way to compare its value to other currencies. The process of measuring the value of currencies is much more nebulous than it appears. If it takes three Brazilian reals to buy a dollar today and four reals next year, it appears that one real is buying less and less, meaning its value is falling. But that is not necessarily the case, because that fall may be partly or fully countered by inflation. If prices are rising much faster in Brazil than in the United States, then the real will feel more and more expensive.

It is thus impossible to accurately measure the value of currencies unless you correct for relative inflation rates. The task grows even more difficult when measuring the value of the real compared not just to the currency of one trade partner but to all its trade partners, from the United States to China, and correcting for different rates of inflation in all these countries. Such a calculation is complex, and the resulting currency values can be confusing and contradictory. In the twelfth-century case prosecuted so abruptly by King Henry, the main reason for the weakness of English sterling was probably high food price inflation after a weak harvest. Unfortunately for the money changers, the king and his wise men did not understand how inflation can erode the value of a currency.

Nine centuries later we have yet to figure out a coherent way to measure the value of a currency corrected for inflation and other variables. Even the most experienced currency experts will admit that there is no consistently reliable measure. In fact, in the global foreign exchange markets, where on average over $5 trillion are traded on any given day, currency valuations don't even feature in the conversations of most traders, who often favor buying the currencies of nations with high interest rates. As one veteran analyst recently put it to my team, "In valuing currencies, nothing works."

The most common measure is the Real Effective Exchange Rate (REER), which attempts to adjust the value of a nation's currency for the rate of consumer price inflation in its major trading partners. There are also competing measures that try to adjust the value of the currency based on different measures of inflation, such as producer prices, or labor costs, or the rate of increase in per capita income, which is the basis of the particularly esoteric Balassa-Samuelson approach to valuing currencies. The minutiae of the different methods aside, the point here is that an analyst's choice of method is subjective, and the results erratic. For instance, in early 2015, as oil prices were falling sharply, the Russian ruble collapsed in value by most of these measures, except for the one that uses labor costs, which made the ruble look expensive. This is the normal state of confusion about the value of currencies.

In an effort to improve clarity, a number of expert sources have attempted to rank how expensive countries are by creating indexes, comparing current prices for things everyone can relate to. The granddaddy of this category is *The Economist's* Big Mac Index, but as McDonald's falls out of style, other analysts have started comparing prices for Starbucks coffee or other globally available goods. Deutsche Bank's annual "Mapping the World's Prices" report uses multiple categories, from the local price of the iPhone 6 and Levi's 501s to the cost of a weekend getaway, a date, and a haircut, but its conclusion still acknowledges the basic subjectivity of the exercise. Its 2015 edition concluded that with a strengthened U.S. dollar, shopping in Europe and Japan "feels a lot cheaper" than it did the year before, at least for Americans.

Getting a feel for the value of currencies is an unavoidably subjective exercise; practical people are wise to be wary of the misleadingly precise numbers that abstract models can produce. Some readers may object that the prices in any country will feel different depending on where the traveler came from. Brazil may feel less expensive to Americans paying in dollars than to Europeans paying in euros or Japanese paying in yen. That can be true at times, but in general a rising currency tends to be rising against most major currencies.

Also, in a world still dominated by the dollar, the most important perspective on any currency is how it feels relative to the dollar. Even though the United States has slipped a bit as an economic superpower—it accounts for 24 percent of global GDP, down from 34 percent in 1998—it is still the sole financial superpower. The dollar is still the world's favorite currency. One-half of the world's economic output comes from countries that use the dollar or have currencies that are closely tied to the dollar, including the Chinese renminbi. And because the Federal Reserve controls the supply of dollars it is, now more than ever, the central bank of the world. Nearly two-thirds of the world's $11 trillion of foreign exchange reserves are held in dollars, and that proportion has barely changed for decades. According to the Bank for International Settlements, 87 percent of all global financial transactions conducted through banks use the dollar on one side. That share may sound impossibly high, but it is accurate, because most global commercial deals are conducted in dollars, even if the deal does not involve an American party. A South Korean company that sells smartphones to Brazil will likely request payment in dollars, because most people still prefer to hold the world's leading reserve currency.

The subjective feel of a currency opens up the whole question of how competitive (read: cheap) the currency is to manipulation by politicians. In the early 2010s, for example, officials in Ankara were trying to make the case that the Turkish lira was very competitive by comparing the inflation-adjusted price of the currency to its price in the 1970s. However, if the starting point of this analysis was shifted to the

1990s, the price of the lira came out looking much higher—and that is certainly how it was beginning to feel to foreigners visiting Ankara or Istanbul. In the absence of an accepted standard for comparing currency values, politicians can pick a yardstick to make any case they want. Outsiders need to rely on faith that they will know an expensive currency when they feel it. The truth is that if a cup of coffee at the corner café feels overpriced, big business deals are likely to feel expensive as well.

One of the more extreme currency price shocks I ever witnessed was in Thailand in early 1998, as the Asian financial crisis was raging. The Thai baht had collapsed by 50 percent on an REER basis within a few short months. I was working in the region at the time and made several reconnaissance trips to Bangkok, where bankers and research analysts from New York and Hong Kong were emerging from the malls with armloads of stuff they bought because it felt so impossibly cheap. Armani and Ferragamo jackets worth more than a thousand dollars in New York were going for the equivalent of a couple hundred. Amateur golfers were walking the streets carrying sets of new Callaway titanium golf clubs, purchased for the equivalent of half off, then going back and picking up another set or two for their relatives and friends back home. Beneath the bargain shopping frenzy, a much more fundamental change was under way.

The Asian financial crisis began in Thailand in part because the baht had grown too expensive, particularly relative to its most important competitors such as China, which had devalued its currency in 1993. The resulting pain was enormous. As the Thai economy ground to a halt, the unemployment rate tripled, property prices fell by half, and the collapsing baht reduced the average income of Thais by more than a third in dollar terms. The mood in Thailand shifted almost overnight from newly rich brio to poverty shock. As bad as Thais felt about their future, however, the baht's collapse made the country look like a bargain again, and within months money was flowing back in significant volumes, a good sign for recovery.

How to Read Money Flows

A second and related question to ask when gauging a country's prospects is: Is money flowing into or out of the country? If the currency feels cheap and the economy is reasonably healthy, bargain hunters will pour money in. If the currency feels cheap, yet money is still fleeing the country, something is seriously wrong. For example, the Russian ruble had collapsed by late 2014 due to the falling price of oil, but Russians were still pulling tens of billions of dollars out of the country every month, fearing that the situation would only get worse. In this case, cheap was not yet a good sign, because it was not yet cheap and stable.

The key to tracking cross-border flows of money can be found in the balance of payments, which is tracked by the IMF and which records all the legal flows of money into and out of a country. Within the balance of payments, the critical category to watch is the current account, which captures how much a nation is producing compared to how much it is consuming. For most countries, by far the biggest entry in the current account is the trade balance, or the money earned from exports minus the money spent on imports. However, the trade balance alone is too narrow a measure to capture the full extent of a nation's international obligations. For that one has to watch the broader current account, because it includes other flows of foreign income that can make those import bills easier or harder to pay, including remittances from locals working abroad, foreign aid, and interest payments to foreigners. The current account thus reveals whether a country is consuming more than it produces and whether it has to borrow from abroad to finance its consumption habits. If a country runs a sizable deficit in the current account for too long, it is going to amass obligations it can't pay and run into a financial crisis at some point. What then is the tipping point?

I first became intrigued by this question after reading a 2000 paper by the Federal Reserve economist Caroline Freund, who in a study of advanced economies found that the current account tends to rise and fall in a somewhat predictable pattern: Signals of a turn for the worse flash when the current account deficit has been rising for about four years and hits a single-year peak of 5 percent of GDP. Soon after exceeding that level, the deficit typically tends to reverse and to fall naturally, simply because businesses and investors lose confidence in the country's ability to meet its obligations, and they pull out money. That undermines the value of the currency and forces locals to import less. The current account deficit then starts to narrow, and the economy slows significantly until falling imports bring the current account back into balance. [2]

Pushing Freund's research on the tipping point forward to include all countries, I screened the available data for 186 nations, emerging and developed, going back to 1960. I tested for various sizes of deficits, over three- and five-year periods, and found 2,300 such observations in all.[*] This search confirmed that when the current account deficit runs persistently high, the normal outcome is an economic slowdown over the next five years. If the deficit averages between 2 and 4 percent of GDP each year over a five-year period, the slowdown is relatively mild. If the deficit averages 5 percent or more, the slowdown is significantly sharper, shaving an average of 2.5 percentage points off the GDP growth rate over the following five years.

This research thus adds supporting evidence for the 5 percent rule. Since 1960 there have been forty cases in which a country saw its current account deficit expand at an average annual rate of at least 5 percent of GDP for as long as five years, and in these cases an economic slowdown was all but certain. Of the forty cases, 85 percent ended in a growth slowdown over the next five years, and in around 80 percent of the cases, there was a crisis of some kind.[†] The growth slowdown hit many

---

[*] I focused only on large economies because the current account in smaller ones can swing sharply with one big investment from abroad, skewing the results. *Large* is defined as an economy representing at least 0.2 percent of global GDP, which in 2015 would be an economy of more than $150 billion.

[†] I say "of some kind" because this definition includes banking, currency, inflation, or debt crises as defined by Carmen Reinhart and Kenneth Rogoff. Data on these kinds of crises is available for 34 of the 40 cases, and 31 of them, or 91 percent, suffered at least one of these crises.

countries rich and poor, including Norway, South Korea, Peru, and the Philippines in the 1970s; Malaysia, Portugal, Brazil, and Poland in the 1980s; and Spain, Greece, Portugal, and Turkey during the period of exuberantly excessive spending in the last decade.

The bottom line: If a country runs a current account deficit as high as 5 percent of GDP each year for five years, then a significant economic slowdown is highly likely, and so is some kind of crisis. Any nation on that path is clearly consuming more than it is producing and more than it can afford, and it needs to dial back. Running sustained current account deficits of more than 3 or 4 percent of GDP can also signal signs of coming economic and financial trouble, just less urgently.

Below the 3 percent threshold, however, a persistent current account deficit may not even be a bad thing depending on where the money is going. Though any deficit shows that money is flowing out of the country, this outflow can be a plus if the money is being spent on productive imports—for example, machinery and equipment to build factories. In that case, the loans financing those purchases are supporting productive investment in future growth. In fact, I have met emerging-world officials who have come to believe that any deficit below 3 percent of GDP is acceptable, while anything higher is cause for concern. At the 2015 IMF spring meetings in Washington, a top official from Indonesia said that its central bank now assumes that if the current account deficit hits 3 percent of GDP, it is time to raise interest rates, in order to restrain consumer spending and thus prevent the country from living beyond its means.

The risks posed by a current account deficit depend on what kind of spending the country is engaging in. If the spending is mainly on imports like luxury goods, which do not fuel future growth, it will be much more difficult for the country to pay the import bills and loans when they come due. One quick way to check where the money is headed is to see if the deficit is rising alongside an increase in investment as a share of GDP. If investment is rising, it is at least circumstantial evidence that the money is not flowing out for frivolous consumption.

Anatomy of a Currency Crisis

The cases in which countries ran a dangerous current account deficit of more than 5 percent of GDP for many years are worth looking at more closely, since they almost always led to a major economic slowdown. These slowdowns played out in unique ways, but the common thread was that the affected countries lived beyond their means for a long period and ultimately could not afford the bills they owed to foreigners. Thailand is a classic case.

In the early 1990s Thailand saw itself as the next Japan, a rising power in manufactured exports. It had already graduated from making textiles to manufacturing cars for the big Japanese automakers and producing semiconductors for personal computers, and the country was convinced that it was destined for greater things. Thais felt even richer than was suggested by their local incomes because the value of the baht was pegged to the strong dollar, which made them feel like kings of the mall anywhere they went.

The strong baht encouraged forms of spending that add greatly to the risk of a widening current account deficit. During this period Thai bankers became famous for their tastes in very particular brands of foreign luxuries, collecting Château Petrus wines and sporting Audemars Piguet watches. Worse, Thais started paying for these extravagances by borrowing heavily in foreign currencies. These loans would become impossible to pay if the baht collapsed, but in the early 1990s Thais brushed off this risk. They believed their boom could last forever and that the dollar peg could therefore last indefinitely. Besides, interest rates were even lower for dollar loans than for baht loans.

The euphoria in Bangkok was such that virtually everyone ignored the warning signs, which in retrospect should have been obvious. Thais were borrowing at lower interest rates in dollars to buy not only luxury goods but also to purchase local real estate and stocks, and prices were shooting up to heights that could last only as long as the strong baht did. Subsequent histories have traced the origins of the baht meltdown to the 1993 decision by China to devalue its own currency, which Beijing orchestrated in order to boost exports at a time when its economy was weakening. The devalued renminbi made Chinese exports much cheaper, allowing China to gain global export market share from Asian rivals, including Thailand. Nonetheless Thais continued consuming as if nothing had changed; between 1990 and 1994 the country's current account deficit rose as a share of GDP by an average of 7 percentage points a year, a rate deep in the danger zone.

Then in the spring of 1995 the dollar started to appreciate against the world's other major currencies such as the Japanese yen and the Deutsche mark, and because the baht was pegged to the dollar, it rose too. During this period Thailand's most important partner for trade and investment was Japan, so the most important measure of the baht was its value in Japanese yen. Over the next two years, the baht felt extremely expensive in yen, and in REER terms it rose more than 50 percent against the yen, discouraging Japanese investors and further slowing Thai exports. Thailand's current account deficit continued to widen, hitting 8 percent of GDP in 1995 and 1996. Questions began to mount about the country's ability to pay its mounting foreign bills and to sustain the exorbitant prices in the Bangkok stock and housing markets. Soon thereafter local and foreign investors panicked about Thailand's stretched finances and started to pull money out of the country.

To fight the destabilizing effects of capital flight, the Thai central bank began spending billions of dollars from its foreign exchange reserves to buy baht, hoping to prevent a precipitous collapse in its value. But as the reserves dwindled, the central bank had to give up the fight and abandon the dollar peg. The baht fell 50 percent against the dollar in 1997, and suddenly all those Thai borrowers couldn't pay the dollar loans they had taken out to buy houses and stock. The stock and real estate markets plummeted, and Thailand was forced to seek a bailout from the IMF in order to pay off its foreign loans. Within months, in a familiar scenario, excesses that had been mounting for years unraveled completely. As the late MIT economist Rudiger Dornbusch put it, crises "take a much longer time coming than you think, but happen much faster than you would have thought."[3]

Anatomy of a Currency Contagion

A current account deficit becomes a clear concern when it has been rising as a share of GDP for many years, and the accumulated bill grows too big to pay. Yet time and again in recent decades, the world has been gripped by currency contagions, in which investors start pulling money out of one troubled country, triggering a pullout from countries in the same region or income class even though those nations can pay their bills. In a way, the serial crises that have rocked the emerging world since the 1970s are one rolling crisis built on the recurring fear that poor nations won't have the money to pay their bills. The Mexican peso crisis of '94 begat the Thai crisis of '97 begat the Argentine crisis of 2002 and many others, trampling more than a few innocent-victim nations along the way.

At the first signs that one emerging-world currency is faltering—as the Thai baht did in 1997—investors often flee from emerging markets in general. They do not pause to distinguish between countries that face a serious current account deficit problem and those that do not. To cite just one recent example, the contagion that swept emerging markets in the summer of 2013 made no distinction between the real trouble in Turkey and the passing problems in India and Indonesia. At that point, India and Indonesia were running current account deficits ranging between 2 to 4 percent of GDP, but all it took was a 10 to 20 percent fall in their currencies to quickly narrow the deficits, in part because their currencies did not feel too expensive to begin with. The direction of change is key, and these countries were much less vulnerable than Turkey or Brazil, where the currencies felt very expensive, and thus were likely to encourage more people to shop and invest overseas and make a persistently large current account deficit even bigger. Yet investors fled blindly from all these countries, as if they were all the same.

They were not. The country most seriously at risk was Turkey, which has an economy almost purpose-built to run up large deficits in the current account. It lacks any deposits of virtually all the essential natural resources and has to import oil, iron, gold, coal, copper, and most other raw materials. Turks also tend to spend heavily on all manner of other imported goods, from cars to computers, and they save relatively little. The national savings rate, which includes savings by households, companies, and government, is less than 15 percent, the lowest among large emerging countries. That means Turks have to borrow heavily from abroad to finance their consumption. And partly because the pool of savings has traditionally been very small, relatively little money is available to invest in local industries, and these industries—including the exporters—are extremely weak. With this combination of weak export industries and heavy demand for imported oil and other resources, Turkey is chronically prone to running up deficits in the current account. In the years after 2008, as global trade slowed and oil prices rose, Turkey once again saw a rapid increase in its current account deficit. By 2013, it was the only major country in the world that had been running a current account deficit that averaged more than 5 percent of GDP for the previous five years, and it faced a flashing red warning on the currency rule.

Does Deglobalization Change the Rule?

Indeed, that warning sign may have been even more urgent than this narrative has suggested so far. There is an important caveat to this rule: The definition of what constitutes a dangerously high current account deficit may well be changing as we speak. The five-year, 5 percent threshold is based on the pattern of currency troubles in recent decades, but in a world disrupted by the global financial crisis of 2008, which has brought global trade growth to a halt and led to a sharp contraction in global capital flows, that pattern may shift. Though we live in a highly interconnected world, growth in global trade flows has slowed quite abruptly. As we've seen, this slump may last quite a while, because of the collapse of global trade talks, the way economies are turning inward, and the fact that China has started to make more of the parts it assembles in its factories at home.

In expert circles, this broad shift in attitudes is feeding a widening debate over the extent to which globalization has given way to "deglobalization." The impact of slowing global trade might not have been big if other global money flows were not in retreat, but they are. Because a current account deficit generally reflects excessive consumption of imports, any country running one has to find foreign currency to pay its import bills, and that currency can enter the country in the form of foreign bank loans, foreign purchases of stocks or bonds, or direct foreign investment in local factories. These flows show up in a separate section of the balance of payments, the capital account, and have dried up even more dramatically than trade since 2008.

Studies done for the Bank of England by the MIT economist Kristin Forbes show that cross-border capital flows have fallen back to levels not seen in more than three decades, when the latest boom in globalization began. This is a striking reversal. In 1980 global annual capital flows amounted to $280 billion, or less than 2 percent of global GDP. Then China opened its doors to global trade and foreign investors, other emerging markets followed, and in the subsequent waves of excitement about this newly open world, capital flows rose to a peak of $9 trillion and 16 percent of global GDP in early 2007. Then came the 2008 crisis and the evaporation of optimism; by 2014, capital flows had fallen back to $1.2 trillion—once again about 2 percent of current global GDP. Judging from the scale of global capital flows alone, the clock has turned back to 1980.

The capital account includes just about every imaginable channel people can use to move money across borders, from bank loans to money secreted away in the Cayman Islands. Normally, analysts and newspaper headlines focus on one aspect of capital flows, the money invested by foreigners in local stock and bond markets, which are technically part of "portfolio flows" but are often referred to as "hot money" because stocks and bonds can normally be sold off very quickly. These flows involve trading in public markets, so they are highly visible. However, this hot money is in fact only one part of overall capital flows, and as Forbes has pointed out it is not the most volatile part. Alongside portfolio flows, the other main capital flows are foreign direct investment and bank loans, and in recent decades bank loans have been the most volatile of all the capital flows. Bank loans are the real hot money.

They are also the key to the recent overall shrinkage in global capital flows. The main reason global capital flows reversed after 2008 is that big banks in the United States, Europe, and Japan are pulling back to their home markets, offering fewer loans overseas. This retreat was driven to some extent by concern about risks in the emerging world but mainly by new regulations imposed after the 2008 crisis. These regulations include requirements that banks hold on to more capital so that, at least in theory, they can better weather the next big global crisis. In the United States, teams of officials from the Federal Reserve now camp for weeks at a time in the office of major investment banks, monitoring whether they are complying with new rules governing the way these banks employ their assets and making sure they do not take too much risk anywhere, including in foreign markets.

Global cross-border bank flows peaked before the crisis at roughly 4 percent of world GDP in 2007, then swung sharply negative the next year, indicating that banks not only stopped lending but started liquidating loans to bring money home, writes *Forbes*. Those flows have yet to recover, and this "deglobalization of banking" will make it increasingly difficult for the United States and Britain to borrow money to support their taste for imported goods. It will also be much more difficult for them to finance their persistent current account deficits, which have averaged about 3 percent in the United States and 2.2 percent in Britain since 1990. The same hurdles now exist for any country that runs a high current account deficit and may be living beyond its means.

Countries will likely find it increasingly difficult to attract the foreign capital flows necessary to pay for their lifestyles, which means they could run into trouble in financing their current account deficits much sooner than they would have in the past. With global trade stagnating, it may be getting tougher for any country to keep its current account in balance by earning export income and easier to fall into a crisis. In the pre-2008 era, the tipping point came when the deficit had been increasing by 5 percent of GDP for five years in a row. In the post-crisis era, the tipping point may come faster and at lower deficit levels—perhaps at the 3 percent mark that central banks officials from India to Indonesia have been increasingly citing as a threshold level.

The Return of Thrift

Even before the optimism of the globalization era gave way to concern about deglobalization, the general consensus among economists was that most nations had gained from opening up to trade, whereas opening up to global capital flows produced mixed results.

At the peak of the globalization boom, rising capital flows made it all too easy for countries to spend beyond their means and drift into financial crises. Back in 1980, how much a country saved and how much it invested had been very closely linked: If investment was growing at a steady pace, then for most countries, savings were also growing at a steady pace. But by the 2000s, that relationship had changed. Rising global capital flows had made available trillions of dollars in new funding each year. Countries no longer needed to save heavily in order to spend or invest heavily, because they could so easily tap the savings of other countries, the basic source of global capital flows. In short, countries like China, where the current account surplus peaked at 10 percent in 2007, were saving enough extra income to finance the often unproductive consumption habits of countries like the United States, where the current account deficit peaked at 6 percent in 2006. The risk was that this torrent of global capital was allowing many countries to spend more than they saved by running up foreign debts.

The old virtues of domestic thrift are now returning. This revival of national savings shows up clearly in the current account, which measures the difference between consumption and production, and that difference reveals how much nations are saving. If nations are consuming more than they produce, running up a current account deficit, they are effectively cutting into savings. Now, with global trade receding, the world's current account imbalances, defined as the absolute value of all current account deficits and current account surpluses, has fallen by $600 billion to $2.7 trillion, or by about a third as a share of global GDP. This shows that a lot less money is sloshing across borders. Since peaking at 6 percent in 2006, the U.S. current account deficit has more than halved to 2.5 percent of GDP, and the country is now much less reliant on funding from overseas. In the nineteen nations of the Eurozone, the average current account deficit reached 1.6 percent of GDP in 2008, but that deficit gave way to a surplus of 2.4 percent by 2014. After having collapsed by 2007, the link between domestic saving and domestic investment has also returned to where it was in 1980. Once again, to the extent countries are investing at all, most are funding that investment largely from their own savings.*

The concern in the post-crisis era is an emerging "savings glut," created by the lack of investment opportunities. A number of forces are contributing to this glut, but two of the most important are slower growth in the emerging world and the related slump in commodity prices. In the 2000s investment increased as a share of global GDP, but all that increase came in the emerging world, where the slowdown in economic growth in the 2010s has been particularly sharp. That is now reducing opportunities for plowing savings into building roads and other investments in emerging countries, many of which are powered by exports of oil and other commodities. Between 2009 and 2014, more than a third of the world's investment worldwide went into commodity

---

* The revival of savings is demonstrated, in technical terms, by the global correlation between domestic savings and domestic investment, which fell from 0.8 in 1980 to –0.1 in 2007 and has since climbed back up to 0.7.

industries, but that level was expected to come down sharply after oil prices collapsed in late 2014.

Though these forces point to slower economic growth in the new era, they also point to more stability. Many countries are relying less on strangers overseas to finance their spending habits, which may be a stabilizing force in a world where rising capital flows—particularly of the hot money variety—had been feeding the magnitude and frequency of currency crises.

Follow the Locals

Even though the rapid expansion of global trade and money flows stopped after the crisis of 2008, many politicians are still quick to blame any local financial crisis on foreigners. It is a common perception that the large shifts in money flows that can cause currency crises are dictated by global players, many of whom emerged on the international scene during the recent decades of go-go globalization. The most powerful among these players are hedge fund moguls, fund managers at various investment firms, sovereign wealth funds that invest the oil profits of petro-states like Saudi Arabia, and pension funds that handle savings for hundreds of millions of working people all over the world. A certain conspiratorial aura prevails around some of these "secretive" new agents of finance. They are often cast as all-seeing eyes—somewhat the way many countries view the CIA—with sources on the ground and technology in the ether that allow them to shape events and outfox rival investors in far corners of the world.

My finding is the opposite: To spot the beginning or the end of currency trouble in emerging markets, follow the locals. They are the first to know when a nation is in crisis or recovery, and they will be the first to move. The big global players mostly follow.

Often crises erupt in emerging countries when investors lose confidence in the economy and start pulling out their money, which undermines the value of local currency and leaves the country incapable of paying its foreign debts. The country then has to run to the IMF for a bailout. Blame often quickly falls on fleet-footed foreigners for triggering the capital flight. This suspicion has arisen in every currency meltdown from the Asian financial crisis of 1997–98—which Malaysia's Mahathir Mohamad pinned on "immoral" and "evil" foreign speculators—to the passing 2013 attacks on the Turkish lira, the Indian rupee, the Indonesian rupiah, and other emerging currencies. Not only national politicians but even global institutions, including the IMF, have attributed these damaging bouts of capital flight to outsiders.[4]

This natural reflex misses a few key steps in the normal sequence of events. To start with, nationalist attacks on immoral foreign speculators imply that locals are loyal and patriotic, while outsiders are flighty and exploitative. This narrative ignores the Lucas paradox, named after the Nobel laureate Robert Lucas, which questions the assumption that money flows tend to move from rich countries to poor ones, driven by wealthy American or European investors seeking high returns in hot growth markets. Lucas pointed out that rich locals in emerging nations also have a strong incentive to move their money to richer countries with more trustworthy institutions and safer investment options, such as U.S. Treasury bonds.

My research supports Lucas's view, showing that locals have been moving money out of emerging stock markets since the records begin in 1995. The data on cross-border flows for twenty-one big emerging countries show that local investors were net sellers in the local stock markets every single year. Though locals in emerging economies did tend to invest the bulk of their money at home, they always sold more local stock than they bought. At the same time, foreigners almost always bought more stock in emerging markets than they sold and were net buyers every year but the crisis year of 2008 and again during the mass exodus of 2015. This should not be that surprising: Both groups were diversifying their bets, with developed world buyers seeking to invest part of their wealth in high-return emerging markets, and emerging-world buyers seeking to invest part of their wealth in safe developed markets. The lesson is that people move their own money mainly out of self-interest, to make more money, and not in order to prove their patriotism or to act out some evil plan to sabotage foreign nations.

In fact, my research shows that in ten out of the twelve major emerging-market currency crises over the past two decades, local investors headed for the exits well before foreigners. As the value of the currency reached its low point, foreigners did capitulate and move much larger sums of money than locals, but they did not lead; they followed on the heels of an earlier exodus. In eight out of those twelve major currency crises, foreigners started pulling out of local investments—calling in loans and dumping stocks and bonds—as the currency was hitting its low point. Instead of anticipating the crisis and making a killing, foreigners sold out at the bottom and lost a fortune.

Capital flight begins with locals, I suspect, because they have better access to intelligence about local conditions. They can pick up informal signs—struggling businesses, looming bankruptcies—long before these trends show up in the official numbers that most big foreign institutions rely on. Balance of payments data show that during Mexico's "tequila crisis" in December 1994, when the currency peg against the dollar came unstuck, locals started to switch out of pesos and into dollars more than eighteen months before the sudden devaluation. Years later Russians began to pull money out of their country more than two years before the ruble collapsed in August 1998.

Savvy locals are also often the first to return. In seven of the twelve major emerging-world currency crises, locals started bringing money back home earlier than foreigners and acted in time to catch the currency on its way up. Another way to think about this pattern is that big global players know a lot less than they like to imagine, and locals are a lot smarter than foreigners give them credit for.

The capital account in the balance of payments also offers telltale signs of when local money is exiting the country in large amounts. As locals begin draining their bank accounts at home, moving cash to the Bahamas and employing other exit channels, the money will show up in the balance of payments as heavy capital outflows. To cite just one example, these flows recently reached astonishing proportions in Russia, even before the price of oil collapsed in late 2014 and signaled clear trouble for the economy. The capital account showed locals were pulling out money in 2012 and 2013 at a pace of $60 billion a year. In 2014 those outflows swelled to $150 billion, more than 8 percent of GDP. In response, the Russian central bank spent more than $100 billion of its reserves to defend the ruble that year.

Rich locals and corporations can also slip money out of troubled countries through illicit channels that show up only in the "errors and omissions" column of the balance of payments. Uncovering these secret flows has become something of a parlor game for forensic economists in recent years. According to Deutsche Bank research, there is strong reason to believe that a good chunk of the money sneaking out of Russia is bound for Britain, which is a favorite destination of Russian oligarchs, owing in part to relatively friendly tax rules and financial regulations.[5] When more money flows out of Russia through irregular channels in the form of "errors and omissions," more money tends to flow into Britain via the same channel. Russia was also believed to be the source of a sudden influx of more than $9 billion into Turkey through the "errors and omissions" channel in 2014, when the ruble was falling and Russians were trying to protect their money from international sanctions imposed on Moscow after its intervention in Ukraine. This flow was a bad sign for Russia but a good one for Turkey, because even if the flows were illicit, money was being put to work in Turkey.

Russia is not even the leader in surreptitious money flows. That dubious distinction goes to China. According to Global Financial Integrity, a Washington-based research firm, China is the top exporter of illicit capital among developing countries. Illicit outflows from China during the decade ending 2012 averaged $125 billion per year, and they have since spiked higher. In a 2015 piece on "the curious case of the missing $300 billion," Goldman Sachs analysts tried to trace how that much money could have slipped out of China in recent years, despite Beijing's stringent efforts to police money flows and a rule that caps the annual amount any individual can ship out of the country at $50,000. Though careful to say that there could be innocuous explanations for how and why this money was getting past China's vigilant gate keepers, the analysts at Goldman concluded that much of it was likely fleeing from a widening crackdown on corruption and illegally made fortunes. [6]

The most likely channel for this stealth capital flight from China was the doctoring of trade invoices, or understating receipts for exports and leaving some of the money abroad. Some of that money was suspected to be moving through the booming coastal city of Shenzhen, where certain gold and jewelry firms were reporting trading volumes that did not match their foreign receipts. A separate study by BNP Paribas research showed that in the first quarter of 2015, the errors and omissions surpassed $80 billion—which is a record for any emerging country. This means outflows through the murky errors and omissions channel were running at an annual rate of $320 billion, or more than 3 percent of China's GDP—an alarming sign.

Even locals who lack access to the flight paths used by big companies and the superrich always have an escape hatch. As fears of a currency meltdown swept emerging nations from Indonesia to Brazil and Turkey in mid-2013, locals used several exit routes. Indians converted rupees into gold, in sums worth tens of billions of dollars each quarter. Ordinary Turks marched down to their banks by the millions, converting their savings from lira into U.S. dollars (to the tune of $22 billion in the last half of 2013, when the lira fell by 20 percent).

This was not the first time that locals successfully anticipated an important shift in a developing nation. During the tumultuous 1990s, domestic investors moved large sums of money out of emerging nations, fleeing the very real risks posed by regimes with a habit of seizing wealth through, for instance, hostile tax collectors, and in economies that were destabilized by high inflation and erratic growth. Since many governments had rules that made it difficult to move capital out of the country, companies and wealthy individuals often found roundabout paths that registered only as "errors and omissions."

When the economic chaos in emerging markets started to subside after 2000, as leaders such as Putin, Lula, and Erdoğan put the financial books in order, the locals once again were early to sense the shift. They brought billions of dollars back home to countries as diverse as Indonesia, South Africa, and Brazil, although again often through back channels. In 2002 global markets were rattled by fear that Lula, who campaigned as a radical leftist, would choose to default on Brazil's debt. But Brazilians focused less on what Lula had said on the campaign trail than on what his team was likely to do: follow a path of economic orthodoxy. Moreover, the Brazilian currency felt very cheap after having lost more than half its value in the preceding three years. With controls in place on how much money Brazilians were allowed to move in and out of the country, they were eager to buy reals and willing to pay more on the black market than the official currency exchanges were charging. This local confidence helped stave off a bigger currency collapse, and foreshadowed the economic rebound that followed.

Fast-forward to April 2015 in Buenos Aires, where Argentine central bank officials tried to persuade me in private meetings that the peso's black market price was a positive sign. They argued that the black market rate, even though it was 40 percent lower than the official rate, was an improvement compared to the year before, when it was 50 percent lower. The bigger story for me, though, was that the black market was still signaling that Argentines lacked confidence in what their government was doing to get the country back on track. The currency was going to have to fall significantly further to persuade locals that their country could be competitive again.

When Money Flows, Flash a Green Light

Even though the central message of this chapter is that a cheap and stable currency is good, currency crises have been a large part of the discussion because those periods indicate that a country has reached a turning point. For a nation that does slip into a currency crisis, the strongest sign of a turnaround is when the current account rebounds from deficit into surplus. That surplus shows the currency is likely stabilizing at a competitively low rate, boosting exports while forcing locals to cut back on imports. The crisis is passing, and the economy can dust itself off and start growing again.

The remarkable similarities in the unfolding of the Asian crisis of 1997–98 and the European crisis of the early 2010s illustrate this point. Like many other currency crises in recent decades, these two echoed each other in the degree of losses they generated and in the way the suffering spread across their respective regions. Back in 1997–98, as the currency contagion spread from Bangkok to Jakarta, Seoul, and Kuala Lumpur, investors fled and currencies crumbled, reaching their deepest bottom in Indonesia. The Indonesian rupiah lost a staggering 80 percent of its value, falling from 2,500 to 16,000 against the dollar; some banks were not able to process the currency trades, because their computers were not programmed to handle an unimaginable five-figure value for the rupiah. The currency meltdown in turn fed a bust in the dollar value of stocks across the region, where at the low point the total value of the four hardest-hit Asian markets fell to just $250 billion.

To put that in perspective, all the companies in Thailand, Indonesia, South Korea, and Malaysia put together plummeted in a few short months to a value lower than General Electric alone. Clearly, this was one of those cases where the global markets were overshooting, but these strikingly low stock valuations were also a sign that the whole country was feeling extremely cheap, owing in good part to a cheap currency, and a turnaround was coming.

The scale of the Asian currency collapse was hardly unusual. Examining again the major currency crises in the emerging world going back to 1990, I found that stock prices in the country at the epicenter of the crisis—such as in Mexico in '94 or in Thailand in '97—typically saw a currency-fueled drop of 85 percent in dollar terms, while the average decline in stock prices across the affected region was 65 percent. The way the Eurozone crisis played out in the region's peripheral economies also exhibited this basic pattern: The stock market fell by up to 90 percent in Greece—the country where the crisis started—and spread across peripheral Europe, including Portugal, Ireland, Italy, and Spain, where the average drop was 70 percent. When the crisis reached its nadir in 2012, the total value of the stock markets of these five European countries was less than the market cap of Apple. The stock market of Greece was worth less than Costco, the big-box U.S. discount store. These values plumb the extremes of what it means to say a country "feels cheap," a moment that often comes at the bottom of a crisis.

In fact, every country in the European drama had its alter ego in the earlier Asian crisis. The central characters, Thailand and Greece, saw equally massive contractions in their economies: Thailand's had contracted by 28 percent at its post-crisis low, and Greece's economy shrank by 25 percent between 2008 and 2015. A similar equivalence of economic suffering held for the second-hardest-hit nations (Indonesia and Ireland), the third-hardest-hit (Malaysia and Italy), and the least hard-hit (Portugal and South Korea, which saw their economies contract by 10 percent each).

The big difference in the stories of these two regional currency contagions, with telling implications for how these episodes normally unfold, was the way they managed their currencies. Put simply, nations that don't try to create an artificially stable financial environment by fixing the price of their currency tend to be more flexible and to bounce back faster. In the decade preceding their respective currency crises, both Asia and Europe tried to make themselves look like safer places in which to lend to and invest by adopting two very different forms of a fixed exchange rate. The Asian countries pegged the value of their currencies in dollars, while the European countries adopted the new continental currency, the euro, anchored by its ties to the continent's largest and most conservative economy, Germany. The plan worked almost too well in both regions, because as confidence in the stability of the currency spread, banks lowered borrowing costs, and locals started borrowing heavily to shop, build houses, and erect factories. This debt-fueled spending and import binge drove current accounts into the red, stirring fears about whether these countries could pay their mounting debts, particularly those owed to foreign banks.

The cycle of collapse and revival unfolded much more quickly in the Asian countries, in large part because they could abandon the dollar peg. Although that move sent currencies and markets crashing, it also helped spark a rebound. After a debilitating year in 1998, by early 1999 recovery was already in sight with current account balances in all the crisis-hit economies back into surplus. In the months before the crisis, these countries had on average a current account deficit equal to 5 percent of GDP. But within a year the East Asian economies notched up a surplus equal to 10 percent of GDP, driven by cheap currencies, falling imports, and exploding exports. After the initial collapse in the Asian currencies, they stopped falling and were cheap and stable enough to help set up their economies for recovery. It took them just three and a half years to recover all the output they had lost in the massive recession that started in 1998.

Jump forward twelve years, and see how Italy, Spain, and the other peripheral European nations had no such quick currency fix. They could not easily abandon the euro, so there was no sudden drop in the value of the currency, and thus no forced, rapid drop in imports or boost to exports. (The euro eventually did start to fall against the dollar, but not until mid-2014.) The only way they could regain a competitive position to generate more export income and reduce their dependence on foreign capital was by making painful choices to cut wages and bloated public payrolls. Economists call this dreaded belt-tightening process "internal devaluation," and it achieves much the same end as a currency devaluation, by restoring export competitiveness. Only it is slower and more politically difficult, particularly in labor-friendly Europe, since it involves tough union negotiations. Five years after the crisis, Europe's peripheral economies were still struggling to recover.

To be fair to Europe, it has faced a much more hostile external backdrop than Asia did. Following the financial crisis in 2008, the global economy experienced its weakest recovery in post–World War II history, and it is hard to export your way to prosperity in such an environment. In 1998 Asia's economies enjoyed not only the option of abandoning their fixed currencies but also the good fortune to make their comebacks at a time when the global economy was strong. A key driver of the recovery in Asia was the fact that the U.S. economy was growing at the unusually rapid clip of 4.5 percent a year in the 1996–2000 period and importing many of Asia's newly cheap goods.

The turning point for the peripheral European countries finally came into view in 2014 as the current account balances showed signs of climbing out of the red and into surplus territory, a signal that these economies were generating the income to pay down foreign debts. Portugal, Spain, and Ireland all registered significant improvements in their current accounts and were on track to post surpluses. Italy and Greece, however, were not.

I visited Greece in May 2015 and found that the reason it was backsliding was that it manufactures little. The sharp drop in its wages and other costs offered no real boost to exports. Falling prices in Greece had, however, made the islands very attractive to tourists, which were overrun with more Chinese and Indian visitors than I have ever seen outside their home countries. But tourism accounts for under 7 percent of Greece's GDP, and while it plays a major role for tiny island nations like the Bahamas and the Seychelles, it has never played an important role in assisting a mid- to large-sized economy bounce back from a financial crisis. Even in the beach destination resort of Thailand, tourism accounted for less than 7 percent of GDP when crisis hit in 1997–98, contributing in just a minor way to Thailand's recovery in the subsequent years.

The freedom of floating currencies also helps to explain why many eastern European nations underwent a very different crisis. Poland and the Czech Republic had cut wages and government spending in preparation for joining the European Union; they went into the 2008 crisis in better financial shape than their richer neighbors, but they had not yet joined the euro, which left their currencies free to fall when the crisis hit. Though the euro still felt quite expensive in the years following the crisis, the Polish zloty and the Czech koruna felt quite cheap. This happy accident of timing helped these countries to recover, particularly when they were competing for export customers with the rest of the emerging world.

Eastern Europe was looking very competitive—that is, feeling quite cheap—compared not only to western Europe but also to emerging-world rivals such as Russia, Brazil, and Turkey. From 2008 to 2013, currency values in most big emerging nations outside Europe rose in inflation-adjusted terms against the dollar, and current account deficits widened in thirteen of the top twenty emerging nations. Most of the seven exceptions were in emerging Europe, including Poland, the Czech Republic, and Hungary. The tough spending cuts slowed imports, while the cheap currency and wage cuts boosted exports, including manufac-tured exports. Poland, with the market-determined value of the zloty declining and wages that were still 75 percent lower on average than those in western Europe, became a major exporter of everything from services to cars and farm products. These forces helped push Poland's current account balance into surplus by 2015, helping the economy reg-ister a robust growth rate of 3.5 percent that year.

Yet because Poland's image was tarnished by its close proximity to the troubled Eurozone, it continued to attract relatively little attention from global investors. It drew so few international business executives that no major global hotel chain saw fit to open a property in Warsaw, the capital of a country of forty million people, which is twice as large as the next biggest nation in eastern Europe. Poland also has the added attraction of low inflation, which helps to stabilize the value of the cur-rency at a low and competitive rate. This combination—a cheap cur-rency and low inflation—is an even more powerful and enduring force in luring money flows than a cheap currency alone.

During my visits to Warsaw in the early 2010s, I saw new restaurants opening in old brick warehouses and other retro chic venues around the capital, but they were filling up mainly with stylish young locals and expats returning from abroad. Just a few years before, so many Poles were emigrating in search of work that the "Polish plumber" had become a controversial symbol for anti-immigration parties elsewhere in Europe. Now the Polish plumbers are coming back home, drawn by the stronger economy and better job prospects, all supported by the competitively valued zloty. The Poles have rediscovered Poland. The foreigners are likely to follow, someday.

You Can't Devalue Your Way to Prosperity

If political leaders often fall prey to the illusion that a strong currency is a symbol of national strength, technocratic leaders who understand that cheap is good at times succumb to the opposite fallacy: that they can make their economy stronger by simply devaluing the currency. This is another form of state meddling—interfering to fix the price of a currency is like interfering to fix any other price in the market, which often punishes such attempts.

It's particularly difficult for a country to devalue its way to prosperity if every other country is trying the same trick. After the crisis of 2008, so many nations tried to improve their competitive position by devaluing their currencies that none managed to gain any lasting advantage. The central banks of the United States, Japan, Britain, and the Eurozone took turns pursuing "quantitative easing" policies that effectively amount to printing more money, in part as a way to devalue their currencies, but each achieved at best a brief gain in export share versus the others.

Markets can punish these attempts to manage currency values in many ways. The most important is that if a country has borrowed heavily in dollars or euros or some other foreign currency, then devaluing its own currency by, say, 30 percent is going to raise its payments on those foreign loans by an equal margin. One of the more persistent questions about the global economy in 2015 was why so many emerging countries, including Brazil, Russia, and Turkey, had gained so little from the recent decline in the value of their currencies. The answer was that they had not fallen far enough to feel unequivocally cheap.

Furthermore, many companies in these countries had been ringing up foreign debt; since 1996, in the emerging world, the total amount of debt owed by private companies to foreign lenders had more than doubled as a share of GDP, and had reached 20 percent or more in Taiwan, Peru, South Africa, Russia, Brazil, and Turkey. For these countries, the drop in the currency values did as much damage as good to the economy; private companies were compelled to spend more for servicing their debt, and less on hiring workers or investing in new plants and equipment.

The world had watched this self-defeating cycle play out before. The Latin American crisis of the 1980s, the first in the series of currency crises that has wracked the emerging world in recent decades, began in part because Argentina, Chile, and Mexico had opened up to foreign loans. This pioneering move produced heady spurts of growth, followed by dizzying problems when these countries could not generate enough foreign income to cover their foreign bills and loan payments. In all these cases, leaders devalued the currency in an attempt to make the economy more competitive, but they ended up pushing many of their own countrymen into default on foreign loans. The process hit bottom in Argentina, when the country defaulted on its national debts in 2002, in the midst of one of the few genuine depressions any nation has witnessed in recent decades. At its low point, currency was in such low supply that Argentines were reduced to setting up barter clubs, including one that met in a vacated luxury mall in Buenos Aires.

Devaluations can do other unintended damage as well. In a country that lacks strong manufacturing industries, the cheaper currency can do little to promote exports, earn foreign currency, and help balance the current account deficit. This is the classic vulnerability of commodity-exporting countries, though recent research shows that, compared to ten or twenty years ago, it is getting more difficult even for manufacturing powers to capitalize on a cheap currency. The reason is the recent global integration of supply chains, which means that many manufacturers buy a significant share of their parts and raw materials from abroad. As a result, exports now contain a larger share of imports, and if manufacturing powers try to gain an export advantage by devaluing their currency, they end up raising the price they have to pay for these imports.

If a country is also highly dependent on imports of basic staples like food and energy, a cheaper currency will make it more expensive to import these essentials, in turn driving up inflation, further undermining the currency and encouraging capital flight. This is the recurring syndrome in, for example, Turkey.

These bouts of capital flight put the government in an awkward position. As foreigners start to follow locals out the door, the central bank often tries to prevent capital flight from precipitating a sudden and destabilizing collapse in the value of the currency. The bank spends billions of dollars from its reserves to buy its own currency, hoping to "defend" the currency, but this ends up draining the reserves and achieving only a temporary pause in the currency's slide. That gives investors a chance to flee the country with partial losses, but their flight keeps exerting downward pressure on the exchange rate. Many currency traders joke that "defending the currency" really means "subsidizing the exit" of foreign investors. This was how the 1997–98 crisis, for example, unfolded in both Indonesia and Thailand. Better, from the start, to let the market decide what price it wants to pay for the currency.

It is the rare country that can deliberately devalue its way to prosperity. This brings us back to the pivotal devaluation in China in 1993, because it was one of those rare cases that led to stronger economic growth with no pain, even in the short term. China had little foreign debt, it did not rely too heavily on imported goods, and most important, it had a strong manufacturing sector, which grew even faster after Beijing devalued the renminbi. This strategy won't work so well in Brazil or Turkey or Nigeria or Argentina or Greece, which have little or no manufacturing base. A cheaper currency in these countries will make imports more expensive and fuel inflation but will do little, or will take a very long time, to encourage growth in exports and jobs due to the lack of export industries.

It is worth pointing out that when Chinese officials were trying to calculate the appropriate value to peg the renminbi to the dollar in 1993, they went to their paramount leader, Deng Xiaoping, who told them to look at the black market rate and use that price to set the value for the currency. The ultimate pragmatist, Deng understood the good sense of using the best available market price to set the value of the currency.

Another interesting case of a successful devaluation was Indonesia, which pulled off a 30 percent devaluation in 1986 because it simultaneously pursued aggressive reforms to promote exports. As Indonesia's former finance minister Muhamad Chatib Basri notes, Indonesia had turned inward during the 1970s but was forced to reform in the 1980s following the collapse in the price of oil, then Indonesia's leading export. Falling oil prices led to a drop in the value of the Indonesian rupiah, which had the effect of reducing the revenues earned by exporters, and transformed them into supporters of trade liberalization. The Indonesian leader Suharto put economic policy in the hands of technocrats, who began cutting tariffs and taxes. They opened doors to foreign investment and instituted an unusually creative answer to corruption among customs agents, by replacing the customs department with a private Swiss inspection company, SGS. At a time when Indonesia was aggressively opening to the world, Basri argues, the rupiah devaluation was one element of a broader reform program that helped set off a manufacturing boom in Indonesia.[7]

One way to think about this rule is that the less developed an economy is, the more sensitive it is to "cheap is good." If a country exports raw materials or, for that matter, very simple manufactured goods such as garments, shoes, or processed foods, for which low prices are often the critical selling point, the more its economic fate will swing with the value of its currency. But if the country makes more expensive goods— particularly branded goods for which customers are willing to pay a premium—then the currency still matters, but less so.

The classic cases are Germany and Japan, which managed to sustain their long runs of strong growth in the 1970s and '80s despite massive currency appreciation, because "Made in Germany" and "Made in Japan" had come to be seen as synonymous with exacting standards and precise engineering. The same story has played out in Switzerland; no currency has appreciated more over the last decade than the Swiss franc, yet the country's share of global exports has remained steady when most other developed countries have seen declines.

The national bank and others have studied "why Switzerland is special" in this regard, and the answer is that the country makes a broad array of exports—including drugs, machinery, and of course watches— that are so high in quality, customers stick with Swiss models even when a stronger franc drives up the price. According to *The Atlas of Economic Complexity*, only Japan makes a more extensive array of sophisticated exports than Switzerland. While in Zurich and Geneva, I've often felt this same unusual insensitivity to price, because even hotel services are delivered with a quality and efficiency that seems to justify the hefty bill. As early as the mid-1990s, I visited the Hiltl restaurant, a Zurich landmark dating to 1898, where waiters were already using handheld devices to transmit orders instantly to the kitchen. The Hiltl is said to be both the oldest vegetarian restaurant in the world and also one of the first to use this handheld technology—a typically Swiss combination.

A somewhat similar evolution toward advanced manufacturing is under way in China, which is working its way up the ladder to make exports that rely less on a cheap currency to hold global market share. Technology and capital goods now comprise half of China's exports, up from 30 percent in 2002. In 2000 nearly 80 percent of the value of publicly traded technology companies was located in the United States,

Europe, and Japan, but that share has since fallen to less than 60 percent, with China, Korea, and Taiwan gaining at their expense.

The way the world has been turned on its head since the crisis of 2008 suggests that the scope for devaluing your way to prosperity is even more limited now. Global trade is no longer expanding, and emerging nations battle one another for finite shares of the fixed trade pie. This is a world in which cheap currencies alone are unlikely to produce many economic stars. Playing games to devalue a currency in this environment could easily backfire. It may still work for a relatively small economy such as Vietnam, in which trade accounts for 170 percent of GDP, and consequently even a small increase in its share of global trade can have a sizable positive impact on economic growth. But in big economies trade matters less than the domestic market.

These growing hurdles are not likely to stop governments from trying to devalue their way to success, but at a time when the global economy is weak, globalization has stalled, and competition is growing more intense, the gambit is increasingly likely to come up empty. Even in China, devaluation is not likely to have the same impact it had in 1993. Since then China has grown to command 12 percent of global exports, the largest share any economy has reached in recent decades, and it is simply too big to expand much further. In fact, because China is so large, when it devalues, the ripple effects tend to force currency falls across the emerging world. In late 2015, when China devalued the renminbi by 3 percent, hoping to revive sagging exports, almost instantaneously the currencies of many other emerging markets fell even more sharply, more than wiping out any competitive gain Beijing might have achieved by the devaluation.

The value of a currency is best determined by the market and can be the simplest real-time measure of how effectively a country can compete on price with its main rivals for international trade and investment. If a currency becomes too expensive, it can lead to a large and sustained increase in the current account deficit, and money will start to flow out of country. The risk of an economic slowdown and a financial crisis is extremely high when the current account deficit has been growing at an average rate of 5 percent of GDP for five years running. But in a world increasingly marked by "deglobalization," the threshold level for a manageable current account deficit could be moving lower, possibly to 3 percent. Even if the current account deficit is below 3 percent, it is still important to understand whether money is flowing out to finance productive purchases like factory equipment or frivolous ones like luxury goods.

To spot the beginning or the end of currency trouble, follow the locals. They are the first to know when a nation is in crisis or recovery, and they will be the first to move. The big global players will mostly follow. When the current account is back in surplus, and the country is once again pulling in enough money from abroad to cover its foreign bills, it's a sign of an impending turnaround in a country's fortunes. Usually it takes a very cheap currency to facilitate this process.

Of course, a free fall in a currency is not a good sign, particularly if the country has substantial foreign debt and does not have a manufacturing base for exports that can benefit from a cheap exchange rate. The ideal mix is a market-determined cheap currency in a stable financial environment underpinned by low inflationary expectations: That combination will give local businesses the confidence to build, banks the confidence to disburse loans at reasonable rates, and investors the confidence to make long-term commitments to the rise of a nation.

9

THE KISS OF DEBT

Is debt growing faster or slower than the economy?

A T THE HEIGHT OF THE ASIAN FINANCIAL CRISIS IN LATE 1997, I requested a meeting in Hong Kong with a provocative character named Robert Zielinski, a bank analyst who had seen signs that the crisis was coming. As early as 1995, he had penned a brief paper warning that many financial crises in the emerging world had been preceded by five consecutive years of debt growing at more than 20 percent a year, and that Thailand was in the midst of just such a credit binge. Few listened to Zielinski at that time— even many of his colleagues at Jardine Fleming, then one of Asia's highest-flying banks, ignored him.

Zielinski did not do much to help spread his own message, given his brusquely unconventional personality. In October 1997, as the Thai baht was collapsing, he reprised his warnings in one of the most offbeat notes I have ever seen from a bank analyst. Instead of delivering a dry recitation of data, this note took the form of a short play called *The Kiss of Debt*, which captured in three pages the basic arc of a credit mania. Set in an unnamed Southeast Asian country, it describes how virtually everyone gets blinded by increasingly good times and low borrowing costs. A banker urges a simple farmer named Ah Hoi to start Ah Hoi

Property Co. Ltd., promising that "a company such as yours" will be a sure hit. A housewife cries, "Buy for me four million of anything! I don't want to miss out." The prime minister tells his concerned finance minister not to worry about funding as they can always borrow more from the banks, which have also lost their senses. Each increasingly irrational step of the way, a chorus in the background sings: "Kiss of debt, kiss of debt, kiss of debt."

Zielinksi was the first to alert me to this warning signal of economic trouble: a period when borrowers and lenders get caught up in a credit mania, and the total amount of private loans grows significantly faster than the economy. It is obvious that credit crises are linked to debt, but there are infinite ways to parse the multitrillion-dollar debt markets, based on who is giving the loans (foreign or local sources) and who is receiving the loans (governments or private companies and individuals), as well as how large the debt burden is and how fast it is growing and over what period of time. The possible combinations are limitless. What Zielinski did was to zero in on how financial crises are often preceded by a sustained boom in borrowing by the private sector, meaning companies and individuals. A decade later I came to wish that I had internalized this message, as private debt grew rapidly in the United States and Europe in the run-up to the global financial crisis—a disaster that would make the Asian financial crisis look small by comparison. I didn't listen to the chorus whispering, "Kiss of debt, kiss of debt . . ."

Over the last three decades, the world has been subjected to increasingly frequent financial crises, each one setting off a hunt for the clearest warning sign of when the financial mine is about to blow again. Every new crisis seemed to produce a new explanation for crises in general. The postmortems after Mexico's "tequila crisis" of the mid-1990s focused on the dangers of short-term debt, because short-term bonds had started the meltdown that time. After the Asian financial crisis of 1997–98, it was all about the danger of borrowing heavily from foreigners, because foreigners had suddenly cut off lending to Thailand and Malaysia when their problems became clear. These varying explanations resulted in much confusion and contributed to the general failure of most big financial institutions to see the credit crisis looming before 2008.

Embarrassed by that failure, the Bank for International Settlements, the European Central Bank, the IMF, and other authorities began to look at the problem anew, and, by 2011, they had moved along separate paths to similar conclusions. One strong thread in their research linked the major credit crises going back to the Great Depression of the 1930s and in some cases even to the "tulip mania" that tripped up Holland in the 1600s. The precursor of all these crises—and thus the most powerful indicator of a coming crisis—was that domestic private credit had been growing faster than the economy for a significant length of time. This is a very important clue.

The authorities also reached another surprising conclusion: Although the total size of a nation's debt—meaning the total of government and private-sector debt—does matter for the economy's prospects, the clearest signal of coming financial trouble comes from the pace of increase in that debt. Size matters, and pace matters more. It was a bad sign for Thailand that by 1997, private debt amounted to 165 percent of GDP, but a debt burden of that size would not necessarily have signaled a crisis if the debt had not also been growing significantly faster than the economy for a sustained period of time. Thailand's debt had been growing steadily even in the late 1980s, but then it took off after 1990. In the five years before 1997, the Thai economy was growing at an annual rate of about 10 percent, but private debt was growing at a rate of around 25 percent. That runaway pace of credit growth reflected the overoptimistic mood and increasingly bad lending and borrowing decisions Zielinski captured in his play, and it revealed that Thailand's debt burden was increasingly likely to spark a crisis. So the clearest signal of the coming crisis was not that private debt hit 165 percent of GDP in 1997, but that it had risen sharply from 98 percent in 1992, a total increase of 67 percentage points. For the purpose of spotting coming trouble, that is the magic number: the five-year increase in private credit as a share of GDP.*

My own research—also belatedly pushed to the front burner after the shock of 2008—refines these discoveries in two important ways. First, it identifies a point of no return, past which private credit has risen so fast over five years that a financial crisis is very likely. Second, it addresses a question the institutional studies did not ask because they were focused on identifying warning signals of a financial crisis, like a collapse in the stock market or the currency. But what if there is no outright crisis, can a credit binge still damage the economy? My research shows that, past the point of no return, the economy is not only likely to suffer a financial crisis but is also virtually certain to suffer a sharp economic slowdown.†

Looking at the available record going back to 1960 for 150 countries, my team and I isolated the thirty most severe five-year-long credit binges. The analysis yielded what connoisseurs of the debt doomsday genre would recognize as a selection of vintage credit crises. Alone, at the top of the list, stands Ireland. There, in the five years between 2004 and 2009, private credit rose by an astonishing total of 160 percentage points as a share of GDP. Also in the developed world, the list includes Japan in the late 1980s and five countries that saw debt spike before the global financial crisis, including Greece, Australia, Sweden, and Norway. Among emerging nations, the list of extreme binges includes Uruguay and Chile in the 1980s, Thailand and Malaysia in the late 1990s, and China today. For these thirty acute cases, private credit grew significantly faster than the economy for five years running

---

* Indeed, certain nations, such as Chile in the 1980s and Indonesia in the early 1990s, suffered crises after a rapid increase in private debt, but to levels that were still relatively low—less than 50 percent as a share of GDP.

† By 2015, I should note, some private financial industry researchers were publishing pieces on the connection between credit binges and slower economic growth, including "Untangling China's Credit Conundrum" from Goldman Sachs that January and "Keeping a Wary Eye on the EM Credit Cycle" by JP Morgan that November.

and increased private credit as a share of GDP by a total of at least 40 percentage points.[*]

In all these cases, a consistent turn for the worse came following the fifth year of the cycle, after the increase in private credit hit the 40-percentage-point threshold. Once they crossed that line, most of these countries—eighteen out of the thirty—went on to suffer a financial crisis within the next five years.[†] These crises hit countries ranging from Greece, where the trouble began almost as soon as private credit crossed the 40 percentage point threshold in 2008, to Thailand, which first crossed the threshold in 1993 and suffered its financial crisis four years later.

The negative impact of an extreme credit binge on the nation's economic growth rate was even more striking. In all thirty cases, including those that did not lead to a financial crisis, the economy suffered a sharp slowdown at some point after the increase in private credit crossed the 40 percentage point threshold.[‡] On average for the thirty cases, the GDP growth rate fell by more than half over the next five years. In Greece, for example, private debt rose from 69 percent of GDP in 2003 to 114 percent in 2008, for a total five-year increase of 45 percentage points. Over the next five years, Greece's average annual GDP growth rate collapsed to negative 5 percent, down from 3 percent before 2008. These slowdowns came when the period of manic optimism gave way to the realization that borrowers and creditors had overindulged at the height of the boom and now faced a painful period of penny-pinching to work off those debts and loans.

---

[*] In most of these cases, GDP growth was strong during the five-year period when credit was growing dangerously fast, so credit growth was the main reason the credit/GDP ratio was rising

[†] Here I use *financial crisis* to mean a banking crisis as defined by Carmen Reinhart and Kenneth Rogoff in *This Time Is Different* (2009), which captures bank runs that force a government to close, merge, bail out, or take over one or more financial institutions.

[‡] In twenty-six of the thirty cases, the average annual rate of growth fell over the next five years. The other four—Malaysia, Uruguay, Finland, and Norway—experienced a serious contraction in the economy, but the recovery came soon enough to lift the average rate of growth for the next five years.

This thirty-for-thirty result is unusually clear and consistent and hints at what may be a law of economic gravity, at least based on patterns in the global economy from the last fifty years. My research also shows that the pace of growth in private credit is an important indicator at the opposite end of the economic cycle, in the period after a credit mania goes bust. If private credit grows significantly *slower* than GDP for five years running, it can create the conditions for an economy to recover strongly. Banks will have rebuilt stores of deposits and will feel comfortable lending again. Borrowers, having reduced their debt burden, will feel comfortable borrowing again.

The critical question to ask about debt: Is private debt growing faster or slower than the economy for a sustained period? A country in which private credit has been growing much faster than the economy for five years should be placed on watch for a sharp slowdown in the economic growth rate and possibly for a financial crisis as well, because lending is running out of control. On the other hand, if private credit has been growing much slower than the economy for five years, the economy should be put on watch for a recovery, because creditors likely have cleaned up their books and are near ready to lend again.

Thailand illustrates both sides of the rule. After the five-year increase in credit-to-GDP crossed the 40-point threshold in 1993, Thailand's average annual GDP growth rate collapsed from 11 percent in the five years before 1993 to just 2.3 percent over the next five years. Nonetheless the credit run-up continued right until the crisis came in 1997. Then bankers and borrowers pulled back, and as they licked their wounds, credit fell as a share of GDP for five years, right through 2001. It was only after that house cleaning that Thailand's recovery started to pick up real momentum.

The Private Sector Leads, the State Follows

The postmortem investigations conducted after the global financial crisis of 2008 have added to our understanding of the workings of financial crises and why they can be traced most consistently to the borrowing of private companies and individuals. The basic answer is that the private sector is where debt manias typically originate. Some trigger—often an invention or innovation—persuades people that the economy is entering a long period of rapid growth, that their future income prospects are bright, and that they can handle more debt. In the United States, credit booms have been triggered by the invention of the diving bell, the opening of canals and railroads, the advent of television, the arrival of powerful fiber optic networks, and the appearance of new kinds of lending tools that allowed people to borrow against the value of their homes.

At first, the impact of the new innovation does in fact boost economic growth and incomes, inspiring bright forecasts that inspire even more borrowing. This cycle of optimism can continue long after the practical impact of the initial innovation has worn off, and economists can tell that impact is wearing off because productivity growth begins to slow. Many businesses will be so caught up in the mania, however, that they will keep building railways or fiber optic lines past the point when current demand for those products justifies investing more in supply. Others start borrowing to build homes and offices, also on the assumption that the boom in demand will continue. Still others jump in offering new kinds of loans to keep the party going.

When debt is growing significantly faster than the economy, even well-run banks cannot possibly dole out so many loans so quickly without making big mistakes. The longer the binge continues, the bigger the errors, as ever dodgier private lenders get in the game, extending credit to increasingly ill-qualified private borrowers and investors—those amateurs described by Zielinski, like the wealthy housewife ready to invest in "four million of anything." When an economic growth spurt is powered by credit excesses, it is prone to crumble.

In the United States before 2008, as we know now, this process of decay in the quality of private credit was epitomized by the rise of "subprime" lenders, some of them pushing loans on deceptively easy terms to unqualified borrowers. Though the subprime market was responsible for only a small portion of home loans in the United States, it was a concentrated backwater of the kinds of loans that often appear in the late stage of a credit mania, offering the opportunity to borrow for no money down, no proof of employment, and no debt repayment record required. Such loans were as fragile as dead leaves, and they became the tinder that lit the debt pile in 2008.

Typically, it is only after private lenders and borrowers get carried away that the government gets involved. As a credit mania gains momentum, the authorities often try to rein in the more egregiously manipulative new lenders and lending practices, but this quickly degenerates into something approximating a game of Whack-a-Mole. Every time the government tries to smack down one kind of shady lender, another one pops up. If the authorities ban subprime home loans, the credit moles start offering supercheap mobile home loans, no down payment and no job history required.

Eventually, the party comes to an end due to some major financial accident, which typically occurs after the central bank is forced to increase the price of money aggressively to clamp down on the excesses. The economy then slows down sharply, and the authorities begin working to ease the ensuing credit crisis by shifting the debt of bankrupt private borrowers onto the government's books. The government's debt also increases as it often attempts to soften the impact of the economic downturn by borrowing to increase public spending. In a detailed 2014 study of financial crises going back to 1870, the economist Alan Taylor and his colleagues concluded: "The idea that financial crises typically have their roots in fiscal [government borrowing] problems is not supported by history." The origin of the trouble is normally found in the private sector, though countries that enter the crisis with heavy government debt will suffer from a longer and deeper recession, simply because the government will find it hard to borrow to finance bailouts or stimulus spending.

This pattern—of debt crises starting in the private sector, and the state playing a supporting role—is now well established. Of more than 430 severe financial crises since 1970, the IMF classifies fewer than 70 (or less than one in six) as primarily government or "sovereign" debt crises. Those include the debt debacles that hit Latin America in the early 1980s, and the scale of those meltdowns helps explain why many analysts are still quick to look for a government culprit behind every debt crisis. The other reason is that by borrowing too heavily to artificially prolong a boom, governments can wind up making the crisis worse.

The Progressive Disease of Debt

The decay produced by debt is a progressive disease. Its symptoms become gradually more intense, depending on how fast the debt is growing and for how long. My research shows that private credit growth did not have to pass the 40-percentage-point increase that characterizes extreme binges to have a severe impact on economic growth. If private credit grew by just 15 percentage points as a share of GDP over five years, the GDP growth rate eased in the next five years, slowing on average by 1 percentage point a year during that period.

As the pace of private credit growth picked up, the scale and likelihood of an economic slowdown increased as well. If private credit grew by 25 percentage points as a share of GDP over five years, the slowdown was quite significant. On average for these cases, the annual GDP growth rate slowed by a third, but with some results that were much worse. In the United States, for example, private credit grew by 25 percentage points between 2002 and 2007—rising from 143 percent of GDP to 168 percent—and the average annual GDP growth rate slowed from 2.9 percent before 2007 to less than 1 percent over the next five years.

As the slowdown spread from the United States to the rest of the world, governments began borrowing to increase spending and fight the widening recession. This followed the usual pattern, with the private businesses and individuals leading the credit cycle and government following. By 2014, despite the general impression that the world had gone through a painful process of "deleveraging," or belt tightening and paying back loans, this was true only in a few countries and industries. Some private borrowers had cut back to an extent, particularly households and financial corporations in the United States. But those cutbacks were offset by new borrowing by nonfinancial corporations and the U.S. government, so total U.S. debts held steady as a share of the economy. And in the emerging world, many governments and corporations were racking up new debts at an alarming pace.

The result was that, worldwide, the debt burden in many countries has grown faster since the global financial crisis than it did during the supposedly reckless years of borrowing that preceded it. Since 2007 the total global debt burden, which includes households, corporations, and governments, has increased from $142 trillion to $199 trillion, and from 269 percent of global GDP to 286 percent, according to a 2015 study by the McKinsey Global Institute. The world as a whole is more deeply burdened by debt than it was at the outset of the 2008 crisis. The total debt burden held steady in the United States, stagnated in Europe, but swelled significantly in key emerging nations. The U.S. Federal Reserve was keeping borrowing costs so low that it was easy for governments in emerging countries to ramp up lending to fight the global slowdown, and it proved irresistible for private companies to pile on new debts. In the five years after the 2008 crisis, private credit rose fast in many of largest emerging markets, for a total increase of more than 25 percentage points as a share of GDP in Malaysia, Thailand, Turkey, and China. In short, these countries reached a stage where the credit rule was signaling a high likelihood of slower growth in the future.

The Record-Setting Binge in China

China however is in a class of its own. According to McKinsey, out of the $57 trillion increase in debt globally since 2007, more than one-third or $21 trillion has been racked up by China. One result of the 2008 crisis was that while China has not overtaken the United States as the world's largest economy, it has overtaken the United States as the single largest contributor to global GDP growth. In the first half of the 2010s, China accounted for a third of the expansion in the global economy, compared to a 17 percent contribution by the United States, an exact role reversal since the 1990s.

The problem is much of China's rise in the 2010s has been facilitated by massive fiscal and monetary stimulus, which entailed a sizable increase in its debt burden. Thus China's debt bomb has become one of the biggest threats to the global economy. Debate rages over how this story will end, with most analysts arguing that a serious slowdown is not a risk, based in part on the extraordinary track record of China's leaders. They have presided over thirty years of virtually uninterrupted growth, even when crises rattled other emerging nations, so surely they will be able to negotiate the debt problem without serious disruption.

History suggests a less rosy outcome.

Before China's current binge, all thirty of the most extreme postwar credit booms led to a serious slowdown. The roster includes two of the most famous Asian miracles—Japan and Taiwan—which were also celebrated for savvy economic leadership and which saw their long runs of strong growth come to an end in a credit binge. Japan and Taiwan both saw private credit expand by at least 40 percentage points as a share of GDP, with Japan crossing that threshold in 1990 and Taiwan following in 1992. This does not augur well for China's chances of avoiding "the kiss of debt."

After the global financial crisis, signs soon started to appear that— for the first time in a long time—China's leaders did not fully grasp what needed to be done. In 2007 Premier Wen Jiabao warned publicly that China's economy had become "unstable" and "unbalanced," because it was investing too large a share of its income, building too many factories and homes, and pouring too much concrete. To many observers, Wen's admission confirmed Beijing's reputation for economic acumen and signaled that China was about to find a new growth model, one less reliant on heavy investment in export-oriented factories and more on encouraging a stronger consumer society. Previous Asian miracle economies like Japan, South Korea, and Taiwan slowed as they matured, and now that China was entering the middle-income rank of nations, it was time for it to slow down too.

When I visited Beijing in early September 2008, shortly after the close of the Summer Olympic Games, the economy was indeed slowing, but from the leadership on down, there was no alarm. Though property prices were showing signs of weakness and a bubble in the Shanghai stock market had just popped, Chinese officials said this kind of turn was normal in a maturing economy. They talked about cutting back on investment, downsizing large state companies, and letting the market play a greater role in the allocation of credit in the economy. In preparation for welcoming the world to the games, China had even eased Internet censorship and ordered polluting plants around the capital to shut down—temporarily—to improve the air quality for the athletes. By the time I arrived, the skies over Beijing were unusually free of smog, and the country seemed very comfortable with its new middle-class status and the natural slowdown in growth that implied.

Two weeks after I left, Lehman Brothers filed for bankruptcy in the United States, and global markets went into a tailspin. Demand collapsed in the United States and Europe, crushing export growth in China, where the leadership suddenly panicked. By that October, China had rolled out its huge effort to keep the economy growing, using both heavy state spending and trillions of dollars in new debt. Reversing course, Wen's government redoubled its commitment to the old investment-led growth model, this time by fueling the engine with debt. The change came virtually overnight. Between 2003 and 2008 credit was not growing faster than the economy and had held steady at about 150 percent of GDP during that period. Then Beijing started urging state banks to pump loans into state companies and unleashed a classic credit mania.

By the time I returned to Beijing in August 2009, the mood had changed completely, to triumphant self-satisfaction. That year the aggressive government campaign to boost spending and lending would keep China's GDP growth rate above the 8 percent target, while the United States and Europe were in recession. In Beijing, taxi drivers and shopkeepers boasted to me that they were tempted to offer Western tourists a discount, just out of pity. People now seemed convinced that their government could produce any growth rate it wanted, no matter what else was going on in the world. Investment was booming again, fueled by a trillion-dollar flow of new loans in the previous twelve months alone, much of it going into the stock and real estate markets, where prices were rising sharply again. Macao casinos were booming. The only people who expressed any concern were bank regulators in Beijing, who were alarmed by the scale of new debt and told me that they were trying to restore some sanity to the increasingly reckless lending practices. The game of Whack-a-Mole was on.

In response to loosened regulations, and the clear signals from Beijing that it wanted more growth at any cost, lenders started offering new kinds of loans, as well as bonds and credit guarantees designed to stretch the new rules to the maximum. New players that came to be known as the "shadow banks" started to appear, many selling credit products promising to deliver yields that were too high to be true. The big state banks responded to the competition by offering "wealth management products" that bundled their loans together with the higher-returning debts of the shadow banks.

To many Chinese, these wealth-management products looked solid because they were issued by familiar banks backed by the all-powerful state, and they appeared to be attractive because they offered returns up to four times higher than bank deposits. To some observers, however, Chinese wealth-management products soon came to resemble the exotic American debt products that pooled together subprime and other mortgage loans into one murky and explosive bundle. These were the products Warren Buffett described as "financial weapons of mass destruction" six years before their implosion helped trigger the U.S. housing and stock market blow-ups in 2007 and 2008.

When Beijing ordered state banks to tighten lending standards, their borrowers and depositors turned in even greater numbers to the shadow banks, which by 2013 would account for half of the trillions of dollars in new credit flows. When the central government began to limit the amount of money that local governments could borrow, they set up shell companies or "local government funding vehicles" to borrow from shadow banks. Soon these local government fronts became the biggest debtors in the shadow banking system. The market for corporate bonds expanded at a furious pace, and most of the "corporations" selling these bonds were in fact fronts for local government.

China also fell into another classic trap of credit manias, when more and more of the borrowed money goes to feed a boom in property prices. In recent decades, recessions have been more likely to originate in debt-fueled property booms, for the simple reason that there has been an explosion in mortgage finance. The Taylor study cited above looked at seventeen advanced economies going back to 1870 and found that the modern boom in global finance has been led by a sharp rise in mortgage lending to households. Over that 140-year period, mortgage lending has risen by a factor of eight, while bank lending to households and private companies for other purposes has risen by a factor of three. Worldwide, home loans now account for more than half of the business of the typical bank. That, says Taylor, explains why economic booms and busts "seem to be increasingly shaped by the dynamics of mortgage credit," with other forms of lending playing only a minor role.

This growing connection between home loans and financial disaster is equally visible in the emerging world. Research by the International Center for Monetary and Banking Studies shows that many postwar economic "miracles," ranging from Italy and Japan in the 1950s to Latin America and Southeast Asia later on, first took off because of strong fundamentals (like strong investment and low inflation) but were sustained by rapidly rising debts and ended in a debt-fueled property bubble. This pattern is well known and is likely one reason why China's bank regulators became concerned almost as soon as Beijing began pumping credit into the economy.

Much of the new lending went straight into real estate, and when I returned again to China in mid-2010, signs of real estate excesses were visible everywhere. Beijing appeared to be the crane capital of the world, even though construction activity usually slows after a city hosts a major event like the Olympics. While driving from the city of Hangzhou to Shanghai for the annual world expo, it was stunning to see apartment buildings coming up many rows deep, all along the nearly two-hundred-kilometer route. The easy loans flowing into Chinese property spurred the sale of about 800 million square feet of real estate that year, more than in all other markets of the world combined. In big cities, prices were rising at 20 to 30 percent a year, driving up the price of a typical apartment to more than ten times the average annual income. Lacking much choice in a country where the stock market is still underdeveloped, a few well-heeled Chinese were buying as many as thirty to forty homes as investments.

Banks often lose sight of the big picture when credit is growing faster than the economy and fuels a property bubble, and Chinese banks were no different. Mesmerized by the rising prices, they started to pay less attention to whether borrowers had enough income to repay loans than to the value of the collateral—often property—that the borrowers put up to secure the loan. This "collateralized lending" works as long as borrowers short on income can keep getting new loans to cover their old loans—based on the rising price of the property or other assets they have offered up as collateral. By 2013, a third of the new loans in China were going to pay off old loans, a merry-go-round that would stop as soon as housing prices started to fall. That October Bank of China chairman Xiao Gang warned that the shadow banking system was starting to resemble a "Ponzi scheme," with loans based on "empty real estate" that would never generate enough return to repay investors.

At the March 2013 party congress, Wen Jiabao stepped down as premier, and as he left, he issued new warnings about China's dire imbalances, saying there was a "growing conflict between downward pressure on economic growth and excess production capacity." Instead of reforming China's investment-driven growth model, however, Wen's government had refueled it with trillions of dollars' worth of new debt. Optimists turned to his successor for hopes of change. The new premier, Li Keqiang, was a dynamic young economist who talked of unleashing market forces, fighting pollution, and reducing inequality. All that seemed to imply (again) that China was ready to let the economy settle into a more mature growth rate, which in turn would allow it to restrain the credit boom.

The return to pragmatism never came. Instead, the leadership revealed its true priority in July 2013, when a top official declared that GDP growth below the official target of 7.5 percent "will not be tolerated." Far from accepting that slower growth is the fate of any middle-class economy, Beijing appeared to embrace the new popular faith that it could produce any growth rate it wanted by executive order. Fixated now on achieving the official growth target or at least appearing to, the government began to report that GDP growth was coming within a few decimal points of 7.5 percent every quarter. And it could not bring itself to shut off the flood of new credit.

Over the course of 2013, the new leadership did take halting steps to restrain lending—for example, by capping bank loans for new homes, restraining purchases of second homes, and pushing other measures to control the real estate price explosion in major cities. But every time the economy showed signs of slowing, the leadership would reopen the credit spigot. The new players jumping into the lending game grew increasingly flaky, including coal and steel companies that had no business branching into finance but nonetheless started guaranteeing billions of dollars in IOUs issued by their clients and partners. Cash-starved companies began to use these IOUs or "assurance drafts" as a form of virtual currency. In 2014 China's central bank estimated that the total value of assurance drafts in circulation had reached the equivalent of $3 trillion.

The credit binge was about to reach new heights. By 2014, the property boom seemed close to peaking, as property prices eased in big cities, but credit was still flowing, lubricated now by the emergence of hundreds of new "crowdfunding" websites with names like "SouFun" that allowed amateur investors to buy a piece of a new mortgage on a deluxe apartment for as little as a few renminbi; one unit of the currency was worth sixteen cents at the time. These websites promised to pay double-digit returns within a matter of weeks. Professional analysts dismissed these offers as implausible, doubting that the lenders had any real connection to the sparkling properties featured in their promotional photos.

By this point, the lending entrepreneurs were shifting their sights to new targets—another move typical in late stages of a credit mania. Credit that had been flowing into property started flowing anew into the stock market, this time with loud and consistent support from the state media, which praised buying stocks as an act of patriotism and good financial sense. Chinese citizens sit on around $20 trillion in savings, and Chinese policy makers wanted to steer some of those savings into stock purchases, in a last-ditch effort to give debt-laden companies a new source of financing. Clearly the aim was to trigger a slow and steady bull run. But the stock market—which had been somnolent for many years—exploded into one of the biggest bubbles in history.

There are four basic signs of a stock market bubble: prices rising at a pace that can't be justified by the underlying rate of economic growth; high levels of borrowing for stock purchases; overtrading by retail investors; and exorbitant valuations. In April 2015, when the Shanghai market had already risen more than 70 percent in the previous six months, the state-run *People's Daily* crowed that the good times were "just beginning." But the market was rallying despite the fact that it had reached the extreme end of all four bubble metrics, which is rare. Stock prices continued to rise, even though economic growth was slowing and corporate profits were shrinking. The amount Chinese investors had borrowed to buy stock equaled 9 percent of the total value of tradable stocks—the highest level of debt-fueled buying for any stock market in history. On some days, more stock was changing hands in China than in all the other stock markets of the world combined. Millions of ordinary Chinese were registering each week as market investors, egged on by those articles in the state media extolling the virtues of buying stock. Two-thirds of the new investors lacked a high school diploma. In rural villages, farmers had set up mini stock exchanges. Some said they spent more time trading than working in the fields.

The Chinese economist Wu Jinglian once said that Chinese stock markets "are worse than casinos, because even casinos have rules."[1] In June 2015 the market started to crash, and in contrast to early 2008, the government intervened aggressively this time—for example, by ordering investors not to sell and threatening those who did sell with prosecution. But Beijing was unable to stop the market's tumble, and as the Shanghai market lost more than a third of its value within a couple of months, the widespread belief that Beijing's authoritarian government could produce any economic outcome it wanted suddenly shifted. Global opinion makers began to question Beijing's reputation for deft handling of the economy, now that its leaders had blown bubbles in the stock, bond, and housing markets. All those bubbles posed a clear threat to the rise of China.

This credit binge had distinctly Chinese characteristics, including the borrowing by local government fronts and the Communist propaganda cheering on a capitalist bubble, but the fundamental fragilities were typical of most manias. There was the obvious moral hazard of a market in which most lenders assumed the government would bail them out if their loans failed, the obvious potential for conflicts of interest and crony lending when the state owns the biggest banks and also their biggest customers, and the familiar spectacle of new lending enterprises popping up faster than the hand of the state could whack them down. These are all important warning signals.

China's credit binge was on the verge of becoming the largest on record in the emerging world. Recall that through 2008 credit growth had remained steady as a share of GDP in China, but after party leaders threw open the credit spigot late that year, the debt burden exploded. By 2013, the five-year increase in private debt had reached a record 80 percentage points as a share of GDP. The next biggest credit binge on record in the emerging world unfolded in the 1990s in Malaysia and Thailand. In Thailand, the five-year increase in private credit to GDP hit 67 percentage points in 1997 and the ensuing slowdown was severe. No country had ever survived a debt binge of such a scale without suffering a severe economic slowdown. It was unlikely China could avoid a similar fate.

There Is No Good Defense Against Extreme Credit Bubbles

At least through 2014, American and European confidence in Beijing's leadership remained so high that the consensus forecasts of private-sector economists for China's growth in the coming years were close to the official Chinese target, then still set at 7.5 percent. The bullish forecasters argued that China was different and could defy its debt burdens because the country had special strengths. It earned a steady stream of foreign income from its powerful export industries, and after running a big trade surplus for many years, it had amassed a war chest of dollars and other foreign currency totaling $4 trillion at the peak. These foreign reserves could be used to pay down debts or to shore up local banks that were running low on capital.

The China bulls further argued that while many emerging countries fell into crisis after borrowing heavily from foreign creditors, Chinese borrowers were in debt mainly to Chinese lenders. In a situation like this, the government could arrange to have bad debts passed around inside the country like a hot potato. And China's regular banks, as opposed to the shadow banks, looked reasonably stable—supported by very large stores of deposits, thanks to very strong domestic savings, which amounted to 50 percent of GDP, compared to a global average of about 22 percent. In short, the bulls argued, China was well positioned to pay off or forgive its own debts.

The historical record casts doubt on the strength of these defenses, not only for China but for any country. Many other nations on the list of the thirty most extreme credit binges enjoyed some of the same advantages, but this did them no good. Taiwan suffered a banking crisis in 1995 despite having foreign exchange reserves that totaled 45 per cent of GDP, a slightly higher level than China had accumulated by 2014. Taiwan's banks also appeared to hold more than ample deposits to back their loans, but that did not avert a crunch. Banking crises hit Japan in the 1970s and Malaysia in the 1990s, even though these countries had high domestic savings rates of around 40 percent of GDP, also well above the global average.

Finally, one of the biggest fallacies offered in China's defense was that although its total debt burden (private and public) looked high, it was not a real threat. By 2015, China's debts had climbed to more than 250 percent as a share of GDP, but this was in the same ballpark as the U.S. burden and a lot smaller than Japan's, which had reached nearly 400 percent. The problem with this comparison was that richer countries can always handle larger debts, for the obvious reason that they have more money in the banks. A debt burden equal to around 250 percent of GDP was pretty normal for a country like the United States, with an average per capita income over $50,000, but it was by far the largest for an emerging nation like China, in the income class of around $10,000. It was also larger than any nation with a per capita income twice as high, including South Korea and Taiwan.

Even if some of the mitigating factors might prevent an outright financial crisis, as debt was continuously rolled over among state-owned entities, a persistent and sharp slowdown still seemed inevitable with a large amount of the new debt going to pay the interest rate on existing loans rather than funding fresh projects. There are no certainties in what leads to the rise and fall of nations. But in the past, every extreme credit binge has resulted in slumping economic growth, often accompanied by a financial crisis.

The Shape of the Slowdown

When a credit crisis hits, the psychology that drove the boom shifts into reverse. People lose faith in the growth prospects of the economy, in their future income, and in their ability to pay off debts. That uncertainty leads to belt-tightening, further slowing the economy.

An economic slowdown after a debt binge can follow a variety of scenarios, involving some combination of a short-term pullback in the economy and a long-term fall in the trend growth rate. The standard scenario is a sharp contraction followed by a recovery to the previous trend growth rate, which was what happened to Sweden after its financial crisis in the early 1990s. The worst cases involve a contraction and then a recovery but to a new, lower trend growth rate, which will in the long run leave the economy significantly smaller than it otherwise would have been. That unfortunately appeared to be the scenario unfolding in the Eurozone after the debt crisis of 2010. It was also the path followed by Japan after its debts peaked in 1990, and by Taiwan after its debts peaked in 1992.

The path a country takes depends in large part on how quickly the government can address the basic debt-to-GDP balance, either by slowing the pace of growth in debt or by reviving GDP growth, or both. In a maturing economy like China, where growth is slowing naturally, the key question is how soon and how aggressively the government can fix the debt problem.

Compared to the other nations on the list of extreme credit binges, one possible path China may follow is that of the other Asian miracle economies, particularly Taiwan, where the mounting debts produced a mild crisis in 1995 and a severe one in 1997. Taiwan responded by pulling back sharply on lending. At the time Taiwan was moving away from the dictatorial version of crony capitalism established by Chiang Kai-shek, and more private players were entering the market, including private banks. They were competing with state banks, making loans based on the economic prospects rather than the political connections of the borrower. The government also canceled a major six-year investment plan, rather than run up its debts to push the projects through. The result was that Taiwan's total debt leveled off, and today it stands at 175 percent of GDP, about where it was at the time of its mid-1990s crises. The economy did slow down to a lower trend growth rate, from nearly 9 percent in the five years before the increase in credit crossed the 40-percentage-point threshold in 1992, to just under 7 percent in the five years after. This was, however, still a strong growth rate for a developing economy, which at the time had an average per capita income of around $15,000.

A worse scenario for China is also possible, however. It is the path of 1990s Japan, which tried to avoid pain at any cost after rising debts led to the collapse of its property and stock market bubbles. Rather than take steps to slow lending growth, or to force banks to recognize and clean up bad loans, Japan bailed out troubled borrowers and covered bad loans with new loans. This daisy chain of bailouts was supported by the *keiretsu*, large conglomerates like Mitsubishi and Mitsui that were built around one bank, whose officials often felt personally obligated to keep their various subsidiaries alive. The bailouts were also aggressively supported by the state. Though private credit growth did slow, government debt started to grow rapidly and has kept growing. Fearing that bankruptcies would lead to unemployment and threaten the ruling party, the government pressured banks to ramp up lending for corporate bailouts and increasingly unproductive investments, including Japan's famous "bridges to nowhere." By the late 1990s, a survey of all publicly traded firms in Japan's construction, manufacturing, real estate, wholesale, and retail industries found that 30 percent qualified as "zombie companies," meaning that they were being kept alive by subsidized loans. This life-support system for failing companies blocked financing for new ones, undercutting Japan's productivity.

The result of these "extend and pretend" debt policies was the worst of both worlds—stagnating growth and rising debt. The continuing effort to prevent any painful reckoning with the credit binge increased

Japan's total debt from 250 percent of GDP in 1990 to 390 percent today. Japan is both perennially vulnerable to debt crises and stuck with a much lower trend growth rate. It suffered a series of bank crises in the 1990s and early 2000s, and its GDP growth rate fell from nearly 5 percent before 1990 to less than 1 percent for the next quarter-century, which represents the worst record for a large developing economy over that period. By 2015, Japan's $4 trillion economy was 80 percent smaller than one would have expected based on its trend growth rate in the 1980s, when it was being hyped as the next world superpower.

This is a possible future for China, if it continues to use debt in a politicized campaign to artificially shore up growth and avoid any painful short-term reckoning. By some estimates 10 percent of the firms on the mainland stock exchange are "zombie companies," kept alive by government support. China has yet to even begin the process of deleveraging, or cutting back debts, which are still growing at a pace of 15 percent a year, more than twice as fast as the economy. History shows that when massive credit binges start to unwind, and credit growth falls below the rate of economic growth, the immediate result is often a recession. But that is a necessary cleansing step, before a new period of healthy credit growth can begin.

The Upside of Credit Booms

Not all increases in debt are for the worse. Capitalism can't work without a credit system that allows small entrepreneurs to borrow to fund big dreams, and there have been many good credit booms, in which credit grew—but not too fast—as a share of the economy and went to fund projects that could boost future growth. Steady credit booms can leave banks with more capital, because they earn a good return on their loans, and with improved lending practices, they offer legitimately creative credit products.

So now to the upside of the rule: If credit has been growing slower than the economy for five years, it suggests that the banking system is healing, creditors are getting ready to start lending again, and a period of healthy credit growth is in the offing. In fact, the more slowly debt has been growing as a share of GDP over a five-year period, the more likely it is that the economy will witness an increase in growth, boosted by healthy credit, in the ensuing years. Many countries have seen this turn for the better in credit and GDP growth in recent decades, including Chile, which was at the bottom of its crisis in 1991, Hungary in 1995, and the Czech Republic, where private credit bottomed out at 30 percent of GDP in 2002. But one of the most dramatic cases of "bottoming out" came in Indonesia after the Asian financial crisis of 1997–98.

In 1997, when the first signs of debt problems appeared in neighboring Thailand, officials of Indonesia's ruling Suharto dictatorship didn't realize how vulnerable their country was. As part of a reform program over the previous decade, the Suharto regime had opened up the nation's banking system to new players, but the poorly designed reforms allowed many industrial conglomerates to establish their own banks, which came to operate as private slush funds. Subsequent waves of investigations revealed that at some banks more than 90 percent of the loans were "connected," or doled out to a bank's parent company, its subsidiaries, or its top officials. In a system based on distributing loans to allies and colleagues, it was hardly surprising that the banks did little vetting of their borrowers. The investigations also revealed that as much as 90 percent of the loans on the books of some banks were "nonperforming"; the borrower had not made a payment in at least nine months.

Often, at the depths of a credit crisis, entrenched powers fight to hold on to the banks that they have run into insolvency and to the fiction that the loans they own still have value. Japan is the classic case, and that is also what happened in Indonesia, but for a much shorter period. The bank restructuring agency set up to dispose of bad loans and to nationalize or shut down failing banks started out by naming thirteen banks that were owned by Suharto's close friends and sons. With Indonesia looking serious about reform, markets expressed relief. Then one of his sons reemerged as head of a different bank along with his old staff; public confidence in the banking system collapsed, and Indonesian businessmen began withdrawing their money and moving it to foreign countries.

So much capital had fled Indonesia by early 1998 that the currency lost 80 percent of its value, and more and more of the politically favored conglomerates could not make payments on their "connected" loans. As the weeks passed, each piece of bad news about the bank investigations—some of them leaked despite Suharto's attempts to keep the process secret—would trigger new runs on the banks. Investigators found that many of the state banks—which held about half of the assets in the system—were insolvent. They did not have enough deposits on hand to back up the loans to their customers, many of whom had ceased making payments anyway. As the extent of the rot became known, the total stock market value of Indonesian banks collapsed to near zero in 1998; in the world's estimation, the Indonesian banking system had basically ceased to exist.

Soon enough bloody street protests broke out, forcing Suharto to resign and tilting the balance of power toward the reformers. Pockets of resistance remained, but the restructuring agency moved faster, completing a transformation of the entire ownership structure of the banks. Suharto's family and their friends were ousted, many of them banned from the industry for life. More than bank reform, this was political revolution. In a historically insular country, foreigners were granted the right to buy 99 percent ownership stakes in banks and to replace the old bosses with competent professionals. During the Asian financial crisis, neighboring Thailand and South Korea also pushed bank reform, but they did so within an existing democratic system; in Indonesia, there was democratic reform of a dictatorial regime, and the old banking system and its kingpins fell alongside the dictator.

In any emerging country, where banks still account for 80 percent of all lending (compared to 50 percent in the United States), a shakeup of banking is a shakeup of society. To restart a banking system from zero, which is where Indonesia found itself, two steps are critical. The bad loans need to be recognized and removed from the books, or the debt burden will act as a drag on lending for years; and the banks need to be "recapitalized," which means provided with fresh capital, which can be done either by the government or by new owners, so that they have money to start making new loans.

Dealing with bad loans always poses a political problem in deciding who will suffer the pain. Authorities can make the borrowers take the hit, by forcing them into default or bankruptcy or by allowing the lender to seize their cars or homes. Or they can press lenders to forgive the debt of the borrower either in its entirety or by offering some relief in the form of easier repayment terms or lowering the total amount owed. After 2008, one reason the United States bounced back faster than Europe is that in most states U.S. law makes it relatively easy for homeowners to default on their mortgages. This helped clear bad debt from the system. One way or another, the beginning of the end of a credit crisis often arrives not when the debts start to be repaid but when they begin to be resolved through forgiveness and relief, or foreclosure and default.

Indonesia resolved bad loans and recapitalized banks with unusual aggression and speed. Given the disrepute into which banks had fallen, it was politically less difficult to inflict pain on them. The government took control of some $32 billion in bad loans, which would eventually be sold for pennies on the dollar, and injected new capital—typically, simple government bonds—into the banks that were in the best shape. Many of the rest were forced either to merge or to close, and within two years the number of banks in Indonesia had fallen from 240 to 164. Four of the worst state banks were folded into one of the stronger ones, Bank Mandiri. Nine of the failed private banks were folded into a transformed Bank Danamon, whose original owner was one of Suharto's closest associates, but who ended up fleeing the country with the authorities close on his heels. He owed more than $1 billion in emergency loans he had received from crony banks.

Another strong signal that a debt crisis is bottoming out can be found inside the banks. Typically, when a bank is disbursing more money in loans than it holds in deposits and relying on outside funding to fill the gap, it could face trouble. If its loans amount to more than 100 percent of deposits, the bank enters a risky zone, and past 120 percent, it faces a crisis warning. After the crisis hits, the ratio of loan to deposits will start falling, as the bank curtails lending, writes off bad loans, and eventually begins to attract deposits again. In general, when total loans fall back under roughly 80 percent as a share of total deposits in the banking system, banks will be poised to start lending again.

This return to banking system balance—with deposits in healthy proportion to loans—has marked the revival in credit and economic growth in many post-crisis countries, including Indonesia. As the crisis approached in 1997, the average loan-to-deposit ratio in the nation's banking system hit 110 percent. After the crisis, the housecleaning was abrupt, as bad loans were wiped from the books and new lending stalled, and the loan-to-deposit ratio fell to 35 percent within a year.

This set the stage for a transformation. Indonesian banks were so badly burned by the Asian financial crisis that they have been branded with a sense of caution that remains today. The banks that were created from the rubble of the dozens that failed at the bottom of the crisis, Danamon and Mandiri, have emerged to become among the best-run and most respected banks in Asia. Meanwhile Jardine Fleming, the investment bank that ignored Zielinski's warnings about the kiss of debt, is long gone. It was one of the first Asian banks to fail as the crisis spread.

Debtophobia

After the humiliation of a debt crisis, badly burned borrowers and banks often fall prey to debtophobia—the fear of taking on debt or giving out credit. Consumers and businesses want only to retire their debts, not to embark on new ventures, while banks are afraid to lend to these shell-shocked customers. Talking to bankers in Thailand and Malaysia in 1998 was like talking to victims of a post-traumatic stress disorder. Many of them preferred to lie low, to buy more safe government bonds and hold them to maturity, rather than take the risk of making new loans. For the next five years, credit grew slowly and retarded the recovery in much of Southeast Asia, where economic growth rates revived but to a pace only one-half to one-third as fast as before the crisis.

After the 2008 global crisis, there was widespread fear that capitalism would grind to a halt, as lenders and borrowers around the world again succumbed to debtophobia. To get a handle on the scale of this threat, researchers dug back into the historical record and found many cases of "creditless recoveries," economies that began to grow again even though credit did not. In fact, in one large IMF study, 20 to 25 percent of the nearly four hundred postwar economic recoveries unfolded without a meaningful revival in credit growth. To some, the fact that economies could revive without credit growth seemed almost magical, and some economists termed them "Phoenix recoveries." It turned out, however, that without credit, a recovery will generally be very weak, with GDP growth rates around one-third lower than in a normal credit-fueled recovery.

Mexico has suffered one of the longest cases of debtophobia in the emerging world. Ever since the string of financial crises that culminated in the peso collapse of 1994, the country has been trying to grow with little credit. The 1994 crisis destroyed Mexican banks as completely as Indonesian banks would be four years later, but the local Mexican owners were not forced out and managed to delay any cleanup of bad loans. At the same time, they never regained the confidence to grant new loans, in part because they had few deposits. The Mexican populace came to distrust bankers so thoroughly that to this day many people don't keep a bank account. Private lending picked up after the early 2000s, but only briefly, when the government forced the sale of Mexico's three largest banks to multinationals like Citibank and HSBC, in the hope of a credit recovery that never came.

The crisis of 2008 scared the multinationals away from lending anywhere, including in Mexico, despite the fact that Mexico's problem was too little credit. By 2014, Mexico had a remarkable twenty-year record of debtophobia, during which private credit shrank as a share of GDP from 38 percent in 1994 to 25 percent, one of the lowest levels in the world. It is no accident that this long period of stagnant credit growth was accompanied by a long period of weak GDP growth, during which neighbors like Chile and Brazil surpassed Mexico in terms of average per capita income.

Mexico's lingering debtophobia has now lasted nearly as long as the one suffered by the United States after the Great Depression. As the British economist Tim Congdon pointed out in 1989, the twenty-five years before the crash of 1929 saw growing American optimism in the economic future, while the twenty-five years after were marked by persistent doubts about the probability and durability of a recovery, and a leading symptom of that doubt was "extreme caution" toward new borrowing and lending.[2]

The normal bout of debtophobia is much shorter than twenty-five years, of course. In a study of all the biggest financial crises going back to the Great Depression, Empirical Research, an independent New York–based consulting firm, found that on average a debt crisis was followed by a period of weak credit and economic growth that lasted about four to five years, after which both credit and GDP growth picked up.[3] This evidence supports the upside of the credit rule, which shows that five-year runs of weak credit growth often lead to a stronger run of economic growth.

The Asian crisis nations illustrate this process well. After 1997 credit fell in the ensuing five years by at least 40 percentage points as a share of GDP in Indonesia, Thailand, and Malaysia. But by around 2001, the gloomy spell of debtophobia started to lift.[*] It takes a trigger to restart a credit boom, some new innovation or change in the economy that gives people reason to believe that their incomes will go up in the future so

---

[*] South Korea, another country at the center of the Asian financial crisis, is excluded here because it followed a different pattern and never saw a decline in credit growth.

they can afford to take on debt and business risks. In Southeast Asia that trigger came from growing signs of financial stability—falling debts and declining government deficits—coupled with booming global prices commodities, which are a critical export for many regional economies. As credit growth picked up in the early 2000s, so did the average GDP growth rate in these three Southeast Asian economies, rising from around 4 percent between 1999 and 2002 to nearly 6 percent between 2003 and 2006.

How Paying Off Debt Pays Off

It's hard to overstate the transformative effect healthy credit growth can have on economic growth in many nations. For much of the 2000s, credit expanded in the emerging world but not too fast as a share of the economy. Remember that even in China credit held steady at about 150 percent of GDP from 2003 to 2008, and economic growth averaged 10 percent a year during that period. Across the emerging world, the combination of healthy credit growth and low inflation was creating the first period of real financial stability many of these countries had ever known.

This stability would transform societies from Russia to Brazil, Turkey, and Indonesia, mainly because high inflation tends to be unpredictable. If lenders cannot even guess the worth of big-ticket items in the future, they will be unwilling to offer long-term loans for houses or cars or businesses or anything else. That still holds true in unusual cases like Argentina, where inflation remains a persistent problem and banks still generally limit the duration of even their long-term loans to a few months. Many of the cornerstones of American middle-class existence, including the five-year car loan or the thirty-year mortgage, are unobtainable luxuries.

For much of the rest of the emerging world, Southeast Asia included, the revival of credit growth in a newly inflation-free environment revolutionized the business of lending in the 2000s. Basic staples of consumer society in the developed world like credit cards, mortgages, and corporate bonds did not exist in most emerging nations as recently as the 1990s. Mortgages were rare in these countries as of 2000 but have since become a multibillion-dollar industry, rising from 0 percent of GDP to 7 percent in Brazil and Turkey, 4 percent in Russia, and 3 percent in Indonesia by 2013. This growing role for credit in a developing economy is referred to as "financial deepening." For countries where people could not buy a car or a house unless they amassed the necessary cash, the introduction of these simple credit products is as important a step into the modern world as indoor plumbing.

The public mood and psychology during a time of healthy credit growth bears no resemblance to the anything-goes atmosphere of a credit mania. In place of shady lenders and unqualified borrowers, responsible lenders are widening the choice of solid loan options available to the average Joe or small business, fueling a period of economic growth that is strong but not too strong to last. When the global financial crisis hit in 2008, all eyes turned immediately to the problems created by the rapid expansion of debt in the United States and Europe. Meanwhile the nations formerly hyped as the "economic tigers" of Southeast Asia had fallen off the global radar, and few noticed that they had reduced their debt burden and were now in a strong position to weather the debt crisis.

Apart from Indonesia, this was also true of Thailand, Malaysia, and the Philippines. These countries had manageable debt burdens and strong banks ready to lend, with total loans that amounted to well under 80 percent of total deposits. Over the next five years the health of the credit system would prove crucial to a nation's prospects for recovery: Nations such as Spain and Greece that had seen the sharpest increase in debt during the global expansion between the 2003 and 2007 boom would post the slowest growth after the crisis; nations such as Philippines and Thailand that had seen the smallest increase in debt during the boom would fare the best.

By 2015, another role reversal was clearly in view. By then the private sectors of developed countries such as the United States and Spain had reduced their debt burden while many emerging markets had been borrowing heavily in an effort to keep growth alive. As emerging-world governments opened up the credit taps in the aftermath of the Great Recession in 2008, debt levels surged but economic growth did not keep up.

This is the flip side of bad investment binges, which are often fueled in their latter stages by too many creditors lending too much money to increasingly unproductive investments, like the building of excess factory capacity or lavish second homes. Before 2007, as we have seen, it took one dollar of new debt to generate one dollar of GDP growth in the emerging world, including in China. Five years after the global crisis, it took two dollars of new debt to generate one dollar of GDP growth in the emerging world, and in China it took four dollars, as more and more lending went into unproductive investments. By 2015, many emerging nations from Brazil to Turkey and Thailand were paying the price for having borrowed too heavily over a short span of time, and excessive debt was a major restraint on their economic prospects.

Rising debt levels can be a sign of healthy growth, so long as debt is not growing too much faster than the economy for too long. The level of debt may matter at some unknown point, but the pace of increase in debt is the most important and clear sign of a shift for the better or worse, and the first signs of trouble often appear in the private sector, where credit manias tend to originate. The psychology of a debt binge not only encourages lending mistakes and borrowing excesses that will retard growth and possibly lead to a financial crisis, but also leaves a mental scar that can last long after the crisis has passed. Once the symptoms of debtophobia start to lift and banks are ready to lend again, the country will feel free of debt burdens and be ready to grow again.

10

THE HYPE WATCH

*How is the country portrayed
by global opinion makers?*

I BEGAN WRITING A NEWSPAPER COLUMN IN 1991, THE START
of a decade that would make me acutely wary of believing headlines and magazine cover stories. At that time the global media were
obsessed with the rise of Japan as the world's dominant economic
power. Japanese companies were outselling their American rivals
on U.S. turf in industries ranging from cars to electronics, and
appeared ready to take over other industries as well. At the peak
of the Japanese bubble in 1989, the value of companies traded in
Tokyo accounted for half the total value on global stock markets,
and Japanese land was just as pricey. A favorite media factoid at the
time was that the land under the Imperial Palace in Tokyo would
sell for more than all the land in California. The Japanese bubble
began to fizzle in 1990, with the crash of the Tokyo stock market
and housing prices, but much of the global media and the political
class kept surfing the wave of hype.

Over two years after the downturn in the Japanese markets, *Time*
magazine in February 1992 ran a cover story on Japan that included
predictions on how the world's second-largest economy could overtake the United States by the year 2000. It quoted Yoshio Sakurauchi,

the speaker of the Lower House of the Japanese parliament, as saying American workers were lazy and illiterate, and that the United States was becoming Japan's subcontractor. The story also cited the pollster William Watts's finding that Americans ranked the Japanese economic threat higher than the Russian military threat. In the U.S. presidential race that year, candidate Paul Tsongas declared: "The Cold War is over and Japan has won."[1]

The Japanese example was a real-time education for me on the essential difference between Wall Street and Fleet Street: their perspective on time. Investors focus on the future, while the news media focus on the present. Their perspectives diverge because their incentives are different. Market players make money by being early to the next big trend, while media commentators make their reputation by credibly explaining the day's headlines. Often, the media warm to a trend only after it has been running for a few years, and has difficulty letting go of the story. Waves of hype do grip the markets, of course; it's just that the news media are geared to capture the current zeitgeist, which reflects the strongest consensus thinking.

Three years after becoming a columnist, I started my career as an investor, and I've been caught ever since between the time horizons of my two passions: writing and investing. By that year, 1994, investors had shifted their attention to new targets in Asia—particularly Thailand, Indonesia, and Malaysia—which appeared poised to join Japan as manufacturing powerhouses. The media were also following the "Asia Rising" story, loudly, with magazine covers celebrating Mahathir Mohamad as "The Master Planner" and countless articles extoling the virtues of "Asian values" such as thriftiness, hard work, respect for leaders, and family loyalty. The media hype continued up to the moment that Southeast Asian currencies and markets melted down in the financial crisis of 1997, when the mood suddenly switched from love to hate, as it so often does. Glowing stories about the new "tiger" economies were replaced by scathing exposés about the multibillion dollar fortune of Indonesian leader Suharto and his family, the corrupt lending practices of Malaysian companies, and investment excesses of Asian "golf course capitalism," a reference to dubious deals struck up between businessmen and politicians over a leisurely round.

The popular media's admiration then swung to the United States, which did look stunningly strong. At the height of the Asian financial crisis in 1998, the U.S. economy expanded at a blistering 5 percent pace, and consumer demand in the United States prevented the world from slipping into a recession. It was almost impossible to interest anyone in emerging economies. Malaysia had the Petronas Towers, then the world's tallest buildings, but American global brands such as McDonald's, with its golden arches, looked like a plausible and less risky vehicle of global economic expansion. This period—from 1998 to 2003—was marked by emotions of hate or at best indifference for many emerging markets.

Time ran a cover in 2003 dismissing Indonesia and the other economies of Southeast Asia as "Tigers No More." Written in the tone of pieces revisiting natural disaster sites five years after the event, the *Time* story effectively wrote off the former tigers. Over the next five years, however, the once crisis-hit countries of Southeast Asia were part of a boom that saw the average pace of growth in emerging economies hit more than 7 percent. During this period, the economic turnaround in emerging countries such as Turkey was ignored by the international press and opinion makers. Though Turkey's moderate Islamic ruling party was pushing economic reform hard in order to gain membership in the European Union, the global media focused instead on its conservative social agenda. Every time Turkey clashed with the EU over a social proposal—to punish adultery, or to ban kissing in public—the media asked whether Turkey could fit comfortably in a political union with more liberal cultures. Meanwhile, Turkey's per capita income would triple over the course of the decade, making it the world's tenth-fastest-growing economy in the 2000s.

Elie Wiesel, the writer and Holocaust survivor, said the opposite of love is not hate; it is indifference. This observation applies well to understanding the hype cycle. The question to ask of any country: How is it portrayed by the global media? The longer an economic boom lasts, the more credible a country's track record appears to the media and the more warmly they embrace it as the economy of the future. The more this love deepens, the more alarmed I get. As we have seen, long runs of sustained growth are rare. And the faster an economy booms, the shorter its growth run is likely to be.

Volumes of research back this firmly established pattern in the rise and fall of nations. One of the most striking versions comes from Credit Suisse, which compiled a database that goes back to 1900—about half a century longer than other efforts. The results reconfirmed the Hobbesian fact that most growth spurts are hard to sustain. Economies—both emerging and developed—that managed to grow at 6 percent a year would typically sustain that pace for four years in a row, those that grew at 8 percent would maintain that speed for three years, and a 10 percent rate normally lasts for two years.

The message of this and similar studies is the same: If a period of strong growth approaches the five-year mark, the default assumption should be that the growth spurt is nearing its end. And yet, many observers assume that strength will build on strength. The praise they shower on economies in the midst of growth booms only sows the seeds of collapse—it makes national leaders too complacent to keep pushing reform and attracts more foreign capital than the country can handle. When a crisis hits, the media's love turns at first to hate. The criticism that follows a crisis is often well founded—the stew of crony capitalist practices exposed by the Asian financial crisis was very real—but a turnaround is still far off. Messes take time to fix.

The next stars often emerge from among countries that have fallen off the media radar—or were never on it in the first place. They start to flourish—or recover momentum—when left alone to put their economic house in order, and it is only after they record several years of strong growth that the media discover them. By then, the run may be nearing exhaustion. The basic rule: the global media's love is a bad sign for any economy, and its indifference is a good one.

A Brief History of Emerging World Hype

Hype about the next hot economies has been proven consistently wrong. In the early twentieth century, people who paid attention to global economic competition were more scarce than they are today, but they were focused on the bright future of Latin America and particularly Argentina, which had already attained first-world income levels by taking advantage of a new British invention—the refrigerated steam ship—to export its beef and crops to the world. Argentina was still one of the richest economies in the world in the 1950s, but it was failing to modernize under the populist misrule of Juan Perón, and the hype was shifting to Venezuela, which would exploit its vast oil wealth in subsequent decades and become a cofounder alongside Saudi Arabia of the OPEC cartel. As oil prices spiked in the 1970s, Venezuela reached an income level close to that of the United States and was touted as the future of Latin America: a rising capitalist democracy on a continent where dictators were taking over in Argentina, Brazil, and later Chile.

Pundits of the 1950s and '60s paid very little attention to Asia, and when they did pay any mind they celebrated the prospects of the Philippines and Burma, both rich in metals, gems and other natural resources. They pitied China and India, and into the mid-1960s many economists dismissed Taiwan as a "basket case" devoid of natural resources, lacking in capital, with a corrupt and discredited government presiding over a largely illiterate population.[2] The world took a similarly dim view of South Korea, seen by commentators in the United States as a "hopeless and bottomless pit," a frontline Cold War state into which Washington was dumping foreign aid dollars with little prospect of generating any economic turnaround. Donors spoke of pouring money down the Korean "rat hole."[3]

These assessments misfired on every salient point—wrong on the future of continents and of countries. Since the 1970s, Asia's average income has been catching up to the West, but Latin America has fallen behind. Argentina continued to tread water, and Venezuela hit the wall when oil prices collapsed in the 1980s. Within Asia, Burma faltered even before the government fell in a 1962 coup that created the failed military state which the generals later renamed Myanmar. The Philippines followed Burma down the tubes three years later, when the kleptocrat Ferdinand Marcos and his equally corrupt wife took power. Meanwhile, their less-noticed Asian neighbors, led by Taiwan the "basket case" and South Korea the "rat hole," were starting to take off. Two decades later, China and then India would also begin their transformations.

The Cover Curse

Weighing hype is another one of those forecasting arts, in which judgments can be aided but not defined by data, such as Google hits and broad media coverage or surveys of leading economists and investor sentiment. In the Internet age, there is no single, iconic measure of mainstream opinion. That distinction used to belong to the covers of the major news magazines, but many American magazine journalists have long recognized the backward-looking nature of their business with a joke: By the time a story reaches the cover of *Time* or *Newsweek*, it's dead.

Even accounting for the jealousy of journalists working at less-iconic publications, I felt there was some truth to this joke, particularly applied to economic stories. It explained how *Newsweek* could write a cover on Sony's "invasion" of Hollywood as the latest sign of Japan's inexorable rise in October 1989, months before the Japanese economy entered a two-decade decline. It is why *Time* would ask whether this is "China's Century—or India's?" in November 2011, the year when all the big emerging economies were starting to slow dramatically.

To test the general proposition, my team and I looked at covers of *Time* published between 1980 and 2010, and found 122 issues in which the cover featured an economic take on an individual country or a region. (*Newsweek* got a pass for lack of access to its archives.) We then determined whether the cover story was optimistic or pessimistic in its spin, and if that sentiment was accurate. The results confirmed some truth in the old joke. If the *Time* cover was downbeat, economic growth picked up over the next five years in 55 percent of the cases. In March 1982, *Time*'s cover invoked "Interest Rate Anguish" over U.S. Fed chief Paul Volcker's decision to hike interest rates, a move now widely lauded as the decisive blow against the stagflation that had gripped the United States. In August 1999, *Time*'s cover on "Japan Returns to Nationalism" saw the country turning inward after a financial crisis, but Japan soon went on to at least briefly pursue reform and pick up some speed under Prime Minister Junichiro Koizumi. And in 2010, *Time* ran a cover on "The Broken States of America," but the U.S. economy picked up speed and outran all other developed economies in the next five years.

On the other hand, if *Time*'s cover spin was upbeat, the economy slowed down over the next five years in 66 percent of the cases. This happened a total of 37 times between 1980 and 2010. After *Time* magazine's cover story on Japan in February 1992, the economy's growth rate fell from more than 5 percent between 1987 and 1991 to a little over 1 percent in the next five years. The May 2006 cover on "The French Way of Reform" argued that France was changing faster than commonly understood, but over the next five years, its growth rate fell by half to less than 1 percent. The "Germany Revs Up" cover of November 2007 was followed by a retreat in Germany's fortunes, and so on.

The point here is not to diminish *Time* or news magazine journalism but to highlight the twin problems of extrapolation and linear thinking. These behavioral biases can blind serious people to major turns in national fortunes, particularly when the good times are under way. Reporters after all tend to follow the lead of market researchers, serious academics, and major institutions such as the IMF. Given its stature, the IMF's forecasts are considered so mainstream that they are often accepted as the global consensus. But they show a systematic tendency to hype the prospects of hot economies, just like everyone else.

In 2013 former U.S. Treasury secretary Larry Summers and his colleague Lant Pritchett issued a frontal assault on the dynamics of hype in "Asiaphoria Meets Regression to the Mean," a paper in which they questioned forecasts that the economies of China and India would increase many times over in the coming decades. Summers and Pritchett virtually pleaded with the IMF and other forecasters to stop assuming that hot countries would stay hot, and to recognize that the single strongest conclusion of postwar research on economic growth is that all economies tend to "regress to the mean," or fall to the historic mean GDP growth rate for all countries. (That mean rate is about 3.5 percent, or 1.8 percent for per capita income growth.) IMF forecasts assume that India and China will not regress but will continue to grow at an only slightly more modest pace, quadrupling in size by 2030, for a combined expansion of about $53 trillion. History, Summers and Pritchett argue, suggests that growth rates in China and India will more likely regress toward the mean, implying that they will only double in size by 2030, for a combined expansion of $11 trillion. That's a $42 trillion gap between extrapolation and regression to the mean, which is the well-established pattern.[4] It is this kind of exaggerated forecast that leads reporters to hype the rise of China and India.

To their credit, some researchers at the IMF were listening. Giang Ho and Paolo Mauro in 2014 published "Growth: Now and Forever?," a report in which they analyzed the forecasting record of the IMF and the World Bank going back to 1990.[5] They discovered that the Summers and Pritchett critique was basically correct. Forecasters seemed to ignore the tendency of economies to regress to the mean, and Ho and Mauro found that "we have had a pretty consistent record of forecasts that turned out to be optimistic." Institutions like the IMF and the World Bank have been issuing forecasts that feed positive media hype for emerging economies, whether they were hot or not, and have "an especially difficult time predicting turning points."

My own review of recent IMF predictions shows how dramatically true this has been in the case of China. In April 2010, the peak year for Chinese GDP growth, the IMF had predicted that the pace of expansion would remain essentially the same, slowing by about half a point over five years to a still blistering 9.5 percent in 2015. Actual growth in China in mid-2015 was some 40 percent lower, at about 7 percent according to official numbers, and even lower, at less than 5 percent according to independent estimates.

After 2010, subsequent IMF forecasts for China were just as optimistic. Every year for the next five years, they predicted a slight drop in the growth rate, and missed the extent of the slowdown by a wide margin. In April 2015, the IMF forecast for China's growth in 2020 was above 6 percent—a floor through which China had probably already fallen. In an age when China has become virtually synonymous with "miraculous boom," it was difficult even for the most serious forecasters to imagine a world in which that economy slows to a normal pace—even as the process was under way.

Though economics was derided by the nineteenth-century historian Thomas Carlyle as the "dismal science," it is in fact suffused with "optimism bias." This ingrained cheeriness is evident in the IMF's long-standing reluctance to forecast recessions. In a study of the IMF's annual economic forecasts for 189 countries between 1999 and 2014, *The Economist* found 220 cases in which an economy grew one year but shrank the next. In its April forecasts for the coming year, however, the IMF never once saw the contraction coming. Even picking random numbers between -2 and 10 would have done better, the magazine found.[6] And this tendency is hardly limited to the IMF: Most economists tend to change their forecasts in small increments, and therefore miss the big shifts. For example, the Philadelphia branch of the Fed conducts a quarterly survey of about fifty leading forecasters, and in early 2008, amid numerous signs that the Great Recession had already begun, including a fall in the stock market, they began to revise their forecasts down, in the usual incremental way. Their average prediction for 2008 growth in the United States was 1.8 percent; only two predicted growth below 1 percent, and not one predicted negative growth for the year. We now know the Great Recession started in 2007.

I suspect that the IMF and the World Bank have a special reason for optimism bias: Many of the countries for which they make forecasts are also essentially their clients. Political elites in those countries would take offense at brutally honest assessments of their economic prospects. I see the same pressures weighing on many independent economists, particularly as emerging nations have grown in clout and reach in recent years. A frustrated economist from a large investment bank recently came to speak with me about China, and he was in a "damned-if-I-do, damned-if-I don't" mood. He complained that if he questioned the 7 percent growth the Chinese government was reporting, he would get an earful from Beijing; but if he didn't question those claims, he would hear it from investors.

Group Hype

Long growth spurts, as we have seen, are improbable in any one country, and even less probable for a collection of countries. This basic fact did not dampen the hype of the last decade. A combination of forces after 2002 helped trigger an emerging-world boom, which saw growth double over the next five years to an average rate of more than 7 percent for the more than 150 countries tracked by the IMF. Forecasters soon projected that the largest emerging economies—Brazil, Russia, India, and China—would expand at a torrid pace, with their average incomes eventually catching up with those of the developed world.

Thus was born the myth of mass "convergence," a worldwide leveling of incomes. This scenario had a beguiling appeal to all kinds of people, from NGOs rooting for the poor to global investors hoping to capitalize on emerging markets, to pundits eager to identify the next big shift in the global balance of power. More than a few observers argued that the rise of emerging nations would hasten the end of America's global dominance, an argument that sounded reasonable enough after the financial crisis of 2008. Two years later, the U.S. economy was growing at an anemic pace, and emerging economies led by China were growing three times faster.

The widening growth advantage of emerging countries sustained the myth of mass convergence, at least for a while. What went largely unappreciated was how unusually rosy the decade between 2000 and 2010 was for the emerging world. In every previous decade going back to 1960, the per capita income of most emerging nations fell relative to the United States. Of the 110 emerging nations in the authoritative Penn World Table, which contains growth data for each country, no more than 45 per cent were catching up to the United States in any decade before 2000, not even during the 1970s commodity boom. All that changed after 2000, when the forces of easy money, surging commodity prices, and rising trade flows swept through the emerging world: Over the next ten years, 80 percent of emerging economies grew fast enough to see per capita income gains relative to the United States.

No wonder the hype for emerging economies started to skyrocket. The five-year period between 2005 and 2010 saw almost freakishly intense growth. Among the 110 emerging countries in the Penn Table, only three were losing ground to the United States in terms of average income, while 107 countries—or 97 percent of the total—were gaining ground. This was unprecedented. The three countries falling behind the United States were Niger, Eritrea, and Jamaica—all minor economies. It seemed that pretty much the whole emerging world was on the rise.

It was wildly implausible to assume that such universal, high growth could be maintained for decades. Convergence is hard enough to achieve for one country. In the last half-century, according to a 2012 study by the World Bank, only thirteen emerging countries have managed to rise from the poor or middle-class and enter the high-income class. By some measures, South Korea has reached the doorstep of developed-world status, and the Czech Republic and Poland are not far off. The mass convergence scenario implied that, within a few decades, so many nations would make the leap from being poor or middle class to rich that the class differences between nations would begin to blur. The vision of a world dominated by nations that are at least comfortably middle class was as utopian as a world without poor people, and about as likely.

As it turned out, 2010 signaled the end of a brief period of super-fast growth for many countries, not the beginning of universal prosperity. Later that year, growth started to slow in the emerging world as global capital flows and trade ebbed, and commodity prices started to weaken. By the middle of the decade, the average growth rate in emerging nations had fallen from a peak of 7.5 percent in 2010 back down to its long-term average of 4 percent, and to around 2 percent excluding China. The United States was expanding faster than that average, and much faster than the limping economies of Russia, Brazil, and South Africa. Far from converging, many of the most hyped emerging economies of the last decade were shrinking relative to the United States. And because their population growth is often faster, these emerging countries were falling behind at an even more rapid pace in terms of per capita incomes.

In the marketplace, all of the "China plays"—investments premised on a straight-line boom in Chinese growth—began to unravel from 2011 onward. Still, none of this impacted public opinion, including expert academic opinion. As part of a panel at the Brookings Institution with several well-known academics in early 2014, I was stunned to hear them talking about the inexorable rise of China, as if the turning point had yet to come. I demurred, but it was not until the collapse of the Shanghai stock market and the devaluation of the yuan in mid-2015 that mainstream global media started to accept the slowdown in China as part of the new reality.

The Special Case of Hype for Commodity Economies

One of my objections to all the hype for the BRICs during the last decade was that this "one acronym fits all" approach to understanding the world made no distinction between manufacturing economies that grow by making things, such as China, and commodity economies that grow by pumping stuff out of the ground. A country like Russia, which exports mainly oil, or like Brazil, which exports iron ore and grains, tends to grow sharply but also to contract severely along with global price swings for their main commodity exports. Tracing this story back five decades, I found a clear connection between commodity price swings and the number of countries growing at catch-up speeds, at least temporarily.

For each decade since 1970, the number of countries that witnessed a rapid convergence in their average incomes with those in the West fluctuated wildly with commodity prices. In the 1970s, when a standard index of commodity prices rose 160 percent, twenty-eight nations converged rapidly.* But when commodity prices stagnated in the 1980s and '90s, the number of rapidly converging nations fell to eleven. As commodity prices doubled after 2000, the first decade of the new millennium turned out to be another golden age for convergence, with thirty-seven nations catching up at a rapid pace.

The problem for commodity-driven economies is that they tend to stop catching up as soon as prices for their main exports fall. The World Bank in 2008 assembled a panel of international economic experts, ranging from former U.S. Treasury secretary Robert Rubin to South African finance minister Trevor Manuel, under the leadership of Nobel laureate Michael Spence. The goal of the Spence Commission was to unravel the secrets of long, steady growth booms, of the kind that had appeared only in the postwar era. The commission identified a list of thirteen economies that had posted average growth of more than 7 percent over at least a quarter-century, but they found that these stories had very different endings.[7] Only six of the thirteen economies continued to grow rapidly until they reached a high income level, and five of the six countries were

---

* "Rapid convergence" defined: We looked at growth in 173 nations going back to 1960 and then ranked these nations by how much their per capita GDP rose compared to per capita GDP in the United States, in each decade. The top quarter of all these observations were designated as "rapid convergence" cases. In these cases, per capita GDP rose by at least 2.8 percentage points, as a share of U.S. per capita GDP, over the decade.

manufacturing export powers, with the quirky exception of Malta. On the other hand, six of the seven economies that stalled before attaining a high income were in the commodity-rich countries of Botswana, Indonesia, Malaysia, Oman, Thailand, and Brazil. Since 1914, Brazil's per capita income has risen and fallen in line with prices for iron ore, sugar, and soybeans, and today it amounts to 16 percent of per capita income in the United States, one point higher than it was in 1914.

One factor that obscures the curse of commodities is that raw materials may appear to play a relatively small role in the economy despite their outsize impact on its growth prospects. The World Bank calculates the income from natural resources at 8 percent of GDP, on average, in low- and middle-income countries, compared to 1.4 percent in the most developed countries. But that 8 percent share can determine an economy's fate if it accounts for a significant portion of exports or government revenues. Commodity price shifts tend to occur rapidly and sharply, suddenly pinching the flow of revenue from oil or cotton or sugar, consequently throwing a nation into crisis—particularly if it needs foreign revenue to service foreign debts. One reason for many of the "lost decades" of weak growth in Latin America is that commodities account for more than half the exports from its major economies.

In many countries the state owns oil, gas, and other commodity-related companies and relies heavily on revenue earned from these companies to fund its operations. A sudden drop in commodity prices can push the government quickly toward economic trouble. Oil officially accounts for only 10 percent of Russian GDP but half of exports and a third of government revenue, and the collapse in oil prices in 2014 threw the economy into a deep recession. Just before oil prices started to plunge that year, President Putin was celebrated on magazine covers as "the most powerful man in the world" following a string of apparent foreign policy successes including the occupation of the Crimea.[8] It was a classic case of hype peaking after the end of a trend: Russia was already falling behind the West in average income, and its oil-fueled recession would accelerate the slump.

The Rosy Disaster Scenarios

Although the fortunes of commodity economies have strong links to volatile price swings, the hype for them is often driven by an emotional form of straight-line thinking derived from the Malthusian disaster scenario. Ever since the English scholar Thomas Malthus first predicted in the early nineteenth century that rising global population would outpace farm output and lead to mass starvation, experts have put forth pessimistic theories every few decades, if not every few years, despite Malthus's prediction never having been realized. Just after a spurt in food prices in 2011, the international organization Oxfam warned that a slower rate of increase in farm output amid rising population would lead to food shortages. Oxfam forecast a doubling of grain prices within twenty years, with millions of more people going hungry by 2030. The implication for the future rise and fall of nations was also evident, with farm nations like Brazil expected to do very well on the back of rising grain and soybean prices.

These scenarios keep getting it wrong for the same reason that Malthus did. They underestimate the capacity of farmers, or oil and steel magnates, or producers of any other commodity to innovate and increase supply. In the post–World War II era, global food prices adjusted for inflation have fallen at an average annual pace of 1.7 percent, in large part because when prices rise, farmers earn more income and invest in better fertilizers and more efficient combines and tractors—to increase supply. The fear of a food price surge in 2011 emerged, once again, from the idea that agricultural progress had hit a wall, with no way to pull more potatoes out of existing fields. That's why farm-output growth was slowing and would continue to decelerate, or so the thinking went.

As usual, this scenario ignored the many ways by which further supply gains are still possible. Crop yields are about half as high in China, Brazil, and the former Soviet countries as in the United States, so output could rise radically if these countries copied foreign methods. Nearly 30 percent of all food and 50 percent of all fruits and vegetables are lost in transit in the emerging world, so better roads in Brazil and Russia could greatly boost the amount of food that reaches the marketplace.

The age-old image of farmers as peasants obscures the fact that modern agribusinesses are quick to adjust investment levels in response to price signals. In fact, studies show that farmers respond faster to market forces than other big commodity suppliers, such as multinational oil companies. The biggest enemy of high prices is high prices, as producers ramp up investment in new supplies.

This is exactly what was happening in 2011: Doomsayers were issuing reports about rising food prices and hunger at the same time that a new flood of investment had already started attacking the threat. Between 2000 and 2010, the world invested $1 trillion to increase production of raw materials, ranging from U.S. shale oil to Brazilian sugar, and new supply pushed prices down. The trend of surging food prices, which rose 66 percent from 2009 to early 2011, soon turned around, and prices fell 30 percent over the next two years.

The sharp decline in the prices of food and other commodities in the current decade have dramatically changed global media sentiment toward countries such as Brazil. At the height of Brazil's economic boom in late 2009, *The Economist* carried a cover story titled "Brazil Takes Off" with an image of the iconic Christ the Redeemer statue soaring into the skies above Rio de Janeiro. Over the next four years, Brazil's economic growth rate fell by more than half and its stock market lost 50 percent of its value in dollar terms. In late 2013, *The Economist* ran a cover with the same Christ statue nose-diving into the ground, asking a bit more tentatively, "Has Brazil blown it?"

The Case for Constant Vigilance

Why is it so difficult for any economy to sustain strong growth? One popular explanation is the middle-income trap, which holds that a poor nation can grow at catch-up speed by making simple improvements such as paving roads but will find it difficult to sustain rapid growth when it hits a middle-income level and needs to develop more advanced industries. The truth, however, is that "development traps" can knock countries off track at any income level. The challenges of creating productive industry—backed by better banks, schools, and regulators, and fueled by steady infusions of investment and credit—do not accumulate and confront an economy all at once. They hound an aspiring nation at every step up the development ladder.

Yet the hype over the middle-income trap has only grown since 2010. A 2013 study by the Berkeley economist Barry Eichengreen and his colleagues noted that a Google search turned up a total of four hundred thousand references to the middle-income trap. Dig into those stories, and one finds warnings about countries ranging from poor ones like Vietnam and India to richer ones including Malaysia, Turkey and Taiwan at risk of falling into the middle-income trap. The concept of the trap is so vaguely and variously defined that it doesn't help narrow down the list of vulnerable countries.

The expression "middle-income trap" was coined by World Bank researchers in 2007, but in September 2013 a new set of researchers at the bank revisited the concept and came away skeptical. They said that the results offered "very little support for the existence" of such a trap and raised doubts about whether it even makes sense to judge middle-income countries based on whether they are on course to catch up to incomes in the West.[9] The researchers found that economies get bogged down at many income levels, not just at the barrier between middle and high incomes. The authors concluded that the idea of a "trap" is a mislabeling of economies that are slowing to a more normal pace of growth, well below the rate required for rapid convergence. Some countries including Bangladesh, Niger, El Salvador, and Mozambique have remained stuck in poverty traps for much of the postwar era at a per capita income level of less than 5 percent that of the United States.

Rich countries can suffer setbacks too. Eichengreen's team found that the likelihood of a slowdown peaks when a nation's per capita GDP reaches 75 percent that of the United States, a level well beyond middle income. Examples of countries that suffered a prolonged seven-year slowdown when they were already quite wealthy are numerous. Japan slowed sharply when its per capita GDP hit $28,000 in 1992, Hong Kong slowed at the $27,000 mark in 1994, Singapore at $35,000 in 1997, Norway at $43,000 in 1998, Ireland and the United Kingdom at $38,000 and $32,000, respectively, in 2003. These slowdowns were often very severe. Ireland's per capita income growth was exploding at an annual pace of 6.6 percent in the seven years before 2003, then collapsed to an average of negative 1.3 percent in the subsequent seven years. There's no buzz phrase for what happened to Ireland, but it could be called a prosperity trap.

In some rare cases, slowdowns can be severe enough to drag newly rich countries back to the middle-income ranks, as has happened at least three times in the last century. Venezuela made the round trip from middle class to rich and back within the last hundred years. Meanwhile, Argentina's average income fell from 65 percent of the U.S. level in the 1930s to less than 20 percent by 2010. The most recent case is Greece, which was demoted into the emerging-market ranks when its finances fell into chaos after 2010, and its per capita income fell from just above to well below the $25,000 mark, the rough cutoff for developed-market status. Greece's fall was due to a protracted financial crisis, which is a common cause for this kind of a tumble.

In any decade, more nations on average fall back to a lower income level than advance to a higher one. Since the late 1940s, many nations have experienced this downward mobility, including the Philippines in the 1950s and Russia, South Africa, and Iran in the 1980s and '90s. The 2012 World Bank study that found only thirteen examples of postwar economies which crossed the threshold into the high-income class also observed that thirty-one countries fell from the middle class into the low-income class. This count includes infamous economic failures as well as war-torn countries like Iraq, Afghanistan, and Haiti.

The way economists put it is that strong growth shows little "persistence." New York University–based economist William Easterly and his colleagues established this fact over twenty years ago, and it has been reconfirmed many times since—but almost always in a negative sense. Summers and Pritchett, for example, analyzed all twenty-eight nations that, since 1950, have experienced periods of "super rapid growth," defined as an average annual per capita GDP growth rate of 6 percent for at least eight years. They found that these booms tend to be "extremely short lived," dying out after a median duration of nine years, and "nearly always" ending in a significant slowdown. Typically, the economy returned to an average annual per capita growth of just over 2 percent, a rate that is "near complete regression to the mean" for all nations.

The story that gets overlooked is the positive one. Countries that are cold in one decade do not necessarily stay cold the next. In any five-year economic cycle, the competitive landscape can change completely. As some nations reach the peak of a debt binge, others will be busy paying off debts, setting themselves up for a strong growth run. New technologies can bring new industries to the cutting edge. New elections can usher in new leaders, for the worse but also for the better. The arrival in recent years of reforming presidents in countries from Italy to Japan has shaken up stagnant regimes and raised the likelihood of better economic growth—not of an Italian or even a Japanese century, but of possibly five good years, perhaps even a full decade. The same goes even for commodity economies, which are poised to boom like a clock, every time prices start moving up. In September 1998, *Time* put the crisis-wracked Russian economy on the cover under the one-word headline "Help!," but over the next five years Russia's growth accelerated from negative 5 percent to positive 7 percent, as oil prices started moving up.

Why the Opposite of Love Is Indifference

Another basic reason that economic stars usually emerge from a cloud of media indifference is that the fastest-growing economies are almost always found among the poorer nations, which tend to be the most widely ignored. The task of generating brisk growth is easier in a poor country, where just building decent roads and other simple steps can boost the economy.

To illustrate the point, I looked at the ten fastest-growing economies in each decade between 1950 and 2010 and found that per capita income of those economies as a group was typically less than $3,500 at the start of their hot decade. Those cases include Nigeria and Turkey during the 1950s; Taiwan and Singapore during the 1960s; Malaysia and Romania during the 1970s; and Egypt and Botswana during the 1980s. The exceptional cases of nations that went on a rapid growth streak when they were already wealthy tended to be commodity economies: Norway and other small, oil-rich economies have made it to the top ten lists by riding oil price spikes. Otherwise, growth superstars in any decade generally arise from relative poverty and the obscurity that goes with it.

This list of the world's fastest-growing economies by decade is remarkable for its number of unsung stars, and for the rate of churn. Rarely did economies stay on the list for two decades in a row. Few expected Brazil to fall off the list after 1980, or for China to jump on. Hardly anyone expected Japan to drop off after 1990, or for Russia to climb aboard the following decade. And every decade tossed up new names—from Iraq in the 1950s to Iran in the '60s and Malta in the '70s—that flamed out in the next decade. More often than not, countries are at the verge of disappearing from the list when the global media are most in love with them, and they are preparing to join the list when they are in the shadows. The next leaders typically emerge from among the past laggards: During this decade the Philippines became the hottest economy in the emerging world, and now formerly stagnant Mexico is the Latin American economy most likely to accelerate in the near term.

Indifference is also a good sign, because when booms go bust, the media come in and conduct an autopsy on the bloated corpse of the economy, laying bare all the excesses of overspending and unpayable debts that a country racked up in the late stages of its boom. The government sets up commissions to close banks and dispose of bad loans, replace corrupt and incompetent figures at leading state companies, and push reform designed to make sure the same crisis doesn't recur.

The house cleaning can take several years, depending on the scale of the crisis. During the Asian financial crisis, for example, the first signs of debt troubles started to appear in Thailand in 1996, and by the next summer the crisis was in full bloom. Some big global investors jumped in and bought Thai stocks in the summer of 1997, acting on the advice first offered by Baron de Rothschild in the 1870s and repeated by others many times since: The best time to buy is "when there is blood in the streets" and prices are presumably at rock bottom. The problem arises when the bloodied country stays that way for some time, as was the case in Asia after 1997, when the crisis spread to other emerging nations and drove down Thailand's stock market by another 70 percent. Many investors who bought into Thailand in the summer of 1997 wound up losing big.

Economies are most likely to turn for the better not during the period of hate but when the media have moved on to the next story, leaving the crisis-hit country alone to work on cleaning up its mess. By the start of the new millennium, the global media had long forgotten the nations felled by the Asian financial crisis, focusing instead on new hotspots, such as the beneficiaries of the tech boom. Meanwhile, new leaders came on board in Russia, Turkey, and South Korea, and many Southeast Asian nations started to stage an export-led recovery fueled by cheap currencies. These new leaders brought current accounts back into balance and brought debts under control, but for many years after the disruptions of 1997 and 1998, it was still hard for the media to see the crisis-hit countries as anything but dysfunctional. In 2000, *Time* put an Indonesian president widely lampooned for falling asleep in meetings on a cover outlining "Wahid's Woes," after which Indonesia's growth jumped from near zero to near 5 percent, as the country cleaned up its banking mess and its cheap currency boosted exports.

Economic growth lacks persistence, but media negativity about certain economies sometimes shows tremendous persistence, which is how success stories get overlooked. In 2003, the global media turned on Russia after Vladimir Putin's government jailed the oil tycoon and democracy campaigner Mikhail Khodorkovsky on what were widely thought to be trumped-up tax and fraud charges. His incarceration and the skullduggery surrounding it turned Russia into a story about Putin's reversion to Soviet-style authoritarianism, even though he still had reformers in key economic positions. The economic boom still had many years left to run, though you would never have known it from reading the international headlines on Putin's Russia.

I have often overlooked countries that are off the global media radar. I missed the economic turnaround in Colombia after Álvaro Uribe became president in 2002 and started to bring peace and order to the war-torn economy. To believe that a country long synonymous with cocaine and murder could be transformed quickly was one leap of faith too far for me. But the condition of "failed state" is not a permanent one.

It's hard to name a supposedly failed state whose economic revival was more roundly ignored by the global media than the Philippines. When I visited Manila in January 2010, I sensed a turn for the better as Filipinos were fed up with the way their country was being surpassed by neighboring economies. They were keen to give a strong mandate to a leader seen as "Mr. Clean," who would reduce record levels of corruption and kick-start investment in a country that was using no more cement per capita than it had eighty years earlier. But the Philippines had been a laggard for so many decades, my journalist friends thought I was joking about its bright prospects. Many still do.

On the other hand, I was worried about the hype that surrounded the election of Narendra Modi as prime minister of India in 2014. Modi led the reader votes for *Time*'s "Person of the Year" in December that year, but the editors declined to give him the honor. No doubt the Indian readers who stuffed *Time*'s ballot box for Modi were disappointed, but appearing on *Time*'s cover would have, in my view, suggested that the euphoria for India was reaching a peak, the kind that often precedes a fall. Modi was already a darling of the international media, which cast him as a reformer who could spark a major economic revival in India at a time when the global economy was desperate for good stories. Hopes were so high that it was hard to find even one financial analyst, whether in Manhattan or Mumbai, with a negative comment on the Indian economy. My sense was that when Modi lost *Time*'s "Person of the Year" cover, India had won.

The Antidote to Hype Is to Apply the Rules

The Economist is an exception to the general rule that magazine covers tend to point in the wrong direction, perhaps thanks to its deliberately contrarian worldview. Looking at 209 covers published between 1980 and 2010, I found that when the British magazine ran an optimistic cover about a country, its economy improved over the next five years in roughly two-thirds of the cases. And when *The Economist* ran a gloomy cover, the economy slowed more than half the time.

In May of 1998 its "Europe takes flight" cover cast the continent as Superman bursting skyward from a toppled phone booth, and the regional economy did accelerate sharply, from a pace of 1.7 percent before 1998 to a pace of 2.6 percent in the next five years. Three months later, when most of the media was still dissecting the golf course capitalism that had caused the Asian financial crisis two years earlier, *The Economist* saw signs of "Asia's astonishing bounce back," which was in the works. In January of 1999 the magazine was among the lonely skeptics arguing for "Why internet shares will fall to earth," but of course they did, leading to recession in the United States and around the world. Two years later it cast incoming prime minister Junichiro Koizumi as "Japan's great hope," and he managed a brief period of reform that helped lift growth from 0.4 percent to a less anemic rate of 1.4 percent.

That's not to say, however, that even this aggressively unconventional magazine did not capture the mainstream consensus many times, including that 2009 "Brazil Rising" cover just before that economy started to collapse. It also got the rise and fall of Africa backward. After Africa posted its second straight decade of disappointing growth in the 1990s, *The Economist* called it "The Hopeless Continent" in a May 2000 cover story. But that year marked the start of a decade in which the number of African economies expanding at an annual average pace of more than 5 percent would jump from fourteen to twenty-eight. Extrapolating from that strong run between 2000 and 2010, the magazine put the continent on its cover in December 2011, this time as "Africa Rising." Neither spin made much sense, because Africa is not one economy but a mélange of fifty-three nations, many with little in common. The same mistake of lumping wildly different economies into one bundle that underpinned the idea of "mass convergence" also formed the basis for the hype over "Africa Rising."

The death knell for this story rang when *Time* ran a cover under the same "Africa Rising" headline twelve months after *The Economist*. At that point Africa was definitely not rising any more. By 2013, the number of African economies growing at faster than 5 percent had slipped to twenty-one from twenty-eight in 2010, and the number running high inflation was on the increase. The Africa story was fragmenting into a more realistic plot, in which its varied economies show a mix of good, average, and ugly growth prospects.

One cause for optimism about Africa after 2000 was the apparent improvement in leadership. A growing number of countries were shedding autocrats and holding democratic elections. But by the turn of the decade it was apparent that these elections turned up few, if any, genuine economic reformers. South Africa's ANC regime was growing stale, having ruled for more than twenty years without being able to lower the unemployment rate, which was stuck at 25 percent. Its leader, Jacob Zuma, was under fire for spending $23 million in public funds to renovate his own home. In Nigeria, the man once seen as the country's first clean president, Goodluck Jonathan, faced questions about his handling of missing oil revenues and of relations with rebellious northern states, where the Islamist extremist Boko Haram insurgency was brewing.

While South Africa and Nigeria are the economic polestars of Africa, the leadership vacuum stretched across the continent. In four of the five years from 2009 to 2013, a London-based NGO, the Mo Ibrahim Foundation, had not been able to find a candidate worthy to receive its African Leadership Award, with only the outgoing president Pedro Pires of the tiny island nation of Cape Verde winning the award in 2011.

With few strong leaders, many African nations were also showing weak results when tested on the other rules. Another basic building block of the "Africa Rising" theme was that many newly elected leaders were bringing wasteful governments under control, but that proved to be wishful thinking once the crisis of 2008 hit. Soon, many African governments started spending heavily to dampen the pain of the slowdown, raising civil service salaries and undertaking other forms of public largesse. The number of African governments running a deficit of more than 3 percent of GDP—the level many experts see as potentially dangerous—rose from a low of eleven in 2008 to twenty in 2013.

At the same time, very few African leaders were investing to wean their economies off the easy windfall profits from oil and other commodities. Between 2000 and 2010, exports from the emerging nations of both Africa and Asia rose by 500 percent, but for Asia about 400 percent of that increase was driven by shipping out larger volumes, in other words by selling more cars, appliances, and other manufactured goods. Africa, on the other hand, prospered by riding the tide of global commodity prices: about 400 percent of the increase in its export revenues came mainly from rising global prices for commodities like cocoa, coffee, and oil. The region had made few new investments in manufacturing plants. In sub-Saharan Africa, commodities account for half of GDP, while manufacturing has been declining and was at just 11 percent of GDP in 2014, down from 16 percent in 1990. This deindustrialization process is the opposite of what any emerging market needs for stable growth and to establish a prosperous middle class.

The "rise" of these economies would end when commodity prices turned, and that started to happen in 2011. As prices for gold, iron ore, and many other commodities slipped, many African nations found it increasingly difficult to balance government budgets and current accounts. As we have seen, the current account deficit signals warnings of a potential currency crisis when it stays at 5 percent of GDP for five years in a row. More and more African countries fell into this danger zone and started facing difficulty in paying their foreign debts. Several African countries including Mozambique, Zambia, and Ghana had to go to the International Monetary Fund in 2014, seeking new or extended loans to help balance their books.

Ghana's troubles were particularly disappointing since it had been feted as one of Africa's brightest stars, but now with higher inflation and heavier foreign debt, its numbers were worse than an also-ran like Zambia. On a visit in 2012, U.S. president Barack Obama lauded Ghana's "wonderful" economic success story, led by an enlightened government, but as writer Adam Minter pointed out in a Bloomberg View column, regular power outages had started to play havoc with the economy that same year, blacking out homes and businesses for eight hours a day, shuttering stores and forcing businessmen to find hotel lobbies with backup generators. Ghana's rise was much more fragile than outsiders had realized, because it was driven by rising prices for oil, gold, and cocoa. As those prices plummeted in 2014, economic growth slowed to its lowest level in two decades, forcing Ghana to go hat in hand to the IMF for a $900 million emergency loan.

But bright spots do exist in Africa. No region so large is ever thoroughly "hopeless." A cluster of economies are ascending along the Indian Ocean, with countries including Uganda and Kenya starting to boost local trade through the East African Community, the new regional common market. Unlike many of their African peers, Kenya and Uganda are importers of many commodities and consequently gained from the fall in prices for oil and other raw materials. Their current accounts were in deficit, but the money they spent on imports was not being frittered away on consumption of luxury goods; it was going to buy machinery, equipment, and other capital goods, which would help drive future growth. Kenya also boasted one of the continent's more promising new leaders, President Uhuru Kenyatta, who took office in 2013 and—despite an international investigation into his alleged role in past tribal violence—was earning high marks from locals for general competence as an economic administrator. Even as the hype for Africa rotated 180 degrees over the last decade, from "Hopeless" to "Rising," the truth was always more complicated: a multilayered plot with fifty-three national storylines, some rising and some almost hopeless.

Mainstream opinion about which nations are rising or falling typically gets the future wrong, because it extrapolates recent trends and grows more enamored of a country the longer the growth run lasts. Often, that love story is cemented by a compelling but one-dimensional explanation. The best antidote to these misleading romances is to check the object of the media's affection against all the rules. Most important, remember that the longer a growth spurt lasts, the less likely it is to continue. The most-loved nations will rarely have the best economic prospects in the next five to ten years. The most-hated nations, on the other hand, are often the object of widespread criticism for a reason, generally an outbreak of political protest or financial crisis that has exposed genuine vulnerabilities and will take some time to address. It is after these crisis-struck nations fade from the media glare and join the ranks of the forgotten countries that they are likely to emerge as the next success stories. The most promising form of hype for any country is none at all.

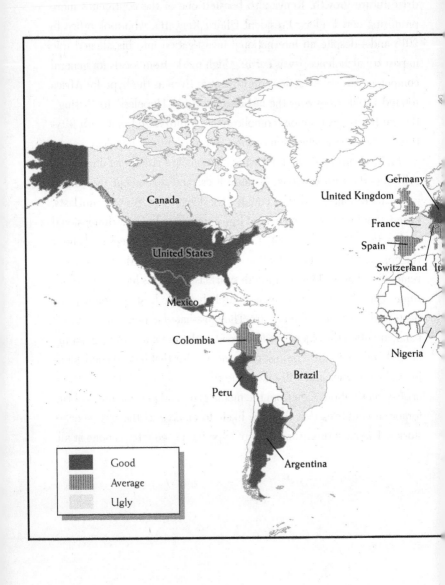

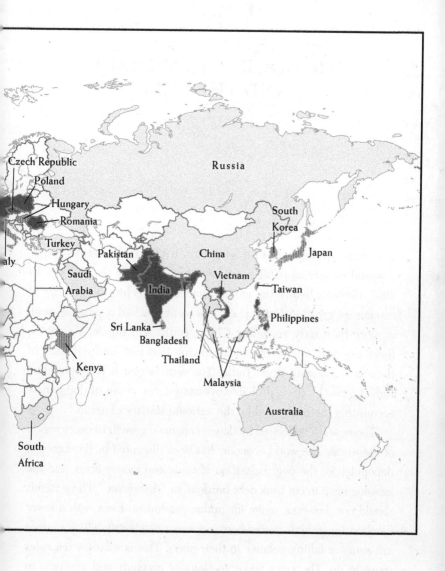

11

THE GOOD, THE AVERAGE, AND THE UGLY

I N THE AC ERA, THERE ARE PRECIOUS FEW NATIONS THAT would qualify as rising stars by the standards of the BC era. In 2007, the year before the global financial crisis hit, the number of economies growing faster than 7 percent reached a postwar peak at more than sixty, including China, India, and Russia. Currently, there are only nine economies growing that fast, and only one of them is reasonably large: India. The next largest is Ethiopia. And India's growth rate is probably overstated, the result of dodgy new accounting methods used by the national statistics bureau.

The new era is defined by slower economic growth in every region of the world. The world economy has been disrupted by the forces of depopulation, the deglobalization of trade and money flows, and the looming need to cut back debt burdens, or "deleverage." These trends should not, however, make for undue pessimism. Even with a lower baseline for growth everywhere, we can still identify which nations are rising or falling, relative to their peers. That is what my ten rules strive to do. The rules make no claim of certainty and aim only to improve the probability of getting the forecast right for the next five to ten years. The forecast itself rests on scores of 1 to 10 for each of the ten rules, and I use the combined scores to rank a nation's economic prospects as good, average, or ugly, compared to other countries in the same income class.

For three decades before the 2008 crisis, the global economy was growing at an average annual pace of over 3 percent, but the potential growth rate of the global economy is now estimated at just under 2.5 percent. The fastest-growing economies are almost always the poorest ones, so the new standards of success still depend on the average income of the nation, but for every category the standard needs to be lowered. For emerging countries with low average incomes—less than $5,000 a year—the definition of good, solid growth should be revised downward by at least 2 percentage points, to any rate above 5 percent. In nations with incomes in the low-to-mid range—between $5,000 and $15,000—a growth rate between 3 and 4 percent can now be classified as a reasonable achievement. And for nations in the middle-income group—$15,000 to $25,000—even 2 to 3 percent is good. Nations with average incomes higher than $25,000 qualify as developed, and for them any rate above 1.5 percent represents relatively strong growth in the AC era.

The new math of economic success will require a shift in mindset for many countries, spoiled as they were during the boom before 2008. The sooner that shift comes, the better for the world. To take one example, it may be some years before we see another major economy put together a sustained run of growth at 7 percent or better. It is critical that leaders and the observers who judge them adopt a more realistic definition of success, lest they put themselves in China's position, wasting money and running up debts in an attempt to attain growth rates that are no longer plausible in the AC era.

What I find striking about the current mood now, in March of 2016, is the complete absence of optimism: When I ask journalist friends to name a country that they view favorably, I often get a blank look. They find it easier to knock a country's economic prospects. I suspect they are judging economic potential by the standards of the BC era, which is why they can't see it anywhere. To help keep things in perspective, it is worth remembering what the Austrian-born economist Joseph Schumpeter had to say: "Pessimistic visions about anything usually strike the public as more erudite than optimistic ones."

No nation is an economic utopia. At any given time, none will score well on all the ten rules, and countries with the best prospects tend to get high scores on six or seven rules at most. Though many economists have looked for it, and some claim to have found it, there is no holy grail, no one key to a prosperous future. The single most reliable indicator I have found is the negative one on the kiss of debt rule, which shows that a major economic slowdown has always materialized when a nation's debt has grown more than 40 percentage points faster than GDP over a five-year period. With this signal now flashing red only for China, even this powerful idea currently applies to one country. A disciplined, balanced, and timely perspective works better than any single metric.

The United States

Opinion polls now suggest that many Americans think their nation is headed in the wrong direction. This sentiment reflects in part the fact that the Unites States has experienced the weakest economic recovery in its post–World War II history. Yet compared with many other developed countries, the U.S. recovery from the crisis of 2008 has been strong, reinforcing the point that we need to think differently about success in the post-crisis world.

Though the share of Americans who are active in the labor force has declined sharply over the last decade, the United States remains a magnet for economic migrants and has a higher rate of growth in the working population than most other developed countries. So the United States still scores relatively well on the rule covering demographics, which says that fewer workers means less economic growth, and the only way a nation can compensate for weak labor force growth is by bringing women, the elderly or migrants into the workforce.

The U.S. government is pursuing the Trans-Pacific Partnership, which brings together twelve nations in a new common market. This would be a step forward according to the rule on geographic sweet spots, which emerge when a county is solidifying its position in global and regional commerce by striking deals and building ports, airports, and other trade channels. Though its prospects are unclear as the political mood turns against free trade, the TPP could accelerate recent gains in the United States, where in the last five years the trade share of GDP has risen from 19 percent to 24 percent. In the near term, however, the benefits will be limited by the creeping deglobalization of trade: In the second half of 2015, worldwide, the growth rate of trade turned negative for the first time since the global financial crisis.

Overall, U.S. prospects still look good relative to other developed countries, but they have shifted to being a bit more mixed in recent months. The factories first rule says that a strong flow of investment is a big plus, particularly if it is going to productive industries like technology and, above all, manufacturing. In this respect, the billions of dollars that have been pouring into tech-driven U.S. businesses has been a very good investment binge, fueling the rise of new methods for extracting oil and gas from shale rock and of the country's world-leading software and Internet companies. By 2015 the top ten companies in the world, in terms of stock market value, were all based in the United States—the first time this has happened since 2002. This dominant American group is led by Apple and includes Facebook, Amazon, Netflix, and Google, which has spawned trend-stamping acronyms like the unfortunate "FANG."

The hype rule comes into play here; admiring global media coverage tends to peak as a nation approaches the end of a boom, to turn harshly negative as crisis hits, and to fade out entirely by the time the nation is ready to rise again. Stories on U.S. tech companies dominate global business news, and together the four FANG firms now have a total stock market value of around a trillion dollars, more than the entire value of the stock markets in Brazil and Russia and only a shade smaller than India's. Those core members of the BRIC nations were hyped in the last decade as the next big thing, but this decade their markets have mostly fallen as their economies have slowed. The hype for the FANG four may signal a coming peak rather than a new strength for the United States.

The rules are indicating a turn for the worse on a few other fronts, too. Shale technology has transformed the United States into the world's largest oil producer, pumping out 12 million barrels a day, up from 8 million at the low point in 2008. The scale of this boom is striking: In 2014, one-third of the investment made by large U.S. companies went into energy, hitting a share very similar to that reached by corporate investment in technology, media, and telecommunications before that bubble burst in 2000. The money that poured into Silicon Valley start-ups in the late 1990s was also a good investment binge, since it left behind productive companies like Google, but its unraveling led in the short term to the 2001 recession.

Now, as oil prices collapse, U.S. energy investments are plummeting, drilling rigs have been silenced from Texas to North Dakota, shale jobs are drying up, and shale boomtowns are turning into ghost towns. Though this oil rush leaves behind a productive new industry, a plus in the long run as it will likely keep a lid on U.S. energy prices, it poses a near-term risk because energy investment was such an important driver of U.S. growth in recent years, and that boost is now largely gone.

The United States has also lost its advantage on the currency rule, which says that cheap is good. Until 2014 the United States was on the right course, with a cheap dollar making exports more competitive while discouraging spending on imports, and forcing the country to live within its means. This turn to thrift shows up in the current account, which measures trade and other foreign transactions and shows a large deficit when a country is borrowing heavily from foreigners to finance its consumption habits. In 2006, the U.S. current account deficit peaked well above 5 percent of GDP, the level that often indicates coming trouble, according to the currency rule. Then, as the crisis hit and the economy slumped, the dollar weakened, and the current account deficit fell to below 3 percent of GDP and out of the danger zone by 2014.

The change for the worse came in 2015 when the dollar surged by more than 20 percent against a basket of major currencies. It now feels expensive compared to the yen, the ruble, the Brazilian real, and the South African rand, among many other emerging-market currencies. The strengthening dollar is beginning to hurt U.S. exports and manufacturing, and it threatens to push the current account deficit back into the warning zone.

Meanwhile, the total debt in the United States—public and private—has remained flat at about 250 percent of GDP over the last five years. This trend is a plus on the kiss of debt rule, which signals trouble when debt is growing much faster than the economy; however, the overall stability conceals pockets of excess. On the upside, U.S. households have been cutting back their debt burden, as have banks and other firms in the financial sector. But the government has been increasing its debts, and so have some other private companies, particularly those involved in the shale energy industry. Outside of the financial firms, U.S. corporate debt has been rising as a share of GDP over the last five years. Though the pace of growth is not in itself too alarming, a disconcerting share of that borrowing has gone to financial engineering schemes like share buybacks to boost stock prices, rather than to productive investments. This decay in the quality of loans is another warning sign under the debt rule.

One of the big wildcards for the United States is the rise of angry populism, a bad sign according to the circle of life rule. Prospects for major reform rise when new leaders are coming to power, particularly after an economic crisis and when they have a mandate to revive growth. But often is not always. In other post-crisis environments, the electorate may demand something more like retribution, rather than reform, if they are angry over rising inequality or fearful of foreign threats. That is the mood in many countries now, the United States included. To an extent not seen in many decades, the 2016 U.S.

presidential campaign has been dominated by populists, led on the right by the real estate billionaire Donald Trump and on the left by Bernie Sanders, who is calling for a political revolution against the "billionaire class."

The language of class warfare rarely bodes well for an economy, especially if it pushes mainstream candidates to adopt more radical positions. Many of the Republican presidential candidates are vying with Trump to stake out the most hard-line positions on issues such as immigration, which could undermine the advantage the United States enjoys as a magnet for foreign talent. Fortunately, as the circle of life rule points out, the rise of radical populists is less threatening to mature democracies, which tend to grow more steadily than emerging nations in part because the political system has enough checks and balances to block radical policy swings.

It's hard to imagine a billionaire even running for the top office in Russia or Mexico, where the resentments over inequality are more raw and exposed. The richest Americans are more admired than hated, in part because the United States still ranks relatively well on the good billionaires, bad billionaires rule. Political uprisings demanding wealth redistribution are most likely in nations where billionaires not only dominate the economy but draw their wealth mainly from political and family connections. Though the wealth of U.S. billionaires amounts to a relatively large 15 percent of GDP, most are "good billionaires"—not family scions but self-made entrepreneurs who generate their wealth outside of corruption-prone industries like mining or construction. That takes some of the edge off the ugly score the United States gets on one aspect of the billionaire rule. Overall, the combined scores on all ten rules still rank the United States in the "good" category among developed nations.

The Other Americas

Regardless of who wins the U.S. election, the mood of the American electorate reflects a post-crisis backlash against established leaders across the world, a normal turn in the circle of political life. Eight of the thirty most populous democracies held national elections in 2015; the seated party lost in five—Nigeria, Argentina, Poland, Canada, and Sri Lanka—and in other countries, including Spain, suffered serious setbacks. This is in contrast to the boom years between 2003 and 2007, when two out of every three incumbent leaders were reelected.

The biggest political shifts are happening where they were least expected. In Latin America, the bad times are pushing countries to the right. Spiraling prices for staple foods and collapsing growth conspired to unseat the left-wing government in Argentina and the left-wing legislature in Venezuela. As the price of onions rule warns, rapidly rising prices for basics like onions doom economic prospects and often unseat leaders, particularly when high inflation is accompanied by falling growth and dwindling living standards. One simple rule of thumb is to watch out for countries where inflation is well above the emerging-world average, which has fallen recently to around 4 percent. In Argentina the combination of 25 percent inflation and zero growth toppled President Cristina Fernández de Kirchner and her populist party, which had been in power for twelve years. Meanwhile, to the north in Venezuela, the pain of 100 percent inflation and negative 10 percent GDP growth ended its socialist party's hold on the national assembly after seventeen years.

In these cases, the rise of fresh leaders can raise the likelihood of progress, starting with the perils of the state rule. Prospects for growth improve when the state is pulling back from meddling in the private sector and focusing its efforts on investing in roads, security, and creating conditions that encourage private business to ramp up investment in productive industries. Strong investment in supply networks—ports, phone systems, factories—allows an economy to grow rapidly without high inflation, the ideal combination.

In Venezuela, the socialists appear unwilling to cede any state power without a fight, so the nation's prospects are still ugly in the extreme. But in Argentina incoming president Mauricio Macri started with a big and promising move. He lifted capital controls, which immediately sent the overvalued peso tumbling to a more competitive price. He cut export taxes, removed tariffs and quotas on farm exports, and raised prices on subsidized power and water. He brought in a new central bank chief and, after years of political interference, vowed to restore the bank's independence, which is critical in the fight against inflation. He fired a team of statisticians that had been accused by the IMF and others of cooking Argentina's economic data. As his own country's prospects shifted rapidly from ugly to good, Macri even called for Venezuela to be suspended from the regional Mercosur trade bloc, signaling the first crack in the leftist front that has mismanaged the major Atlantic economies of South America for over a decade.

The surviving member of that front is the Workers' Party in Brazil, and after being reelected in late 2014, President Dilma Rousseff now faces the risk of impeachment. Her approval ratings have fallen from a 2013 high of 60 percent to 10 percent. Rousseff is the only major world leader whose approval rating is lower than the inflation rate. Decimated by falling commodity prices, the economy is contracting sharply and facing its worst downturn since the 1930s.

Brazil's long record of state interference in the economy has reached a new peak. Before Rousseff took power, Brazil ran a primary budget surplus, but under her guidance that surplus has decayed into a deficit equal to 10 percent of GDP, the highest for any large economy in the world. To control the rising deficit, Rousseff has been forced to propose emergency deficit reduction measures. But because nearly 70 percent of the budget goes toward social entitlements and salaries, there is little room to cut spending. Rousseff's deficit reduction plans thus focus on tax increases, which are likely to further hurt the economy. The president's political stock is so low there is no way she can propose any serious reform of a perilously generous state that, for example, still allows many Brazilians to retire in their early fifties.

The combination of a clumsy state and chronically high borrowing costs has depressed investment in Brazil for years, a bad sign on the factories first rule. In a developing country an investment level around 25 to 35 percent of GDP is good for growth, particularly if the money is going into productive industries like manufacturing or technology. In Brazil's case, investment as a share of the economy has stagnated for many years below 20 percent of GDP. Far from building new manufacturing plants, Brazil is more reliant than ever on sales of soybeans, sugar, and other commodities, which now account for 67 percent of exports, up from 46 percent in 2000. Though Brazil does have a small niche of well-known and globally competitive industrial companies, they are the exception to its overwhelming dependence on commodities. In global media and markets, Brazil has gone from widely admired to widely disparaged, the poster child for all the ills bedeviling emerging economies.

On the hype rule, it is a good sign when the global media stop criticizing a crisis-wracked country and just ignore it. While Brazil is for now hated by the media, there are some positive signs. In particular the Brazilian currency feels cheap. The cheap is good rule identifies locals as the first people to sense when a falling currency signals more instability to come, and they start pulling money out of a country. But rich Brazilians are staying put: a good sign. Unlike wealthy Russians, who have taken every opportunity to pull money out of a similarly devastated commodity economy, wealthy Brazilians are bargain hunting for investments at home, as are buyers from the United States and China. In São Paulo, hotels that cater to international business people are renting rooms for two hundred dollars a night, down from over a thousand dollars a night at the peak of the commodity boom. At a recent meeting in New York, a São Paulo–based billionaire volunteered that he is investing heavily at home because "Brazil is for sale."

Follow the locals in Brazil, and they lead to other signs of a possible turn for the better. In São Paulo malls, Brazilian-made clothes are now selling for less than clothes made in China, which has the most expensive currency in the emerging world. This growing competitive advantage has been very slow to turn around Brazil's current account deficit, in part because it has one of the most closed economies in the world. But after a long delay, the current account deficit is shrinking. The deficit hit 5 percent of GDP in early 2015 but a year later is running below 3 percent, out of the danger zone. By some of the more optimistic estimates, the deficit could turn to surplus in 2017, a turning point that often signals more stable growth to come.

Though Brazil is far from becoming a geographic sweet spot, it is at least starting to rethink policies that shut it off from the world, with trade counting for an extremely low 20 percent of GDP. Between 2000 and 2015, while its rivals were cutting dozens of trade deals, Brazil cut two. The first sign of relaxation in Brazil's closed stance came in November of 2015, when on a trip to Turkey for the G-20 summit, Rousseff is said to have explored possible trade deals with European countries. All told, Brazil has not changed course enough to rise out of the ugly class, but it has lifted itself off the bottom, mainly due to the rapid fall of its currency and the sudden evaporation of hype for what some global commentators had started calling "God's own country."

The collapse in commodity prices has fragmented the prospects in the neighboring region of the Andes. Among the hottest stars for much of the past decade, now only Peru's prospects still look good, while Colombia has fallen to average and Chile to ugly. Meanwhile, the Latin country with the highest scores on the rules is Mexico.

In recent years, while the left-wing axis of Brazil, Venezuela, and Argentina cut itself off from global markets and railed against the United States, Mexico was racing to open doors to the world and profit from closer ties to its giant neighbor. Heavy U.S. investment in manufacturing plants has helped Mexico reduce its reliance on oil, which now accounts for 10 percent of exports, down from 40 percent in the 1980s. Mexico is thus the rare case of an economy reducing its ties to petroleum, as most others continue to ride the wild ups and downs of oil prices.

When I met President Enrique Peña Nieto before his election in 2012, he was being criticized in the local media as a vacant pretty boy with a soap opera wife. But he had a coherent plan to double Mexico's growth rate by breaking up the oligopolies that still hold back the economy. His progress has been retarded by scandal, including a sweetheart real estate deal involving his wife, and by bad luck—he opened the oil sector to new foreign investment just as prices were about to fall. But some of his reforms are beginning to bear fruit.

Peña Nieto's team came in as arrogant reformers, refusing to take calls from power players in the old system, but they since have learned to work with them. The government passed landmark legislation to break up monopolies in industries like telecoms, reduce the power of unions, open up sectors such as energy to foreign investors, improve tax collections, and invest more heavily in public infrastructure.

Like so many countries in the AC era, Mexico's challenge begins with the fact that people matter now more than ever, as population growth slows worldwide. Mexico's working-age population has been growing at a rate of 1.2 percent, which is weak for a sizable emerging country. To sustain a growth rate of above 3 percent, Mexico has to rely on raising its productivity, and that in turn requires increasing investment in infrastructure, equipment, and training. Peña Nieto's team is working toward increasing the investment rate, which has stagnated for years around 20 percent of GDP, with projects such as a new $12 billion international airport for Mexico City.

To address the high cost of electricity, which is 100 percent more expensive in Mexico than it is across the border in Texas, the government plans to build new pipelines to bring cheap U.S. natural gas to Mexican power plants and to build more electric production capacity. Coupled with the falling value of the peso and increasingly competitive wages, the prospect of falling electricity costs is attracting investors like Kia, the large Korean automaker. In 2015 Kia chose Mexico over Brazil and the United States as the site of a plant that will eventually be capable of producing one million cars a year.

Within North America, car production is shifting rapidly from north to south, and from Canada to Mexico, as the Mexican government improves port facilities and aggressively cuts trade deals. Its forty-five free trade agreements are double the number cut by the United States, and Canadian officials have conceded that Mexico is winning the regional race on trade deals. Just about every major car company in the world, from BMW to General Motors and Toyota to Kia, is now in Mexico, building or expanding plants from Chihuahua in the north to Puebla in the south. The geography rule rewards nations that promote regional balance in growth, and few countries are spreading the wealth across provinces better than Mexico.

Mexico has been like a plane waiting to take off for years now, but with reforms already in place, its prospects certainly look better than most countries, particularly those in Latin America. While Brazil and its other southern neighbors are gripped by stagflation, Mexico has an inflation rate well below the emerging-market average, and the economy is growing at a pace of around 3 percent, which in the AC era is good for a country with an average income of around $10,000.

South Asia

The place to look for the next winners is always among the recent laggards, according to the hype rule. In recent decades few countries have fallen farther off the global media radar than those in South Asia. The exception is India, which has been flattered by spasms of hype for many years, most recently when Prime Minister Narendra Modi took power in May 2014 and promised major economic reform. However, India's smaller neighbors remained out of the picture. Pakistan, Bangladesh, and Sri Lanka made international news, respectively, for issues like terror, sweatshops, and prosecuting war crimes. These storylines obscure the economic reality, which is that Bangladesh, Sri Lanka, and Pakistan are contributing to the quiet rise of South Asia.

Together, the nations of South Asia are growing at an average annual pace of close to 6 percent, very good by the standards of the AC era, even for these low-income countries. Leaders in the region are pushing reform, credit growth is under control, and working-age population growth is strong, particularly in Pakistan and Bangladesh. Unlike most emerging regions, falling commodity prices help South Asia, where all the economies are commodity importers. Low oil prices are keeping inflation rates in check even as economic growth accelerates—the ideal combination. In 2015 South Asia had the highest concentration of accelerating economies in the world.

The whole region is emerging as a geographic sweet spot. Since 2008 many emerging economies have been hurt by rising wages and have seen their share of global exports decline, but Bangladesh, Pakistan, and Sri Lanka are benefiting tremendously as manufacturers look for cheaper wages outside of China. Bangladesh is now the second-leading exporter, after China, of ready-made clothes to the United States and Germany. And as China and Japan maneuver for influence in the Indian Ocean, they are investing billions in new ports in these nations, all of which offer prime locations near the major East-West trade routes, an essential element of a geographic sweet spot. After Beijing recently announced plans to build a $46 billion "economic corridor" connecting ports on the southern coast of Pakistan to western China, Japan beat out China for rights to build Bangladesh's first deep-water port at Matarbari.

Investment in Sri Lanka and Bangladesh is now at or near 30 percent of GDP, right in the stable zone for promoting strong growth without inflation, and a significant portion of that investment is going into factories. Pakistan has a weaker record for both investment and manufacturing, which represents just 12 percent of GDP, but the mood has transformed amid signs that the fragile Pakistani state appears to be taking steps to tamp down extremist violence. Since the 2014 Taliban massacre of more than a hundred schoolchildren in Peshawar, one no longer hears ordinary Pakistanis distinguish between "good" and "bad" members of the Taliban rebellion. Public revulsion seems to have inspired Pakistan's army to crack down, and the number of terrorism-related fatalities fell to ten a day in 2015, down from thirty a day in 2009.

On a 2014 trip the risks of travel inside Pakistan were so high, our security detail confined my team to its Karachi hotel. A year later, they were allowed to wander the country, accompanied by guards who did not bother to arm or dress for combat. One bodyguard showed up in blue suede shoes. Even the bloody March 2016 bombing in Lahore did not destroy the brighter mood of locals, who say the big news is how the coup-prone military has matured. It is focusing on security and leaving the task of managing the economy to the civilian government of Nawaz Sharif, who appears likely to finish out his term in 2018. That would be an unusual sign of progress in coup-prone Pakistan.

Since coming to power in 2012 Sharif has overseen a decline in the inflation rate to less than 3 percent, a fall in the government budget deficit from 8 percent to 5 percent of GDP, and in the current account deficit from 8 percent to less than 1 percent of GDP, well into the safe zone. Critics attribute those deficit reductions to falling oil prices and credit any progress under Sharif to the fact that his reform program faces quarterly review by the IMF, as a condition of a 2013 emergency loan. The legitimate concern is that the reforms will end when IMF oversight does, but for now it seems the Pakistan government will engage with the IMF for a few more years.

The new burst of Pakistani optimism is inspired less by Sharif than by the decline in violence and the infusion of Chinese money, which could go a long way to address the investment shortfall in a small economy. China's $46 billion "economic corridor" plan is scheduled to build new roads, railways, and power plants across the country within just twenty years. Pakistan may not be able to complete so many projects that fast, but spending even half that sum could double the current rate of foreign investment. Hotels from Karachi to Lahore are packed with Chinese delegations working on the economic corridor. Like its neighbors, Pakistan is on pace to see growth pick up in the coming years.

Though the change in mood is less dramatic, Bangladesh is heading in a similar direction. With exports and investment strong, it is running a current account surplus. Population trends are even better. Through 2020, very few countries in the world are expected to see working-age population grow at or near 2 percent a year—the pace set in most miracle economies in the past. Two of them are in South Asia: Pakistan and Bangladesh.

Just as important, the three small South Asian players have managed to keep growth alive without transgressing the debt rule. They have seen modest growth in private credit as a share of GDP over the last five years, and their banks have healthy balance sheets. The rule says that banks are generally in good shape when their outstanding loans amount to no more than 80 percent of deposits, suggesting that they have enough deposits on hand to make new loans. All the South Asian banking systems are at or below that level. This marks the region as a land of entrepreneurial opportunity in a world where so many big emerging countries have seen a sharp and dangerous expansion of credit in the last five years.

South Asia has been dogged by political instability since the independence movements of the 1940s, and the economic risks of authoritarian rule still loom over the countries that make up this coup-prone region. On average, authoritarian governments are no more or less likely than democracies to produce long runs of strong growth, but they produce much less steady growth and tend to experience volatile swings from very strong to very weak growth. This risk faded last year in Sri Lanka after voters rejected President Mahinda Rajapaksa's bid for a fourth term. Relieved local business executives, who did not dare criticize Rajapaksa when he was in power, say his defeat lifts the "Mugabe risk"—the threat that Sri Lanka would end up with a disastrous dictator like Robert Mugabe, whose thirty-five-year reign in Zimbabwe has seen wild boom and bust cycles that have left the nation in ruins.

India's prospects are holding steady and it continues with its long tradition of confounding both optimists and pessimists. When Modi first arrived in office, his supporters hoped that he would rattle the status quo, while critics feared that he would prove to be too aggressive and authoritarian for the world's largest democracy. Two years into his term, Modi has moved with surprising caution on economic matters, staying well within the old Indian habits of incremental change. He has done some positive but obvious things, like reducing fuel subsidies, and has promoted a culture of competitive federalism among the states. He seems to understand the importance of stable prices and has left the central bank alone to focus on fighting inflation.

But India under Modi also offers plenty of fodder for pessimists. One of the biggest obstacles to faster growth is a state banking system that controls 75 percent of all loans, more than double the emerging-world average. In a country with deep socialist roots, privatizing even some loss-making state banks is seen as too heretical a step, despite the clear signs of mismanagement. A striking 15 percent of state bank loans have gone bad. Credit growth is held back by the sclerotic banking system, and Indian businesses remain very wary of investing at home.

New investment is coming mainly from foreigners, whom Modi has courted aggressively. In August, Foxconn—the world's largest electronics maker—announced plans to invest $5 billion in new plants and R&D centers in Maharashtra. That's a plus, but in any large economy, investment is driven mainly by locals, and the Modi government has courted them mainly with slogans. It started out promoting "Make in India" to boost manufacturing, but lately it has swapped that pitch for one targeted at technology, "Start Up India." The concern in tech centers of India is that, having flourished without state help or interference, they may now be subject to unwanted attention.

Weak investment tends to make an economy vulnerable to inflation, because the failure to build adequate networks of roads and factories means output can't keep up with demand when economic growth accelerates. India over the past few years has been a classic case of an inflation-prone country. Under Modi, the new inflation-fighting mandate of the central bank has combined with falling oil prices to bring the inflation rate down from double digits to 5 percent. That's a marked improvement, but it's still well above the emerging-world average.

On the geography rule, South Asia has long been hampered by the extremely low level of trade within the region, and Modi has been bolder in dealing with neighbors than he has been at home. He has reached out to forge closer trade and diplomatic ties to Bangladesh and to old rivals in Pakistan. Widen the lens to include the rest of the world, however, and the story is less promising. Since 2010 India has implemented over five hundred protectionist measures, more than any other country in the world according to the Centre for Economic Policy Research, a nonprofit network of economists based in Europe.[1]

India is as much a continent as a country, with 29 states that are as varied and often much more populous than the states of Europe. Today much of the real economic action is in the hands of chief ministers from states such as Haryana and Andhra Pradesh, who are traveling from New York to Beijing pitching for investments. This explains why despite all the mixed messages from the national capital, India is probably growing at a rate between 5 and 6 percent, much less than the government claims but still a good outcome for a low-income country in the AC era. With its small South Asian neighbors picking up momentum, the entire region is demonstrating relatively strong growth, and doing it all without attracting much attention as a group. It is another big plus that the major media are not talking up the "South Asian Tigers." At least not yet.

Southeast Asia

Outside of the Indian subcontinent, there is no region in the world where every country is enjoying reasonably high growth with stable inflation. Next door in Southeast Asia, the picture for the nations clustered around the South China Sea is the usual mix of good, average, and ugly. The region is home to one of the most widely overlooked success stories in the world, the Philippines, which is five years into a run of strong growth, yet shows none of the signs of excess—whether in credit, or investment, or inflation, or current account deficits—that normally signal the end. Though global investors have been pouring money into Philippine stocks and bonds, the international media have largely ignored this bright spot in the doldrums of the AC era. Investment is increasing with no signs of a credit mania. Economic growth is running at more than 6 percent with inflation barely above one percent. The Philippines is very unusual in the emerging world for the light touch of the state, which offers no subsidies for electricity or gas and has no ownership stake in major banks or in any of the companies on the Manila stock market.

The Philippines was a laughingstock for so long that it may take some more years for the media to recognize its transformation under the leadership of President Benigno Aquino III. It is always a bad sign in the circle of life when even successful leaders hang on to power too long; Aquino plans to step down in 2016, in accord with the law and on schedule. His upcoming departure has created some uncertainty, since the candidates to succeed include a mix of reformers and old-school patronage politicians. For now, however, the Philippines is still in the good stage of the cycles that govern political leadership, the role of the state, credit, investment, inflation, and money flows, and has a fast-growing working-age population. The former laggard is now a global frontrunner, and this run still has legs.

The next best prospects in Southeast Asia belong somewhat surprisingly to Indonesia, which is at least not imploding like other large commodity economies. Russia, Brazil, and South Africa all began drifting toward recession when global commodity prices started to fall in 2011. But Indonesia, which exports copper, palm oil, and other raw materials, has slowed only half a step. It is protected by a relatively low per capita income of just $3,500, which makes growth easier, and the fact that it has a larger domestic investment and consumption base than other countries in its class.

In 2014, Indonesians voted in a fresh leader as president, the maverick outsider and former furniture maker Joko Widodo, and after some early mistakes he seems to be gaining momentum. In keeping with the saying that bad times make for good policy, Widodo pushed reform hard only after falling commodity prices slowed the economy. He cut energy subsidies, one of the worst giveaways of meddling states, and plans to use the proceeds to build roads and other infrastructure, in order to attract more investment in manufacturing industries. He reshuffled an incompetent cabinet of technocrats who had, for example, delayed releasing investment funds on the grounds that the new ministry which would handle those investments did not yet have an official name. In a late 2015 meeting with President Obama at the White House, Widodo agreed to join the Trans-Pacific Partnership, a big step toward openness for a traditionally insular country. Once implemented, the partnership will require him to reform dysfunctional aspects of the economy, including rules that require the government to buy from state-run companies and that make it difficult for foreigners to work in Indonesia.

Sweeping trade deals can provide national leaders political cover to push tough reform, on the grounds that they have no choice but to meet their international obligations. Widodo plans to make up for collapsing export revenue by ramping up investment in roads so inadequate it takes six hours to drive the fifty kilometers from an industrial zone outside Jakarta to the nearest port. The current account deficit has fallen below 3 percent and the currency feels cheap. The population is young and growing, but it will peak and start aging around 2025, so the challenge for Indonesia is to get rich before it gets old.

Close behind Indonesia in the rankings stands Vietnam, which scores very differently on the rules for everything from politics to credit. The Communist Party has reigned since the end of the Vietnam War with no sign of letting go. Though there is now some talk of privatizing state companies, they still account for a third of the economy. To counter the global downturn, the government is intervening more and now has a fiscal deficit equal to 6 percent of GDP, more than twice the emerging world average. It has also unleashed a torrent of credit over the past decade to prop up growth, and the ostrich-like central bank has responded to a rising tide of bad loans by underreporting them.

Communist Party politics are so murky it is hard to know which leader is really calling the shots in Vietnam. Yet the nation remains free of social unrest so long as the party continues to improve living standards, which it has, bulldozing new roads with authoritarian zeal. Vietnam has an average income one-third that of Indonesia, but the highways are already much better. It now takes twenty minutes by car from the new terminal at Hanoi's international airport to the city center, thanks to the recent opening of a sweeping eight-lane motorway and a bridge that has halved the driving distance to about ten miles.

The Vietnamese see themselves as the next China, evolving rapidly from an agrarian economy into an export manufacturing powerhouse. After spiking to a dangerously high 40 percent of GDP in the go-go years of the last decade, investment has come down to 28 percent of GDP. That is right in the 25 to 35 percent sweet spot for sustaining high growth with low inflation in a developing country. Inflation has fallen to less than 2 percent from peaks above 20 percent as recently as 2011. Foreign direct investment amounts to 6 percent of GDP, the highest level in Southeast Asia, and most of it does go into manufacturing: everything from cars to smartphones. Vietnam was a divided country not so long ago, but factories are now sprouting up everywhere, from Hanoi in the north to Ho Chi Minh City in the south, reflecting unusually strong regional balance in growth.

Today, when locals in Beijing talk about how slowing growth at home could spill over China's borders, it is a bit surreal to hear their neighbors in Hanoi predicting that growth is going to accelerate this year and next, and claiming that their country's exports are going to get a boost from the Trans-Pacific Partnership. Vietnam is a striking example of a geographic sweet spot, moving quickly to link all of its provinces to global and regional trade routes. The boom is real, but Vietnam's prospects rest on high scores for the two rules governing factories and geography. Its rise thus looks more uncertain than that of more balanced economies, like the Philippines.

It is often the case that former stars decay into laggards, and this process seems to be infecting neighboring countries like Malaysia and

Thailand. These countries are slipping in the Southeast Asian rankings in part because of political factors. Malaysian Prime Minister Najib Razak has been embroiled in corruption scandals and seems oblivious to how seriously falling commodity prices undermine his nation's economy, which relies on exports of palm oil and petroleum. On a visit to New York in October of 2015, one of my colleagues asked him whether the collapse in the value of the ringgit is offering any boost to his nation's embattled manufacturing sector. He answered by missing the point, saying that the cheap ringgit is great for tourism, which cannot be an important contributor to growth in a country as large as Malaysia. Pressed on the manufacturing question, he seemed at a loss. An aide at the back of the room pitched in to help, but he spoke about investment in oil and other raw materials. The crowd left with the impression that Malaysia is missing an opportunity, because the cheap currency coupled with the right reforms could supercharge Malaysian manufacturing.

In Thailand, the economy has long been insulated from political upheavals by the stabilizing effect of a strong manufacturing sector and the jobs it creates, but that may be changing. In May of 2014 the Army staged the country's nineteenth coup since the 1930s, and the military leaders seemed almost apologetic in private meetings, promising elections would come soon. Instead, they started maneuvering to write a new constitution that would permanently sideline their rural foes and gut democratic institutions, creating a politburo-type government and a single agency to run state companies in banking, energy, transport, and other industries. This unfolding triumph of the urban elite is reflected in the fact that the capital city of Bangkok is ten times more populous than the second city of Chiang Mai and still growing. Under the geography rule, this is a dangerous sign of regional inequality for a midsize country like Thailand.

Thailand should be using its location at the commercial heart of Indochina to broaden opportunity across the country, but amid the political battles between capital and countryside the economy seems to have been forgotten. This time, even the permanent civil servants who normally keep the economy running through the coups and post-coup periods can't keep momentum going. The junta is reviving the controlled military economy of the 1980s, and growth is slowing sharply. The population is aging rapidly and incomes are falling, but street protests have disappeared due to the heavy army presence. Thai businesses are sitting on their wallets, waiting to see how the new constitution shakes out; investment is slumping; and building projects are stalled. Credit nonetheless grew much faster than the Thai economy over the past few years, because households have been borrowing heavily, and Thailand now faces one of the worst debt hangovers outside China and Turkey. All this suggests that the growth rate is likely to remain anemic in coming years.

East Asia

An even more striking case of a "leader to laggard" story is unfolding in East Asia, home of the original miracle economies. The key is China, where the Communist Party is talking the right language of "supply-side reform," implying a reduction of the investment excesses built up during the boom years, but still seems unwilling to tolerate the short-term pain required to make that adjustment—or even tolerate the natural slowdown in growth that happens when a nation reaches a lower-middle income level, as China has.

Its average income is approaching $10,000, and the leadership has lowered its growth target to 6.5 percent for 2016, which would be ambitious even for a poorer country in the AC era. Late last year, some provincial officials admitted they had doctored numbers in order to meet these growth targets. The most important reform China could adopt is to scrap the growth target, which is driving leaders to force-feed the economy with debt it can no longer digest efficiently.

A growth target of more than 6 percent is particularly ambitious for China now that its working-age population growth has hit a major turning point, shrinking in 2015 for the first time since the UN started keeping records in 1950. In the postwar period, major economies with a shrinking working-age population have posted an average growth rate of just 1.5 percent, and have never sustained a growth rate of 6 percent or better. It seems unlikely China can buck its bad demographics either.

The debt rule continues to flash a bright red warning. Debt binges as large as China's have always led to economic slowdowns, and often have been accompanied by financial crises of some kind. No developing country has run up debts as rapidly as China has done since 2008, and its debt is still growing twice as fast as its GDP. Much of that credit continues to fund increasingly unproductive investment, which accounts for well above 35 percent of GDP, the upper limit of the safe zone for stable growth.

In 2013, investment in China peaked at an all-time high—47 percent of GDP—having climbed steadily from less than 25 percent in 1970. This represents another alarming turning point. My research shows that the pace of economic growth typically falls by half in the five years after an investment peak above 40 percent of GDP. The industrial sector now accounts for an unusually large share of the Chinese economy, and after slowing sharply last year it is now on track to contract in 2016, which would represent the first industrial recession in China since it began opening to the world in 1978.[2]

Following the locals also suggests trouble. Beijing recently devalued the renminbi, hoping to revive industry and exports, and thwart a sharp bout of capital flight. Instead, the devaluation proved too small to calm nerves, and the Chinese started shipping money out even faster. In 2015, $640 billion fled China, most of it in the last six months of the year, and much of it covered up by doctored export receipts and other tools locals use to hide illicit capital flows. This scenario has played out with dire consequences before, since in ten out of the twelve major emerging-market currency crises going back to 1990, local investors headed for the exits well before foreigners.

The flight of capital represents a loud vote of no confidence in the government's ability to manage a deteriorating economic situation. In

China's case, the flows are so large that they are felt across the world. Wealthy Chinese are using the pricey renminbi to buy property and push real estate prices to near bubble levels everywhere from San Francisco to London. At Australia's two largest developers, 40 percent of the buyers are speculators and three out of four speculators are Chinese, some arriving on package tours to shop for second homes outside China.

China's economic growth path has come to resemble a ping-pong ball bouncing down stairs, popping up when the government rolls out new stimulus measures, only to fall to an even lower level. If there is one good sign for China, it is that the global media are by now all over the story and asking whether the economy is headed for a "hard landing." By some estimates China grew at a pace below 4 percent in 2015, which to locals feels like a recession after so many years of double-digit growth, so I would argue that the economy has already hard-landed. The question is whether it is also headed for some kind of financial crisis, which could come in the form of a pop in the bond market bubble, or a currency crisis if rapid capital flight leads to a collapse in the value of the renminbi. Whether it has a crisis or not, China's economic growth prospects now rank among the ugliest in the emerging world.

The impact of China's hard landing is being felt around the world, because China this decade displaced the United States as the lead driver of global growth. Forty-four countries now rely on China as their main export market, up fourfold since 2004, compared to thirty-one that rely mainly on the United States. Today every one-percentage-point slowdown in China's economy reduces global GDP growth by nearly half a percentage point, with emerging markets bearing the brunt.

Among the hardest hit are the commodity exporters, followed by immediate neighbors like Taiwan and South Korea, which not only trade heavily with China but also have an intricate web of investments in factories there. Neither country is in trouble, however. Credit growth is stable in Taiwan, and banks are flush with deposits. South Korea continues to shine on the factories first rule, expanding its manufacturing prowess into aerospace, new branches of the computer chip industry, and pharmaceuticals. One of its largest conglomerates is investing billions to become the world's largest manufacturer in the booming market for bio-similars—or near copies of existing biological drugs.

On balance though, the rules point to a somewhat muddled future for South Korea and Taiwan. Feted in the past for growing rich while remaining egalitarian, both countries have seen a rising backlash against inequality. South Korean president Park Geun-hye came to office promising "economic democracy," but in late 2015 she faced mass protests for undercutting job protections and coddling the billionaires who own the nation's leading industrial conglomerates. Anger over growing inequality, rising costs of property, and the previous government's image of cozying up too much to China also helped bring a fresh leader to power in Taiwan, Tsai Ing-wen of the Democratic Progressive Party. In the past the rise of a DPP candidate has always alarmed the markets, fearful that this pro-independence party would set off clashes with China, which still claims sovereignty over Taiwan.

When I met her in Taipei in 2014, however, Tsai came off as a pragmatic reformer and assured me that she had no intention of rocking the status quo. It may well be that she has the street credibility to complete the controversial China trade deals that helped topple her predecessor. Moreover, Tsai plans to diversify Taiwan's trade links beyond China by signing on to the Trans-Pacific Partnership with the United States, which could make her country more well-rounded as a geographical sweet spot. However, at a time when the working-age population is shrinking in both Taiwan and South Korea, and slowing global trade is buffeting their traditional source of growth—exports—it is hard to imagine how these countries can grow at a rapid pace in the coming five years. The prospects of these former miracle economies now look decidedly average.

The population trends are even more adverse in Japan, yet at the margin the story there may be more encouraging. China surpassed Japan as the world's second-largest economy in 2010, but this crisis of status provoked a revival of sorts in Japan, as the circle of life rule predicts. Two years later, frustrated Japanese voted in Prime Minister Shinzo Abe, who came to power promising to reawaken the economy by firing "three arrows": more government spending, looser monetary policy, and reform to make the nation more open and competitive.

Many of Abe's reforms go to the heart of Japan's problems. The state is interfering less and taking aggressive steps to bolster the rapidly aging workforce, the high level of debt is at least not rising further, the yen is dirt cheap, and the economy is opening to trade and competition in ways that are often overlooked. To help its global companies compete abroad, the Abe government cut corporate taxes from 40 percent to 32 percent and is targeting a further cut to 29 percent, a little lower than in Germany. To fortify a rapidly aging workforce, Abe has pushed "womenomics," including a revamping of childcare systems. The share of adult women who participate in the work force is up from 60 percent in 2010 to 65 percent today—surpassing the United States, where the share is stagnant at 63 percent. In addition, the Abe government is talking about creating special economic zones with looser rules for foreign workers, particularly for those involved in care for the elderly. This test run may uncover how far Japan would be willing to open its doors to economic migrants.

The Abe government is also a joint author with the United States of the Trans-Pacific Partnership, which is at its core a Japanese-American plan to write the rules of fair trade before China can. Abe is already looking at ways to open long closed backwaters of the Japanese economy, including a plan to cut subsidies for powerful but inefficient rice farmers. His government has also thrown open its doors to tourists, using lower taxes, simpler visa requirements, and the appeal of the suddenly cheap yen to lure more visitors. Since 2011 the number of foreign visitors has risen from 8 million to 20 million, and over the last year more than half that surge came from China alone. The train from Narita International Airport to Tokyo recently added public service announcements in Chinese, a striking shift for bitter rivals that still joust over blood feuds dating to World War II.

This is a powerful testament to the economic impact of rapidly shifting currency values, which are now pulling tourists from China—carrying the most expensive currency in the developing world—to Japan—the country with the cheapest currency in the developed world. Tokyo has been transformed into a bargain basement, and *bakugai*, or "explosive buying," was named the most popular buzzword of 2015, when tourists were snapping up everything from cosmetics to high-tech toilet seats. Money is flowing into Japan, and home prices have stopped falling for the first time in twenty-five years. This is a healthy sign on the price of onions rule, suggesting that Japan's long and destructive bout of deflation could be at an end.

Even the kiss of debt is not quite as threatening for Japan as its astonishing total debt burden—390 percent of GDP—might lead one to imagine. The public debt burden is indeed unusually high at 220 percent of GDP, nearly double that of the next most-indebted government in the developed world, which is Italy's. But remember, the key signal is the *pace of increase* in debt, which has been very slight over the past five years, and banks are flush with deposits (now more than enough to cover new loans).

Japan is defying its caricature as the country that never changes, but its progress on a host of rules is still only enough to move it up from ugly to average. Several critical weaknesses will continue to limit its prospects. With Japan's working-age population projected to decline by nearly 1 percent a year through 2020, it scores terribly on the demographic rule. While Japan's proximity to China was a real advantage on the geographic sweet spot rule, it is not anymore. Investment is growing, but weakly. The currency has been cheap for over a year and—though it is attracting tourists—has yet to do much to boost exports. Japan sends nearly a quarter of its exports to China, more than any other developed economy, and that will be a drag on growth as Chinese demand shrinks. Still, even a move up from ugly to average represents real progress in a world where the prospects of so many economies are in decline.

The developed economy with the most sharply deteriorating

prospects is an Asian neighbor, Australia. Along with Canada, Australia is proof that the curse of commodities is not confined only to poor countries. Both Australia and Canada had ridden the tide of high prices for oil, gas, and other commodities before 2011, and entered into debt and spending binges typical of these frenzied booms. Following the collapse in commodity prices, both countries are going through a painful adjustment.

Canada looks slightly better than Australia on the rules, owing to geography and factories. In 2015, Canada tossed out a ruling party that had grown stale after ten years in power and ushered in a new prime minister, Justin Trudeau, who was feared by the markets as a "socialist" but appears to understand what Canada needs. He has talked about weaning Canada from dependence on oil, opening the economy by joining the Trans-Pacific Partnership with the United States, and investing more in roads and factories. The manufacturing sector is relatively large, and though it is losing competitiveness, it is not as troubled as Australian manufacturing. Perhaps Canada's biggest advantage is that its economy is tied through trade mainly to the United States, while Australia's main links are to China, which is slowing much more rapidly than the United States. Geographic sweet spots are not static—they grow more or less sweet with the rise and fall of neighbors and shifting trade patterns.

Australia's fall from good to ugly has been rapid. It has gone a quarter-century without suffering a recession, and that long run of success fed a case of severe complacency. Even the major positive for Australia—a relatively fast population growth rate boosted by open immigration—is under threat. Anti-immigrant sentiment is a growing force in Australian politics, despite the fact that the number of migrants is falling. Migration now adds 0.7 percent to the population each year, down by half since 2008, as trouble in commodity industries dries up job opportunities.

Like many emerging economies, Australia had indulged itself during the commodity price boom. As debts mounted in recent years,

Australia was investing heavily, but mainly in real estate and commodity industries like iron ore, not in factories first. Australians borrowed heavily to buy stocks and houses, driving up home prices by more than 50 percent between 2010 and 2014, the highest increase in the developed world over that time. The price surge was further fueled by those package tours for real estate shoppers out of China. As the price of onions rule shows, consumer price inflation is not the only kind that matters, because there is an increasingly strong link between rapid inflation in real estate prices and economic busts. In 2015, investment in real estate amounted to well over 5 percent of Australia's GDP, a level that has often signaled bubbles in the past.

During the boom years in Australia, wages rose sharply, as did the value of the Australian dollar, which undercut the competitiveness of what few factories the country had left. The anemic manufacturing sector represents 8 percent of GDP, the lowest level for a major developed country, and it is declining. In 2013 and 2014, Ford, GM, and Toyota announced that they were shutting down car production in Australia, driven out by the high costs, and based on their current plans the auto industry could be dead in Australia by 2017. Meanwhile, the car industry was flourishing elsewhere. Over the same period, Ford and Nissan followed early moves by Renault and Volkswagen to expand manufacturing operations in Europe, particularly Spain.

Europe

The prospects of Europe's largest powers are mixed, with Germany looking quite good, Britain rather average, and France decidedly ugly. Germany continues to coast along largely on the strength of the Hartz reforms that starting in 2002 lowered its labor costs and made its exports more competitive. Since Angela Merkel became chancellor in 2005, her main contribution has been to sustain this momentum. The state budget is in balance, inflation is stable, and Germany largely avoided a credit binge after 2008. The result is a banking network that has a few weak links, concentrated in the provincial Landesbanken, but no systematic problems and relatively few bad loans. Meanwhile, a steady flow of investment continues to fuel an extraordinary export machine.

Germany has turned itself into the geographic heart of European manufacturing, with supply networks branching out into the lower-cost labor markets of eastern Europe. Its billionaire class controls vast wealth but generates the majority of it in the kinds of productive industries that are most likely to generate good jobs and least likely to generate a political backlash against growth.

Bad billionaires in corruption-prone industries control only 1 percent of billionaire wealth. Merkel's finest hour, however, may have been one of her last; she resisted the right-wing backlash against the million-plus refugees who poured into Europe in 2015 and kept Germany's doors open wider than any other country in the world. That's exactly what Germany needs to rejuvenate an aging workforce and counts as a bold positive under the people matter rule. The resulting controversy lowers Merkel's chances of landing a fourth term in 2017, but that's not necessarily bad for Germany. Under the circle of life rule, replacing a long-standing leader with a fresh one is generally a plus.

Germany certainly looks stronger than Britain, which seems to be evolving into a larger version of Singapore, an island economy driven by services. Growth is powered to a large degree by the financial service industries in London, which accounts for 20 percent of the economy. Manufacturing accounts for 9 percent of GDP in Britain, second lowest among big developed economies after Australia but without the potential boost from resource wealth. In 2016 there is a widespread sense that the country is turning inward, with the government of Prime Minister David Cameron committed to holding a referendum on whether Britain should leave the European Union, in part so it can limit benefits to refugees. Popular anger over rising wealth inequality—London is home to 80 billionaires, one of the highest concentrations in the world—has pushed the Labour Party to the extreme left. It also put pressure on the conservative government to consider intervening more in the economy, for example by slapping new regulations on global banks.

Meanwhile the domestic economy in Britain is showing signs of excess: Real estate prices have soared to record highs, rising more than twice as fast as wages. Tales abound of students from China and Russia renting London apartments at monthly rates higher than the average yearly income in the UK. Though consumer price inflation is low, prices for homes and other assets raise serious inflation concerns. The pound feels expensive at a time when the euro feels cheap, further undercutting British competitiveness. There are, however, rules on which the UK looks good. Its companies and households have cut back sharply on private debt, which is down by 33 percentage points as a share of GDP since 2010. Its trade relationships are quite strong, and it scores relatively well on the people matter rule. Britain's population growth is strong for a rich country, and it is a magnet for economic migrants (despite its closed door to war refugees). Overall, Britain's growth prospects look about average.

The global political backlash against incumbent rulers is also playing havoc with the European rankings, pressuring states to interfere more in the economy and close borders. The widely feared rise of extremist parties on the right and left did not topple leaders in any major country in 2015. The center held. Europe as a whole, with growth running at about 1.5 percent and inflation under control, is not a continent ripe for takeover by right-wing extremism, as many fear. The governing parties in Britain and France both survived election challenges from fringe parties. Nonetheless, the rise of populist parties did force countries like Italy, Portugal, and Spain to dial back on competitive reforms.

One of the biggest shifts came in Spain, which fell over the course of last year from the top of the developed-world rankings to average. After the global financial crisis started to hit Europe hard in 2010, Spain was one of the countries stuck with huge debts. It was forced to reform. The positive side of the debt rule is that a large decrease in the debt-to-GDP ratio can set up a country for a new round of lending and growth, and in the five years between 2011 and 2015, private debt fell by 30 percentage points as a share of GDP in Spain, one of the sharpest drops in the developed world. Wages and labor costs also came down as Spaniards paid down debt. During this period, with global manufacturers expanding plants in Spain, it was one of the few developed countries to see its share of global export manufacturing expand. By last year, however, Mariano Rajoy's center-right government had lost most of its enthusiasm for tough reform, and then in the December 2015 elections it lost its parliamentary majority and its leverage. With progress stymied, Spain's progress now rests on the momentum of past reforms, and its prospects have slipped.

France is also trending downward according to the rules, particularly on the perils of the state. Already the largest government in the world, state spending had expanded from 51 percent of GDP in 2000 to 57 percent in 2015, and reforms proposed by the government to cut the bureaucracy and red tape are mostly half measures. The government for example, planned to lift the rule that bans retail stores from opening on Sunday, but only for twelve Sundays a year. Along with Italy, France has been losing competitiveness and has seen its labor costs rise by 5 percent since 2010. France has also seen one of the developed world's largest debt increases in the AC era, with private debt up by 16 percentage points as a share of GDP over the last five years.

Though France has a large foreign population, it has struggled to integrate the Muslims living in its urban areas, and the relationship soured further in late 2015 following the deadly attacks on Paris by gunmen proclaiming allegiance to the Islamic State. With that, the prospect of further immigration to address France's aging problem faded, as fear of terrorism and support for the right-wing nationalist parties rose. Today France is widely seen as the new sick man of Europe—the label that had attached to Britain in the 1970s and Germany in the 1990s.

To the east, Poland, the Czech Republic, and Romania have capitalized on their proximity to Germany and the rich markets of western Europe. Though fewer and fewer Western companies are still "offshoring" plants to China, they are still moving into eastern Europe. With relatively low labor costs and cheap currencies, these countries continue to attract investment from German industrial giants looking to build car and other manufacturing plants. Across the region, exports are strong, current account balances are close to being in balance or in surplus, and foreign debts are low. The Czech Republic's economic prospects now rank among the best of the large emerging nations. It did not have a debt binge either before or after 2008, so it avoided both stages of the recent global credit manias.

Poland has worked to cut back its debt burden sharply over the last five years, and the region's largest economy still looks good according to many of the rules, with business investment rising even as it stagnates in most other emerging economies, and dynamic billionaires expanding operations into Germany and Switzerland. However, Poland is clear proof that no nation is an economic utopia. Just when it seemed the country had everything going for it, on the circle of life rule the situation deteriorated, with serious consequences.

The shift came in October 2015 following the election victory of the conservative Law and Justice Party, which raised alarms across Europe when it said it would no longer fly the EU flag at presidential press conferences. The new government is moving to raise taxes on bank profits in a way that could hurt lending in the economy, and to assert political control over the state media and the judiciary. Its decision to pack Poland's top court with new appointees has unnerved the foreign community. Though fears that Law and Justice will "destroy Polish democracy" appear overblown, and the party quickly diluted its generous promises to lower the retirement age and pay large baby bonuses, its mix of loud populism and occasional pragmatism do undercut Poland's prospects. Before the election, the country scored well on eight rules, but now it looks good on six, with the politics turning ugly and the state bureaucracy tightening its hold on the economy.

Just south of Poland lies Romania, another striking case of an economy rising from a long period of stagnation but still widely ignored. Though Romania did run up debts after 2008, it has dialed back with unusual vigor. At a time when countries from India to China are still struggling with how to force banks to admit the full extent of their bad loans, Romania is imposing a definition of "bad" so stringent it arguably makes Romanian banks appear to be in worse shape than they really are. Romania is also aggressively downsizing its post-Communist state, and until recently it remained one of the few countries in the world that dared to sell majority, rather than partial, stakes in its state companies.

Romania shares the vulnerability that looms over all of eastern Europe, which is that its workforce is aging rapidly. Up to the last days of his regime in 1989, the Communist dictator Nicolae Ceauşescu was forcing Romanians to have more children, by imposing heavy taxes on adults who remained childless after the age of twenty-five. Proving how difficult it is for governments to increase fertility rates, Romania nonetheless stands today alongside Poland and the Czech Republic as one of the most rapidly aging societies in the emerging world; the UN projects that its working-age population will contract by 1.2 percent a year through 2020. At that rate, even dramatic moves to bring women or migrants into the workforce cannot offset population decline. Still, Romania is changing so determinedly for the better across a range of rules that its prospects look good.

The rise of these former Soviet satellites stands as a silent rebuke to their former overlords in Moscow, who are heading in the opposite direction. Nothing dramatizes the diverging fates of Russia and its lost dominion more sharply than this fact: In 2015, while eastern Europe as a whole enjoyed falling inflation and rising growth, Russia sunk into stagflation, with the economy contracting at a rate of 3 percent and inflation running at a rate of 15 percent. Among major countries, Russia now has one of the lowest scores on the rules.

Its leader, Vladimir Putin, is in his fourth term and has long since grown stale. He has abandoned economic reform in favor of expensive foreign military adventures to reassert Russian influence in the Middle East and eastern Europe. Boosted by propaganda trumpeting

Russia's recent territorial grabs in Ukraine and intervention in Syria, Putin remains stunningly popular—his approval ratings are officially reported at 90 percent, at a time when economic troubles are undermining the popularity of other leaders all over the world. According to the circle of life rule, however, there is nothing worse than a stale leader who has overstayed his economic usefulness but is well positioned to hold power indefinitely.

Putin's basic failure is that he never diversified an economy that remains dependent on oil, and it has collapsed with oil prices. To bring in cash, the government is now talking about selling minority stakes in Aeroflot and other state companies, but there is no sign it will relinquish ownership control. Russian manufacturing barely exists as a competitive export industry. Despite the oil price collapse, Russia remains more top-heavy with billionaire wealth than any other emerging nation, and 67 percent of the total billionaire wealth comes from politically connected industries like oil. Countries rarely score a completely ugly "1" on any rule, but right now Russia scores that low on the rules for politics, the state, bad versus good billionaires, and demographics. Russia also has one of the world's fastest-shrinking working-age populations. Its best score comes on the currency rule, because cheap is good and the ruble has plummeted along with the price of oil.

At the height of the oil boom, Moscow was a spectacle of petro-decadence, with Bentleys and Maybachs jamming the streets and caviar flowing till dawn. By late last year, when oil had fallen from $110 to under $50 in less than eighteen months, a new reality had dawned. The ruble had lost more than half its value against the dollar, and Moscow hadn't felt so cheap in years. Or so modest. During a trip in the fall of 2015, my colleagues were driven around in a sensible sedan, the Toyota Camry. With the ruble falling, so many disappointed Russians had to cancel Mediterranean vacations that tourism chief Oleg Safonov felt compelled to remind them that "the need for beaches" was a recent fad: "Our forefathers, even the wealthy, did not go en masse to foreign seas."

In keeping with the sober mood, Putin has been playing defense on the economic front. His promotional material trumpets his role as defender of Russian greatness in a hostile world, and to maintain that pose he is making sure Russia is not beholden to foreigners. Though Russia is rapidly running up private debt at home, a bad sign on the debt rule, it has also repaid billions in loans from foreigners over the last year. And rather than drain the treasury to defend the ruble in currency markets, the Putin government wisely let it float a year ago, allowing its value to drop. Though the price of oil is falling in dollars, each dollar in oil revenue is now worth twice as many rubles, which is what matters for the government budget. Coupled with cuts in government spending, the falling ruble has improved the outlook for the government deficit dramatically. As recently as 2014, Russia needed oil prices of at least $100 a barrel to generate enough revenue to balance its budget, but now it can balance the budget at an oil price of around $50. That is a strong bulwark against foreign pressure, particularly at a time when major oil producing countries from Nigeria to Saudi Arabia still need an oil price of around $80 for their budgets to balance.

The problem with Putin's economic strategy is that it is all defense against foreign influence, with no offense to spark growth at home. On two of the biggest concerns in the AC era—deleveraging and depopulation—Russia ranks poorly among emerging countries, with a rapidly aging population that has been running up private debts at home. On the third big concern—deglobalization—Russia has become one of the greatest obstacles to world trade. Between 2008 and late 2015, Russia imposed nearly five hundred trade protection measures, second most in the world after India.

Even Putin's top aides acknowledge in private that as Russia's GDP growth rate fell to 2 percent in early 2012, long before oil prices collapsed, the economy is not being held back only by oil. Ministry of Finance officials once presented us a grim chart, showing that investment has been falling steadily over the last few years to less than 20 percent of GDP, one of the weakest rates among large emerging economies. And there is no plan to change that.

Turkey and the Middle East

A story quite similar to Russia's is unfolding in Turkey. While it has no oil or other natural resource wealth, Turkey shares stagflationary characteristics with the commodity-heavy economies. Recep Tayyip Erdoğan came to office as a charismatic reformer who understood what Turkey needed to control spending and beat hyperinflation, but he is in his thirteenth year in a national leadership position and has grown stale. His government is tightening its control over the economy, and he seems to have lost his grip on economics. Erdoğan has over the past couple of years gotten into public spats with the central bank, arguing bizarrely that the proper response to higher inflation was to lower interest rates. He has also argued that lower rates insulate Islamic banks from violating the Muslim injunction against usury, suggesting that religion was starting to trump economics in Turkey.

Turkey is thus another former star now deeply mired in the ugly group. It is in the midst of the second-largest credit binge in the world, after China, with private credit up more than 35 percentage points as a share of GDP over the last five years. Since Turkey imports all its oil, the collapse in oil prices should have pushed the current account out of the red very quickly. Turkey is such a weak exporter, however, the current account has adjusted rather slowly with the deficit only now on track to move below 5 percent of GDP and thus out of the danger zone. With the economy faltering, and inflation rising, Erdoğan's ruling AK Party lost its parliamentary majority last May, only to regain it in snap elections seven months later, when it exploited public fears over terror attacks and the rise of the Islamic State. Victory in these heated circumstances is likely to encourage the AK Party's populist and nationalist tendencies. That leaves Turkey with genuinely strong scores on just two rules, people and geography, given the good growth in its work force and the well-balanced growth across the country.

Turkey, however, no longer gains as much as it once did by virtue of proximity to the oil-rich nations of the Middle East, particularly those in the Gulf region, which also face danger ahead. A cheap currency is best when its price is determined by the market, not the government, and one basic problem for Saudi Arabia and the other Gulf monarchies is that they peg their currencies to the dollar. As a result, the fall in oil prices did not bring down the value of their currencies or help keep their budgets in balance, as it did in Russia.

The Gulf economies' budget problems grew as they increased public spending in a bid to forestall the political unrest that continues to sweep the Arab world. Last January Saudi Arabia crowned a new king, who immediately began doling out new perks, including a bonus equal to about two months' pay to soldiers, pensioners, students on government stipends, and every government employee, or over half of the population. Last year the government budget, which ran a double-digit surplus as recently as 2012, fell into a deficit amounting to 15 percent of GDP, the worst in any large emerging economy. Many of the kingdom's neighbors are in a similar position, and the Gulf is now the opposite of South Asia: It is the only subregion in the world where all the economies are likely to decelerate in coming years.

Africa

It never makes sense to talk about emerging countries in large groups, and Africa has fifty-three nations, two-thirds with populations under 20 million and nearly half with economies that generate less than $10 billion in GDP each year. That's one-third the size of the economy of Vermont. With a few exceptions, particularly South Africa, these countries lack well-developed institutions, produce very spotty statistics, and are hard for outside analysts to get an accurate read on. But the trends that can be measured are turning for the worse. The number of African economies growing faster than 6 percent fell from twenty-two in 2010 to nine in 2015. The number with inflation higher than 10 percent has risen from four to ten.

Many of Africa's economies are caught in the rise and fall of commodity prices: During the boom years they didn't invest the windfall in new industries. When commodity prices started to fall in 2011, the currencies collapsed, but without strong industries the falling currency did little to boost exports. Instead, the falling currency made it more difficult to pay back foreign debts that many of these countries had piled up during the good times.

South Africa, the second-largest economy in Africa after Nigeria and a major exporter of commodities including gold, diamonds, and iron ore, shares with other commodity-oriented economies such as Russia and Brazil the problems of weak investment, a falling currency, a stale ruling party, and a meddlesome government. President Jacob Zuma recently changed finance ministers twice in one week, casting about for one who would endorse his ambitious spending projects without terrifying the markets. However, in contrast to its commodity economy peers, South Africa has unusually strong financial institutions and particularly well-run large banks, which never let credit growth run out of control after 2008.

The South African rand has declined so sharply in inflation-adjusted terms that it feels like one of the cheapest currencies in the world. Dinner in one of Cape Town's world-class restaurants can come to less than thirty dollars per head. The country is suffering a much milder case of stagflation than some other big commodity economies: GDP growth is weak but still positive, and inflation is under double digits and it is not negating the gains to competitiveness from the fall in the currency. Overall, South Africa looks a bit less ugly judging by the rules than a country like Russia.

South Africa's slowdown is otherwise emblematic of the troubles that reemerged on its home continent after 2011, when news magazines were hyping the "Africa Rising" theme. As this story fragments into good, average, and ugly plotlines, a glance at a map of the continent shows that the good stories are emerging in the east, around Kenya, and the worst are welling up in the west, around Nigeria.

In 2015, Nigeria was bathed in a brief flicker of positive hype when Muhammadu Buhari won the presidency on promises to clean up one of the world's most corrupt countries. I was wary this time because his predecessor, Goodluck Jonathan, had made similar promises. Instead Jonathan became a case study in how not to manage a commodity economy, letting oil profits slip into the wrong hands. Even Jonathan's predecessor, the notoriously corrupt Olusegun Obasanjo, had managed during his term to build up the savings held in Nigeria's foreign exchange reserves. After Jonathan took power in 2010, those reserves were slowly drained from $50 billion to $33 billion, despite growing revenue from rising oil prices.

When the oil price boom ended in 2014, Nigeria was left with dangerously low foreign reserves. By 2015 most large oil exporting nations had combined savings, stored in foreign exchange reserves and sovereign wealth funds, which at least matched the size of the economy. In Nigeria those savings had fallen to 8 percent of GDP. Much of this shortfall was due to theft, and the result is that Nigeria now has enough savings to cover its looming budget deficits for barely more than a year.

A former general, Buhari came in promising to attack corruption and the terrorist rebels of Boko Haram, and both of those moves are vital to creating a foundation of trust and security in the economy. But he may underappreciate how deeply the curse of oil has eroded his nation's growth prospects. The government earns 70 percent of its revenue from oil, and the collapse in the oil price means the government deficit is likely to approach 5 percent of GDP this year. Falling oil export revenue is pushing the current account into deficit for the first time in a decade. Like other nations in Africa, Nigeria needs to find a way to break the bad saving and investing habits typical of a nation with an abundance of natural resources.

To the east, in contrast, Kenya is now one of the few African countries that still has a chance to see growth pick up speed this decade. Kenya is an oil importer, so it gains from falling prices and is not threatened by the oil curse. It has a reform-minded leader in Uhuru Kenyatta, who came to power in a peaceful 2013 election and has managed to attract investment. He recently appointed a new central bank chief, who is cleaning up weak links in the financial system and has shuttered frail banks. Though Kenya looks bad on the currency rule—the shilling feels expensive and the current account deficit is well above 5 percent of GDP—it is moving in a positive direction on several others. Investment is up from less than 19 percent of GDP in 2009 to nearly 24 percent, and is rising into the sweet spot. New power plants have halved the electric bill for Kenyan consumers. Multinational companies and investors see Kenya as the anchor of the East African Community, a promising regional common market. It is also an important stop on the new "maritime silk road" under development by China, which is building a new road from the Kenyan port at Mombasa to the capital city of Nairobi, a distance of 275 miles. Kenya therefore ranks well on most of the rules from geography to factories first and has a huge advantage on people matter, with a working-age population expected to grow at an average pace of 3 percent a year through 2020, one of the fastest rates in the world.

The Myth of the Long Term, Revisited

At the start of this decade, some observers thought we were at the dawn of an "African Century," but as the boom has unraveled and uncertainty has come to grip the globe, these sweeping forecasts for entire regions, spanning many decades, have fallen out of fashion. That might be a healthy sign, if optimism had not been replaced by an almost equally unbridled pessimism about almost every country on the planet. While growth is likely to be lower across the world as depopulation, deglobalization, and deleveraging accelerate, some nations will continue to rise even in this slow-growth world.

In the developed world, the list of nations with relatively good prospects includes Germany and the United States; in the large class of middle-income nations, much of eastern Europe and Mexico seem well poised for growth; among low-income nations, the relative stars are likely to emerge from South Asia, East Africa, and parts of Southeast Asia. That is how these nations stack up at this moment in time—March 2016—but the rankings could change suddenly with an untimely assassination, an unorthodox shift in economic policy, a startling invention, or some act of providence. Also, if a global recession does materialize this year, as currently feared, it will be difficult for any country to achieve a "good" growth rate in the near future. But this phase too shall pass, given that global recessions typically last a year, and the outlook here is for the next five years.

The rules are designed to capture these dynamic changes, which is why I monitor and update the scores regularly, and why I do not presume to suggest that any nation will remain in the good, average, or ugly camp for more than the next five years. The noted psychologist and author Philip Tetlock has put thousands of predictions to the test over recent decades, and in his book *Superforecasting* presents evidence confirming both the obvious point that forecasts get less reliable the farther they reach into the future and the less obvious point that they become no more accurate than random guesses beyond five years. For the practical purpose of tracking the rise and fall of nations, the time frame needs to be short enough to be plausible, but also long enough to be useful for planning and policy purposes.

In the next five years, the global economy disrupted by the crisis of 2008 will start giving way to a new set of circumstances entirely. The AC era shall pass, and conditions will likely be radically different in 2020. The way nations rank based on the rules will change, and the details of the rules will evolve, but I believe the basic concept will endure. The most reliable way to track the rise and fall of nations is through a system of rules focused on a practical time frame.

To those who thirst for more far-out forecasts, remember that very few countries ever rise steadily for many decades, and those precious few generally stay within the sweet spots and out of the red zones outlined in the rules, one year at a time. That was the case with the handful of East Asian "miracles," which grew for decades because they kept pushing reform proactively, and grew in a balanced away, without serious violations of the rules on inflation, credit, investment, or anything else. Eventually, though, the miracles too will fade. Every nation is destined to go through periods of expansion and decline, and none is destined to rise, or fall, forever. In an impermanent world, the only constant is the turning of the economic and political cycles that govern the future.

THE GEOGRAPHIC SWEETSPOTS

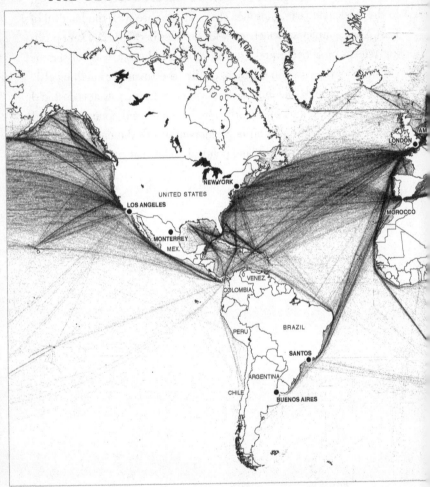

The lines represent the major global shipping routes as of 2015.

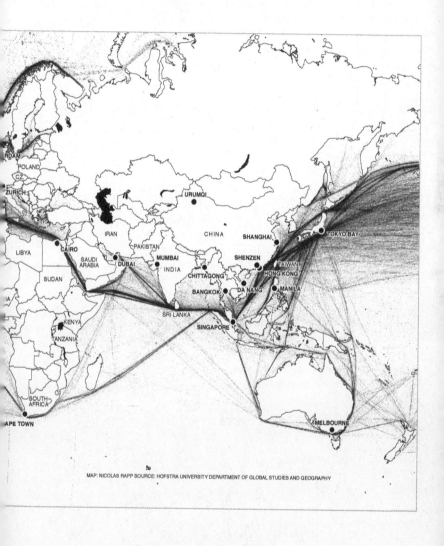

MAP: NICOLAS RAPP SOURCE: HOFSTRA UNIVERSITY DEPARTMENT OF GLOBAL STUDIES AND GEOGRAPHY

ACKNOWLEDGMENTS

For the first two decades of my alternative career as a writer, I was resigned to author Christopher Hitchens's advice: "Everybody does have a book in them, but in most cases that's where it should stay." I was comfortable writing op-eds, but the thought of writing a book seemed much too daunting. All that changed thanks to Tony Emerson, who left his job as the editor of *Newsweek International* in 2010 to help me pen *Breakout Nations*. He has since become my partner in crime for all my writing ventures. Once the book writing bug gets to you, there is no letting the ideas stay in you. *The Rise and Fall of Nations* is my latest project again made possible with Tony's help.

Led by Jitania Kandhari, I am fortunate to have arguably one of the best research teams to help me think about the way the world is working. I have interacted with Jitania since 1998 and can only marvel at her boundless energy and enthusiasm for economic research. I am eternally grateful to her for being there for me whenever I have needed any guidance or assistance. She is supported by Steven Quattry, who must be the most well-read person I have ever met. His interests go well beyond the field of economics and politics, and his lateral thinking has contributed significantly to my understanding of the world. I would also like to thank team member Soham Sengupta for his fast and clear answers to any question.

It is hard to imagine, though, how I could get anything done without Paul Weiner. He has been the team's quartermaster and more for over a dozen years and has been involved in all my endeavors. His organizational skills were once again critical in putting this book together in New York, and quick-thinking Christine Dsouza plays a similar role in Mumbai.

Ever since I started writing in 1991, my sister Shumita Deveshwar has been there to constantly support me, from storing clippings of relevant newspaper articles as part of a mini-library at home to offering critical comments on all the pieces I have written. Before Tony arrived on the scene, Shumita would drop everything to edit my articles at virtually a moment's notice, and even for this book she took out large chunks of time to improve the prose. There is nothing that I can possibly do to repay the unconditional support I have received from her as well as from my parents, who have indulged my idiosyncratic behavior from the get-go.

My close friend and mentor Simran Bhargava has probably had the biggest influence on my thinking and writings over the years. She also taught me how, in Rudyard Kipling's words, to keep your head when all about you are losing theirs. Simran spent hours reading and rereading drafts of the chapters, and her way with questions triggers the mind to come up with more insights and anecdotes. Simran is a simpatico and has instilled in me the basic lesson of writing that if you can't explain something simply, it means you haven't understood it well enough.

There are few acts as selfless as reading someone else's book line by line and offering detailed feedback. I have been incredibly fortunate to find many people who have been so generous with their time. Pierre Yared of Columbia University devoured the manuscript in a week and made some of the most discerning observations that I could hope for, helping me to sharpen the narrative. I would like to thank Amy Oldenburg for making this introduction and also for all her support in my writing endeavors. Dorab Sopariwala, counted as one of India's most respected researchers with an amazing eye for detail, along with Rahul Sharma, who has worked in various leading editorial roles, went over the manuscript with a fine-tooth comb and offered some very valuable suggestions. My friend Sabah Ashraf too scoured the book and came up with key big-picture observations.

My colleagues at work, Ashutosh Sinha, Paul Psaila, Jim Upton, Swanand Kelkar, and Amay Hattangadi, all spent a meaningful amount of time scanning the text and helping to improve it. I would like to thank the following other members of my team for their contributions on specific chapters and topics: Tim Drinkall, Eric Carlson, Cristina Piedrahita, Gaite Ali, Pierre Horvilleur, Vishal Gupta, Jorge Chirino, Samuel Rhee, Munib Madni, May Yu, and Gary Cheung. Cyril Moulle-Berteaux has long been my intellectual sparring partner and I brainstormed with him on many ideas for *The Rise and Fall of Nations*. He has the best analytical mind of anyone I know, and I am grateful to him for his thoughts on various topics touched upon in the book.

I was delighted to have some of the sharpest editors in the business find it worth their while to take such interest in this project. Stuart Proffitt at Allen Lane and Brendan Curry at Norton took an inordinate amount of time both to streamline the prose and to save me from any blushes. Once again, facilitating all this was my agent, the legendary Andrew Wylie, and I am gratified to be part of his roster. I am also obliged to Andrew's associate in London, James Pullen, for his support in this venture.

As both an investor and a writer, I am fortunate to have access to reports prepared by various research firms across the world and also opportunities to speak with the analysts working at these firms. While it is hard for me to list the names of all the analysts I have spoken with in connection with the book, I would like to particularly thank Dan Fineman.

Fareed Zakaria is an inspiration to many people in the sphere of current affairs, and I have been lucky enough to have him as a close friend. Over long dinner conversations, we have tried to solve many of the world's problems. More significantly, he has repeatedly emphasized to me the importance of writing a book by stressing the role it plays in "deepening one's intellectual capital." Fareed's words and constant encouragement have been vital for me to put pen to paper.

When I look back at all the people who have helped me in this project, I am struck by the magnanimity that exists in this world. I can't be grateful enough to the remarkable set of people who have carved time out to indulge me in my passion for writing. While thanking each of one of them for their immense contribution, I am reminded of this exchange between two senior politicians from the same alma mater. When signing the college yearbook at a reunion, one wrote, "I am who I am because of the college." To which the other followed with the line "Why blame the college?" Similarly, the people acknowledged here are not to blame if my book does not appeal to you in the end.

NOTES

On Methodology

For the various GDP growth analyses in the book, I used different data sources depending on the time period I was looking at. For example, if the analysis went back only as far as the 1980s, I tended to use the IMF WEO database, as it is updated twice a year and is standard in academic research. If the analysis looked farther back in time, I tended to use the World Bank data set, which has data back to the 1960s. In examining real per capita growth, which is necessary for work on convergence, I tended to use the Penn World data tables, which has data going back to 1950. For some of the pre-1950 GDP data, I used the Maddison database. Also, throughout the book, figures for debt as a share of GDP are based on data that exclude debts in the financial sector, in order to avoid possible double counting.

Introduction

1   Mark P. Lagon and Arch Puddington, "Democracy Takes a Global Hit," *Wall Street Journal*, January 27, 2016.

2   Arthur Miller, "The Year It Came Apart," *New York Magazine*, December 30, 1974.

3   Harry Wu, "China's Growth and Productivity Performance Debate Revisited—Accounting for China's Sources of Growth with a New Data Set," The Conference Board, Report no. EPWP1401, February 2014.

4   Ghada Fayad and Roberto Perrelli, "Growth Surprises and Synchronized Slowdowns in Emerging Markets: An Empirical Investigation," International Monetary Fund, 2014.

5   Lant Pritchett and Lawrence Summers, "Asiaphoria Meets Regression to the Mean," National Bureau of Economic Research, Working Paper no. 20573, October 2014.

6   "Goodhart's Law," BusinessDictionary.com.

7   James Surowiecki, *The Wisdom of Crowds: Why the Many Are Smarter Than the Few and How Collective Wisdom Shapes Business, Economies, Societies, and Nations* (New York: Doubleday, 2004).

8   Ned Davis, Ned's Insights, November 14, 2014.

9   "Picking Apart the Productivity Paradox," Goldman Sachs Research, October 5, 2015.

Chapter 1: People Matter

1   Rick Gladstone, "India Will Be Most Populous Country Sooner Than Thought," *New York Times*, July 29, 2015.

2   Charles S. Pearson, *On the Cusp: From Population Boom to Bust* (New York: Oxford University Press, 2015).

3   Tristin Hopper, "A History of the Baby Bonus: Tories Now Tout Benefits of Program They Once Axed," *National Post*, July 13, 2015.

4   Richard F. Hokenson, "Retiring the Current Model of Retirement," Hokenson Research, March 2004.

5   Andrew Mason, "Demographic Transition and Demographic Dividends in Developing and Developed Countries," United Nations Expert Group Meeting on Social and Economic Implications of Changing Population Age Structures, August 31–September 2, 2005.

6   "Women, Business, and the Law 2014," World Bank, 2013.

7   Peter Hessler, "Learning to Speak Lingerie," *New Yorker*, August 10, 2015.

8   "Fair Play: More Equal Laws Boost Female Labor Force Participation," International Monetary Fund, 2015.

9   Jim Yong Kim, "CNBC Excerpts: CNBC's Sara Eisen Speaks with World Bank Group President Jim Yong Kim on CNBC's 'Squawk Alley' Today," transcript of interview by Sara Eisen, CNBC, October 1 2015.

10   Caglar Ozden and Mathis Warner, "Immigrants versus Natives? Displacement and Job Creation," World Bank, 2014.

11   BCA Research, "The End of Europe's Welfare State," Weekly Report, June 26, 2015.

12   Carl Benedikt Frey and Michael Osborne, "The Future of Employment: How Susceptible Are Jobs to Computerisation?," Oxford University Programme on the Impacts of Future Technology, September 17, 2013.

13   David Rotman, "How Technology Is Destroying Jobs," MIT Technology Review, June 12, 2013.

14   John Markoff, "The Next Wave," *Edge*, July 16, 2015.

Chapter 2: The Circle of Life

1 Fareed Zakaria, *The Post-American World and the Rise of the Rest* (New York: Norton, 2008).

2 Jonathan Wheatley, "Brazil's Leader Blames White People for Crisis," *Financial Times,* March 27, 2009.

3 Global Emerging Markets Equity Team, "Tales from the Emerging World: The Myths of Middle-Class Revolution," Morgan Stanley Investment Management, July 16, 2013.

4 "The Quest for Prosperity," *Economist,* May 15, 2007.

5 Saeed Naqvi, "A Little Left of Self Interest," *The Friday Times,* June 26, 2015.

6 William Easterly, *The Tyranny of Experts: Economists, Dictators, and the Forgotten Rights of the Poor* (New York: Basic Books, 2014).

Chapter 3: Good Billionaires, Bad Billionaires

1 "Global Wealth Report 2014," Credit Suisse Research Institute, 2014.

2 Richard Fry and Rakesh Kochhar, "America's Wealth Gap between Middle-Income and Upper-Income Families Is Widest on Record," Pew Research Center, December 17, 2014.

3 "The World's Billionaires," *Forbes,* 2015.

4 Andrew Berg and Jonathan Ostry, "Inequality and Unsustainable Growth: Two Sides of the Same Coin?" IMF Staff Discussion Note, 2011.

5 Bradford Johnson, "Retail: The Wal-Mart Effect; Information Technology Isn't the Whole Story Behind Productivity," *McKinsey Quarterly* (Winter 2002).

6 Robert Peston, "Inequality Is Bad for Growth, Says OECD," BBC News, May 21, 2015.

Chapter 4: Perils of the State

1 Roger Altman, "Blame Bond Markets, Not Politicians, for Austerity," *Financial Times,* May 8, 2013.

2 Ahmed Feteha, "Welcome to Egypt's Fake Weddings: Get High, Leave Lots of Cash," *Bloomberg News,* June 23, 2015.

3 Ronald Coase and Ning Wang, *How China Became Capitalist* (London: Palgrave Macmillan, 2013).

4 Jun Ma, Audrey Shi, and Shan Lan, "Deregulation and Private Sector Growth," Deutsche Bank Research Report, September 13, 2013.

5 Anders Aslund, "How Russia Mismanaged the Financial Crisis," *Moscow Times,* February 27, 2013.

6 Amy Li, "Premier Li Keqiang Makes Case for Deeper Economic Reforms over Stimulus," *South China Morning Post,* May 1, 2014.

7   Liz Matthew, "Manmohan Singh Should Have Put Foot Down, Cancelled 2G Licences," *Indian Express*, November 8, 2014.

8   Yannis Palaiologos, "Syriza Must Let Markets and Meritocracy Rule," *Financial Times*, May 12, 2015.

Chapter 5: The Geographic Sweet Spot

1   Rickards, James. *Currency Wars: The Making of the Next Global Crisis* (New York: Portfolio/Penguin, 2012).

2   Antonia Ax:son Johnson and Stefan Persson, "Do Not Fight Free Trade— It Makes Countries Richer," *Financial Times*, July 23, 2015.

3   Daron Acemoglu, Simon Johnson, and James Robinson, "The Rise of Europe: Atlantic Trade, Institutional Change, and Economic Growth," *American Economic Review* 95, no. 3 (2005): 546–79.

4   John Boudreau, "The Biggest Winner from TPP Trade Deal May Be Vietnam," *Bloomberg News*, October 8, 2015; Eurasia, July 2015.

5   Victor Essien, "Regional Trade Agreements in Africa: A Historical and Bibliographic Account of ECOWAS and CEMAC," *NYU Global*, 2006.

6   Moisés Naím, "The Most Important Alliance You've Never Heard Of," *Atlantic*, February 17, 2014.

7   Ibid.

8   Peter Zeihan, *The Accidental Superpower: The Next Generation of American Preeminence and the Coming Global Disorder* (New York: Twelve, 2014).

9   Sumana Manohar, Hugo Scott-Gall, and Megha Chaturvedi, "Small Dots, Big Picture: Is Trade Set to Fade?," Goldman Sachs Research, September 24, 2015.

Chapter 6: Factories First

1   Dani Rodrik, "The Perils of Premature Deindustrialization," *Project Syndicate*, 2013.

2   Ejaz Ghani, William Robert Kerr, and Alex Segura, "Informal Tradables and the Employment Growth of Indian Manufacturing," World Bank Policy Research Working Paper no. 7206, March 2, 2015.

3   Jaithirth Rao, "How They Killed Our Factories," *Indian Express*, January 20, 2014.

4   Ejaz Ghani and Stephen D. O'Connell, "Can Service Be a Growth Escalator in Low-Income Countries?," World Bank Policy Research Working Paper, 2014.

5   Ramana Nanda and Matthew Rhodes-Kropf, "Investment Cycles and Startup Innovation," *Journal of Finance Economics* 110, no. 2 (2013): 403–18.

6   Ebrahim Rahbari, Willem Buiter, Joe Seydl, and George Friedlander, "Poor Productivity, Poor Data, and Plenty of Polarisation," Citi Research, August 12, 2015.

7   Tom Burgis, *The Looting Machine: Warlords, Oligarchs, Corporations, Smugglers, and the Theft of Africa's Wealth* (New York: PublicAffairs, 2015).

Chapter 7: The Price of Onions

1   Helge Berger and Mark Spoerer, "Economic Crises and the European Revolutions of 1848," *Journal of Economic History* 61, no. 2 (June 2001): 293–326.

2   Martin Paldam, "Inflation and Political Instability in Eight Latin American Countries," *Public Choice* 52, no. 2 (1987): 143–68.

3   Marc Bellemare, "Rising Food Prices, Food Price Volatility, and Social Unrest," *American Journal of Agricultural Economics,* June 26, 2014.

4   "World Bank Tackles Food Emergency," BBC News, April 14, 2008.

5   Neil Irwin, "Of Kiwis and Currencies: How a 2% Inflation Target Became Global Economic Gospel," *New York Times*, December 19, 2014.

6   Jim Reid, Nick Burns, and Seb Barker, "Long-Term Asset Return Study: Bonds: The Final Bubble Frontier?," Deutsche Bank Markets Research Report, September 10, 2014.

7   Irving Fisher, "The Debt Deflation Theory of Great Depression," *St. Louis Federal Reserve,* n.d.

8   David Hackett Fischer, *The Great Wave: Price Revolutions and the Rhythm of History* (New York: Oxford University Press, 1996).

9   Claudioo Bordio, Magdalena Erdem, and Andrew Filardo, "The Costs of Deflations: A Historical Perspective," Bank of International Settlements, 2015.

10 "Toward Operationalizing Macroprudential Policies: When to Act?" chapter 3 in *Global Financial Stability Report* (International Monetary Fund, September 2011).

11 Òscar Jordà, Moritz Schularick, and Alan Taylor, "Leveraged Bubbles," National Bureau of Economic Research, Working Paper no. 21486, August 2015.

Chapter 8: Cheap Is Good

1   Ed Lowther, "A Short History of the Pound," BBC News, February 14, 2014.

2   Caroline Freund, "Current Account Adjustment in Industrialized Countries," *International Finance Discussion Papers* (U.S. Federal Reserve, 2000).

3   Rudi Dornbusch, interview by *Frontline*, PBS, 1995.

4   Paul Davidson, "IMF Chief Says Global Growth Still Too Weak," *USA Today*, April 2, 2014

5   Oliver Harvey and Robin Winkler, "Dark Matter: Hidden Capital Flows That Drive G10 Exchange Rates," Deutsche Bank Markets Research Report, March 6, 2015.

6   "EM Macro Daily: China Capital Outflow Risk—The Curious Case of the Missing $300 Billions," Goldman Sachs Global Investment Research, January 13, 2015.

7   Muhamad Chatib Basri and Hal Hill, "Ideas, Interests, and Oil Prices: The Political Economy of Trade Reform During Soeharto's Indonesia," *World Economy* 27, no. 5 (2004): 633–55.

Chapter 9: The Kiss of Debt

1   "China's Rigged IPOs," *Wall Street Journal*, December 2, 2015.

2   Tim Congdon, "The Debt Threat," *Economic Affairs* 9, no. 2 (January 1989): 42–44.

3   Michael Goldstein, Laura Dix, and Alfredo Pinel, "Post Crisis Blues: The Second Half Improves," Empirical Research Partners, November 2011.

Chapter 10: The Hype Watch

1   Barry Hillenbrand, "America in the Mind of Japan," *Time*, February 10, 1992.

2   John F. Copper, *Historical Dictionary of Taiwan (Republic of China)*, 4th ed. (Lanham, MD: Rowman and Littlefield).

3   Young-lob Chung, *South Korea in the Fast Lane: Economic Development and Capital Formation* (New York, Oxford University Press, 2007).

4   Lant Pritchett and Lawrence Summers, "Asiaphoria Meets Regression to the Mean," National Bureau of Economic Research, Working Paper no. 20573, October 2014.

5   Giang Ho and Paolo Mauro, "Growth: Now and Forever?," IMF, Working Paper no. 14/117, July 2014.

6   "A Mean Feat," *Economist*, January 9, 2016.

7   Commission on Growth and Development, "The Growth Report: Strategies for Sustained Growth and Inclusive Development," World Bank, 2008.

8   "Russian President Vladimir Putin Tops Forbes' 2015 Ranking of the World's Most Powerful People," *Forbes*, November 4, 2015.

9   Fernando Gabril Im and David Rosenblatt. "Middle Income Traps A Conceptual and Empirical Survey." World Bank Operations and Strategy Unit, Working Paper no. 6594, September 2013.

Chapter 11: The Good, the Average, and the Ugly

1 Simon J. Evenett and Johannes Fritz, "The Tide Turns? Trade, Protectionism, and Slowing Global Growth," Centre for Economic Policy Research, November 2015.
2 Charlene Chu, "China Roadmap—Something's Gotta Give," Autonomous Research, January 4, 2016.

BIBLIOGRAPHY

Introduction: Impermanence

Anderson, Jonathan. "The Globalization Collection." EM Advisers Group, May 8, 2015.

Baweja, Bhanu. "The Tricks of Trade: A Structural Change?" UBS Research, November 13, 2013.

Booth, Robert. "Education and Skills Have Long-Term Effect on Cities' Economic Well Being." *Guardian*, July 12, 2012.

Burton, Katherine. "Hedge Funds Shut at Fastest Pace Since 2009 on Poor Performance." Bloomberg News, December 2, 2014.

Cates, Andrew, Bhanu Baweja, and Sophie Constable. "Globalization's Challenges." UBS Research, July 22, 2015.

Clark, David. "The Forward March of Democracy Halted? World Politics and the Rise of Authoritarianism." Henry Jackson Society, 2015.

Cookson, Clive, and Tyler Shendruk. "Animal Energetics: The Price of the Hunt." *Financial Times,* October 10, 2014.

Davis, Ned. "Using Crowd Psychology and the Stock Market to Call the Economy." Ned Davis Research, November 14, 2014.

Donnan, Shawn. "IMF and World Bank Warn of 'Peak Trade.' " *Financial Times*, November 18, 2014.

———. "Peak Trade and China's Role in Five Charts." *Financial Times*, November 19, 2014.

"Economics Needs to Reflect a Post-Crisis World." *Financial Times*, September 25, 2014.

Fayad, Ghada, and Roberto Perrelli. "Growth Surprises and Synchronized Slowdowns in Emerging Markets—An Empirical Investigation." International Monetary Fund, Working Paper no. 14/173, September 17, 2014.

Fordham, Tina M. "Taking It to the Street." Citigroup Research, May 2014.

Galston, William. "Modern Autocrats Are on the March." *Wall Street Journal*, June 23, 2015.

Garman, Christopher, and Jonathan Dill. "Reform Tracker." Eurasia Group, October 2014.

Grene, Sophia. "Nouriel Roubini: Dr. Doom Condemns Cute Investment Labels." *Financial Times*, July 26, 2015.

Hanushek, Eric A., and Ludger Woessmann. "Education and Economic Growth." In *Economics of Education*. Amsterdam: Elsevier, 2010.

Ignatius, David. "Hope for Democracy in the Arab World." *Washington Post*, August 9 2013.

"The Increasing Importance of Developing Countries in the Global Economy." *World Trade Report*, 2014.

Jerven, Morten, and Magnus Ebo Duncan. "Revising GDP Estimates in Sub-Saharan Africa: Lessons from Ghana." *African Statistical Journal* 15 (August 2012).

Kaletsky, Anatole. "Wrong, INET?" *The Economist*, November 22, 2010.

Kennedy, Robert. "Is a 'Human Population Bomb" Ticking." Al Jazeera, June 12, 2012.

Kurlantzick, Joshua. "The Great Deglobalizing." *Boston Globe*, February 1, 2015.

Lagon, Mark P. and Arch Puddington. "Democracy Takes a Global Hit." *Wall Street Journal*, January 27, 2016.

Lu, Ming, Zhao Chen, Yongqin Wang, Yan Zhang, Yuan Zhang, and Changyuan Lao. *China's Economic Development: Institutions, Growth and Imbalances*. Northampton, MA: Edward Elgar Publishing, 2013.

Lund, Susan, et al. "Financial Globalization: Retreat or Reset?" McKinsey Global Institute, March 2013.

Manyika, James, et al. "Global Growth: Can Productivity Save the Day in an Aging World?" McKinsey Global Institute, January 2015.

Mauboussin, Michael J., and Dan Callahan. "Learning from Freestyle Chess." Credit Suisse Research, September 10, 2014.

Miller, Arthur. "The Year It Came Apart." *New York*, Dececember 30, 1974.

O'Neill, Jim. "Building Better Global Economic BRICs." Goldman Sachs Global Economics Paper no. 66, November 30, 2001.

Peters, Heiko, and Stefan Schneider. "Sluggish Global Trade—Cyclical or Structural?" Deutsche Bank Research, November 25, 2014.

"Picking Apart the Productivity Paradox," Goldman Sachs Research, October 5, 2015.

Schofield, Mark. "Global Strategy and Macro Group Theme Book." Citigroup Research, April 2015.

Sharma, Ruchir. "Going In for the Big Kill." *Newsweek*, October 2, 2006.

———. "Can India Still Be a Breakout Nation." *Economic Times*, December 10, 2012.

———. "The Ever-Emerging Markets: Why Economic Forecasts Fail." *Foreign Affairs* 93, no. 1 (2014).

———. "China's Stock Plunge Is Scarier Than Greece." *Wall Street Journal*, July 7, 2015.

Studwell, Joe. *How Asia Works: Success and Failure in the World's Most Dynamic Region*. New York: Grove, 2013.

Surowiecki, James. *The Wisdom of Crowds: Why the Many Are Smarter Than the Few and How Collective Wisdom Shapes Business, Economies, Societies, and Nations*. New York: Doubleday, 2004.

Tilton, Andrew. "Still Wading Through 'Great Stagnations.' " Goldman Sachs Global Investment Research, September 17, 2014.

———. "Growth Recovery and Trade Stagnation Evidence from New Data." Goldman Sachs Global Investment Research, June 5, 2015.

Vogel, Ezra. *Japan as Number One: Lessons for America*. New York: Harper & Row, 1979.

"What Is the Trade Slowdown Telling Us?" Gavekal Research, September 30, 2015.

Wu, Harry. "China's Growth and Productivity Performance Debate Revisited—Accounting for China's Sources of Growth with a New Data Set." The Conference Board, Report no. EPWP1401, February 2014.

Zurayk, Rami. "Use Your Loaf: Why Food Prices Are Crucial in the Arab Spring." *The Guardian* 16 July 2011: n. pag. Print.

Chapter 1: People Matter

Abramson, David. "Accelerating Wage Growth—Should We Be Worried?" BCA Research, May 11, 2015.

Acemoglu, Daron, and David Autor. "What Does Human Capital Do?" *Journal of Economic Literature* 50, no. 2 (2012): 426–63.

Adams, Tim. "And the Pulitzer Goes to . . . a Computer." *Guardian*, June 28, 2015.

Aghion, Philippe, Alberto Alesina, and Francesco Trebbi. "Democracy, Technology, and Growth." National Bureau of Economic Research, Working Paper no. 13180, June 2007.

Alderman, Liz. "In Europe, Fake Jobs Can Have Real Benefits." *New York Times*, May 29, 2015.

Anderson, Jonathan. "Institutional Winners and Losers." EM Advisers Group, December 18, 2014.

———. "How to Think About China." EM Advisers Group, February 5, 2015.

Anderson, Thomas M., and Hans-Peter Kohler. "Demographic Transition Revisited: Low Fertility, Socioeconomic Development, and Gender Equity." Population Studies Center, Working Paper, May 15, 2015.

Andreessen, Marc. "This Is Probably a Good Time to Say That I Don't Believe Robots Will Eat All the Jobs." Blog.pmarca.com, June 13, 2014.

Andrews, Nick. "Being Polish." Gavekal Dragoomics, July 17, 2014.

Aoki, Dajia. "Can Japan Overcome Decline in Labor Force." UBS Research, August 6, 2015.

"Asia's New Family Values." *Economist*, August 22, 2015.

Bandhari, Pranjal. "The Camel, the Tent and Reforms." *Live Mint*, October 7, 2015.

Berezin, Peter. "The End of Europe's Welfare State." BCA Research, June 26, 2015.

Bernstein, Jared. "Before Blaming the Robots, Let's Get the Policy Right." *New York Times*, February 17, 2014.

Brooks, Rob. "China's Biggest Problem? Too Many Men." CNN, March 4, 2013.

Butler, William. "Women in the Economy: Global Growth Generators." Citigroup Research, May 2015.

Cates, Andrew, Bhanu Baweja, and Sophie Constable. "Globalization's Challenges." UBS Research, July 21, 2015.

Chatterji, Aaron, Edward Glaeser, and William Kerr. "Clusters of Entrepreneurship and Innovation." National Bureau of Economic Research, Working Paper no. 19013, May 2013.

Chaudhary, Latika, Aldo Musacchio, Steven Nafziger, and Se Yan. "Big BRICs, Weak Foundations: The Beginning of Public Elementary Education in Brazil, Russia, India, and China." National Bureau of Economic Research, Working Paper no. 17852, February 2012.

Credit Suisse Demographic Research, n.d.

Czaika, Mathias, and Christopher Parsons. "The Gravity of High-Skilled Migration Policies." International Migration Institute, May 21, 2015.

"Dominant and Dangerous." *Economist*, October 3, 2015.

Eberstadt, Nicholas. "The Demographic Future: What Population Growth—and Decline—Means for the Economy." *Foreign Affairs*, November 1, 2010.

Elekdag, Selim, et al. "Corporate Leverage in Emerging Markets—A Concern?" International Monetary Fund, October 2015.

Fatima, Ambreen, and Humera Sultana. "Tracing Out the U-Shape Relationship Between Famale Labor Force Participation Rate and Economic Development for Pakistan." *International Journal of Social Economics* 36, nos. 1–2 (2009): 182–98.

Fernandes, Sharon. "India, Second Biggest Loser of Rich Citizens." *Times of India*, July 14, 2015.

Frey, Carl Benedikt, and Michael Osborne. "The Future of Employment: How Susceptible Are Jobs to Compensation." Oxford Martin School, September 17, 2013).

Fulwood, Alice, and Edward Teather. "Malaysia by the Numbers." UBS Research, October 2015.

Garland, Kris. "Demographics Matter." Strategas, September 22, 2015.

"Gary Marcus on the Future of Artificial Intelligence and the Brain." Hosted by Russ Roberts. Library of Economics and Liberty, December 15, 2014.

Gibbs, Richard. "The Momentum of Migration." Macquarie Research, December 3, 2014.

———. "Global Intuition: Maximizing Migration Trends." Macquarie Research, March 5, 2015.

Gladstone, Rick. "India Will Be Most Populous Country Sooner Than Thought." *New York Times*, July 29, 2015.

"Global Demographics and Labor Force Trends, Global Value, Earnings Quality, MBS, Construction Activity." Ned Davis Research, November 19, 2015.

Golub, Jonathan. "Demographics to Drive Slower Growth, Higher Stocks." RBC Capital Markets Research, July 27, 2015.

Gonzales, Christian, et al. "Fair Play: More Equal Laws Boost Female Labor Force Participation." International Monetary Fund, February 23, 2015.

Goodhart, Charles. "Latin America: What Your Peers Are Reading." Morgan Stanley Research, September 15, 2015.

Grey, C. G. P. *Humans Need Not Apply* (film). 2014.

Grindal, Alejandra, and Patrick Ayers. "Why Demographics Matter." Ned Davis Research, July 23, 2015.

Gupta, Shekhar. "Modi and the Art of the Sell." *Indian Express*, December 18, 2012.

Haberman, Clyde. "The Unrealized Horrors of Population Explosion." *New York Times,* May 31, 2015.

Harari, Yuval Noah, and Daniel Kahneman. "Death Is Optional." *Edge*, November 25, 2015.

Hausmann, Ricardo. "The Tacit-Knowledge Economy." *Project Syndicate,* October 30, 2013.

Hessler, Peter. "Learning to Speak Lingerie." *New Yorker,* August 10, 2015.

Hokenson, Richard F. "Retiring the Current Model of Retirement." Hokenson Research, March 2004.

————. "Rethinking Old Age Economic Security." Evercore ISI Research, July 30, 2015.

————. "Long Term Unemployment: A Global Perspective." Evercore ISI Research, August 18, 2015.

————. "The European Refugee Predicament." Evercore ISI Research, September 17, 2015.

Hopper, Tristin. "A History of the Baby Bonus: Tories Now Tout Benefits of Program They Once Axed." *National Post*, July 13, 2015.

Ip, Greg. "Economy's Supply Side Sputters." *Wall Street Journal*, February 18, 2015.

Jain, Tanvee Gupta. "Thank You, Overseas Indians." Macquarie Research, December 2, 2013.

Kapur, Ajay Singh. "China—Accumulating Risks, Caveat Emptor." Bank of America Research, May 27, 2015.

Kennedy, Robert. "Is a Human Population Bomb Ticking?" Al Jazeera, June 12, 2012.

Khosla, Vinod. "How to Win at Leapfrog." McKinsey & Company, December 2013.

Kim, Jim Young. "CNBC Excerpts: CNBC's Sara Eisen Speaks with World Bank Group President Jim Yong Kim on CNBC's 'Squawk Alley' Today." Transcript of interview by Sara Eisen. CNBC, October 1 2015.

Kochhar, Kalpana, et al. *India's Pattern of Development: What Happened, What Follows?* International Monetary Fund, 2006.

Last, Jonathan V. "America's Baby Bust." *Wall Street Journal*, February 12, 2013.

————. *What to Expect When No One's Expecting: America's Coming Demographic Disaster.* New York: Encounter Books, 2013.

Lau, Kinger. "Why Korea Will Continue to Outperform Taiwan." Goldman Sachs Global Investment Research, September 10, 2012.

Laurent, Clint. "India—The Young and the Restless." Macquarie Research, September 18, 2015.

Lawson, Nigel. "Apocalypse Later." *Wall Street Journal*, July 27, 2015.

Lochner, Lance. "Non-Production Benefits of Education: Crime, Health, and Good Citizenship." National Bureau of Economic Research, Working Paper no. 16722, January 2011.

Lubas, Amy, and Veneta Dmitrova. "Is Dwindling Productivity Here to Stay?" Ned Davis Research, May 14, 2015.

Mackie, David. "Euro Area Population, Participation, and Slack." JP Morgan Research, November 21, 2014.

Magaziner, Daniel, and Sean Jacobs. "South Africa Turns on Its Immigrants." *New York Times*, April 24, 2015.

"Malaysia's Misguided Immigration Policy." Foreign Policy Associations, 2011.

Markoff, John. "The Next Wave." *Edge*, July 16, 2015.

Markus, Andrew. "Attitudes to Immigration and Cultural Diversity in Australia." *Journal of Sociology* 50, no. 1 (2014): 10–22.

Mason, Andrew. "Demographic Transition and Demographic Dividends in Developing and Developed Countries." United Nations Expert Group Meeting on Social and Economic Implications of Changing Population Age Structures, August 31–September 2, 2005.

Meeker, Mary. "Internet Trends: Morgan Stanley Executive Women's Conference." Kleiner Perkins Caufield Byers, October 1, 2013.

Minder, Raphael. "Car Factories Offer Hope for Spanish Industry and Workers." *New York Times*, December 27, 2012.

Nair, Prashant. "Indian Pharma in a Global Context." Citigroup Research, August 14, 2013.

Ninan, T. N. "Only 'Above Average.'" *Business Standard*, July 25, 2014.

"No Country for Old Men." *Economist*, January 10, 2015.

Noronha, João. "Brazil Strategy: Navigating Turbulent Times." Santander Research, August 12, 2015.

O'Hare, Maureen. "Danish Moms Urged to Send Their Kids on Baby-making Vacations." *CNN*, October 1, 2015.

Ozden, Caglar, and Mathis Warner. "Immigrants versus Natives? Displacement and Job Creation." World Bank, 2014.

Patel, Raj. "The End of Plenty Review." *New York Times*, July 24, 2015.

Pathiparampil, Bino. "India-Pharma: US Market Remains a Great Opportunity." IIFL Institutional Equities, 2013.

Pearson, Charles. *On the Cusp: From Population Boom to Bust*. New York: Oxford University Press, 2015.

"Picking Apart the Productivity Paradox." Goldman Sachs, Global Macro Research, October 5, 2015).

"PISA Scores: Why Would You Invest in Greece Instead of Poland?" Renaissance Capital, December 4, 2013.

Redenius, Jeremy. "The Challenges to Feeding the World May Not Be So Challenging After All." Bernstein Research, December 6, 2013.

Redman, Alex. "Latin America in 2015: The Most Challenged Emerging Market Region." Credit Suisse Research, March 9, 2015.

Roberts, Russ. *Gary Marcus on the Future of Artificial Intelligence and the Brain*. Library of Economics and Liberty, 2014.

Robertson, Charles. "What's Wrong with Russia." Renaissance Capital, January 24, 2013.

Rotman, David. "How Technology Is Destroying Jobs." *MIT Technology Review*, June 12, 2013.

Roy, Amlan. "Indonesia: Are Good Demographics Adequate for Growth and Investments?" Credit Suisse Demographics Research, March 9, 2015.

———. "A Perspective on Migration: Past to Present." Credit Suisse Demographic Research, September 30, 2015.

Salsman, Richard M. "Social Security Is Much Worse Than a Ponzi Scheme—and Here's How to End It." *Forbes*, September 27, 2011.

Saltar, Daniel. "The Focal Point: New Russia—New Focus." Renaissance Capital, October 21, 2013.

Schneider, Jim, et al. "Fortnightly Answers Questions: Where Is Everybody Going?" Goldman Sachs Research, September 3, 2015.

Shedlock, Michael. "47% of Chinese Billionaires Want to Leave China Within 5 Years." *Financial Sense*, September 5, 2014.

Stephen, Craig. "Rich Chinese Line Up to Leave China." *Market Watch*, February 9, 2014.

Stephens, Bret. "Nobels and National Greatness." *Wall Street Journal*, October 14, 2013.

Tabuchi, Hiroko. "Sony's Bread and Butter? It's Not Electronics." *New York Times*, May 27, 2013.

Tiglao, Rigoberto. "PH Has Highest Fertility Rate in Our Region." *Manila Times*, April 8, 2014.

Toohey, Tim, and Andrew Boak. "Population: Cutting Potential Growth; Forecasting Housing Surplus." Goldman Sachs Global Investment Research, April 15, 2015.

Verme, Paolo. "Economic Development and Female Labor Participation in the Middle East and North Africa: A Test of the U-Shape Hypothesis." World Bank, 2014.

Wan, Fan Cheuk, and Alexander Redman. "Asian Family Business Report 2011." Credit Suisse Research, October 2011.

Weafer, Chris, and Mark Adomanis. "Special Report—Demographics." *Macro-Advisory*, January 2015.

Weir, Fred. "Russia Needs Immigrants, But Can It Accept Them?" *Christian Science Monitor*, October 27, 2013.

"Women, Business, and the Law 2014." World Bank, n.d.

Yadav, Gaurav. "Indonesia's Industrialization." Bank of America Research, January 21, 2015.

Yeoh, Brenda, and Weigan Lin. "Rapid Growth in Singapore's Immigrant Population Brings Policy Challenges." *Migration Policy*, 2007.

Yin, David. "Singapore Needs Immigrants, Says Jim Rogers." *Forbes Asia*, June 6, 2013.

Chapter 2: The Circle of Life

"2014 EM Elections Update." Morgan Stanley Research, December 2013.

Acemoglu, Daron. "Development Won't Ensure Democracy in Turkey." *New York Times*, June 2013.

Acemoglu, Daron, and James Robinson. "Economics Versus Politics: Pitfalls of Policy Advice." National Bureau of Economic Research, Working Paper no. 18921, March 2013.

Aghion, Philippe, Alberto Alessina, and Francesco Trebbi. "Democracy, Technology, and Growth." National Bureau of Economic Research, Working Paper no. 13180, June 2007.

Alexiadou, Despina, and Hakan Gunaydin. "The Politics of Economic Adjustment: Technocratic Appointments and Representation in Economically Advanced Parliamentary Democracies." EPSA Conference, University of Pittsburgh, 2013.

Anderson, Jonathan. "One Hell of an Argentina Rally." EM Advisors Group, April 2015.

"Argentina's Economy: The Austerity Diet" *Economist*, August 23, 2001.

Baweja, Bhanu. "The Weakest Link in EM." UBS Research, December 2014.

Burke, Paul, and Andrew Leigh. "Do Output Contracts Trigger Democratic Change?" Institute for the Study of Labor, 2010.

Cardoso, Eliana, and Vladimir Kuhl Teles. "A Brief History of Brazil's Growth." Getulio Vargas Foundation, 2010.

Crockett, David. *"The Contemporary Presidency*: 'An Excess of Refinement': Lame Duck Presidents in Constitutional and Historical Context." *Presidential Studies Quarterly* 38, no. 4 (2008): 707–21

Dell, Melissa, Nathan Lane, and Pablo Querubin. "State Capacity, Local Governance, and Economic Development in Vietnam." National Bureau of Economic Research, March 2015.

Dhune, Sadanand. "Don't Bet on India to Elect the Thatcherite." *Wall Street Journal*, June 2, 2013.

———. "India's Modi and the Market." *Wall Street Journal*, November 21, 2013.

Diamond, Larry. "Facing Up the Democratic Recession." *Journal of Democracy* 26, no. 1 (2015): 141–55.

Dill, Jonathan, and Christopher Garman. "Emerging Markets Reform Tracker." Eurasia Group, October 2014.

"Directional Economics: The Problem with Political Longevity." Renaissance Capital, August 2013.

Easterly, William. *The Tyranny of Experts.* New York: Basic Books, 2014.

Easterly, William. "Benevolent Autocrats." National Bureau of Economic Research Working Paper, May 2011.

"Elections in Brazil, India, Indonesia and South Africa in 2014: Potential Catalysts for Market Turnarounds." Morgan Stanley Research, October 2013.

"EM Monthly: New Voices vs Old Leaders." Eurasia Group, July 2013.

"Emerging Markets: New Phase of Politics Will Lead to More Divergence." Eurasia Group, November 2012.

Fayad, Ghada, Robert Bates, and Anke Hoeffler. "Income and Democracy: Lipset's Law Revised." International Monetary Fund, 2012.

Feteha, Ahmed. "Welcome to Egypt's Fake Weddings: Get High, Leave Lots of Cash." *Bloomberg News*, June 23, 2015.

Freeland, Chrystia. "Some Cracks in the Cult of Technocrats." *New York Times*, May 23, 2013.

Friedman, Thomas. "The Other Arab Awakening." *New York Times*, November 30, 2013.

Fry, Richard, and Rakesh Kochhar. "America's Wealth Gap between Middle-Income and Upper-Income Families Is Widest on Record," Pew Research Center, December 17, 2014.

Fukuyama, Francis. "The Middle Class Revolution." *Wall Street Journal*, June 22, 2013.

———. "At the 'End of History' Still Stands Democracy." *Wall Street Journal*, June 6, 2014.

Garman, Christopher. "New Voices vs. Old Leaders: How the Middle Class Is Reshaping EM Politics." Eurasia Group, July 2013.

———. "Emerging Markets Strategy." Eurasia Group, November 2014.

Global Emerging Markets Equity Team. "Tales from the Emerging World: The Myths of Middle-Class Revolution." Morgan Stanley Investment Management. July 16, 2013.

Goldstone, Jack. "Understanding the Revolutions of 2011." *Foreign Affairs*, May–June 2011.

Greenspan, Alan. "Never Saw It Coming." *Foreign Affairs*, November–December 2013.

Guha, Ramachandra. "A Strongman Is Not the Solution to India's Troubles." *Financial Times,* November 17, 2013.

Giuliano, Paola, Prachi Mishra, and Antonio Spilimbergo. "Democracy and Reforms: Evidence from a New Dataset." International Monetary Fund Working Paper, July 2010.

Hellevig, Jon. "Aware Group Research on the Effects of Putin's Tax Reforms." Awara Group Research, April 2014.

Iyigun, Murat, and Dani Rodrik. "On the Efficacy of Reforms: Policy Tinkering, Institutional Change, and Entrepreneurship." National Bureau of Economic Research, Working Paper no. 10455, April 2004.

Klein, Ezra. "The Protests in Turkey, Brazil, and Egypt Shouldn't Surprise You." *Washington Post,* July 2, 2013.

Lagon, Mark P., and Arch Puddington. "Democracy Takes a Global Hit." *Wall Street Journal,* January 27, 2016.

Laidler, Ben. "LatAm Strategy—Interesting Charts." HSBC Research, June 2014.

Lansberg-Rodriguez, Daniel. "Latin America Is a Region Plagued by Incumbents." *Financial Times,* October 15, 2014.

Matekja, Mislav. "Europe Year Ahead 2013." JP Morgan Research, December 3, 2012.

Mian, Atif R., Amir Sufi, and Francesco Trebbi. "Resolving Debt Overhang: Political Constraints in the Aftermath of Financial Crisis." National Bureau of Economic Research, Working Paper no. 17831, February 2012.

Mithcell, Daniel. "Russia's Flat Tax Miracle." Heritage Foundation, March 2003.

Mousavizadeh, Nader. "The Presence of Leadership." *New York Times,* March 2, 2013.

Naqvi, Saeed. "A Little Left of Self Interest." *Friday Times,* June 26, 2015.

Page, Jeremy. "China Spins New Lessons from Soviet Union's Fall." *Wall Street Journal,* December 10, 2013.

Perkins, Dario. "No Italian Renaissance." Lombard Street Reseach, June 2014.

"Peru's Roaring Economy: Hold On Tight." *Economist,* February 2, 2013.

Pilling, David. "China and the Post-Tsunami Spirit Have Revived Japan." *Financial Times,* May 8, 2013.

———. "India's Modi Fills a Void of Congress Party's Making." *Financial Times,* September 25, 2013.

Polan, Magdalena. "EM Markets: EM Macro Daily." Goldman Sachs Research, September 12, 2013.

Putin, Vladimir. "Answers to Questions for Participants in the Russian Meetings." Interview, World Economic Forum, 2001.

"The Quest for Prosperity." *Economist,* May 15, 2007.

Rapoza, Kenneth. "Why Lula Was Better for Brazil than Dilma." *Forbes,* December 9, 2013.

Rosenberg, Mark. "African Frontiers: Diverging Political Trajectories Highlight Varying Growth Paths in 2014." Eurasia Group, 2014.

"Russia: A Smooth Political Transition." Goldman Sachs Research, October 2007.

Sharma, Ruchir. "Booms, Busts, and Protests—Normal Life in Emerging Countries." *Financial Times,* July 1, 2013.

Sharma, Ruchir. "India's Cycle of Recklessness and Reform." *Wall Street Journal,* February 28, 2013.

Smith, Tony. "In Brazil, Chafing at Economic Restraints." *New York Times,* March 17, 2004.

"A Strongman Cometh." JP Morgan Research, November 2012.

Summers, Lawrence. "Second-Term Presidents Cost America 40 Lost Years" *Financial Times,* August 10, 2014.

———. "Bold Reform Is the Only Answer to Secular Stagnation." *Financial Times,* September 7, 2014.

"Technocrats—Minds Like Machines." *Economist,* November 19, 2011.

"Turkey: Business Climate Will Gradually Erode with Erdogan Presidency." Eurasia Group, July 2014.

"Turkey's Delight: A Growing Economy." *Bloomberg News,* August 31, 2003.

"Turkish PM's Top Aide Says Erdoğan One of Only Two World Leaders." *Today's Zaman,* August 29, 2013.

Wang, Zhengxu. "China's Leadership Succession: New Faces and New Rules of the Game." European Institute for Security Studies, 2012.

Wolf, Martin. "Legitimate Business Unlocks Mexico's Growth." *Financial Times,* June 3, 2014.

"World of Work Report 2013: Repairing the Economic and Social Fabric." International Labor Organization, 2013.

Wyatt, Caroline. "Bush and Putin: Best of Friends." BBC News, June 16, 2001.

Chapter 3: Good Billionaires, Bad Billionaires

Alderson, Arthur, and Kevin Doran. "How Has Income Inequality Grown." Indiana University, 2010.

"All Men Are Created Unequal." *Economist,* January 7, 2014.

Allegretto, Sylvia A. "The State of Working America's Wealth." Economic Policy Institute, 2011.

Anderson, Jon Lee. "The Comandante's Canal." *New Yorker,* March 10, 2014.

Berg, Andrew G., and Jonathan Ostry. "Inequality and Unsustainable Growth: Two Sides of the Same Coin." International Monetary Fund, 2011.

Chilkoti, Avantika. "India's Wealthy and How They Spend It." *Financial Times*, July 14, 2014.

Da Costa, Pedro Nicolaci. "Stiglitz: Fed's Zero Rate Policy Boosts Inequality." *Wall Street Journal*, June 4, 2015.

Dehejia, Vivek. "Is India's Rising Billionaire Wealth Bad for the Country?" Reuters, October 30, 2012.

Dhume, Sadanand. "India's Gilded Distration." *Wall Street Journal*, November 29, 2012.

Donovan, Paul. "Inequality in a Time of Crisis." UBS Research, October 9, 2013.

Ferranti, David De, et al. *Inequality in Latin America and the Caribbean: Breaking with History?* World Bank, 2003.

"Forecasting Inflation: Temporary and Structural Changes Interact." Citigroup Research, May 14, 2015.

Fry, Richard, and Rakesh Kochhar. "America's Wealth Gap between Middle-Income and Upper-Income Families Is Widest on Record," Pew Research Center, December 17, 2014.

Galor, Oded. "Inequality, Human Capital Formation and the Process of Development." National Bureau of Economic Research, Working Paper no. 17058, May 2011.

Glaeser, Edward, and Claudia Goldin. "Corruption and Reform: An Introduction." National Bureau of Economic Research, Working Paper no. 10775, September 2004.

"Global Wealth Report." Credit Suisse, 2015.

Grant, Will. "Chavez Boosts Food Price Controls." BBC News, March 4, 2009.

Hatzius, Jan. "Better Times for Middle Incomes." Goldman Sachs Global Investment Research, March 27, 2015.

Jain, Samir. "For the Rich, Investing in Hotels Reap Intangible Gains." *Times Group*, January 6, 2015.

"Juan Velasco Alvarado." *Encyclopaedia Britannica*.

Lee, Hyun-Hoon, Minsoo Lee, and Donghyun Park. "Growth Policy and Inequality in Developing Asia: Lessons from Korea." ERIA Discussion Paper 2012–12, July 2012.

Leibbrandt, Murray, Ingrid Woolard, and Arden Finn. "Describing and Decomposing Post-Apartheid Income Inequality in South Africa." University of Cape Town, 2012.

"Luis Echeverría Alvarez." *Encyclopaedia Britannica*.

Malpass, David. "How Big Government Drives Inequality." *Wall Street Journal*, January 15, 2014.

Nuzzo, Carmen, Elga Bartsch, Paul Campbell Roberts, and Jessica Alsford. "Sustainable Economics: Mind the Inequality Gap." Morgan Stanley Research, 2015.

Pani, Marco. "Hold Your Nose and Vote: Why Do Some Democracies Tolerate Corruption?" International Monetary Fund, 2009.

Parks, Ken. "Argentina Moves to Trim Costly Utility Subsidies." *Wall Street Journal*, March 27, 2014.

Pikkety, Thomas. *Capital in the Twenty-First Century*. Cambridge, MA: Harvard University Press, 2013.

"Putin Publicly Humiliates Business Tycoons Solving Social Crisis in Russian Town." *Pravda*, June 5, 2009.

Robertson, Charles. "Will Anti-Corruption Legislation Prolong Corruption?" Renaissance Capital, December 5, 2012.

Sharma, Ruchir. "For True Stimulus, Fed Should Drop QE3." *Financial Times*, September 10, 2012.

Sharma, Ruchir. "Liberals Love the 'One Percent.'" *Wall Street Journal*, July 30, 2014.

Sharma, Ruchir. "What the Billionaires List Tells Us." *Forbes*, March 13, 2013.

Stand, D. W. "Why Inequality Keeps Rising: Inequality in Emerging Economies." Organization for Economic Cooperation and Development, 2011.

Swanson, Ana. "Why Some Billionaires Are Bad for Growth, and Others Aren't." *Washington Post*, August 20, 2015.

Thornhill, John. "Vladimir Putin and His Tsar Quality." *Financial Times*, February 6, 2015.

"To Those That Have." *Economist*, April 18, 2015.

"Upgrading Long Term Trajectory from Negative to Neutral on Credible Signals of Policy Moderation." Eurasia Group, July 14, 2015.

Chapter 4: Perils of the State

Acemoglu, Daron, Ufuk Akcigit, Nicholas Bloom, and William Kerr. "Innovation, Reallocation, and Growth." National Bureau of Economic Research, Working Paper no. 18993, April 2013.

Acemoglu, Daron, James Robinson, and Thierry Verdier. "Can't We All Be More Like Scandinavians?" National Bureau of Economic Research, Working Paper no. 18441, October 2012.

Altman, Roger. "Blame Bond Markets, Not Politicians, For Austerity." *Financial Times*, May 8, 2013.

Anderlini, Jamil. "China Has Wasted 6.8 Trillion Dollars in Investment." Reuters, November 27, 2014.

Anderson, Jonathan. "No North African Renaissance." EM Advisers Group, May 1, 2015.

Aslund, Anders. "How Russia Mismanaged the Financial Crisis." *Moscow Times*, February 27, 2013.

Batson, Andrew. "China: Can Reforms Revitalize the Private Sector?" Gavekal Dragonomics, October 16, 2014.

Chang, Ha Joon. "State Owned Enterprise Reform." United Nations, Department of Economic and Social Affairs, 2007.

Coase, Ronald, and Ning Wang, *How China Became Capitalist*. London: Palgrave Macmillan, 2012.

D'Souza, Juliet, William Megginson, and Robert Nash. "The Effects of Changes in Corporate Governance and Restructuring on Operating Performance: Evidence from Privatizations." *Global Finance Journal*, 2005.

Ezdi, Asif. "Dealing with Dual Nationality." *News International,* November 14, 2014.

Feteha, Ahmed. "Welcome to Egypt's Fake Weddings: Get High, Leave Lots of Cash." *Bloomberg* June 23, 2015.

Gonzalez-Garcia, Jesus, and Francesco Grigoli. "State Owned Banks and Fiscal Discipline." International Monetary Fund, October 2013.

"Greek Deal Maybe Yes, End-June, But Fundamentals Are Looking Worse Than Ever." Renaissance Capital, June 15, 2015.

Ha, Eunyoung, and Myung-koo Kang. "Government Responses to Financial Crises: Identifying Patterns and Policy Origins." World Development, 2014.

Hammer, Joshua. "'The Full Catastrophe' by James Angelos." *New York Times,* June 19, 2015.

Hassan, Mirza, and Wilson Prichard. "The Political Economy of Tax Reform in Bangladesh: Political Settlements, Informal Institutions, and the Negotiations of Reform." International Center for Tax and Development, 2013.

"How to Raise China's Return on Capital." Dragonomics, December 2013.

Jones, Randall, and Satoshi Urasawa. "Sustaining Korea's Convergence to the Highest Income Countries." Organization for Economic Cooperation and Development, 2012.

Joshi, Sandeep. "Wiser by Vodafone Verdict, Pranab to Tax Overseas Transactions." *Hindu,* March 17, 2012.

Li, Amy. "Premier Li Keqiang Makes Case for Deeper Economic Reforms over Stimulus." *South China Morning Post,* May 1, 2014.

Jun Ma, Audrey Shi, and Shan Lan. "Deregulation and Private Sector Growth." Deutsche Bank Research Report, September 13, 2013.

Matthew, Liz. "Manmohan Singh Should Have Put Foot Down, Cancelled 2G Licenses." *Indian Express*, November 8, 2014.

Naim, Moises. "In Brazil, Turkey, and Chile, Protests Follow Economic Success." *Bloomberg News*, June 27, 2013.

"New Mediocre." Lombard Street Research, November 6, 2014.

"The $9 Trillion Sale." *Economist*, January 11, 2014.

" 'Overkill' by Institutions Has Hampered Growth: Jaitley." *Business Standard*, April 27, 2015.

Palaiologos, Yannis. "Syriza Must Let Markets and Meritocracy Rule." *Financial Times*, May 12, 2015.

Poddar, Tushar. "How to Reduce Fiscal Deficit." *Economic Times*, February 10, 2015.

Sharma, Ruchir. "Time for Slash and Burn to Rejuvenate Markets." *Times of India*, February 14, 2011.

———. "How Emerging Markets Lost Their Mojo." *Wall Street Journal*, June 26, 2013.

———. "China's Illusory Growth Numbers." *Wall Street Journal*, October 30, 2013.

Steinberg, Chad, and Masato Nakane. "Can Women Save Japan?" International Monetary Fund, 2012.

Studwell, Joe. *How Asia Works: Success and Failure in the World's Most Dynamic Region*. New York: Grove, 2013.

Weatley, Jonathan. "Brazil's Leader Blames White People for Crisis." *Financial Times*, March 27, 2009.

Yepes, Concepcion, Pete Pedoni, and Xingwei Hu. "Crime and the Economy in Mexican States: Heterogeneous Panel Estimates (1993–2012)." International Monetary Fund, 2015.

Chapter 5: The Geographic Sweet Spot

Abhluwalia, Montek. "Regional Balance in Indian Planning." Planning Commission, 2013.

Alegado, Siegfrid O. "BPO Companies Turning to Cebu." *GMA News*, November 5, 2013.

Anderson, Jonathan. "How to Think About Emerging Markets (Part 2)." Emerging Advisers Group, September 4, 2012.

———. "A Bit of Cold Water on Brazil Reform Euphoria." EM Advisers Group, September 19, 2014.

———. "Myths and Realities of Mexican Competitiveness." *Jonathan Anderson*, September 29, 2014.

———. "Things Look Better in East Africa." EM Advisers Group, May 4, 2015.

"ASEAN and China: Strengthening Economic Links." HSBC Economics, August 5, 2014.

"Bangladesh: Getting Back to Business." HSBC Research, June 29, 2015.

Boudreau, John. "The Biggest Winner from TPP Trade Deal May Be Vietnam." Bloomberg News, October 8, 2015.

"China's Foreign Ports: The New Masters and Commanders." *Economist*, June 8, 2013.

Cowan, David. "Thinking about North Africa in 2015–2016." Citigroup Research, April 27, 2015.

Crabtree, James. "Sri Lanka Sees Benefits of China's Maritime Silk Road Plan." *Financial Times*, September 17, 2014.

Davis, Bob. "The U.S–China Disconnect on Trade Deals." *Wall Street Journal*, May 3, 2015.

"End of an Era for Oil and the Middle East." BCA Research, April 9, 2015.

Essien, Victor. "Regional Trade Agreements in Africa: A Historical and Bibliographic Account of ECOWAS and CEMAC." NYU Global, 2006.

"Fortnightly Thoughts: Brighter Lights, Bigger Cities." Goldman Sachs Global Investment Research, November 21, 2013.

Fujita, Masahisa, and Paul Krugman. "The New Economic Geography: Past, Present, and the Future." *Papers in Regional Science* 83 (2004): 139–64.

Glaeser, Edward L., and Albert Saiz. "The Rise of the Skilled City." National Bureau of Economic Research, Working Paper no. 10191, December 2003.

Guha, Ramachandra. "Ideas of Public Service." *Telegraph,* July 11, 2015.

Holland, Robert. "Why Hasn't Globalization Killed Manufacturing Clusters." Harvard Business School, 2015.

Johnson, Antonia Ax:son, and Stefan Persson. "Do Not Fight Free Trade—It Makes Countries Richer." *Financial Times*, July 23, 2015.

Kapur, Devesh. "Western Anti-capitalists Take Too Much for Granted." *Financial Times,* July 23, 2014.

Khanna, Parag. "The End of the Nation-State?" *New York Times,* October 12, 2013.

Kroeber, Arthur. "Four Shades of Latin America." GK Research, March 12, 2013.

Lissovolik, Yaroslav. "Discerning Russia's Regional Potential." Deutsche Bank Research, October 4, 2013.

Manohar, Sumana, Hugo Scott-Gall, and Megha Chaturvedi. "Small Dots, Big Picture: Is Trade Set to Fade?" Goldman Sachs Investment Research, September 24, 2015.

Maughan, Tim. "The Dystopian Lake Filled by the World's Tech Lust." BBC News, April 2, 2015.

"Mercosur RIP?" *Economist,* June 14, 2012.

Naím, Moisés. "The Most Important Alliance You've Never Heard Of." *Atlantic,* February 17, 2014.

"New Frontiers." *Economist,* January 11, 2014.

"The New Masters and Commanders." *Economist,* June 8, 2013.

"The Nuclear Deal's Other Winner." *Economist,* July 25, 2015.

Rickards, James. *Currency Wars: The Making of the Next Global Crisis.* New York: Portfolio/Penguin, 2012.

"Russia Equity Strategy—Discerning Russia's Regional Potential." Deutsche Bank Research, October 4, 2013.

Shapiro, Jesse. "Smart Cities: Quality of Life, Productivity, and the Growth Effects of Human Capital." National Bureau of Economic Research, Working Paper no. 11615, September 2005.

Sharma, Ruchir. "Europe's Flying Geese." *Economic Times,* November 19, 2007.

"The Tricks of Trade: A Structural Change?" UBS Investment Research, November 13, 2013.

Zakaria, Fareed. "America's Prospects Are Promising Indeed." *Washington Post,* November 20, 2014.

Zeihan, Peter. *The Accidental Superpower: The Next Generation of American Preeminence and the Coming Global Disorder.* New York: Twelve, 2014.

Chapter 6: Factories First

Anderlini, Jamil. "Property Bubble Is a 'Major Risk to China." *Financial Times,* August 25, 2014.

Anderson, Jonathan. "The EM Agricultural Investment Boom." EM Advisers Group, October 31, 2014.

———. "Still Happy with Disinflation." EM Advisers Group, May 14, 2015.

Bradsher, Keith. "China's Housing Resists Efforts to Spur Market." *New York Times,* December 18, 2014.

Burgis, Tom. *The Looting Machine: Warlords, Oligarchs, Corporations, and the Theft of Africa's Wealth.* New York: PublicAffairs, 2015.

———. "Nigeria Unraveled." *Financial Times,* February 14, 2015.

Carroll, Christopher. "Precautionary Saving and the Marginal Propensity to Consume Out of Permanent Income." National Bureau of Economic Research, Working Paper no. 8233, April 2001.

Carroll, Christopher, Jody Overland, and David Weil. "Saving and Growth with Habit Formation." *American Economic Review* 90, no. 3 (2000): 341–55.

Chen, Nan-Kuang. "Asset Price Fluctuations in Taiwan: Evidence from Stock and Real Estate Prices 1973 to 1992." *Journal of Asian Economics* 12, no. 2 (2001): 215–32.

"China's Ghost City Index Holds the Future." China Investment Network, October 13, 2014.

Crooks, Ed. "US Shale Oil Industry Hit by $30bn Outflows." *Financial Times*, September 6, 2015.

"The Daily—A Better Class of Bubble." Gavekal Dragonomics, December 1, 2014.

DeBusschere, Dennis, and Brian Herlihy. "Disruptive Technologies and Their Impact on the Economy." ISI Group, May 9, 2014.

Evans-Pritchard, Ambrose. "Devaluation by China Is the Next Great Risk for a Deflationary World." *Telegraph*, February 4, 2015.

Flowers, Andrew. "If a Computer Can Diagnose Cancer, Will Doctors Become Obsolete?" FiveThirtyEight, August 22, 2014.

Garchitorena, Rafael, and Carissa Mangubat. "Manufacturing: A New Growth Driver?" Deutsche Bank, September 24, 2012.

Ghani, Ejaz, and Stephen O'Connell. "Can Service Be a Growth Escalator in Low-Income Countries?" World Bank Policy Research Working Paper, July 1, 2014.

Ghani, Ejaz William Robert Kerr, and Alex Segura. "Informal Tradables and the Employment Growth of Indian Manufacturing," World Bank Policy Research Working Paper no. WPS7206, March 2, 2015.

Haussman, Ricardo, et al. *The Atlas of Economic Complexity*. Cambridge, MA: Harvard University Press, 2012.

Krane, Jim, and Mark Agerton. "The U.S. Shale Boom Takes a Break." *Foreign Affairs* May 26, 2015.

Li, Cao. "Under Xi, China's Wave of 'Weird Architecture' May Have Peaked." *New York Times*, December 19, 2014.

Lubas, Amy, and Veneta Dimitrova. "Is Dwindling Productivity Here to Stay?" Ned Davis Research Group, May 14, 2015.

Meyer, Gregory. "Harsh Realities Finally Push US Champions of Shale Oil into Retreat." *Financial Times*, November 1, 2015.

Moskvitch, Katia. "How Israel Turned Itself into a High-Tech Hub." BBC News, November 21, 2011.

Nanda, Ramana, and Matthew Rhodes-Kropf. "Investment Cycles and Startup Innovation." *Journal of Finance Economics* 110, no. 2 (2013): 403–18.

"Nigeria: Looking Down the Abyss." BCA Research, January 28, 2015.

Pilling, David. "China May Be in Much Better Shape than It Looks." *Financial Times,* October 16, 2013.

Rao, Jaithirth. "How They Killed Our Factories." *Indian Express*, January 20, 2014.

Rodrik, Dani. "The Future of Economic Convergence." National Bureau of Economic Research, Working Paper no. 17400, September 2011.

———. "No More Growth Miracles." *Project Syndicate*, August 8, 2012.

Rowden, Rick. "The Myth of Africa's Rise: Why the Rumors of Africa's Explosive Growth Have Been Greatly Exaggerated." *Foreign Policy*, January 4, 2013.

Saeed, Saquib. "A Pakistani's Perspective: Why Bangladesh Is Doing Better than Pakistan." *Tribune* June 2, 2014.

Schofield, Mark. "Citi Macro Views: Global Strategy and Macro Group Theme Book." Citigroup Research, January 2015.

Scott, Margaret. "The World According to Japan: From a Faux Holland to Petite Pyramids, the Japanese Indulge in the Exotic—in the Safety of Their Own Back Yard." *Los Angeles Times*, November 21, 1993.

"The Service Elevator." *Economist*, May 19, 2011.

Spense, Michael. "Labor's Digital Displacement." *Project Syndicate*, May 22, 2014.

Tandiyono, Felicia. "ASEAN Infrastructure: Indonesia vs Thailand." JP Morgan Research, November 5, 2014.

Technion. *100 Years of Science and Technology*. 2011.

Timmons, Heather, and J. Adam Huggins. "New York Manhole Covers, Forged Barefoot in India." *New York Times*, November 26, 2007.

Titon, Andrew. "How India Can Become the Next Korea." Goldman Sachs Global Investment Research, April 11, 2014.

———. "Growth Recovery and Trade Stagnation—Evidence from New Data." Goldman Sachs Global Investment Research, June 5, 2015.

"US Shale: Calm Before the Storm." *Financial Times*, December 3, 2015.

"What Next for the Start-up Nation?" *Economist*, January 21, 2012.

"Why Africa Is Becoming Less Dependent on Commodities." *Economist*, January 11, 2015.

Chapter 7: The Price of Onions

Anderson, Jonathan. "OK, Seriously, What Will It Take to Get Brazilian Inflation Down?" EM Advisers Group, March 1, 2014.

———. "The Food Glut Charts (2014 Edition)." EM Advisers Group, October 31, 2014.

Bellemare, Marc. "Rising Food Prices, Food Price Volatility, and Social Unrest.",*American Journal of Agricultural Economics*, June 26, 2014.

Bergen, Mark. "Line of Credit." *Caravan Magazine*, October 1, 2013.

Berger, Helge, and Mark Spoerer, "Economic Crises and the European Revolutions of 1848," *Journal of Economic History* 61, no. 2 (June 2001): 293–326.

Bloom, Nick, Stephen Bond, and John Van Reenen. "Uncertainty and Investment Dynamics." *Review of Economic Studies* 74, no. 2 (2006): 391–415

Borio, Claudio, Magdalena Erdem, Andrew Filardo, and Boris Hofmann. "The Costs of Deflations: A Historical Perspective." Bank of International Settlements, 2015.

Cesa-Bianchi, Ambrogio, Luis Cespedes, and Alessandro Rebucci. "Global Liquidity, House Prices and the Macroeconomy: Evidence from Advanced and Emerging Economies." Bank of England Working Papers, 2015.

Cochrane, John H. "Who's Afraid of a Little Deflation?" *Wall Street Journal*, November 17, 2014.

Druckenmiller, Stanley, and Kevin Ward. "The Asset-Rich, Income-Poor Economy." *Wall Street Journal*, June 19, 2014.

"Falling Prices Are Good for Workers." Lombard Street Research, January 23, 2015.

Fischer, David Hackett. *The Great Wave: Price Revolutions and the Rhythm of History*. New York: Oxford University Press, 1996.

Fisher, Irving. "The Debt Deflation Theory of Great Depression." St. Louis Federal Reserve, n.d.

Gavae, Charles. "Back to MV=PQ." GK Research, January 9, 2014.

Hatiuz, Jan. "Revisiting the Risk of Another Bus." Goldman Sachs Global Investment Research, November 3, 2014.

Irwin, Neil. "Of Kiwis and Currencies: How a 2% Inflation Target Became Global Economic Gospel." *New York Times*, December 19, 2014.

Kay, John. "History Is the Antidote to Fear of Falling Prices." *Financial Times*, January 27, 2015.

Lubin, David, Guillermo Mondino, and Johanna Chua. "Emerging Markets Macro and Strategy Outlook: Can EM Grow If World Trade Doesn't?" Citigroup Research, February 27, 2015.

Luhnor, David. "The Two Latin Americas." *Wall Street Journal*, January 3, 2014.

Maheshwari, Vivek, Nimish Joshi, Bravesh Shah, and Rohit Kadam. "Taste of India: E-Tailing, A Virtual Reality." CLSA Research, January 10, 2014.

Minack, Gerard. "The Wrong Soft of Inlation." Minack Advisors, August 22, 2014.

"Mission Impossible: 2% Inflation." BCA Research, August 20, 2015.

Mohanty, Deepak, A. B. Chakraborty, Abhiman Das, and Joice John. "Inflation Threshold in India: An Empirical Investigation." RBI Working Paper Series, 2011.

"OPEC Annual Statistical Bulletin 2015." 2015.

Paldam, Martin. "Inflation and Political Instability in Eight Latin American Countries 1946–83." *Public Choice* 52, no. 2 (1987): 143–68.

Redenius, Jeremy, Catherine Tubb, and Noelle Guo. "The Challenges to Feeding the World May Not Be So Challenging After All." Bernstein Research, December 6, 2013.

Reid, Jim, Nick Burns, and Seb Barker. "Long-Term Asset Return Study: Bonds: The Final Bubble Frontier?" Deutsche Bank Markets Research Report, September 10, 2014.

Schofield, Mark. "Challenging the Consensus on Inflation." Citigroup Research, June 29, 2015.

Scott, David. "Deflationary Boom—Some Random Thoughts and Questions." Cha-am Advisors, March 2, 2015.

Sharma, Ruchir. "The Oil Shock with No Pain." *Newsweek*, October 31, 2005.

———. "Cracking Inflation Should Be India's Priority." *Financial Times*, December 8, 2013.

Stephens, Bret. "Book Review: 'The Myth of America's Decline,' by Josef Joffe." *Wall Street Journal*, November 6, 2013.

Ward, Justin. "Commodity Super Cycle Analysis." Wells Fargo Research, January 15, 2015.

Warsh, Kevin, and Stanley Druckenmiller. "The Asset-Rich, Income-Poor Economy." *Wall Street Journal,* June 19, 2014.

Wilson, Dominican. "Emerging Markets: EM Macro Daily—Who in EM Can Live the Australian Dream?" Goldman Sachs Global Investment Research, February 26, 2014.

"World Bank Tackles Food Emergency." BBC News, April 14, 2008.

Chapter 8: Cheap Is Good

Ahmed, Shaghil, and Andrei Zlate. "Capital Flows to Emerging Market Economies: A Brave New World." Federal Reserve, June 2013.

Basri, M. Chatib, and Hal Hill. "Ideas, Interests, and Oil Prices: The Political Economy of Trade Reform During Soeharto's Indonesia." University of Indonesia and Australian National University, 2004.

Davidson, Paul. "IMF Chief Says Global Growth Still Too Weak." *USA Today*, April 2, 2014.

"Don't Catch Falling Knives." BCA Research, July 29, 2015.

"EM Macro Daily: China Capital Outflow Risk—The Curious Case of the Missing $300 Billions." Goldman Sachs Global Investment Research, January 13, 2015.

Forbes, Kristin. "Financial 'Deglobalization'?: Capital Flows, Banks, and the Beatles." Bank of England, 2014.

Freund, Caroline. "Current Account Adjustment in Industrialized Countries." International Finance Discussion Papers, 2000.

"Global Macro Jottings: Financial Deglobalization." VTB Capital, November 20, 2014.

Harvey, Oliver, and Robin Winkler. "Dark Matter: The Hidden Capital Flows That Drive G10 Exchange Rates." Deutsche Bank Markets Research, March 6, 2015).

Hyman, Ed. "Bond Yields Up But S&P Advances." Evercore ISI, February 18, 2015.

"Is That a Kleptocrat in Your Balance of Payments?" *Financial Times Alphaville*, March 10, 2015.

Kaminsky, Graciela, Saul Lizondo, and Carmen Reinhart. "Leading Indicators of Currency Crises." International Monetary Fund, 1998.

Keohane, David. "China, When a Hot Money Outflow Threatens to Become a Torrent." *Financial Times Alphaville*, May 13, 2015.

Lowther, Ed. "A Short History of the Pound." BBC News, February 14, 2014.

"NRIs Sent Home $65 Billion in Past Six Months:Lord Swraj Paul." *Press Trust of India*, April 22, 2015.

"Pushing the Limits of International Trade Policy." World Bank, 2014.

Sanyal, Sanjeev. "The Random Walk: Mapping the World's Prices 2015." Deutsche Bank Research, April 14, 2015.

Sharma, Ruchir. "And Then There Were None." *Economic Times*, September 5, 2000.

———. "Why Europe Will Bounce Back in 2013." *Financial Times*, December 18, 2012.

———. "Don't Expect Emerging Markets to Be Flooded in Cheap Money." *Financial Times*, May 20, 2013.

Singh, Shweta. "Mexico Has a Competitive Edge." Lombard Street Research, August 1, 2014.

Chapter 9: The Kiss of Debt

Abiad, Abdul, Giovanni Dell'Arrica, and Bin Li. "Creditless Recoveries." International Monetary Fund, 2011.

Akarli, Ahmet, and Michael Hinds. "Turkey's Dormant Fault Line." Goldman Sachs Research, May 10, 2013.

Alessi, Lucia, and Carsten Detken. "Quasi Real Time Early Warning Indicators for Costly Asset Price Boom/Bust Cycles: A Role for Global Liquidity." *Economic Journal of Political Economy* 27, no. 3 (2011).

Anderlini, Jamil. "China: Overborrowed and Overbuilt." *Financial Times*, January 29, 2015.

Anderson, Jonathan. "Back on the Wrong Track." EM Advisers Group, September 11, 2013.

———. "The Auto Theory of Central Europe." EM Advisers Group, April 9, 2014.

Biggs, Michael, Thomas Mayer, and Andreas Pick. "Credit and Economic Recovery: Demistifying Phoenix Miracles." DNB Working Paper, 2009.

"Boomophobia." CLSA Research, 2007.

Borio, Claudio, and Mathias Drehmann. "Assessing the Risk of Banking Crises—Revisited." *Bank for International Settlements Quarterly Review*, March 2, 2009.

Broda, Christian, and Stanley Druckenmiller. "The Fed's Faulty 1937 Excuse." *Wall Street Journal*, April 15, 2015.

Buttiglone, Luigi, Philip Lane, and Lucrezia Reichlin. "Deleveraging? What Deleveraging?" Center for Economic Policy Research, 2014.

Caballero, Ricardo J., Takeo Hoshi, and Anil Kashyap. "Zombie Lending and Depressed Restructuring in Japan." *American Economic Review* 98, no. 5 (2008): 1943–77.

Calderón, César, and Megumi Kubota. "Gross Inflows Gone Wild: Gross Capital Inflows, Credit Booms and Crises." World Bank Policy Research Working Paper, 2012.

Calvo, Guillermo, Alejandro Izquierdo, and Ernesto Talvi. "Phoenix Miracles in Emerging Markets: Recovering without Credit from Systemic Financial Crises." National Bureau of Economic Research, Working Paper no. 12101, March 2006.

Caprio, Gerard, Daniela Klingebiel, Luc Laeven, and Guillermo Noguera. "Banking Crisis Database." World Bank, 2003.

Chancellor, Edward, and Mike Monnelly. "Feeding the Dragon: Why China's Credit System Looks Vulnerable." *GMO*, January 2013.

"China Faces the Kiss of Debt." Email to Dev Kar, May 13, 2015.

"China's Property Problems." Goldman Sachs Global Investment Research, October 21, 2014.

"China's Rigged IPOs." *Wall Street Journal*, December 2, 2015.

Dell'Arriccia, Giovanni, Deniz Igan, Luc Laeven, and Hui Tong. "Policies for Macrofinancial Stability: How to Deal with Credit Booms." International Monetary Fund Staff Discussion Note no. 12/06, June 7, 2012.

Demirgüç-Kunt, Asli, and Enrica Detragiache. "The Determinants of Banking Crises." *International Monetary Fund Staff Papers* 45, no. 1 (March 1998).

Dobbs, Richard, Susan Lund, Jonathan Woetzel, and Mina Mutafchieva. "Debt and Not Much Deleveraging." McKinsey Global Institute, 2015.

Dumas, Charlie. "Eurozone Needs a Debt Relief Conference." Lombard Street Research, December 22, 2014.

"82nd Annual Report: Rebalancing Growth." Bank for International Settlements, June 24, 2012.

"The Elephant in the Room." JP Morgan Research, September 2, 2015.

"The Future History of China's Deleveraging." Gavekal Dragonomics, July 2014.

"Global Financial Stability Report: The Quest for Lasting Stability." International Monetary Fund, April 2011.

Goldsmith, Raymond W. "Financial Structure and Development." National Bureau of Economic Research, 1969.

Hensley, David, David Mackie, and Zina Bushra Sajid. "Special Report: Hazard Ahead: The EM Credit Cycle Has Turned Down." JP Morgan Research, November 7, 2015.

He, Dong, and Robert Neil McCauley. "Transmitting Global Liquidity to East Asia: Policy Rates, Bond Yields, Currencies and Dollar Credit." Bank for International Settlements, Working Paper no. 431, October 2013.

Jordà, Òscar, Moritz Schularick, and Alan Taylor. "The Great Mortgaging: Housing Finance, Crises, and Business Cycles." National Bureau of Economic Research, Working Paper no. 20501, September 2014.

———. "Leveraged Bubbles." National Bureau of Economic Research, Working Paper no. 21486, August 2015.

Kaplan, Robert. "China's Perilous Tangle of Military and Economic Fortunes." *Financial Times*, July 27, 2014.

Kindleberger, Charles, and Robert Z. Aliber. *Manias, Panics, and Crashes: A History of Financial Crises*. 6th ed. London: Palgrave Macmillan, 2011.

Laeven, Luc, and Fabián Valencia. "Systemic Banking Crises Database: An Update." International Monetary Fund, Working Paper no. 12/163, June 2012).

Laponte, Pierre, and Alex Bellefleur. "When the Music Stops Playing for Chinese Credit." *Pavilion*, October 2, 2014.

Lowenstein, Matthew. "China's Shadow Currency." *Diplomat*, December 12, 2013.

Lund-Jensen, Kasper. "Monitoring Systemic Risk Based on Dynamic Thresholds." International Monetary Fund, Working Paper no. 12/159, June 2012.

McKinnon, Ronald. *Money and Capital in Economic Development*. Washington, DC: Brookings Institution Press, 1973.

Mendoza, Enrique G., and Marco E. Terrones. "An Anatomy of Credit Booms: Evidence from Macro Aggregates and Firm Level Data." International Monetary Fund, Working Paper no. 08/226, April 6, 2008.

Mian, Atif, and Amir Sufi. *House of Debt: How They (And You) Caused the Great Recession, and How We Can Prevent It from Happening Again*. Chicago: University of Chicago Press, 2014.

Murphy, David, and Lei Chen. "Default at the Gate." *CLSA*, September 29, 2014.

"New Mediocre." Lombard Street Research, November 6, 2014.

Peek, Joe, and Eric S. Rosengren. "Unnatural Selection: Perverse Incetives and the Misallocation of Credit in Japan." National Bureau of Economic Research, Working Paper no. 9643, April 2003.

Pettis, Michael. *Avoiding the Fall: China's Economic Restructuring.* Washington, DC: Carnegie Endowment for International Peace, 2013.

Reinhart, Carmen M., and Kenneth S. Rogoff. "Banking Crises: An Equal Opportunity Menace." National Bureau of Economic Research, Working Paper no. 14587, December 2008.

———. "From Financial Crash to Debt Crisis." National Bureau of Economic Research, Working Paper no. 15795, March 2010.

———. "Financial and Sovereign Debt Crises: Some Lessons Learned and Those Forgotten." International Monetary Fund, December 24, 2013.

"Risks to Growth from Build Ups in Public Debt." Goldman Sachs Global Investment Research, March 7, 2012.

Rodrik, Dani. *One Economics, Many Recipes: Globalization, Institutions, and Economic Growth.* Princeton, NJ: Princeton University Press, 2007.

Savary, Mathieu. "Give Credit Where Credit Is Due." BCA Research, November 27, 2015.

Schularick, Moritz, and Alan Taylor. "Credit Booms Gone Bust: Monetary Policy, Leverage Cycles, and Financial Crises 1870–2008." National Bureau of Economic Research, Working Paper no. 15512, November 2009.

"Shanghai Surprises." *Wall Street Journal*, December 10, 2014.

Sharma, Ruchir. "China Has Its Own Debt Bomb." *Wall Street Journal*, February 26, 2013.

———. "China's Debt Fueled Boom." *Financial Times*, January 27, 2014.

Strom, Stephanie. "Clouds Hanging Over Sogo Bankruptcy Lift a Bit in Japan." *New York Times*, July 15, 2000.

Taylor, Alan M. "Credit, Financial Stability, and the Macroeconomy." National Bureau of Economic Research, Working Paper no. 21039, March 2015.

———. "The Great Leveraging: Five Facts and Five Lessons for Policymakers." *Bank for International Settlements, July* 2012.

Timmons, Heather. "The Secret Factor in China's Housing Bubble? Mistresses." *Aeon Magazine*, October 14, 2013.

Wolf, Martin. "Credit Cannot Outgrow GDP Forever, Even in China." *Financial Times*, April 1, 2014.

———. "We Are Trapped in a Cycle of Credit Booms." *Financial Times*, October 7, 2014.

Zhang, Joe. "China's Economy Is Choking on a Surfeit of Stimulus." *Financial Times*, November 10, 2014.

Zhao, Longying. "Chinese Housing: Tough Comparisons." Empirical Research Partners, July 9, 2014.

Chaper 10: The Hype Watch

Acemoglu, Daron. "Constitutions, Politics, and Economics." National Bureau of Economic Research, Working Paper no. 11235, March 2005.

Agenor, Pierre-Richard, Otaviano Canuto, and Michael Jelenic. "Avoiding Middle-Income Growth Traps." The World Bank: Economic Premise, November 2012.

"America's Future." *Economist*, July 9, 2009.

Anderson, Jonathan. "Hard Thinking on China's Traps, Reforms, and the Plenum." EM Advisers Group, November 4, 2013.

————. "The Inexorable End of Africa." EM Advisers Group, April 3, 2014.

Birrell, Ian. "Africa Is Refuting the Usual Economic Pessimism." *Wall Street Journal,* April 16, 2014.

Cevik, Serhan, and Mohammad Rahmati. "Breaking the Curse of Sisyphus: An Empircal Analysis of Post-Conflict Economic Transitions." International Monetary Fund, 2013.

Chung, Young-Iob. *South Korea in the Fast Lane: Economic Development and Capital Formation.* New York: Oxford University Press, 2007.

Commission on Growth and Development. "The Growth Report: Strategies for Sustained Growth and Inclusive Development," World Bank, 2008.

Copper, John F. *Historical Dictionary of Taiwan (Republic of China),* 4th ed. Lanham, MD: Rowman and Littlefield, 2015.

Cowen, Tyler. "Why Texas Is Our Future." *Time,* October 28, 2013.

Dennis, Geoffrey. "Emerging Markets: The Earnings Challenge in 2013." Citigroup Research, January 4, 2013.

"Do Poor Countries Really Get Richer?" *Economist,* September 19, 2014.

Dornbusch, Rudi. Interview by *Frontline*, PBS, n.d.

Eichengreen, Barry, Donghyun Park, and Kwanho Shin. "When Fast Growing Economies Slow Down: International Evidence and Implications for China." National Bureau of Economic Research, Working Paper no. 16919, March 2011.

————. "Growth Slowdowns Redux: New Evidence on the Middle-Income Trap." National Bureau of Economic Research, Working Paper no. 18673, January 2013.

Felipe, Jesus, Utsav Kumar, and Reynold Galope. "Middle-Income Transitions: Trap or Myth?" ADB Economic Working Paper Series, 2014.

Fernandez, Dave. "Myanmar: Clouds Begin to Lift." JP Morgan Research, May 18, 2012.

Gill, Indermit, and Homi Kharas. "An East Asian Renaissance." World Bank, 2007.

"Growth US Tight Oil Production Will Present New Challenges Both in North America and Globally." Eurasia Group, November 28, 2012.

Hillenbrand, Barry. "America in the Mind of Japan." *Time,* February 10, 1992.

Ho, Giang, and Paolo Mauro. "Growth: Now and Forever." International Monetary Fund, 2014.

Im, Fernando Gabril, and David Rosenblatt. "Middle Income Traps A Conceptual and Empirical Survey." World Bank Operations and Strategy Unit, Working Paper no. 6594, September 2013.

Joffe, Josef. "China's Coming Economic Slowdown." *Wall Street Journal,* October 25, 2013.

Kraay, Aart, and David McKenzie. "Do Poverty Traps Exist? Assessing the Evidence." *Journal of Economic Perspectives* 28, no. 3 (2014): 127–48.

Lomax, John, and Wietse Nijenhuis. "Not in a (Middle-Income) Trap." HSBC Research, 2013.

Magnus, George. "Hitting a BRIC Wall: The Risk of the Middle Income Trap." UBS Investment Research, January 21, 2013.

Mahbubani, Kishore. "Why Singapore Is the World's Most Successful Society." *Huffington Post,* August 4, 2015.

"A Mean Feat," *Economist,* January 9, 2016.

Mondino, Guillermo, and Fernando Diaz. "When Do Recessions Turn into Depressions? A Note on Growth Mean-Reversion in EM." Citi Research, February 18, 2016.

Moore, Elaine. "'Supranationals' Borrow at Record Levels." *Financial Times,* September 24, 2014.

O'Neill, Jim. "Why China Will Disappoint the Pessimists Yet Again." *Bloomberg News,* September 25, 2013.

———. "Who You Calling a BRIC?" *Bloomberg News,* November 12, 2013.

Partlow, Joshuya, and Gabriela Martinez. "Mexican President's Popularity Slips Despite Legislative Wins." *Washington Post,* September 3, 2014.

Pritchett, Lant, and Lawrence Summers. "Asiaphoria Meets Regression to the Mean." National Bureau of Economic Research, Working Paper no. 20573, October 2014.

Raiser, Martin. "Relaunching the European Convergence Machine." *Globalist,* January 29, 2013.

Rodrik, Dani. "No More Growth Miracles." *Project Syndicate,* 2012.

Roy, Nilanjana S. "Of Indian Elections, Onions and Salt." *New York Times,* November 20, 2013.

Ruhashyankiko, J. F. "Africa Knocking at IMF's Door." Goldman Sachs Global Investment Research, September 10, 2014.

"Russian President Vladimir Putin Tops Forbes' 2015 Ranking of the World's Most Powerful People." *Forbes,* November 4, 2015.

Sharma, Ruchir. "The Third Coming." *Economic Times,* October 3, 2012.

————. "The Oil and Gold Booms Are Over." *Bloomberg News,* May 5, 2013.

Subramaniam, Arvin. "Too Soon to Mourn Emerging Markets." *Financial Times,* October 7, 2013.

"Timeline: Reforms in Burma." BBC News, April 22, 2013.

Wolf, Martin. "Why China's Economy Might Topple." *Financial Times,* April 3, 2013.

Yap, Cecilia, Siegfrid Alegado, and Karl Lester. "Philippine Growth Rises for Best Three Years Since Mid-1950s." *Bloomberg News,* January 28, 2015.

Zakaria, Fareed. *The Post-American World and the Rise of the Rest.* New York: Norton, 2008.

INDEX

Page references in *italics* refer to table and maps.

ALLEN LANE
an imprint of
PENGUIN BOOKS

Recently Published

Anthony Gottlieb, *The Dream of Enlightenment: The Rise of Modern Philosophy*

Marc Morris, *William I: England's Conqueror*

Gareth Stedman Jones, *Karl Marx: Greatness and Illusion*

J.C.H. King, *Blood and Land: The Story of Native North America*

Robert Gerwarth, *The Vanquished: Why the First World War Failed to End, 1917-1923*

Joseph Stiglitz, *The Euro: And Its Threat to Europe*

John Bradshaw and Sarah Ellis, *The Trainable Cat: How to Make Life Happier for You and Your Cat*

A J Pollard, *Edward IV: The Summer King*

Erri de Luca, *The Day Before Happiness*

Diarmaid MacCulloch, *All Things Made New: Writings on the Reformation*

Daniel Beer, *The House of the Dead: Siberian Exile Under the Tsars*

Tom Holland, *Athelstan: The Making of England*

Christopher Goscha, *The Penguin History of Modern Vietnam*

Mark Singer, *Trump and Me*

Roger Scruton, *The Ring of Truth: The Wisdom of Wagner's Ring of the Nibelung*

Ruchir Sharma, *The Rise and Fall of Nations: Ten Rules of Change in the Post-Crisis World*

Jonathan Sumption, *Edward III: A Heroic Failure*

Daniel Todman, *Britain's War: Into Battle, 1937-1941*

Dacher Keltner, *The Power Paradox: How We Gain and Lose Influence*

Tom Gash, *Criminal: The Truth About Why People Do Bad Things*

Brendan Simms, *Britain's Europe: A Thousand Years of Conflict and Cooperation*

Slavoj Žižek, *Against the Double Blackmail: Refugees, Terror, and Other Troubles with the Neighbours*

Lynsey Hanley, *Respectable: The Experience of Class*

Piers Brendon, *Edward VIII: The Uncrowned King*

Matthew Desmond, *Evicted: Poverty and Profit in the American City*

T.M. Devine, *Independence or Union: Scotland's Past and Scotland's Present*

Seamus Murphy, *The Republic*

Jerry Brotton, *This Orient Isle: Elizabethan England and the Islamic World*

Srinath Raghavan, *India's War: The Making of Modern South Asia, 1939-1945*

Clare Jackson, *Charles II: The Star King*

Nandan Nilekani and Viral Shah, *Rebooting India: Realizing a Billion Aspirations*

Sunil Khilnani, *Incarnations: India in 50 Lives*

Helen Pearson, *The Life Project: The Extraordinary Story of Our Ordinary Lives*

Ben Ratliff, *Every Song Ever: Twenty Ways to Listen to Music Now*

Richard Davenport-Hines, *Edward VII: The Cosmopolitan King*

Peter H. Wilson, *The Holy Roman Empire: A Thousand Years of Europe's History*